The Priest and the Prophetess

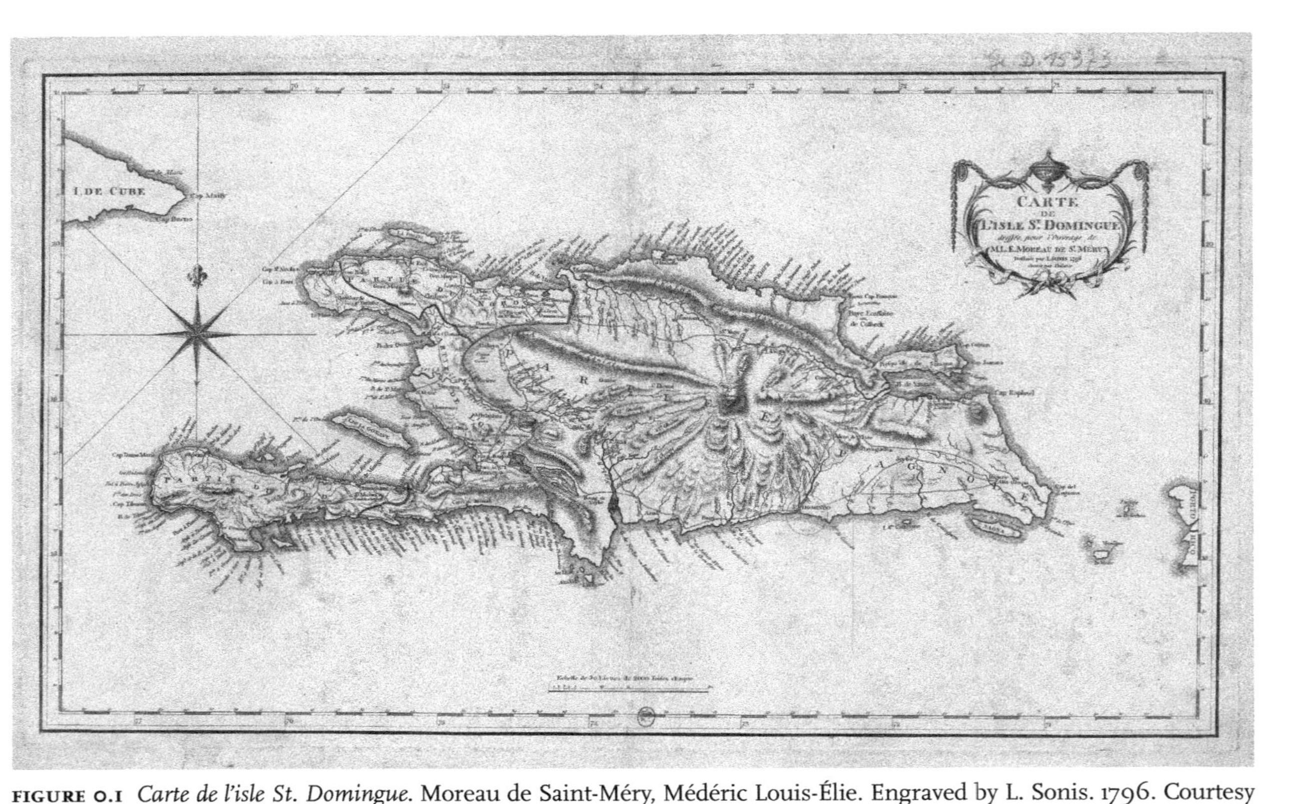

FIGURE 0.1 *Carte de l'isle St. Domingue.* Moreau de Saint-Méry, Médéric Louis-Élie. Engraved by L. Sonis. 1796. Courtesy of La Bibliothèque Nationale de France.

The Priest and the Prophetess

Abbé Ouvière, Romaine Rivière, and the Revolutionary Atlantic World

TERRY REY

OXFORD
UNIVERSITY PRESS

Oxford University Press is a department of the University of Oxford. It furthers the University's objective of excellence in research, scholarship, and education by publishing worldwide. Oxford is a registered trade mark of Oxford University Press in the UK and certain other countries.

Published in the United States of America by Oxford University Press
198 Madison Avenue, New York, NY 10016, United States of America.

CIP data is on file at the Library of Congress
ISBN 978-0-19-062584-9

This book is dedicated in loving memory to Margaret Mitchell Armand, Nadine Bricourt, Karen McCarthy Brown, Francesca Canfield, Christopher T. Gray, Otto Maduro, Nathalie Moussignac, and Angelania Ritchelle, and prayerfully to the radical Catholic futures of my godchildren, Dani Beanga Denambili, Nia Vivian Hammond Fuller, Frantz Joseph Fabien, Trésor Thierry Kongawi, Joseph Sergio Lawrence Rey, Christopher David Stone, and Aidan Sweet.

Contents

Acknowledgments

WITH A NOD to John Donne, I affirm with conviction that "no book is an island," meaning that I have something of a continent's worth of thanks to express here. The good chunk of my life that has been invested in the research and writing of *The Priest and the Prophetess* I will never get back, and I regret having not shared more of it with those who are dear to me in myriad ways. But hopefully the book will be received by all of them and you as a humble token of sincere gratitude, a labor and expression of love.

Above all, I thank my beautiful wife, María, for her insight, patience, support, love, friendship, and spirit. No one inspires me more. And our children, Nathaniel, Thoraya, and Isabella, have often tolerated my cloistered scholarly existence when I should have been helping them with homework or driving them places: *Mèsi anpil, timoun mwen yo!* I'm also very grateful to our family in Mexico City for taking me to watch CF América crush their opponents in Estadio Azteca when I really needed such a break, and to our family in Port-au-Prince for making me in a real sense Haitian.

Temple University, my alma mater and intellectual home, has been very kind to me, and I am honored to be a member of the tenured faculty at this august institution in North Philadelphia. Many Temple colleagues have generously shared ideas, insights, and contacts that have made this book much better than it otherwise would have been. Accordingly, for all of their collegiality and support, I appreciatively acknowledge the following Owls: Zain Abdullah, Rebecca Alpert, Alicia Cunningham-Bryant, Elizabeth Hayes Alvarez, Kathy Biddick, Khalid Blankinship, Lucy Bregman, Hai-Lung Dai, John Davies, Kevin Delaney, Ken Dossar, Talissa Ford, Jane Anna Gordon, Lewis Ricardo Gordon, Doug Greenfield, Justin Hill, Priya Joshi, Nyasha Junior, Dave Krueger, Brett Krutzsch, Mark Leuchter, Laura Levitt, Vasiliki Limberis, Diane Maleson, John Raines, Fred Rowland, Jeremy Schipper, Noah Shusterman, Bryant Simon, Teresa Soufas, and Leonard Swidler. I've also been very fortunate to have had two excellent research assistants for this project at Temple in Holly Gorman and Yiang-Yin Li.

Beyond Temple quite a few scholars have been of immeasurably vital help to me in the crafting of this book, none more so than Jim Sweet. Jim is really more of a brother than a friend, and he has in effect trained me as a historian, which I suppose makes me Phillip Curtin's intellectual great-grandson. Likewise I'm grateful for the friendship and encouragement of John Clark, a.k.a. Kongo Johnny, another Africanized brother from the Southland, who long ago saw that I was onto something with this Romaine-la-Prophétesse character and encouraged me to think of him afrocentrically. John Garrigus also read the entire manuscript and offered invaluable feedback, as did three anonymous reviewers whom I wish I could thank by name here.

Other scholars of African, French, and Haitian history and religion have been wonderfully supportive with their feedback, hence *mèsi anpil* to Dimitri Béchacq, Joseph Byrnes, Stefania Capone, Donald Cosentino, Watson Denis, Leslie Desmangles, Ernst Even, Donna Evleth, Carolyn Fick, David Geggus, Léon-François Hoffmann, Laënnec Hurbon, Ira Lowenthal, Randy Matory, Liza McAlister, Jacob Olupona, Deborah O'Neil, Jeremy Popkin, Kate Ramsey, Karen Richman, Rob Taber, John Thornton, and Drexel Woodson. Writing with Deborah and Karen has been among my greatest joys in life, and I really miss sipping *Twazetwal* in Port-au-Prince with Ira, Alexis Gardella, and Luca Spinelli Barrile. In Haiti, furthermore, I have been ever inspired by the support, friendship, and activism of Joel Jean-Baptiste (*Kreyon Pèp La!*), Rachelle Beauvoir-Dominique, and Yolette Mengual.

This book obviously owes a great deal to the good people at Oxford University Press, none more so than Theo Calderara, my editor, Drew Anderla, Marcela Maxfield, Glenn Ramirez, and Alyssa Russell. Despite some ups and downs along the way, Theo has kept the faith in this project and provided me with wonderful guidance and arranged for no fewer than four historians of the Haitian Revolution to read and comment on earlier drafts of the manuscript. It has been a true pleasure working with Theo and Oxford and I am altogether honored and delighted to publish with them.

Real historians—among whom I now feel entitled to count myself, despite having been trained in religious studies and philosophy—spend far too much time in archives, and this has been a rather tedious experience for me, one to which I will never subject myself again. It has been abundantly fruitful, though, largely because of the gracious and expert assistance of those in the know, of the archivists whose value to our understanding of our species' literate past is simply beyond compare. I regret that I did not write down the names of all of the archivists and librarians who have helped me in places like

Paris, Philadelphia, and Port-au-Prince, but that should not dull the sparkling word of thanks to them that I write here and now. Meanwhile, I do recall their names and am every bit as grateful to: Roy Goodman of the American Philosophical Society; Nicole Contaxis of the Historical Society of New York; Tom Lisanti of the New York Public Library; Kaitlyn Pettengill of the Historical Society of Pennsylvania; Danielle Aloia and Arlene Shaner of the New York Academy of Medicine; and Maryjane Green of Old St. Joseph's Church. My understanding of eighteenth- and nineteenth-century Episcopalianism and Freemasonry was also greatly enhanced by several other archivists, namely Gwynedd Canaan, Brian F. Johnson, Tom Savini, and Glenys Waldman.

In a similar vein, I am indebted to a number of scholars and genealogists in Georgia and South Carolina, places that I had never expected this project to take me. Dennis Taylor and Jerome Reel of Clemson University were very kind to respond helpfully to my inquiries, as was Beau Shuler, of the Pascalis family. Especially deep is my gratitude to the friendly folks of Aiken, South Carolina, a town whose street grid was designed by Dr. Felix Pascalis' son, Cyril Ouvière, and I owe a great deal of thanks in particular to Janet Robinson of the Aiken County Public Library, to Brenda Baratto, Ashley Oswald, and Mary White of the Aiken County Historical Museum, and to Todd Lista for working with the Museum to shoot the portrait of Felix Pascalis that appears in Chapter 7. Thanks elsewhere in the Southland is directed to Jerry Byrd and Carl Anderson, in Atlanta, as well.

On first glance, it might appear even more surprising than South Carolina that this book project also brought me virtually to Warsaw. This is because the marvelous painting that graces its cover, January Suchodolski's 1845 *The Battle of San Domingo*, is housed in the Polish Army Museum, which generously provided me with a high-resolution copy. Many thanks, thus, to the Museum and especially to Aleksandra Dzwonek for the image and permission to publish it, as well as for providing the following helpful contextualization for the painting:

> After Poland lost her independence in 1795, Polish patriots in exile, with the consent of the French Republic, formed the Polish Legions in Italy numbering about 7,000 soldiers. With the signing of the treaty of Lunéville in 1801, the Legions, whose republican attitude ... had become inconvenient to Napoleon, were consequently renamed [the] 113th and 114th French demi-brigades and sent to the isle of San Domingo (today's Haiti) to quell the anti-French slave revolution. During the heavy fighting of 1802–1803, most of the 5280 Poles were killed or died of yellow fever; only between 200 and 300 returned to

> Europe and about 400 remained in San Domingo. The Poles' kindness to captured Haitian rebels secured them an exception from the exile of all whites (except Poles and Germans) included in the Haitian Imperial Constitution published by Emperor Jacques I Dessalines.
>
> The descendants of the Polish soldiers live in Haiti to this day—mostly in the vicinity of the mountain village of Cazale.

Though the battle painted by Suchodolski in particular and Polish participation in the Haitian Revolution in general occurred after the story told here leaves Saint-Domingue, the image does depict many aspects of the topography and military culture covered in several chapters of *The Priest and the Prophetess* and could just as well be a scene from Romaine-la-Prophétesse's extraordinary conquests. That it depicts Poles engaged in battle with Africans in itself reflects some of the remarkable, far-reaching, and sometimes unexpected encounters that shaped the revolutionary Atlantic world, furthermore, like that of the priest and the prophetess.

It is customary to conclude narratives like this by stating that all the mistakes in this book are my own, so there you have it: they are mine and mine alone. Now I can get back to ethnography and to surfing. Good history is too hard to write, though it does help when you have a good story to tell and good friends who are excellent historians. I'm in awe of those scholars who really do this for a living and do it well. I'll thus close by saying to them: Good luck with the dead, especially with illiterate visionaries like Romaine-la-Prophétesse and those who followed her/him into the chapels and onto the battlefields of life.

Men anpil chay pa lou... sort of.

The Priest and the Prophetess

Introduction

La vie est le fruit du hasard.
Et le hasard est divin.
—FRANKETIENNE[1]

AS THEY ROSE with the sun on New Year's Day 1792, the careworn residents of Léogâne, a small but important coastal city in the French Caribbean slave plantation colony of Saint-Domingue, discovered that they were now ruled by a black insurgent leader, a Dominican man named Romaine Rivière who claimed to be a Catholic prophetess and the Virgin Mary's godson. The leading citizens of the town, whites and free people of color alike, had signed a treaty to this effect the day before, thus leaving their uncertain fate in the hands of a charismatic religious visionary whose mission from God was to shatter white power, secure political rights for free blacks and coloreds in the colony, abolish slavery, and bolster both the Catholic Church and a teetering kingdom across the Atlantic Ocean. For several months Romaine's followers, free coloreds (blacks and mulattoes) and escaped slaves, had been occupying, pillaging, and torching homes and plantations throughout the region, slaughtering whites and unallied free coloreds and slaves along the way. At least 2,000 people were left dead in their wake, perhaps many more.

Prohibited by this tumult from lifting anchor and hoisting sail, the fate of three American cargo ships anchored just offshore shortly after the treaty's signing was also in the balance. During the second week of January, French colonial authorities had commissioned Captain Cambis with the task of sailing *La Surveillante* to Léogâne to escort the vessels away from the militarily occupied town to safe harbor in Port-au-Prince. Mediating messages from his godmother, Romaine prophesied that *La Surveillante* had an additional objective: to bombard his people as it disembarked. Word of his prophecy spread and provoked uproar among his acolytes, who abducted several of the ship's officers, leaving one of them bloodied. Negotiations ensued "to calm the general effervescence," however, and *La Surveillante* left without further incident.[2]

Birthplace of the powerful female Taino cacique Anacaona in 1464, Léogâne had never seen anything quite like this in its extraordinary history. The Spanish had at one point made *Yaguana* the seat of their colonial enterprise on the island, which was called by Anacaona's people *Ayiti* (Taino: highland), a land that the Columbus expedition claimed as part of Spain in 1492, renaming it La Isla Española (Hispañola). Spanish colonists also constructed in Léogâne one of the oldest churches in the Americas—and the oldest in Haiti—St. Rose de Lima.[3] Nearby, in 1504 the governor general, Nicolás de Ovando, burned 300 Native American chiefs alive for allegedly conspiring to overthrow the colonizers.[4] Following a brief incursion by Dutch adventurers that forced the Spanish to abandon Léogâne,[5] by 1660 it was taken over and resettled by French buccaneers and then established as a colonial foothold for the French crown by Bertrand D'Ogeron, governor of Tortuga, in 1665.[6] In 1697 Léogâne, along with the entire western third of the island, was formally ceded to the French, who named their new colony Saint-Domingue, briefly making Léogâne its capital. By 1786 the population of the Parish of Léogâne—whose growth was fueled by the lucrative coffee and sugar industries—counted "1,064 whites, 1,520 affranchis, and 16,492 slaves,"[7] and the city featured "a four-hundred seat theater" owned by "a mulatto woman and theater aficionado."[8] An Indian queen, Spanish conquistadors, Dutch adventurers, racist genocide, French pirates, sugar barons, African slaves, and a theater—Léogâne had indeed seen a great deal in its history, but never anything quite like Romaine-la-Prophétesse.

Renowned for its fertile soil, the Plain of Léogâne was home to Saint-Domingue's first sugar refinery and by the mid-eighteenth century was producing some of the world's finest sugar and, in the surrounding mountains and hills, some of its finest coffee, thanks in part to a sophisticated irrigation system. This made the Plain's main town, Léogâne, an important center of commerce and a key to France's imperialist transformation of the sparsely populated and renegade backwater of Saint-Domingue into a prosperous plantation colony. Dominguan cities reflected this prosperity. Take Léogâne itself, for instance, whose center took the form of "a regular hexagon, fortified with a good wall and 10 bastions after the modern form; and in one of the points of the road, is a fort, of a triangular figure, called De la Punta. A river, which runs into the sea, passes through the middle of town."[9] By the time the Haitian Revolution would break out in the summer of 1791, Léogâne had become "one of the most important towns in the West Province, consist(ing) of between 300 and 400 houses laid out in 15 streets."[10]

On the eve of the Haitian Revolution, Saint-Domingue's slave plantations were producing over 75,000 tons of sugar annually, the colony's main export, helping to make it the most lucrative of Europe's "New World" colonies. Léogâne's contribution in 1789 amounted to about 4,000 tons of sugar, along with over 95,000 tons of coffee, nearly 70 tons of cotton, and 2 tons of indigo, alongside relatively minor productions in leather, molasses, and rum.[11] The rapid expansion of sugar production required a simultaneous increase in the size of the colony's enslaved workforce, such that by then roughly half a million slaves toiled on Saint-Domingue's plantations, over half of them African-born. A Swiss visitor published the following oft-cited description of the brutality that he witnessed there:

> There were about one hundred men and women of various ages, all of them busily digging ditches in a cane field, most of them naked or covered in rags. The sun beat down directly on their heads: sweat flowing from throughout their bodies, their limbs weighed down by their heavy tools and by the resistance of earth hard enough to break their tools, they still made a great effort to overcome all of these obstacles. A deafening silence reigned among them, the suffering etched on their faces, but the time for rest had not yet come. The merciless eye of the slave driver watched over the workforce, and several foremen with long whips stationed among the slaves meted out severe lashes on those who looked too tired to keep up pace or who had to slow down, men and women, young and old alike indistinctly.[12]

Some victims of this atrocious injustice fought back. Resistance to slavery and all of its accompanying brutality was mounted from the very moment when Africans were captured in their homeland and throughout their ordeal of being enchained, shoehorned onto slave ships, and forcibly brought across the Atlantic Ocean to the Americas. Various forms of sedition (from foot-dragging and marronage, to the poisoning of livestock and armed insurrection) quickly became familiar features of colonial Atlantic slaving societies. Saint-Domingue, a source of unsurpassed wealth that contributed centrally to financing the construction of modernity itself, was also a powder keg. Although organized armed uprisings involving slaves occurred in Hispaniola as early as 1522, and several others erupted during the 25-year period between 1679 and 1704, such violent insurrections were actually somewhat infrequent in Saint-Domingue; they were nevertheless seemingly always on the minds of planters and slaves alike.

The most significant of the prerevolutionary resistance movements in the colony was that led by an African named François Makandal, an escaped slave who for nearly 20 years struck fear in the hearts of Dominguan whites by employing poison and leading his maroon followers in raids of their plantations. Some believed that his ultimate motivation was messianic rule over the entire colony, and in this respect Makandal has interesting parallels to Romaine-la-Prophétesse. Although in the end he was captured and burned at the stake in 1758, Makandal's legacy remains so strong that even today the word *makandal* is a cognate for poison in Haitian Creole.[13]

Haiti's national foundation mythology celebrates one particular slave uprising in Saint-Domingue above all others for transforming disjointed outbursts of black resistance into a national revolution—the Haitian Revolution—namely, the momentous nocturnal gathering and sacrificial ritual orchestrated by Boukman Dutty and Cécile Fatiman in August of 1791 at Bois Caïman. Though the role of religion at Bois Caïman is debated among historians, Boukman and Fatiman were real people, and they indeed contributed decisively to the insurrection's spread. And though the kind of charismatic leadership that they, and Makandal before them, displayed would remain instrumental over the course of the Haitian independence struggle, it was especially during the early years of the Revolution that such forms of religiously inspired leadership of deep African roots made their most resounding impact. In fact, as the insurrections became more organized, unified, and orchestrated via coherent military strategy, its ascendant leaders, like Toussaint Louverture and Jean-Jacques Dessalines, effectively and sometimes quite violently acted to curb the influence of African spirituality on the struggle. Earlier, however, especially in 1791–1792, African religious forms, many of them Catholic or combined with Catholic forms, served the insurgents very effectively as a unifying force, as an inspiration for superhuman feats of courage, and, perhaps most importantly, as a platform from which charismatic prophets could rise in stature to strike back against white supremacy and racial oppression. At this, Romaine-la-Prophétesse was unsurpassed.

Romaine-la-Prophétesse first came to my attention about 25 years ago, when I was conducting historical and ethnographic research for a doctoral dissertation on Marian devotion in Haiti.[14] In that study I was centrally concerned with the contested uses of the Virgin Mary by various factions, classes, races, and nationalities in the many social, political, and cultural struggles that one may trace throughout Dominguan and Haitian history. Of course, no struggle in this history was more significant than the Haitian Revolution. I quickly became fascinated by the subject of religion in the Revolution, especially in the form of the "embodied moral arguments" of religiously inspired leaders of the 1791 insurgencies that sparked the epochal conflict.[15] There, too, one finds the Virgin Mary. Among all the African and Creole religious leaders involved in world history's only successful national slave revolt—an amazing, valiant, violent, and creative bunch in their own right—Romaine distinguished himself and beckoned me then, as he does now, by claiming to be the Virgin Mary's "godson." Ever since then I have planned to write a book about Romaine-la-Prophétesse, however brief that his appearance at the beginning of the Haitian Revolution might have been, and despite the relatively scant data about him in the historical record. Based on some of that data and secondary source literature, in 1998 I published a journal article on the prophetess, which remains, until now, the only extensive scholarly study of Romaine and his religion; in thoroughly revised and expanded form, much of the material from that article appears scattered throughout this book, especially in Chapter 2.[16] Since that publication, I have managed to access and analyze hundreds of primary source documents that I had missed prior, including relevant notarial records, parish registries, eyewitness accounts, and a few letters written by the prophetess to the priest, Abbé Ouvière, and by other parties in contact with them, and they add much to our understanding of Romaine's place in the complex and confusing politics and culture of the 1791 insurrections in Saint-Domingue's West Province.

An even much fuller picture began to emerge as I researched the life, influence, and writings of Abbé Ouvière, a French Catholic priest and physician who briefly served as an advisor to Romaine-la-Prophétesse and to the leaders of the loosely related free colored civil rights movement, which had formed a confederacy and mustered an army of troops 4,000 strong in the fall of 1791 at Croix-des-Bouquets and Bizoton. As it turns out, the priest was every bit as intriguing a personage as the prophetess. A trusted, literate, white visitor to the insurgent camp that Romaine had established on his coffee plantation at Trou Coffy in the mountains above Léogâne, the priest is much more amply represented in the archives than the prophetess, reflecting how "[i]nequalities experienced by the actors lead to uneven historical power in the inscription of traces," as Michel-Rolph Trouillot observes.[17] Two of the most important parts of the story that I tell in this book are (1) how these two men (one a Frenchman from Aix-en-Provence, across the ocean, and the other an African-descended immigrant from the Spanish colony of Santo Domingo, across the border) came together in Saint-Domingue via Catholicism; and (2) how Romaine's Trou Coffy insurgency, which at one point counted several thousand rebels, conquered two of the colony's cities, Jacmel and Léogâne—astonishing feats the likes of which neither Makandal nor Boukman had ever accomplished. In fact, no other black insurgent leader in the entire colonial history of the

Americas ever conquered and ruled a single coastal city, let alone two of them, underscoring both the uniqueness of Romaine-la-Prophétesse and the power of religion in stirring and sustaining insurrection in the revolutionary Atlantic world—or in any world, for that matter.[18]

But Ouvière's life beyond the Haitian Revolution necessarily takes us much further. On a personal level, it took me home, in fact; for, it was while doing research in Philadelphia, where I live and teach, that I discovered that Abbé Ouvière fled the Caribbean in 1793 and settled right here in the City of Brotherly Love, William Penn's "Holy Experiment," which was every bit a nodal point of the revolutionary Atlantic world as Saint-Domingue, and which was then the "Athens of America." As such, the archive has transformed a book project originally about a prophetess into *The Priest and The Prophetess.*[19] And though formerly conceived of as a book about the Haitian Revolution, because Romaine disappeared from history in 1792 and Ouvière disappeared from Saint-Domingue that same year, while the Revolution had still more than another decade to go, this is instead a book about the revolutionary Atlantic world, but one set largely in Saint-Domingue and intended to affirm Haiti's place at the very heart of that world.

The priest and the prophetess thus united in one of what Robin Blackburn describes as the "strange and unexpected associations between those brought into some sort of communication with one another by Atlantic commerce and its tributaries: maroons, smugglers, the 'brethren of the coast', deserters, naval ratings fleeing the lash, seamen jumping ship, religious or political dissidents, soldiers of fortune and renegade priests, Quakers and Freemasons, devotees of the enlightenment and disciples of African cults."[20] Such a process indeed brought the paths of Abbé Ouvière and Romaine Rivière to cross. And while I had long believed that the story of the priest and the prophetess was at heart one of Catholic inspiration and conspiracy against a colonial slave regime, of an insurgent black maroon in cahoots with a radical white cleric, I now see that this says as much about my own desire as it does about the historical reality; although both men were Catholic and to some measure abolitionists, and though it was indeed Catholicism that led to their union, in reality one of them owned slaves and the other was sent to Paris in 1792 to lobby for the rights of slave owners before the National Assembly, as we'll see. Over and above being about one of the "strange and unexpected associations" to unite strange bedfellows in the revolutionary Atlantic world, the story of the priest and the prophetess is part of Haiti's rich Catholic heritage and reflects how Catholicism played an important role in the triumph of the Haitian Revolution, the institutional Catholic Church's complicity in the transatlantic slave trade notwithstanding.

Despite the fact that most of the giants of the Haitian Revolution, from Romaine and Jean-Francois, to Toussaint Louverture and Jean-Jacques Dessalines, considered themselves Catholic and their militant endeavor to be largely conducted in favor of the Church, much scholarly literature on Haiti overstates the reach of the African-derived religion of Vodou, past and present, and exaggerates the role of Vodou in the Haitian Revolution as a "*foyer de resistance*,"[21] thereby obscuring or flat out denying the important contribution that Catholicism also made to the abolitionist cause in Saint-Domingue.[22] In fact, some scholars have painted an ahistorical diptych in which Vodou is the black "African" religion of resistance and the true religion of "Haitians," while Catholicism is the white "European" religion of domination and a colonial imposition.[23] Jean Fouchard, who more than anyone else inspired me to write this book, invitingly opening a door in writing that "Romaine-la-Prophétesse awaits his historian,"[24] states quite categorically that the "shameful, practical and realistic reasons" behind the Catholic missionary endeavor in Saint-Domingue were

> to tear the greatest number of blacks possible from their ancestral religion, from their beliefs and most notably from Vodou which, in spite of unexpected arguments about this subject, *singularly* facilitated, in its mysterious gatherings of slaves, secret maneuvers tending toward freedom, *le marronage*, and this voiceless and active struggle wrought through poison and fire, to culminate in the general uprising of the slaves.[25]

Yet in reality, as we'll see in Chapter 5, one of the very "reasons" for which the Jesuits were in fact expelled from the colony in 1763 was for allowing syncretic Afro-Catholic religious practice among slaves and for providing space for "mysterious gatherings of slaves, secret maneuvers toward freedom." Surely, therefore, at least as far as religion is concerned, Vodou neither sparked nor "facilitated" the Haitian Revolution "*singularly*."

Though Vodou is indeed revolutionary and visionary in many ways, it is not clear that it was as pivotal to the Revolution as certain scholars would have us believe.[26] Some excellent historical research suggests that the Bois Caïman (Haitian Creole: Bwa Kayiman) ceremony either is entirely mythic or that it took place but perhaps not where or when it is often assumed.[27] That said, the question of the role of Vodou in the Haitian Revolution, whether at Bois Caïman or Trou Coffy, should be raised more broadly as the question of the role of religion in the Haitian Revolution, holistically considered, because not only is there a Catholic dimension to the Vodou question, there are also both Vodouist and Catholic dimensions, often intertwined, to the religion question itself. The broader optic of religion allows for a richer portrait not only of the multifarious and fascinating Dominguan sociocultural reality that Laurent Dubois refers to as "a new set of religious developments" then unfolding in Saint-Domingue,[28] but also of the contributions that other religious forms made to the antislavery cause in the colony, like Islam, Protestantism (especially Quakerism), Freemasonry, Taino shamanism, and perhaps even Judaism. Obviously of a much lesser influence than Vodou and Catholicism, traces of each of these religions can nonetheless also be found embedded in the ideology and actualization of insurgency in Saint-Domingue: Makandal (and perhaps even Boukman, though more likely Cécile Fatiman) might have been a Muslim; French abolitionist propaganda that circulated in the colony drew much of its inspiration from English and American Quakers; and the French civil commissioner Etienne Polverel, who along with his fellow commissioner Léger Félicité Sonthonax would declare slavery abolished in Saint-Domingue in 1793, was a Freemason, as some believe Toussaint Louverture himself to have been.[29]

Just as a broader optic of religion thus sheds new light on the nature of the 1791–1792 rebellions in Saint-Domingue, recent important advances in the study of the transatlantic slave trade provide much sounder and more robust data on the ethnicity of Africans in the colonial Americas than previous generations of scholars had to work with. As a result, historians and anthropologists are now better equipped to explore the specific African religious forms that featured in Dominguan society and that have shaped both Haitian Catholicism and Vodou. Most studies of Haitian religion have thus far been anthropological, and where they do explore history, they emphasize the West African influences on the emergence of Vodou.[30] This is perfectly understandable, for during the first several decades of the importation of slaves to Saint-Domingue, most victims were indeed taken from West Africa, and to an ethnographer Vodou in Haiti even today looks a great deal like traditional religion in West Africa, while many of the *lwa* (spirits) who are venerated in Haiti are also venerated in places like Benin, Togo, and Nigeria. Thanks especially to the groundbreaking work behind David Eltis' *Transatlantic Slave Trade Database*, however, today we have a clearer picture of the ethnic composition of Africans in Saint-Domingue (and throughout the colonial Americas), one that would suggest that Central Africans had a much more prevalent architectural role in Vodou's origins than previously assumed.[31] Even still, scholarly analyses of the impact of Central Africa on Dominguan religion have, for the most part, limited their scope to "traditional" Kongolese influences on Vodou, all but totally ignoring the forceful historical reality of popular Catholicism among West Central Africans, who in fact comprised roughly half of Saint-Domingue's African population on the eve of Haitian Revolution—a form of religion that thousands of them brought with them from Africa.[32] Thus in Chapter 2 the question of Kongolese Catholicism on Romaine-la-Prophétesse and the Trou Coffy insurgency is carefully explored.

Though important and centrally orientational, my focus on religion in this book is nothing more, or less, than a main category of analysis, and it is not intended as any overarching claim about its supremacy over other symbolic or cultural systems in shaping the course of revolutionary Atlantic history. This is but a small part of a conversation, after all, and future archival discoveries will take the conversation further, as will evolutions in research technologies and advancements in theory and method. For, just as poststructuralist and postcolonial theory has strongly challenged longstanding notions about race, gender, and ethnicity, for example, so too has it formidably challenged our understanding of religion.

I am well aware of recent debates in religious studies and anthropology about "genealogies of religion," and I find much of the argumentation in these and other debates about the so-called Western construction of religion to be compelling, the usually less-concerning problematic of the term "Western" notwithstanding. That I am making the case in this book that religion played a central role in inspiring the Haitian Revolution, of course, demands clarification of what precisely I mean by the term. While not disagreeing with Talal Asad that "there cannot be a universal definition of religion, not only because its constituent elements and relationships are historically specific, but that definition is itself the historical product of discursive processes,"[33] for the purposes of this project—not so much as definition but as orientation—I adopt a combination of two attractive definitions of the term *pluralized*, the latter of which is shaped in part by Asad's concerns with "genealogies of religion": Thomas Tweed's definition of religions as "confluences of organic cultural flows that intensify joy and confront suffering by drawing on human and suprahuman forces to make homes and cross boundaries;"[34] and Ananda Abeysekara's definition of religion as "embodied moral arguments."[35] Thus fused, these definitions are especially suitable to my analysis because the two chief subjects of this book, the priest and the prophetess, drew powerfully on "organic cultural flows" and "human and suprahuman forces" to squarely, and in Romaine's case quite violently, "confront suffering," thus they respectively embodied African and Creole and Catholic and Enlightenment moral arguments against social injustice. They did so, furthermore, as healers—Romaine as an herbalist, shaman, and social reformer, and Ouvière as a Catholic priest and physician.

Still, the epistemological question remains as to whether my use of the term "religion" is somewhat anachronistic; that is, am I applying a concept whose meaning in my own twenty-first-century culture is generally understood to mean one thing that would be foreign to, and thereby uncritically imputed into, the intellectual and popular cultures of the revolutionary Atlantic world? I accept the risk of this as real, though I am not persuaded by depictions of Haitian Vodou as a "non-Western" religion,[36] nor am I convinced that what I mean by the term "religion" today is substantively any different from what Baron Pamphile Lacroix meant by the term when writing in the early nineteenth century his observations about the very slave insurrections that are a main focus of this book: "As such, religion, opinion, color, prejudices, and interest were all employed to harm public morale and to spread the elements of discord and revolt."[37] It should be noted that this comment comes directly after Lacroix's discussion of Romaine-la-Prophétesse, furthermore, and that it is doubtful that this white observer, as an "enlightened" Frenchman, would have used the term "religion" in reference to Romaine had he not understood the prophetess to be Catholic—however "heretical" that he might have been—instead of some species of pagan savage.

It was religion indeed that brought the priest and the prophetess together, specifically their shared Catholic faith. A cultivated Frenchman, the priest was also a physician, scientist, editor, and author who published on a wide range of topics and eventually developed a reputation as one of the world's leading experts on yellow fever. Though variously identified by contemporary observers, historians, and novelists as a "charlatan," "shaman," "fanatic," "imposter," "voodoo priest," "sorcerer," "bitch," "she-devil," "mad man," and "the Muhammad of Saint-Domingue," meanwhile, I argue that first and foremost Romaine was a charismatic and prophetic Catholic catechist, spiritual medium, herbalist, and social healer, even though he is most remembered for his religious "fanaticism" (or his putative Vodouist heroism) and for the death and destruction wrought by the insurgency that he led out of Trou Coffy. From the biblical prophet Amos and Joan of Arc, to José María Morelos and Malcolm X, there is a long history in our world of supremely gifted and visionary individuals who saw religiously inspired violence as a necessary means toward social healing. I propose that Romaine-la-Prophétesse should be placed in, and even celebrated as, part of this lineage.[38]

Like Kongolese prophets before him in Africa, none more so than Beatriz Kimpa Vita (1684–1706), Romaine sought to heal society by bolstering his church and restoring a fractured kingdom, which were linked objectives that animated other revolutionary leaders in Saint-Domingue. As such, the prophetess was one of the colonial Africana healers whom James Sweet calls "a sort of 'superconductor' for the dialogic tensions and ruptures outlined in the linking of pre-colonial African histories to the colonial and the post-colonial."[39] As a healer of formal European training himself, for his part, Abbé Ouvière reflects similar "tensions and ruptures," not only in Saint-Domingue but also in France and the United States. Thus, in addition to their Catholic faith, the priest and the prophetess shared in common their respective self-understandings as healers, underscoring the variegated ways in which Catholicism was perceived by many as a vehicle for biophysical and social therapy and healing in the revolutionary Atlantic world.

In following Alyssa Goldstein Sepinwall's study of Abbé Henri Grégoire, I suggest that the lives of Romaine-la-Prophétesse and Abbé Ouvière may also serve our historical understanding as "window, agent, and symbol."[40] Romaine provides a unique window through which we may view both Catholic and African religious forms and their currency in Saint-Domingue. As agent, he drew inspiration from said forms for leading one of the Haitian Revolution's most devastating insurgencies, however short-lived that the Trou Coffy rebellion might have been. And as symbols, the prophetess and the priest together reflect the powerful confluence of religious and political ideals in the revolutionary Atlantic world, a world in which race functioned to both stymie and inspire their explosively sputtering but world-transforming realization.

Though the second half of his life unfolded in the United States of America and thus departs from the previous chapters that were written in France and Saint-Domingue, this in itself makes Abbé Ouvière such a fascinating window into the deep interconnections between France, Saint-Domingue, and the United States in the revolutionary Atlantic world. When the priest arrived in Philadelphia, then the new nation's capital, in the spring of 1793, he carried a letter of introduction from a French aristocrat to President George Washington, and he found himself in a city "awash with French people, French goods, and French culture."[41] Philadelphia's wealthiest man and leading philanthropist, Stephen Girard, was a Frenchman whose fortune was made on the backs of slaves whom he owned in Saint-Domingue, for example, while French jurist Médéric Louis Élie Moreau de Saint-Méry's *Description topographique, physique, civile, politique et historique de la partie française de Saint-Domingue,*[42] our most important single source of information about the colony, was first published in Philadelphia, the city in which he then resided, in 1797–1798.

The priest and the prophetess were thus two men from two different societies of two different races, in an increasingly racially dichotomous, revolutionary world, whose lives came together explosively for a few days at the beginning of the Haitian Revolution. Catholic faith united them, as did enlightenment ideals of freedom and a more just social order, all propelled by reason and a calling to heal. The chapters that follow explore the social, political, and religious forces that shaped their relationship, while weaving the respective biography of each extraordinary man.

Though the sociopolitical cauldron in which they were brewed was common, two distinct and largely unrelated insurrectionary movements broke out in Saint-Domingue in the summer of 1791, marking the beginning of the Haitian Revolution. Slaves led a massive revolt in the North Province, while in the South and West Provinces free coloreds took up arms to fight for their full civil rights as French citizens. Chapter 1 details the rise of Trou Coffy in the Jacmel insurgent theater, followed by discreet chapters, 2 and 3, that are respective biographies of the prophetess and the priest. Chapter 4 treats Trou Coffy in the Léogâne insurgent theater, also in the colony's West Province, while considering insurrectionary activity elsewhere in the West and also in the South Province, by way of context. Providing an important contextualization for understanding Romaine Rivière's relationship with Abbé Ouvière, meanwhile, Chapter 5 provides an analysis of the political engagements/disengagements of other Catholic priests with/from insurgents in Saint-Domingue in 1791–1792. Chapter 6 details the fall of Trou Coffy and the relationship between the priest and the prophetess, while Chapter 7 traces the subsequent harrowing transatlantic journeys of the priest in 1792, paving the way for Chapter 8, which summarizes his formidable career as a scientist and physician in America, as Dr. Pascalis, and the light that his writings shed on the place and function of race and religion in the revolutionary Atlantic world. We return to Romaine-la-Prophétesse and his place in fiction and imagination in Chapter 9, prior to going to Haiti and New York to wind things down in our Conclusion. *Bon lecture!*

I

The Rise of Trou Coffy and the Jacmel Insurgent Theater

Depi ou nan labotwa, fòk ou aksepte san vole sou ou.

—HAITIAN PROVERB[1]

Overview

WITNESSES TO THE horrors that ravaged Saint-Domingue beginning in the summer of 1791 were quick to identify the unfolding drama as *"la guerre"* and to see what was at stake: namely, everything. Although whites sometimes exaggerated black violence in the colony, everyone had good reason to fear for their lives, as a spectacular racial revolution was indeed in the offing. With notable recent exceptions, the regional focus of most scholarship on Saint-Domingue and the Haitian Revolution understandably has been on the colony's North Province, home to Saint-Domingue's most celebrated city and busiest port, Cap-Français, where dramatic slave uprisings cataclysmically brought the once prosperous French plantation enterprise to ruin.[2] The racial composition of most of the South's and West's insurgencies (mostly free coloreds, instead of enslaved blacks) and their motives (full citizenship and civil rights for free coloreds, rather than the abolition of slavery) differed considerably from those behind the slave rebellion in the North.

In actuality there were thus two distinct armed rebellions that broke out in Saint-Domingue in 1791–1792, that of the North and that of the South and West, leaving French state authority in the colony breached and bursting open two doors through which, a dozen years later, the revolutionaries would ultimately storm to independence. And while the Haitian Revolution is rightly celebrated as world history's first and only successful national slave uprising, free colored insurgents in the South and West Provinces, though liberating slaves and sometimes forcing them to join their ranks, generally neither perceived of their struggle in such terms nor envisioned a future time of peace in which their prosperity would not require slave labor. In Saint-Domingue's West Province, the insurgent movement inspired and led by Romaine-la-Prophétesse at Trou-Coffy was clearly the largest and the most feared and devastating, and it was led by a free black man who owned slaves but was nevertheless divinely inspired to abolish slavery on the island.[3]

This chapter details and contextualizes the rise of the Trou Coffy insurgency and its incursions in the Jacmel theater. Trou Coffy is most famous for its mysterious leader, Romaine-la-Prophétesse, its successful conquest of the city of Léogâne in early 1792, and its seizure and destruction of numerous slave plantations located in the surrounding plains and hills. These tumultuous events included countless killings of whites and any mulattoes and blacks who were unallied with or resistant to the insurgent cause. A close reading of the archival material reveals that the Trou Coffy insurgency was also centrally instrumental in a well-planned military campaign against, and ultimately the occupation of, the city of Jacmel, located on the colony's southern coast yet administratively situated in Saint-Domingue's West Province. Led by Romaine out of Trou Coffy, this campaign involved the orchestration of several rebel camps closer to Jacmel, whose troops would siege the city and leave much of it and its neighboring plantations in heaps of ashes. Like Trou Coffy, these insurgent camps were based on plantations, ones either owned by sympathetic free coloreds or seized from whites.[4] They were comprised mainly of mulatto and free black militants and in some cases even white malcontents, who were presumably members of a class of socially marginalized French and white Creoles known collectively as *petits blancs* (lit: little whites), a community that was reviled by nineteenth-century historian Beaubrun Ardouin as "an ignorant class depraved by hatred and jealously who developed into a horde of bandits."[5] Over time, as these insurgent groups raided more and more plantations, the number of blacks in their ranks swelled when they freed slaves and either invited or forced them to join the rebellion. In some cases, they killed those slaves who refused to do so.

It is difficult to say just how many militants were camped at Trou Coffy at the peak of its power, or in any of the other insurgent camps in the West province in 1791/1792, but all tolled there were clearly at least 10,000 throughout the region, 13,000 by one estimate, far more than the quite limited French garrisons in Léogâne and Jacmel could deal with, to be sure.[6] Father J. P. M. Bloüet, the curé of the parish of Jacmel, indicated in November of 1791 that his city had been "besieged for quite some time by more than three thousand armed brigands, whites, blacks, and mulattoes, supported by heavy artillery."[7] Another contemporary observer estimated that more broadly across the West there were in the "rebel camps . . . more than 5000 armed men of color, not counting the whites who are allied with them."[8] In the South Province, meanwhile, a few thousand more militants terrorized the city of Les Cayes and surrounding plantations, orchestrating raids from several insurgent camps that were quite similar in makeup and motive to those in and around Léogâne and Jacmel.[9]

Although there is no clear evidence of any orchestration between the insurgent camps in the South Province around the city of Les Cayes and those in the West that were tied to Trou Coffy, they were all in some way expected to answer to the most influential free colored leaders in Saint-Domingue, who by November of 1791 had mustered a formidable army in the West Province and whose most important leader, Julien Raimond, was then in Paris lobbying the National Assembly for their cause.[10] In Saint-Domingue, meanwhile, the free colored civil rights movement was led by Pierre Pinchinat, its president, and André Rigaud, its ablest military commander. Most of the "combined army" of their Confederacy (drawing troops from multiple parishes in the West and South Provinces) was based primarily in Croix-des-Bouquets, just north of Port-au-Prince, and in Bizoton, just to the west. Besides their ties to these command centers of the Confederacy, the insurgent camps of the West and the South bore other notable similarities, thus it is helpful by way of context to outline some of the contours and actions of those in the South before discussing those in the West in general and the Trou Coffy insurgency in particular. But what, it must be asked, provoked these free colored uprisings in the first place, and for what cause was the Confederacy taking up arms and enlisting troops?

Causes of the 1791 Insurgencies in the South and West Provinces

The outbreak of the Haitian Revolution in 1791 was nothing like the black and white, black versus white conflict that it is often presumed to have been.[11] There were indeed whites who died for the cause of black liberation, and blacks who died protecting white slave owners, in addition to the masses of black slaves rebelling against a white power structure that brutally oppressed them. What greatly complicates understanding the Revolution are the free people of color, a mostly mixed race population that grew tremendously in the decades just prior to the Revolution, and their distinct political aims. In the South and West Provinces they took up arms and organized revolts against the Franco-Dominguan white economic and political elites at the very same time that the momentous slave revolts in the North Province brought

France's most prosperous colony to its knees and into the cauldron of revolution, but they did so for different reasons: not to abolish slavery, but at a minimum to secure their full civil rights as French citizens and, for some, to supplant whites as the dominant class in the colony.

By the watershed year of 1789 and the outbreak of revolution in France, the size of Saint-Domingue's population of free coloreds had grown to roughly equal that of whites in the colony, to about 30,000, and they "owned one-third of the plantation property, one-quarter of the slaves, and one-quarter of the real estate property."[12] Notwithstanding their expanding numbers, even when combined with those of the white population, on the eve of the Haitian Revolution freepersons were greatly outnumbered by slaves, by roughly ten to one. Most of the free people of color were mulattoes, and almost all slaves were black and the majority of them African-born, while most, but certainly not all, whites in the colony, and countless more in France, prospered thanks to slavery.

Up until the second half of the eighteenth century the most affluent among the *gens de couleur libres* had enjoyed a Saint-Domingue in which social achievement was open to them and in which class, rather than race, determined the social station of the free. Though racism had certainly existed from the very beginning of the colony and was central to its inception, on the heels of the Seven Years' War between the British and French Empires, racial animosity between whites and mulattoes intensified in Saint-Domingue.[13] As of 1763, increasingly restrictive legislations were passed to inhibit the social and political advancement of free coloreds and to safeguard white supremacy in the colony. Free people of color were forbidden from holding any public office or positions in courts of law, or to practice law at all for that matter. They were also barred from potentially lucrative professions in medicine, pharmacy, and goldsmithing.[14] Though it paled in comparison to the oppression suffered by African and Creole slaves in Saint-Domingue, the growing legalized discrimination against free people of color was humiliating, extending even to what clothes they could wear in public and, infinitely worse yet, it imperiled their freedom. Even the wealthiest among them, like the Ogé family in the North Province and the Raimond family in the South, were now at risk of being enslaved. This was clearly a people who had much to fight for, and they were about to take up arms.

Proclaimed in Paris in in August of 1789, *The Declaration of the Rights of Man and of the Citizen* stirred debate about the social and political status of free people of color in Saint-Domingue. Its assertion that "men are born free and remain free and equal in rights" stood in obvious contradiction to the social and political realities of Saint-Domingue and thus provided moral fuel for both the free colored civil rights movement and the abolitionist cause, which were on the verge of turning spectacularly violent. While in the metropole the National Assembly briefly considered the possible ramifications of the *Declaration* for its colonies, for free coloreds in Saint-Domingue the implications were as powerful as they were clear, and the impact of their interpretation of and response to events in France helped spark the Haitian Revolution in 1791.[15]

Free coloreds' interpretations of the *Declaration* provoked outrage among whites that soon escalated into physical violence in Saint-Domingue. For example, "a mulatto named Lacombe was hanged by them for having presented a humble exhortation in which he demanded the application of the principle *of the rights of man* in favor of his class." According to Ardouin, furthermore, "This petition was deemed to be incendiary because it opened with the words 'In the name of the Father, the Son, and the Holy Spirit'," reflecting a powerful merger of enlightenment ideals and Christian social ethics in the minds of the racially and politically marginalized of Dominguan society. "Thus this religious catchphrase, which this unfortunate soul imagined would move them to recall that in the eyes of the Divinity all men are equal, turned out to be his crime, for the whites, already become the gods of Saint-Domingue, did not affirm this equality as proclaimed by the religion of Christ."[16]

In September of 1789, Vincent Ogé, a Dominguan free colored working alongside of Raimond in Paris, presented to the National Assembly a document entitled *Cahier contentant les plaintes, doléances & reclamations des citoyens libres & proprietaries de couleur, des Îles & Colonies françaises* (Register containing the complaints, grievances, and demands of the free colored citizens and landowners of the French Islands and Colonies).[17] The document articulated the political aims of the Dominguan free coloreds, none more pressing than that of gaining seats for their own elected representatives in the National Assembly.[18] But Ogé soon lost his patience with the sputtering diplomacy in Paris, and just over a year later he returned to Saint-Domingue to take up arms for his people's cause. Along with another free colored named Jean-Baptiste Chavannes, a small-scale planter who had gained military experience in the American Revolution, Ogé mustered a force of several hundred insurgents in the North Province and sieged the town of Grande Rivière. In short order, French colonial administrators sent a large battalion to crush the rebellion, forcing Ogé and Chavannes to flee and seek asylum across the border. Spanish authorities extradited them to Saint-Domingue, however, and the two insurgent leaders were tried and executed in a ghastly public spectacle, broken on the wheel and decapitated, their heads placed on display as a gruesome warning to anyone else who might be entertaining the thought of fighting for their rights. In France, news of this horrific execution incited indignation and spurred increased sympathy for the cause of the *gens de couleur* in Saint-Domingue; it also "worsened relations between them [whites] and the free colored population in the island, preparing the way for the insurrection that broke out in the West province, where the two groups were almost equal in size, in August 1791."[19]

Raimond had by then been in Paris for more than six years, engaging in diplomacy on his Creole people's behalf as the drama of the French Revolution played out and the Haitian Revolution began.[20] The wealthy mixed-race indigo planter from Aquin circulated in France's prevailing political circles, and his writings went far in shaping revolutionary thought about the "rights of man" as they extended to free coloreds in the Americas, especially in Saint-Domingue, influencing the likes of Abbé Henri Grégoire, even though Raimond did not share Grégoire's abolitionism. The free people of color most attuned to Raimond's exhortations were his political colleagues in France and his ethno-economic brethren in Saint-Domingue, who endeavored to unify their struggle diplomatically, politically, and, when they saw no other choice, militarily. Raimond's lobbying efforts helped compel the National Assembly's March 28, 1790 decree that all property owners in the colonies of at least 25 years of age, regardless of color, be granted voting privileges, and its May 15, 1791 decree to extend full civil rights to *gens de couleur libres.*

For obvious reasons, the May 15 decree was arguably the most significant political development for Saint-Domingue's free coloreds in the colony's history. This was true for both wealthy planters and for merchants and farmers of lower socioeconomic standing, like Romaine Rivière. In this sense being comparable to Chavannes, Romaine was a small-scale coffee farmer whose relationship to slavery was drastically different from that of wealthy Dominguan mulattos like Ogé and Raimond, who considered themselves French and who were little influenced by African or local peasant/slave culture or identity. It is thus unimaginable that the likes of Chavannes or Romaine could ever have uttered or echoed anything like Raimond's proslavery assurance that "one can hardly imagine that I would want to suddenly ruin my whole family, which owns between 7 and 8 millions in property in Saint-Domingue," by way of promoting abolition.[21] The free colored rebellion of 1791 was thus not at all sprung from a unified social movement, which helps explain why Pierre Pinchinat's ascendant Confederacy ultimately failed to incorporate Romaine-la-Prophétesse and the Trou Coffy insurgency. As important, and contributing to the volatile sociopolitical cauldron out of which the Haitian Revolution would explosively percolate, the May 15 decree also exacerbated racial animosity throughout the colony, driving various factions among the free to take up arms for their respective causes, just as black slaves in the North Province were plotting their own massive insurrection.

During the very month when slaves in the colony's North Province launched their colossal revolt, in August 1791, the organization of the free colored civil rights movement culminated with a large gathering at the parish church in Mirebalais, in the West Province. There, delegates from throughout the colony elected Pierre Pinchinat as their president and convened a council of 40 representatives before the Colonial Assembly; they also "swore upon the last drop of their blood to protect the elected representatives against any attack or harassment while exercising their duties," as Carolyn Fick explains.[22] Though declared illegal by the highest ranking French official in Saint-Domingue, the governor general Philibert Rouxel François de Blanchelande, the council of 40 quickly signed concordats with mulattoes in Croix-des-Bouquets and Port-au-Prince and organized a chain of command for their Confederacy and its "combined army," with key military bases established in Bizoton and Croix-des-Bouquets. War was clearly on the brink.

Blanchelande's declaration that the Mirebalais free colored assembly was illegal had little concrete effect in the face of the Confederate Army's swelling to count some 4,000 troops, leaving whites with "no alternative but to come to terms with the mulattoes on a provincewide basis."[23] In mid-October, a conciliatory treaty between whites and mulattoes was brokered, which pledged, most importantly, to reinforce the decree of May 15 that had been passed in Paris. In the interim, however, the National Assembly had rescinded that decree, while the white Provincial Assembly in Port-au-Prince and the national guard maneuvered to block its implementation on their own. Chaos and mayhem ensued, riots erupted, and by the third week of November the city was largely in ruins and many free coloreds had been exiled or slaughtered.[24]

Just prior, at a September 1791 convention, around the very time that the Trou Coffy insurgency would begin, free coloreds had again outlined their demands, as summarized here by Ardouin:

1. that the whites would recognize *the equality of their political rights* rights that are guaranteed by natural law, the principles of the French Revolution, and the decrees of March 28, 1790 and May 15, 1791, as well as by the Code Noir.
2. that the privacy of correspondence be inviolable; a right that the whites had abused;
3. that *freedom of the press* be consecrated, save for legal responsibility;

4. that all *proscriptions* pronounced against the men of color be by decree, judgment, confiscations, etc., be annulled;
5. that future measures be taken to reverse all judgments pronounced against Ogé, Chavannes, and their compatriots.... [25]

That, in a word, is what they would soon be fighting for, though a closer look at the ground level, on the battlefield, reveals additional motives among those plotting insurrection. Like the insurgent black leaders in the North Georges Biassou and Jean-François Papillon, many free colored insurgents in the West understood themselves to be fighting not only for their rights but also for their king in France, whose reign of course began to seriously teeter as of 1789;[26] and, as we will see momentarily, this was certainly also the case for Romaine-la-Prophétesse and his followers at Trou Coffy. In addition, black insurgents in the North "were aware of the [French] Revolution's hostility toward the Church, and there is little reason to doubt the sincerity of their conviction that in opposing the whites, they were upholding the cause of religion,"[27] as surely was Romaine in the West, who was likewise poised to muster an army at Trou Coffy to defend the Catholic faith.

One of the real challenges of transatlantic diplomacy in the revolutionary Atlantic world was that news took so long to cross the ocean. When the National Assembly learned of staunch resistance to the May 15 decree in Saint-Domingue, they created a "National Civil Commission" of three military officers, Ignace-Frédéric de Mirbeck, Philippe-Rose Roume de Saint-Laurent, and Edmond de Saint-Léger, and sent them to the colony to impose the Assembly's will on whites who clamored against the decree's expansion of free coloreds' civil rights. But by the time that the Commission finally arrived in Saint-Domingue, in November 1791, the Assembly had suspended the May 15 decree, on September 24, and Mirbeck, Roume, and Saint-Léger immediately "found themselves confronting entirely new and far more serious problems: violent revolts of the slaves in the North Province and of the free population of color in the West."[28] Worse yet, from their perspective, the Commissioners were not accompanied by any military battalions from France, so were their diplomatic efforts to fail, which by then seemed and, in fact was, inevitable, they would need to rely on French troops already in the colony and/or muster forces among local Creoles.

With news of the suspension of the May 15 decree further fueling their rage, more free coloreds in the South and West Provinces of Saint-Domingue became militants and joined the insurgency already underway, either on their own or as foot soldiers in the Confederate Army. They were intent on taking what they believed to be legally and morally theirs, namely their civil rights as

French citizens, and any white elites in the colony who stood in their way simply had to be eliminated. This was stated explicitly by insurgents connected to Romaine-la-Prophétesse, who, according to one eyewitness, "announced that their intention was to take over all of Jacmel and to destroy all of the whites with the exception of a few old ones." More broadly speaking, Romaine's followers indicated that "they wanted to roast all of the whites, that the country was now theirs ... that soon they would manage to destroy the whites, that there would be a procession on every plantation to bring the blacks to recognize them and to restore order."[29]

Insurgent Camps in the South Province

The South Province of Saint-Domingue was the most remote in the colony, in terms of distance from the commercial and porting hub of Cap-Français, and hence from France, and the administrative capital of Port-au-Prince. Just as the South was thus largely left to fend for itself economically throughout Dominguan history, which contributed to a lively smuggling trade there, so too was it left to its own devices when forced to defend its cities and plantations from free colored insurgents and rebelling slaves in 1791 and 1792. For instance, an attempt by authorities in Les Cayes to protect some of the neighboring plantations against the rebels by sending a battalion of 300 armed men toward the end of 1791 failed to disperse the "brigands" and only "served to further fuel their ferocity." Numerous are the letters and reports (mostly written by whites and sometimes exaggerative of putative black or colored ferocity) in the archive to the Colonial Assembly in Cap-Français desperately pleading for help in the face of mounting "general revolt": for soldiers, arms, ammunition, and, by January of 1792, even food, out of a well-founded fear of "the horror of famine." Insurgents had been bombarding ships, blocking supply routes, and seeking to force whites and unallied free coloreds out of the city of Les Cayes, and their enemies had much to fear: "Our suffering is at its worst. Our patience, our efforts, and our proposals for peace to the armed men of color in the hills above la Ravine Seche have done nothing but pushed them to every excess.... Our situation is dire, and if help doesn't soon arrive ... we will be unable to evade a fatal subversion."[30]

The rebel camp at Ravine Sèche was one of several such militant bases around the city of Les Cayes and the smaller coastal towns of Aquin, Côteaux, Port-à-Piment, Port-Salut, St. Louis, and Torbeck, and the region's plantations. Among them, the most feared and influential was, like Trou Coffy in the West, located on the plantation of the insurgent who led it, a mulatto planter named Gérard Prou. The Prou plantation had been transformed into Camp Prou as early as late 1790, and by November 21, 1791, its insurgents had "raised the flag of rebellion," becoming "an illegal and vexing mob" and "making incursions into neighboring plantations."[31] Similar to the military objectives of the Trou Coffy insurgency, the Camp Prou militants' chief aim was to take over the region's main city, in Prou's case Les Cayes. Furthermore, the Prou insurgents raided Les Cayes not just for food, weapons, and other material things but also for spiritual things that it might obtain from the city's Catholic church. The stated demands of the Prou insurgents included half of the city's cannons with their ammunition and "to enter the city, 500 strong, drums beating, flags flying, to become the public defense force, to be received at a distance of 200 paces from the city by unarmed white citizens, who will give them the osculatorium."[32] Once a common feature of the Catholic Mass, an osculatorium is a wooden or metal tablet engraved with the image of the Virgin Mary, some other saint, or the Crucifixion that is passed around the congregation and kissed during the Peace Greeting. One can only speculate as to the specific reasons why the Prou insurgents desired the osculatorium from the Our Lady of the Assumption Church in Les Cayes, but it would be in keeping with the religious culture of many, if not all, rebel camps in Saint-Domingue for it to have been perceived of as both a protective and legitimating piece of religious capital.[33] In the Haitian Revolution, as it were, high-caliber cannons and Catholic ritual paraphernalia went hand-in-hand as weapons of great effect in the struggle for social justice.

In a society in which black slaves greatly outnumbered free residents, white, black or mulatto, by roughly ten to one, only the most desperate of predicaments would compel planters to arm their slaves to defend themselves against imminent attacks. Yet, this is precisely what slave owners in the South did after the insurgents had pillaged and torched several plantations, leaving an untold number of people "pitilessly massacred." Because they believed that their situation was desperate and about to get even worse, local whites decided to give weapons to 10 percent of their slaves. And speaking of weapons, for their part, the insurgents realized that achieving their objectives, which included by one account taking over the entire South Province and leaving the North and West provinces under white control, would require more firearms than they had, so in December they commandeered a ship and set out to intercept an arms shipment bound for Les Cayes, off the coast of Aquin. A French corsair attacked the insurgents' boat in the Bay of Aquin on December 26, however, opening fire and sinking the pirated vessel.

Outraged over the incident, on the last two days of the year the insurgents, "vile and execrable murderers" that they were said to be, embarked on a campaign "to water the entire plain with the blood of those poor white colonists."

Many were "seized, taken and subjected to the most frightful torments, and unspeakable cruelties unknown even in the most barbaric nation." Torbeck "was transformed into a theater of bloody scenes of horrible, premeditated death sentences for the whites." In one instance, allegedly "not satisfied with simply executing their victims, they cut them up into strips and salted them and they drink their blood mixed with tafia." The insurgents also "ordered slaves to no longer work for their masters, telling them that they were free." Some slaves refused and endeavored instead to protect their masters, like a group from "plantations surrounding Laborde [who] actually went to the white's military camp to join them in their combat against the mulattoes," and like a female slave who managed to hide an Englishman named King for several days and eventually deliver him to safe haven in Les Cayes. An elderly blind Frenchman, Monsieur de la Pivardiere, was not so fortunate, meanwhile, being killed despite the pleas of a 14-year-old slave boy who tried to save him; for his effort, the boy "was massacred with him." Two fleeing *commandeurs d'ateliers* (slave overseers), likely Creole slaves themselves, were captured by the insurgents and had their hands cut off.[34] Not even younger children were spared the insurgents' fury: With their parents forced to watch, two white siblings, aged four and twelve, were killed and gutted. The victims' stomachs were then fastened as hoods over their parents' heads before they, too, were summarily executed.[35]

Another group of mulatto and free black militants that terrorized the South Province, one in close collaboration with Camp Prou, was that led by Joseph Blek at Camp Mercy. Blek's insurgent campaign had extended to the extreme western tip of the province, to Dame Marie and Tiburon, before he was arrested, on February 18, 1792, during a raid on his camp that left four whites dead. He was examined by a doctor and cleared for interrogation the next morning by Jean-Baptiste Louis Mongin, *"avocat et parelement lieutenant de la Sénéchaussée de St. Louis gran prévot de la commission prevotale de la partie du Sud de Saint-Domingue,"* and his jury of other state functionaries with less bombastic titles. A Creole mulatto who had lived for some time in France (most likely for his education) and returned to Saint-Domingue in 1788, Blek was understandably cautious during questioning, as it was surely clear to him that his life was on the line.[36]

Blek did say a few things, however, and a confiscated letter that he had written sheds additional light on his motives and activities. Writing to a "compatriot," Blek had outlined a strategy for stealing cannons from St. Louis to deliver them to insurgents under his command in Dame Marie, part of an effort to mount a defense against a force of 700 soldiers then sailing to attack Camp Mercy, some of them English: "I am working to get a wagon to go on

Monday or Tuesday to try and get the cannons in St. Louis. You should see the necessity, as I do, of having 24 calibers to defeat our enemies and to bring our tyrants to reason." Blek also revealed that Camp Prou had supplied Camp Mercy with its ammunition, which itself derived from Grand Goâve; that Camp Prou was led by Gérard Prou; and that Camp Mercy was made up of "seventy to eighty men of color and four or five hundred Swiss," or absconding slaves who were hired as mercenaries, along with two surgeons.[37] Asked why the Mercy insurgents killed just about every white person that they came upon during a raid of Port-à-Piment, meanwhile, Blek said that he wasn't there but blamed blacks under the command of Justo Rancoll for that particular massacre, an assault that also left three black and two mulatto insurgents wounded and one black dead. Though he couldn't answer the question as to why the rebels "fired upon the king's ships each time they ported at Les Cayes," Blek did further reveal that Gérard Prou was the mastermind behind the sack of Port-à-Piment, while fingering a one Augstin Bellande as the culprit behind the torching of the area's plantations. And why did the rebels set fire to them? "To kill the whites."

For obvious reasons, Blek's captors were keen to gather as much intelligence from him as possible about Camp Mercy, and via their probing they learned that the number of militants in the camp had recently increased with the arrival of "ten mulattoes who came from Jérémie with a prodigious quantity of blacks." In terms of the camp's arsenal, at first Blek offered that they possessed but a single cannon, only later confessing that there were in fact four or five, and that the Mercy insurgents had "only about 80 guns," as well as a stockpile of lances and machetes. The interrogation also successfully elicited information about a third insurgent camp in the area, Camp Gerard, and key intelligence about the largest of the three, Camp Prou, where evidently Blek had been stationed prior to mustering troops at Camp Mercy. For instance, Gérard Prou's efforts to bring cannons from St. Louis to his camp had failed, but another leader of Camp Prou, Pierre Prou, perhaps Gérard's brother, did manage to secure three barrels of gun powder for the cannons that were already there. Pressed on the identities of other camp leaders, Blek named Dasque Morel Charlier and his brother Narcisse. The camp had "five or six sentries posted at a good distance," furthermore, to watch for attackers, and in the event that any were seen, Narcisse was to be alerted and the plantation bell would be rung to rouse the militants to arms.[38]

Though clearly "violent" and intent on devastating the white-dominated industry and prosperity of the South Province, the free colored insurgents at Camps Mercy and Prou were nothing like the "vexing mob" that municipal authorities in Les Cayes portrayed them to be. The camps had, after all, "councils" and officers (Narcisse was a "general major"), and their defense and excursions were carefully orchestrated. Like other insurgent gatherings in the West, Camp Mercy had some contact with the mulatto leadership in Croix-des-Bouquets—"not much," according to Blek, though he had signed some kind of treaty that they had sent to him just four days prior to his arrest, one that was being prepared for presentation to the National Civil Commission, led by the three *commissaires* recently sent from France to, among other objectives, explore the possibility of quelling the various rebellions then raging in Saint-Domingue. Camp Prou's written correspondence, meanwhile, even carried an official stamp bearing the letters "NLR." Blek did not know what they stood for but explained simply that the stamp "was the mark of Camp Prou, which was used to give leaves and permissions." Asked why he had left Camp Prou in the first place and went to Camp Mercy, finally, Blek simply lamented, "he didn't like war, especially this war."

One thing that Joseph Blek apparently liked very much and deeply revered was the Catholic Church. When the Prou and Mercy insurgents returned to their camps after their deadly raid on Port-à-Piment, Blek was alarmed to see that, in addition to the booty that one would expect the victorious raiders to bring home from such assaults, the blacks under Rancoll's charge had pillaged the church and brought with them "the sacred vessels."[39] Their motives for having done so are unclear, though some of the items were surely made of gold and thus might have enticed the pillagers as valuable in purely material terms; it is also possible that they hoped to arrange for Mass to be said in Camp Prou or Camp Mercy and wanted the items for that purpose, as was the case in Trou Coffy, where church paraphernalia had been acquired from the St. Rose de Lima Church in Léogâne for the Eucharistic services in the chapel that Romaine-la-Prophétesse had constructed on his plantation.[40] Or, they might have desired the items for employment as protective amulets, perhaps an early instance of a widespread feature of Haitian religious culture to this day, something noted as early in 1704 in the French Caribbean by the Jesuit missionary Père Labat, in regards to slaves' deep reverence for, and repurposing of, Eucharistic bread and holy water as powerful charms.[41] Beyond Haiti and throughout the Catholic world, holy oil has historically been among the items most often taken from churches for popular use as a protective ointment. This has been especially the case among thieves, furthermore, and thus, not surprisingly, the Camp Mercy insurgents took some from the church in Port-à-Piment.[42]

Whatever the motives of Rancoll's blacks in taking the sacred vessels, Blek pulled rank, seized them, and "searched in vain for the *curé* [parish priest] to give them back," an effort that would presumably have required him to make a perilous trip to post-raid Port-à-Piment. And despite Blek's witting or unwitting failure to remember a number of details that his captors pressed him for—the names of the two surgeons at Camp Mercy, for instance—he clearly knew which sacred vessels were in his possession and held them in high esteem, as evinced by his dropping everything in the midst of a rebellion to wander in search of a Catholic priest to restore them to their rightful place: "Interrogated as to what kind of vessels? Responded that there was a monstrance, an incensory, and the incense holder, a ciborium, a box of holy oils, but that he never found the chalice."

That the insurgents of Camps Mercy and Prou held Catholic liturgical objects and priests in high regard is unsurprising, as this was common among black and free colored rebels in Saint-Domingue. That they stole such objects from a church was, however, exceptional. As David Geggus observes, "During the Revolution there is no evidence of damage to churches by the insurgents, nor even of theft of sacred vessels in areas the blacks controlled."[43] Geggus also notes that Catholic priests almost always enjoyed the protection of the rebels and were never mistreated by them, and this was clearly the case with the curé of Port-à-Piment, who seems to have been the only white person spared in the gruesome raid, judging by Blek's seeking him out to return the sacred vessels to him. Blek couldn't find the priest, however, so he "wrapped them up and sent them to Camp Prou." It is unknown, meanwhile, if the Camp Prou insurgents ever succeeded in obtaining the osculatorium from the church in Les Cayes; one thing is certain, though: They would have taken good care of it had they done so, even if they might have fetishized it. In any case, a sense of humanity leads one to hope that Blek's Catholic faith was at least of some comfort to him when, following his interrogation, "on February 8, 1792, he was *pummeled, tarred, and roasted alive*" by enraged whites in Les Cayes.[44]

The arrival of the national civil commissioners in the colony in late November of 1791 spawned concerted efforts to quell the uprisings in the South and West Provinces and/or to have them subsumed by the Confederacy. Much to the chagrin of Les Cayes's white residents, the commissioners enlisted the Confederate general André Rigaud to oversee a plan to disarm or at least pacify the insurgents in the South, while an April 4 decree in Paris restored the civil rights of free coloreds, temporarily alleviating tensions between whites and mulattos in Saint-Domingue. Surely not helping matters, though, the first thing Rigaud did once arriving on scene, on March 2, was to station a cannon on a hill overlooking Les Cayes and bombard the city for an entire day. Contrary to the commissioners' intentions, his very arrival only served to further embolden the insurgents.[45] Even with the dispersal of Camp Mercy in February 1792, the region was wracked by "new fires, new raids, and new atrocities."[46] What had begun as a civil war pitting free coloreds against whites was inexorably turning into a massive slave revolt. By the time that Governor Blanchelande embarked with a battalion for the South Province to repel the insurgency there, in early August 1792, an insurmountable number of slaves had joined the insurrection. His efforts thus failed miserably, and Blanchelande returned to France humiliated, was received as a traitor, and faced the ignominy of being among the first persons beheaded by guillotine during the Reign of Terror, on April 15, 1793. In the South Province of Saint-Domingue, meanwhile, insurgent camps grew and new ones formed, "from which the leaders surveyed their remaining troops, waiting and watching for a new opportunity to strike."[47] The Haitian Revolution was well underway.

The Rise of Romaine-la-Prophétesse and the Trou Coffy Insurgency

It was in the sociopolitical context described above, especially the growing racial animosity between whites and free coloreds in Saint-Domingue, that Romaine-la-Prophétesse rose to prominence and his insurgent movement at Trou Coffy emerged. Though the next chapter of this book is devoted entirely to the question just who Romaine was, a few words on this matter are here in order, along with a brief explanation of how the rebel camp at Trou Coffy developed in the first place. In an earlier article on the subject I had argued that Romaine may have been Kongolese, or at least that many of his followers were and that his appeal to them could be partially explained in Kongolese religious terms.[48] Although I remain convinced that Kongolese religious thought was important to his charisma and congregation, subsequent research indicates definitively that Romaine was himself not Kongolese, for church and notarial records clearly and consistently indicate that he was a "free black" who was born on the Spanish side of the island around 1750.[49] And while there are some (albeit fewer) primary source documents that refer to Romaine as being a *griffe* (meaning one-fourth white and three-fourths black), rather than a black, it is important to remember that racial classifications in Saint-Domingue were ambiguous and shifting, and that someone who might be taken as a *griffe* (*grif, griffon*) by one observer could just as well be seen as a black or mulatto by another.

There is greater consistency in the archive about Romaine's ethnic identity, meanwhile, as being "Spanish," meaning that he was an immigrant from the Spanish side of the island of Hispaniola. Importantly, this is how he was identified by the observer who knew him best, and one of only two authors of any of the documents in the archive, apart from the parish and notarial records, who actually met the prophetess in person, Abbé Ouvière. Ouvière, in fact, did not even allude to Romaine's race in his earliest report on Trou Coffy, just offering instead that the prophetess was "a Spaniard," tout court.[50] His designation is clear evidence to conclusively affirm that Romaine-la-Prophétesse was born and raised on the Spanish side of the island of Hispaniola and not anywhere in Africa or Saint-Domingue. He migrated across the border seemingly in search of fortune, lured by the coffee boom in the 1770s–1780s in the colony's West Province. This, at any rate, is where Romaine Rivière enters the historical record, as the owner of a small coffee plantation in a place called Trou Coffy, located in the hills above the Plain of Léogâne.

Contemporary observers described Trou Coffy as being about "eight leagues from Léogâne," situated "in a deep, narrow valley, of difficult access, surrounded by mountains" and resembling "the ancient crater of a volcano."[51] Abbé Ouvière further elaborated that it was "near the summit of a mountain that was dominated by an infinity of some other smaller hills, partly covered and reaching down all the way to the sea at the south" and "covered with beautiful orchids of coffee."[52] I have located Trou Coffy to be part of today's Communal Section of Fondwa (Fr: Fonds d'Oei; lit: Goose Depths), in the Commune of Léogâne in Haiti's West Province, just as had M. L. E. Moreau de Saint-Méry in the late eighteenth century, more specifically "between Coq Qui Chante and Fondoir."[53] Judging from the very few times that Trou Coffy appears in the Léogâne and Jacmel church registries, it would appear that the place was quite sparsely populated in the colonial era.[54]

Most of Haiti is very hilly and mountainous, and virtually every ravine, dale, nook, and cranny in the nation's mountains and hills has been named, in some cases numerously, whether formally or informally. In Haitian Creole, "*twou*" can refer either to a ravine or a small bay, while "*nan*" usually refers to a ravine or small valley and has no maritime referent. *Twous* usually differ from ravines and *nans* in being more circular or square in surface shape than ovular or elongated. Trou Coffy was (and is) obviously the former, and Fondwa's elevation is nearly 2,000 feet.[55] In scoffing at the name of the parish of Trou in the North Province of Saint-Domingue (today called Trou du Nord), meanwhile, the Jesuit Father Margat explained almost apologetically in a 1743 letter to his order's superior in France that the first French "colonists were not elegant when it came to naming places, as is too often seen in the ridiculous names that they gave to different districts. They call TROU here any and all gaps of decent width that extend between two mountains and empties onto some plain."[56] As for "Coffy," two possibilities for the origin of word spring immediately to mind: (1) it was a rich coffee-planting zone, though coffee in

French is *"café,"* and in light of their being almost no English place names anywhere in Haiti, one could reasonably doubt this derivation; and (2) Koffi is a common personal name in West Africa, and thus Trou Coffy might derive its name from an African woman or man associated with the location.

Many insurgent camps in revolutionary Saint-Domingue were, like Trou Coffy, described by those who feared them as being of very difficult access. In topographical terms, however, that was sometimes an overstatement. The mayor of Léogâne, Villards, for instance, managed to visit from his city in September of 1791, as did Abbé Ouvière three months later. After his brief

FIGURE 1.1 A black Dominguan, member of the free colored class to which Romaine-la-Prophétesse belonged and for which he fought, asserts his liberty.

stay in the notorious camp in late December 1791, furthermore, the priest explained that Trou Coffy was "inaccessible" not so much because of topography but because of "terror,"[57] though later in life he would describe getting there during a stormy night to have been a rather harrowing experience, an ascending journey on horseback that meandered "through some narrow paths and along the edges of cliffs that only the instincts of the horses and the familiarity of their guides could navigate."[58] It was that kind of familiarity that enabled Romaine's troops to effectively and stealthily circulate throughout the mountains and plains between Jacmel and Léogâne, in any case, and their tactics of raiding, often by night, and retreating to their naturally well-fortified redoubt at Trou Coffy reflects the African military experience that some of them surely drew upon. In this respect, Romaine's band were hardly unique among the earliest waves of slave and/or free colored insurgents in Saint-Domingue, as they skillfully employed guerilla tactics that took full advantage of the topography in posting troops and launching ambushes and assaults.[59]

Abbé Ouvière's are the only descriptions of Trou Coffy that I have found in the primary source material offered by someone who had actually visited the place. By the priest's account, Romaine's coffee plantation possessed a "*grande caze*" (big house) and was situated in a "tilted corner" (*coin renverse*) and "surrounded" on all sides by high mountains.[60] In addition to the big house, which seemed to the priest to be "an old habitation that Romaine had taken over to ensure the security of his assembly," the camp "appeared to be covered with huts or small huts, by whose lights I could count them."[61] One would imagine that the huts were originally small dwellings for slaves, and that the plantation also featured some kind of a barn for storing cultivated coffee awaiting transport to port or market, as well as outhouses, a kitchen, a grater mill, a peeling mill, a winnowing mill, carpentry and masonry workshops, a large basin for washing coffee, and drying racks, as well as pens for poultry, a pasture for cattle, and a stable for horses. In addition to a cistern or pond, gardens, orchards, and walks, there must have also been some forest on the property as well, for, as P. J. Laborie, who was a coffee plantation owner himself, informs in his detailed how-to book *The Coffee Plantation of San Domingo*, "A tract of standing woodland, which will always be useful in the most advanced periods, must always be left within reach."[62] Though we cannot presently say how many slaves might have labored on Romaine's plantation, by way of context it is worth considering that "the average coffee plantation in Saint-Domingue had only 33 slaves and many had less than two dozen."[63]

Although like several other scholars I once thought that Romaine-la-Prophétesse had occupied an abandoned church at Trou Coffy, I no longer believe that there ever was one there, abandoned or other.[64] Saint-Domingue had relatively few churches, and most of them were in the colony's cities and towns. The prophetess did, however, arrange for the construction of a chapel on his plantation, according to Father Bloüet, the curé of Jacmel.[65] Though in his letters to the priest the mayor of Léogâne, Villards, never mentioned the chapel at Trou Coffy, Father Menetrier, the curé of Léogâne, described it to Abbé Ouvière as being "very pretty."[66] One could judiciously speculate, furthermore, that chapels were more common on plantations owned by free coloreds like Romaine than those owned by whites, for "free coloreds tended to be strongly pious," as Stewart King explains, taking "up Roman Catholic piety just as whites were drifting away from it."[67] Léogâne's parish registries between 1780 and 1792 corroborate this observation, as relatively few whites seem to have bothered having their children baptized, whereas hundreds of free colored parents did; Romaine himself sponsored no fewer than nine free colored godchildren, for instance, between 1784 and 1791.[68]

What sparked the Trou Coffy insurgency in the first place? It appears that the movement began not so much as a unified insurgency but as a feud between Romaine, a free black, and a neighboring white planter, Monsieur Joseph-Marie Tavet, one of the wealthiest and most powerful *habitants* in the region. Fearful of repercussions from mounting tensions between whites and free coloreds elsewhere in the colony, especially Port-au-Prince, Tavet amassed about 100 armed men on his plantation. In reaction, and aware of "the mistreatment that the whites of the colony never ceased to mete out against the people of color," the prophetess felt "obliged to become their leader to protect them."[69] Thus inspired, Romaine summoned his free colored contacts and friends, and some *petits blancs,* from Jacmel, Léogâne, Grand Goâve, and Petit Goâve to his plantation, with arms, which soon resulted in "an even much larger" gathering on his plantation than that which had amassed on Tavet's. The Trou Coffy movement surged from that point on, especially once the prophetess began receiving messages from the spirit world that transformed him into a warlord:

> The Trou Coffy camp continued its excursions and its acts of brigandage. The leader of these villains managed to maintain order so well, like another Mohammed, by surrounding himself with the device of religion, with all the trappings of a cult, with himself as its minister, bestowing on himself the gift of prophecy. Knowing as we do the blacks and their penchant for superstition, we can see how easily they obeyed this imposter with veneration.[70]

Not surprisingly, Monsieur Tavet's plantation would be among the first that Romaine would target, with his troops "surrounding its *cazes* and striking Sieur Constant several times with sabers, leaving him maimed," on or around September 24, 1791.[71] Following their prophetess' command, "they penetrated further into the plantation, completely destroying it and burning it. The noise of this violence announced with many excuses that these devastators had only villainy as their motive." And as such, "the Mohammed of Saint Domingue," the Virgin Mary's godson, launched his mission to conquer Jacmel, Léogâne, and the entire island.[72]

Soon the number of rebels joining the Trou Coffy insurgency grew dramatically, and they would spend the next six months wreaking havoc throughout the region, eventually sieging both the cities of Léogâne and Jacmel, as we shall see.[73] Romaine's closest collaborators, members of his high command, numbered at least six, all but one of them free coloreds, none of whom had seemingly ever been slaves or maroons: *Colonel Général* Elie Courlogne, Alexandre Boursiquot, Henry Charpentier, Gros Poisson, and Soliment.[74] The sixth and the exception was a *petit blanc* named Delisle de Bresolle, who "called himself the *capitaine general* of the free people of color," a violent man whose efforts to carve out a fortune for himself in Saint-Domingue seemingly hadn't by then panned out, thus impelling him to vent his rage by joining the insurgency.[75] In the Jacmel insurgent theater Delisle would emerge as "one of the principal chiefs of the brigands," and it is clear that no member of the Trou Coffy insurgency played a larger role in the siege of the city of Jacmel.[76] A letter dated March 1, 1792, could be read as placing Delisle in Romaine's camp at Trou Coffy; at the very least, it demonstrates that he was certainly in communication with Romaine-la-Prophétesse throughout the insurgency.[77]

Trou Coffy and the Jacmel Insurgent Theater

Led chiefly by free coloreds who understandably felt threatened by increasing racial discrimination against them in Saint-Domingue, insurgent camps like Prou in the South Province and Trou Coffy in the West devastated these parts of the colony though their violent raids on plantations and towns, killing many in their wake, cutting off supply routes to their enemies, and destroying virtually an entire season's harvest in what had been a tremendously lucrative planting region. In the case of the West Province, the Trou Coffy insurgency, based on Romaine's coffee plantation, was the most feared and destructive of the militant camps, being, in conjunction with satellite camps that ultimately answered to the prophetess, responsible for the siege of Léogâne, the occupation and torching of Jacmel, and the pillaging and devastation of plantations throughout the surrounding mountains and plains. In effect, the Trou Coffy insurgency unfolded in two distinct but overlapping theaters of military operation, one centered on Jacmel and the other on Léogâne. Along the south coast, meanwhile, the insurgency's swath of death and destruction reached from Marigot, located roughly 25 kilometers to the east of Jacmel, to Bainet, located about 45 kilometers to the west of the city.

In his official report to the French state on the *"troubles"* in Saint-Domingue, which was published in Paris in four volumes between 1796 and 1799, the attorney and legislator Jean-Philippe Garran de Coulon explains that Trou Coffy's assaults on Jacmel began as follows:

> The city of Jacmel, located a short distance from the infernal redoubt of Trou Coffi, where Romaine had established the seat of his tyranny, has more than once witnessed its territory ravaged by the incursions of the villains directed by this imposter; and the whites as well as the men of color in the surrounding area were quick to adopt his principles of anarchy and of ferocity in allying themselves with him.[78]

Put somewhat more philosophically, Garran attributed the "gruesome examples" of "Trou-Coffi" to "a sentiment so sadly tied to so many other affections of the human heart," namely "vengeance . . . which knows practically no limits once it has taken its first step."[79]

One of the most valuable archival documents for understanding the insurgency in and around Jacmel in 1791–1792 is a 47-page report entitled *Précis des faits qui se sont passés dans la paroisse de Jacmel et sa dépendance, depuis le commencement de septembre 1791 jusqu'à ce jour—onze mars 1792* ("Summary of events that occurred in the Jacmel parish and environs, since the beginning of September 1791 up to today, March 11, 1792"). From this report we learn that as of September 1, 1791, "the people of color and the free blacks of the *dépendance de Jacmel,* without providing the municipality with any explanation as to why, banded together in arms in several places, notably at la Grande Rivière and la Gosseline, where they opened fire on a number of whites." Within a week, the rebels began burning area plantations and killing anyone who stood in their way, like, for example, a mason at Sieur Lautine's plantation named Jean, who was beheaded, and "Sieur Deshayes, a planter [*habitant*] in Grand Harpon."[80] Deshayes was also decapitated, and his "head was placed on display on the fence of the so-called Romain chief of Trou Coffy." In a telling act that was both symbolically and literally cogent, "these brigands cut the whips of the slave drivers." As was reported among insurgents throughout all three of Saint-Domingue's provinces, furthermore, Romaine's troops "said to the slaves that the King had granted them their freedom, that it it was no longer necessary to work."

Toward the end of September insurgent camps had formed near "Grande Riviere, Rivière de Gauche, La Gosseline, Jacmel Mountain, and Trou Coffy," and their raids were designed to pillage weapons and supplies, torch plantations, and to slaughter anyone unallied with their cause. One of the first in the area to be targeted was *habitation* Reynaud, which was raided and burned to the ground by "45 brigands armed with sabers, guns, and pistols" at the break of day on September 23. The insurgents stormed the big house and other buildings and "opened fire on anyone they fell upon," taking Sieur Reynaud and his children's tutor hostage; their lives were only spared "due to the pleading and weeping of Madame Reynaud and her children, who were themselves mistreated and subjected to saber slashes." The following day, the insurgents raided a bakery in Grande Riviere owned by a man named Jean Portier, taking all the bread, wine, and tafia, along with "a gun and a pair of pistols," while evidently leaving Portier himself unharmed, perhaps because he had cooperated with the insurgents and handed over these coveted things without objection.

By the time of the bakery incident in Grande Rivière, municipal officials in Jacmel clearly realized both the mounting threat that the insurgency represented and the position of primacy that Trou Coffy had assumed among various rebel camps throughout the region. Hence, they decided to attempt to quell the violence through diplomacy before things escalated to the level that they had already reached the previous month in the North Province, the epochal and immense slave uprising around the colony's crown jewel city, Cap-Français. Yet, unlike the insurrectionary slaves in the North Province, the mulattoes who launched the insurgency in the West, as in the South, "did not want to stir up a revolution in Saint-Domingue," as John Garrigus explains. "But that is exactly what they ended up doing."[81]

Soon after the insurgent raids in and around the city began, the *"Municipalité"* of Jacmel organized a delegation of "forty men and some brigades of the *maréchaussé*," the local constabulary tasked usually with hunting down escaped slaves, and sent them toward Trou Coffy with the aim of entering into negotiations and hopefully securing a peace treaty with Romaine-la-Prophétesse. Led by Monseiur Quirion, "major general of the national guard of Jacmel," the negotiating party made their way to Coq Qui Chante, just two leagues south of Trou Coffy, where they camped out on Tavet's desolate, devastated plantation. Along the way they evidently began entertaining plans to attack Trou Coffy outright rather than seeking peace through diplomacy, as

Quirion sent word from Coq Qui Chante to authorities in Léogâne about their mission and requested "reinforcements to conquer and force the brigands gathered at Trou Coffy to disband." For their part, the surviving residents of Coq Qui Chante also wrote to the king's representative *(commandant par le roi)* in Léogâne, M. de Villards, indicating that they wished for negotiations with Romaine to take place. The response from Léogâne was probably not what they had been hoping for; for one thing, no additional troops would be sent, while for another, Villards instructed the Jacmel delegation "to take no further action until he arrived on the scene," for some reason adding what should have seemed obvious, "that he condemned the activities of the people at Trou Coffy."

Accompanied by three men of color, Mayor de Villards soon arrived in Coq Qui Chante and instructed Quirion to name four *commissaires* from among his own charges to go with him to "Camp Cophy . . . to deal with the miscreants." As they neared Trou Coffy, Villards insisted on walking alone ahead of the others "because he was known to these brigands." The insurgents not only knew him, but they also recognized him as the king's representative, for upon seeing the mayor approach the camp they broke out into ecstatic cries of "Long live the King! Long live our sad King!" The insurgents' deep royalism was thus resoundingly manifest in the high esteem in which they held the mayor, which greatly impressed and probably surprised the delegates from Jacmel, to whom "it seemed that Sieur de Villards enjoyed very high consideration and that he had much authority [among the insurgents]." Negotiations with Trou Coffy quickly proceeded and appeared to have gone swimmingly: "the brigands promised to henceforth be tranquil, to free the prisoners, return what they had stolen, and to disband as soon as the Jacmel detachment left." The detachment returned to Jacmel the next day, along with the prisoners they had freed and a sense of hope that an important step toward restoring peace and order to the region had been taken. It was a false sense of hope, alas, because "the promises that the miscreants had made were not kept at all, except for the freeing of the prisoners."

Within days of the ill-fated negotiations "a battalion of men of color and free blacks descended upon several plantations in Coq Qui Chante, where they murdered Sieur Dugage, a local, Langeudoc, an old octogenarian from Léogâne, and La Mazare, manager of the Dupiton plantation." Though Trou Coffy is not explicitly blamed for these attacks, given the camp's close proximity to Coq Qui Chante, it is certain that Romaine's followers indeed carried them out; in one of their signature moves, furthermore, "they cut the whips of the slave drivers."

Meanwhile in Jacmel, the very next day, on September 25:

> [A]t nine o'clock in the morning, men of color and free blacks with guns, sabers, and pistols spread out in different parts of the city, the largest number to the fort; one detachment of about 30 men of color went to the prison and freed five or six mulattos and free blacks and took them away, [men] who had been arrested as accomplices and accused of various thefts and murders; then they went down to the road along the seaside where they broke into several people's homes and opened fire . . . they mortally wounded Sieur Lenoir, who was sick in bed, and others were rather gravely wounded.[82]

Father Bloüet identified Henry Charpentier as "a young mulatto already renowned for his cruelties" who led the attack on the seaside homes. Charpentier allegedly acted "with the intention of killing fifty to sixty whites" and was the one who had shot Lenoir, "his own landlord." Panic swept the city, and whites along the seaside fled to ships anchored in the bay. "Reinforced by all the other brigands," Charpentier and company pillaged homes and businesses and opened fire on "the widow Minot," who tried to escape "by diving into the sea at the risk of being taken and devoured by sharks or ravaged by the waves, the likes of which here are unimaginable. In a word, the rage of these traitors has reached its height and threatened to devour any whites who didn't make it to ships in the harbor."[83] Those who fled into the woods, meanwhile, "were hunted down with dogs." Once calm was restored, local officials sought to file charges against Charpentier, "but he was never arrested or brought to justice." "Calm" here is a relative term, as "the fires continued, as did the pillaging and the murders in distant quarters, the roads along the grand riviere de Jacmel and the josseline [i.e., La Gosseline] were littered with the mutilated cadavers of whites."[84]

Just following the late-September violence in and around Jacmel, nearer to Bainet and Petit Goâve, at least three whites were killed on plantations by "blacks in insurrection," according to parish funerary records, and buried in Bainet on October 10, 1791.[85] There is evidence that these attacks were orchestrated out of Trou Coffy, and it is not difficult to imagine that news of events in Jacmel inspired something of a clamor in Bainet that incited the slaves in question to take up arms and kill their masters with the intention of joining the ascendant rebel movement. The attack on Bainet was the work of a member of Romaine's inner circle, moreover, Alexandre Boursiquot, "the most infamous *homme de couleur* who had massacred in the parish of Daynette [Bainet] 30 whites in a single day," as one French official alleged.[86]

Garran likewise implicates Boursiquot, along with other free coloreds from Jacmel, in the slaughter, describing the event in grisly detailed based on the testimony of one white man who was fortunate enough to escape with his life:

> Forty-seven whites . . . were arrested by the men of color of Baynet . . . they were then tied in this state to long pole, and taken while being whipped one league out of the city, where they were shot by the men of color. One particular circumstance seems to exacerbate the atrocity of this murder. There is reason to believe that it had been premeditated months in advance. A letter from a man of color who was, it is said, one of the leaders of Trou-Coffi, wrote to one of the *habitants* of Baynet toward the end of the year prior, entreating him to leave with all of the good citizens, following the uselessness of their efforts for peace, because in twenty-four hours the town will be subjected to flames and blood.[87]

News of the massacre of mulattoes during the catastrophic violence in Port au Prince in November reverberated throughout the West and South Provinces, likely tossing more fuel onto the rage behind the Bainet killings and a renewed thirst for revenge among the insurgents for the spilt blood of their "brothers." Free blacks and mulattoes who resided in Jacmel, "who had previously been on good terms with the whites . . . now began organizing themselves in armed defense as well, whereupon the whites attacked and drove them out of the city."[88] Undoubtedly, many of these banished mulatto *jacmeliens* joined the insurgents in their efforts to not only take over the city but also to exterminate their enemies in the process. Some of them bunkered in at Camp Pasquet, whose leadership position would soon be assumed by one of Romaine's officers, Gros Poisson.[89] A renewed fervor swept Trou Coffy, where perhaps Romaine-la-Prophétesse was receiving fresh messages from the Virgin Mary to ramp up his efforts to conquer Jacmel. By late November, "daily complaints" were being lodged to Monsieur Vissière, Jacmel's military commander, about "how the gathering . . . at Trou Coffy relentlessly committed murder, theft, and arson," including the pillaging and torching of several additional plantations in Coq Qui Chante. With the insurgency spreading along the south coast and with free colored rage on the rise, meanwhile, on December 2, whites "of every age and sex" in Sal Trou, near Belle Anse, were forced to flee in canoes because of "the furor of the people of color and free blacks, who had killed many and torched several plantations," rowing in the Caribbean Sea to seek refuge in Jacmel, a distance of some 80 kilometers.[90]

Among the many atrocious crimes that the archival sources allege to have been committed by the Trou Coffy insurgents, one of the most pivotal occurred during the second week of December in 1791. After further attempts at diplomacy had failed to produce "anything more than a war that was more horrible and cruel than ever," on the evening of December 9,

> a mob went to the plantation of Sieur Propice, one league from this city. After treating themselves to supper and liberating the slaves, they fired three shots which killed him, and they cut off his head, which they displayed on the fence of his plantation in front of the main road, then pillaging the place, making off with a good deal of money that Sieur Propice had there and taking all of his horses.

In response, Jacmel sent a detachment of white troops and loyal *gens de couleur* to the Propice plantation, arresting several of the planter's slaves on suspicion that they had conspired in his murder. The city also convened the General Council of the Commune, inviting representatives "of both clans" from around the area to decide what course of action to take, resulting in increased patrols in and around the city, tight surveillance over people of color, and the declaration of martial law.

Just days later, on December 14, Romaine and his second-in-command, a free colored man named Elie Courlogne, "sent two letters from Trou Coffy," one addressed to the municipal authorities and the other to the commander general of the *gens de couleur*, by which they demanded that the subjects arrested in connection with the murder of Sieur Propice be released from prison. They justified their demand out of concerns for "humanity, which should guide all of our actions." Dramatically punctuating their demand, the next morning, "a free black named Brunet, armed with a saber and a pistol," stormed into Jacmel screaming "that the horse that he was riding was Sieur Propice's, that he defied anyone who would dare try to take it from him, and that in two hours all whites would be murdered if they didn't arrange for the release of all prisoners and if they didn't leave on the ships anchored offshore." Brunet raced about town on the late Propice's horse while firing shots into the air and volleying insults "at all the citizens," before speeding off. The local military commander sounded the alarm, ordering everyone to grab their weapons and take refuge in the fort, while "many others who were aboard the ships came ashore to join their brothers." But nothing happened, for the time being at least, and a tense calm descended upon the city.

According to one letter signed by Tavet and other local elites, by early January the city of Jacmel was "surrounded by five camps of mulattoes, one at the Pasquet plantation, one at La Gosseline, one at the Remour plantation," and another at Cayes Jacmel, all of them also consisting in part by then of "a large number of blacks that they took from our work sites and have armed against us."[91] Listed here are the insurgent camps closest to Jacmel, though city officials knew and in fact had stated earlier that Trou Coffy was the camp that was to be most feared, one that "harbored lively hostilities" against them and seemingly occupied some measure of authority over the others.[92] There was now every reason to believe that the insurgent camps surrounding the city were Trou Coffy satellites.

Within a few weeks of the Brunet affair, periodically insurgents from these camps would mount further attacks on the city, perhaps whenever they needed food or other supplies, and life in Jacmel became increasingly harsh and insecure. Even when things were relatively quiet, travel outside the city was a risky affair, as the insurgents posted troops to prohibit supplies from getting through or simply to rob and at times kill those who had no choice but to be on the road. Father Bloüet experienced this firsthand: "Upon returning from some rounds that were necessitated by my ministry, I was myself stopped and frisked by a foreign mulatto, who didn't recognize me personally but who recognized my garb." Thus realizing that Bloüet was a Catholic priest, the foreign mulatto insurgent released the curé unharmed.

The number of insurgents in the Jacmel theater grew as liberated slaves joined their ranks, with new rebel camps emerging in the surrounding area as well. Especially alarming to the residents of Jacmel was news that as of Christmas 1791, an insurgent camp had been established on the DesMarattes plantation, under the leadership of Alexandre Boursiquot, "within cannon fire range of the city."[93] The rebel camps on the Pasquet and DesMarattes plantations were indeed soon buzzing with activity.[94] Their opportune locations enabled the insurgents to orchestrate new incursions onto neighboring plantations and to move forward with plans to take over the city. Meanwhile, Boursiquot and several collaborators "wrote a letter from Camp Pasquet to the municipal authorities in which they expressed their desire for an inviolable peace but that they wanted first to exchange prisoners.... The municipality replied that they could send our prisoners and those in our custody would be faithfully returned."[95] But, as with the failed negotiations with Romaine and Trou Coffy three months earlier, Jacmel's agreement with Boursiquot and Camp Pasquet would only lead to the release of a few prisoners, while peace of any kind, inviolable or other, would prove to be elusive. In fact, the violence and destruction was about to get worse. A few days after the prisoner exchange, a city delegation was lured out of Jacmel to participate in negotiations with "Sieur Delisle" on a plantation just outside the city, near la Creste à Palmiste. Delisle de Bresolle, a *petit blanc,* was said to be possessed by "a mortal hatred of the *grands blancs creoles,*" which evidently fueled his participation in the free colored insurgency around Jacmel.[96] Wary because of reports that Delisle had "a few days prior delivered the most violent speech against the whites," the delegation was accompanied by an armed detachment. That precaution was of little avail, though, for as soon as they came within view of the occupied plantation, the rebels ambushed them and opened fire. Seven members of the delegation were left dead.[97]

Although I have found no evidence that Romaine-la-Prophétesse personally participated in any raids, either in the Jacmel or Léogâne theater, he is clearly identified in several primary source documents to be the leader of the Trou Coffy insurgency, holding the rank of "*Commandant Général,*" which, coincidently and by way of illustration, was the rank that the Marquis de Lafayette held during his participation in the American Revolution.[98] On the ground in the Jacmel theater, meanwhile, the field marshal with the greatest authority and influence appears to have been Delisle, a "*mésaillé*" who, thanks to his whiteness, is one of the very few "brigands" to be at times referred to in the archives with the title of respect "*Sieur*" (Sire or Sir).[99]

La municipalité de Jacmel went on the counteroffensive on January 4, 1792, assembling a detachment of dragoons and dispatching it with a cannon to attack a group of insurgents who had just raided and occupied the La Conte plantation. No sooner had they reached the edge of the plantation, however, that they were fired upon by the insurgents, who put up "a vigorous resistance." The dragoons responded with cannon fire, which eventually succeeded in forcing the rebels to retreat to the DesMarattes plantation, where "they took cover in the bushes." Indicative of how effective were collaborations between the various insurgent camps in the area, by nightfall "they were joined by a considerable reinforcement from Camp Pasquet." This would force the dragoons to abandon any plan that they might have had to further pursue the insurgents by raiding their camp at *habitation* DesMarattes, or at least to postpone it.

With several more plantations having been pillaged and torched in the interim, military commanders in Jacmel decided to mount a full-scale offensive on Camp Pasquet, which by then possessed at least two cannons. On January 17, the day after Delisle had led "a large number of people of color" in raiding the plantation of Sieur Feraud in Cap Rouge, the Jacmel dragoons attacked Camp Pasquet, driving the rebels to scurry to DesMarattes and managing to seize their cannons. Five members of the Jacmel detachment were killed in the battle. The next day, meanwhile, in an incursion from the east, Delisle led a contingent of mulattoes from Cayes Jacmel, joined by another led by Cadet Raffy, and raided and occupied the Cyvadier plantation, "in such a way that we now find ourselves blocked in," as city officials reported. "From that point on we could no longer send our servants to the river . . . and needed to send an armed detachment to gather the water that we needed."

By January 19, the insurgents had stationed as many as 12 cannons close enough to the city to begin profusely bombarding Jacmel. Another detachment of dragoons set out on a counteroffensive, only to be repelled by an ambush shortly after embarking. The writing on the wall was clear: "The enemy was readying for an attack, with everyone gone to his post. In effect, they mounted their artillery at several spots on a hill, to the northwest and within gunshot ranges of the fort, from which they began to fire upon us at six o'clock" in the morning. That night, the insurgents used the cover of darkness "to slip into the city with torches and incendiary devices, and they torched the north and northwest parts of the city in a gust of terror." Penetrating further into the streets of Jacmel during the course of the night, burning houses and businesses along the way until five o'clock the next morning, they left the city "covered by flames and smoke." Other insurgents who had occupied the Beaudoin plantation to the east, likely Delisle's troops, fired even more cannonballs on the city and proceeded toward the church, freeing slaves along the way, setting fire to the courthouse, and "stationing themselves in the Garraud house on the seaside and in front of the fort, to kill us if the fire chased us from our post, as they had hoped, and if we needed to flee, but they were fooled in their hope." The fort held initially, but Jacmel was devastated, with 130 of its houses reduced to cinders.

The attacks intensified on January 21, with upward of "13,000 mulattoes and negroes" raiding "in the most undaunted manner at four o'clock in the afternoon." They surrounded the city and the fort, prohibiting anyone from fleeing, and their efforts were bolstered by shots fired from cannons that had been stolen from Marigot, which a Catholic priest who was allied with the rebels, Abbé Aubert, had positioned in the hills above. Heavy fighting ensued, and though the insurgents greatly outnumbered their enemies in the garrison, who amounted to just 1,150 in all, "400 of which were negroes that are faithful to their owners," they suffered many casualties. Until 5:30 the following morning, Jacmel was a scene of carnage, with the rebels only relenting on occasion, "at times retreating from the fort to the town, to burn their dead, and those that were dangerously wounded."[100]

Reflecting the havoc that Trou Coffy wreaked on the city of Jacmel, the parish registry indicates that the first white victim to be inhumed was Joseph Maure, a businessman from Provence who was killed while defending the fort "against the actions, attacks, and murders that the people of color exercise."

Maure was buried in the town cemetery on January 5, the day after he was killed. With the violence swelling, however, it became too dangerous to conduct funerals in the cemetery, so municipal authorities decreed that Father Ferriere, who was filling in for a curiously absent Father Bloüet, should proceed to bury the mounting dead within the walls of the fort. Thus, on January 23, "unable to get ourselves to the normal cemetery," Ferriere presided over the burial of Sieur Pierre Cambrun, one of at least two dozen who died "in the attack and in the general arson committed by the people of color" and were buried in the fort, some of them having fallen in a second major attack launched on February 10. All but one of these victims were white men between the ages of 16 and 47, with several having succumbed to their wounds while being treated in the local hospital; the other was a five-year-old girl named Marie Catherine Simonet, who died in the city on February 19, 1792. Jacmel had become a killing field, such that Father Ferriere performed only funeral services, and neither baptisms nor weddings, during the first few months of 1792. Though he was finally able to recommence burying the dead in the cemetery as of April 4, Ferriere did not perform the year's first wedding until April 16 or the first baptism until May 5; in the interim, he had buried 41 people.[101] It is unclear whether Sunday Masses at the Saints James and Philip Cathedral had likewise been disrupted by the insurgent raids, though surely they must have been.

Sometime during the January attacks on Jacmel news reached Trou Coffy that the national civil commissioners had arrived in the colony and offered amnesty to the insurgents if they would lay down their arms and cease their assaults. In the meantime, the commissioners wrote to assure local authorities that they had reached truces with several principals of the insurgency in the West, and that even the dreaded Delisle had written to them, on February 11, suggesting that he was prepared to accept the offer. Nevertheless, and whatever Delisle's true intentions might have been, things had by then spun quite out of control, and violence continued to rock Jacmel and environs.[102] As in the South, the free colored insurgency in the West Province had drawn many slaves into the rebellious maelstrom. They would increasingly appropriate the struggle on their own terms, soon to transform it into a bona fide slave insurrection aimed at toppling an unjust regime—an aim that they shared with the free coloreds—and at securing their own liberation permanently—an aim entirely their own and an effort that helped pave the way to ultimate victory in the Haitian Revolution the following decade.

As 1791 gave way to 1792, meanwhile, Romaine increasingly set his sights on taking over the city of Léogâne, while Delisle remained focused on Jacmel. Delisle's siege of the Cyvadier plantation effectively cut off the supply route into Jacmel from the east, leaving the city entirely surrounded by insurgents and now bombarded by cannon fire from the nearby hills. All that remained for the insurgents to achieve their principal objective, the total conquest of the city, was to gain control of the fort, the last white stronghold and something of an obsession for Delisle. On February 29, several slaves from neighboring plantations met on *habitation* Leyman, near Cap Rouge, in the hut of a slave named Heleine, with another slave named Tarquin evidently doing most of the talking. The slaves discussed the prospects of absconding from their plantations and joining the insurgency, noting with interest how Delisle had offered "six portugueses" (gold coins worth roughly 133 livres each) for the head of any white person holed up in the Jacmel fort. Reflective of strategic differences in the insurgent leadership, furthermore, they spoke of how Cadet Raffy had recently had an argument with Delisle and "reproached him for having torched the plantations of M. Feraud and Beauvoir, the former at Cap Rouge and the latter in the hills above Cayes Jacmel, in the quarter of Festel. He said that he should have just contented himself with taking the food supplies of the whites who were absent." Delisle was reproached by Raffy for having gone too far, and not without reason, for if the insurgents would ultimately rule the West Province, it would certainly have been advantageous for plantations to remain functional to restore some semblance of an economy, rather than starting entirely from scratch.[103]

Judging from the military titles taken by Romaine and members of his inner leadership circle, it would appear that Delisle was third or fourth in command of the Trou Coffy insurgency. Much like his superiors, furthermore, Delisle actively courted the collaboration of a white French Catholic priest—actually in Delisle's case two of them, Père Aubert, who had commandeered the cannons from Marigot for the attack on Jacmel, as mentioned earlier, and Père Blacé, the curé of Cayes Jacmel. Deemed by Trou Coffy's enemies as being "as deceitful" as Delisle, Père Blacé dined with the *petit blanc* and was enlisted to stay "among the brigands" and even to perform marriages for some of them with slave women on one of the plantations that they had sacked.[104] It is quite likely that Delisle was among those men who were married to slave women by Blacé. The marriages were doubly radical, in that by law they would have manumitted the women who entered them. In any case, Delisle's close association with two subversive Catholic priests suggests that Romaine's "*capitaine general*," a white Frenchman, joined forces with the prophetess not just out of his own disdain for wealthy whites and free coloreds but perhaps also out of his own radical Catholic faith.

Whatever may have been the chain of command at Trou Coffy in the Jacmel insurgent theater, the rebellion ultimately bombarded, torched, and starved *la municipalité* de Jacmel into submission. Bereft of food and still without any military reinforcements, the whites and allied free colored and loyal slaves of Jacmel were now at the mercy of the likes of Boursiquot, Delisle, Romaine, and their followers. It was such a desperate situation that the remaining whites were left with no choice but to surrender the fort, while, for their part, the free colored insurgents had built one of their own in Marigot.[105] In effect, Trou Coffy had conquered Jacmel—in fact, they also destroyed it. Léogâne would suffer much the same fate. But before turning our attention to that drama, let us now consider the biographies of Romaine-la-Prophétesse and Abbé Ouvière and then explore the relationships between other insurgent leaders and Catholic priests at the beginning of the Haitian Revolution.

2

Romaine-la-Prophétesse

The lower the social class, the more radical are the forms assumed by the need for a savior.

—MAX WEBER[1]

Overview

ROMAINE RIVIÈRE WOULD be king.[2] At least that is what he, as Romaine-la-Prophétesse, godson of the Virgin Mary, declared and what his followers believed. Their belief is but faintly echoed in the archive, however, which more resoundingly portrays them as superstitious dupes and the mysterious warlord as a murderous and manipulative charlatan—a "Muhammad of Saint-Domingue" who preached "an infernal doctrine" and caused some of the most violent scenes in a most violent world.[3] Subsequent writers have generally accepted and echoed the disparaging portrayal of Romaine in the primary source literature, while more recently a few historians have sought to let some of the evidence tell his story, adding a slender but much more objective sketch to our understanding of one of the most influential insurgent leaders in the Haitian Revolution. Unheard in all of these portrayals are the voices of those who were drawn to him, as are Romaine's own motivations and intentions. Yet once we sift through his contemporary chroniclers' assumptions about the prophetess' alleged "fanaticism" and the "ignorance" and "gullibility" of his followers, some of these subaltern voices and ideas can be at least faintly heard by carefully considering the mechanics of Romaine's charisma. Such a reckoning requires focusing careful attention on the African religious background of many who were drawn to the prophetess and on the political aspirations and religious lives of free colored followers and the black slaves that joined his insurgent movement at Trou Coffy.

Through an analysis of a range of primary source documents, including notarial and parish records, eyewitness accounts, and correspondence to, from, and about him, this chapter first elucidates the identity of Romaine-la-Prophétesse, particularly his legal status, race, ethnicity, sexuality, politics, and religion. Four sections follow that respectively treat several important issues pertaining to Romaine and the "revitalization movement" that he inspired and led out of Trou Coffy: the question of the role of marronage; the religious culture of the Trou Coffy insurgency; African dimensions of his message and movement; and royalism.[4] What emerges is a portrait of a remarkable man in a revolutionary world who felt inspired by the Virgin Mary to take up arms to defend his people, king, and Church.

Identifying the "Hermaphroditic Tiger"

As an insurgent leader Romaine-la-Prophétesse enters the historical record in the summer of 1791, though the free black Creole from the Spanish side of the island had already been in Saint-Domingue for many years. Notarial records indicate that "Romain Riviere" had purchased ten *carreaux* (roughly 32 acres) of land in Trou Coffy in July 1784 from a free mulatto named Maurice Cavalier for the sum of 4,000 livres "in money and animals."[5] By comparison, "a *carreau* of good farmland in Limonade cost about 300 *livres*," while "a new male slave cost between 1,800 and 2,500 *livres*."[6] Presumably, land in Limonade, in the North Province, would have been exploited for the cultivation of sugar, whereas higher land for the cultivation of coffee was less valuable in Saint-Domingue. That said, because the contract for land transaction between Cavalier and Rivière does not provide details of any buildings or planted fields on the property, it would seem that Romaine had purchased a tract of land that he later developed as a small-scale coffee-planting enterprise, rather than an already-functioning farm or plantation.

About a year later, the prophetess got married, on August 22, 1785, to a woman named Marie Roze Adam. Their wedding ceremony was performed by Father Sauvage, curé of Léogâne, in the Church of St. Rose de Lima, with Pierre Douault, Paul Lagetiere (sp?), Pierre Glaise, and Charles François Lemaire standing as witnesses. According to Sauvage's entry in the Léogâne parish registry, Romaine's bride was a *mulatresse*, "a Creole of the age of forty-three years," whom the prophetess had purchased from her master, Sieur Rene Guindet, on the tenth of that month, along with their three children, for the sum of 6,000 livres.[7] In effect, the prophetess purchased them as slaves, and once he married Marie Roze they were legally manumitted. Their notarial marriage contract stipulates, furthermore, that "the future groom" was a "*habitant*" who owned 40 *carreaux* of land at Trou Coffy, suggesting that the 10 *carreaux* he had purchased from Cavalier earlier that year was adjacent to 30 that Romaine already owned. The prophetess also owned at least two slaves, two horses, and furniture.[8] For her part, "the future bride" possessed "only . . . clothes and jewelry" and a few other items valued in total at 900 livres.[9]

One of the most striking bits of information contained in Romaine's wedding contract is that he and Marie-Roze had "of their production three living children . . . Louis-Marie, eleven years old, Pierre-Marie, nine years old, and Marie-Jeanne, seven years old, all of them *grifs*." In effect, these were the prophetess' biological children, meaning, among other things, that Romaine (or "Romain," as he is named in the notarial records) had been in Saint-Domingue as early as 1772, the year of the conception of his first child with Marie Roze. As such, the prophetess had been in the colony for at least 19 years when the Trou Coffy insurgency broke out. That each child was named in part for the Virgin Mary also suggests that Romaine's Marianism was deep and had a long history prior to the emergence of the Trou Coffy insurgency; thus, accusations that the prophetess opportunistically feigned and exploited religious faith to fan the fires of violent fanaticism are, at the very least, questionable.

The fact that Romaine entered into a long-term relationship with an enslaved woman, managing to impregnate Marie Roze three times within a five-year period (1772–1777), raises interesting, though perhaps ultimately unanswerable, questions about his presence on the Guindet plantation. Was he on Guindet's payroll as some kind of employee? Or could he have been a regular trading partner of Guindet's? A few additional notarial records have Romaine purchasing slaves and buying (for 6,600 livres) and selling (for 3,600 livres) a 25-*carreaux* plot of land, along with a 17-year-old Kongolese slave named Augustin, in Grande Marre in 1787.[10] By then the Léogâne notary, Rozond, was no longer requiring Romaine to demonstrate proof of his free status, writing instead that the *"habitant"* was "justified as such by diverse certificates already entered into the undersigned notary's records." All of this indicates that by the second half of the 1780s Romaine Rivière had established himself as a respectable coffee grower and trader around Léogâne, such that it is not difficult to imagine him regularly visiting the Guindet plantation for professional reasons. In Marie Roze and their children, furthermore, he had even more compelling reasons to do so, over and above any business that he might have conducted with Guindet.

All seven of the notarial records and all ten of the entries in the Léogâne parish registry that mention "Romain Riviere" identify him as a *negre libre*—a free black—and one says that he was "of the Spanish nation." The earlier documents, in which the notary had required proof of his free status, indicate that Romaine presented "a baptismal record from the curé of the parish of Our Lady of Thirty Graces in the Spanish part of Saint-Domingue."[11]

Unfortunately, the dates of Romaine's birth and baptism are nowhere mentioned, nor do any of the notarial or parish records indicate his age, but Abbé Ouvière reckoned that he was "about 40 years of age" at the time of the Trou Coffy insurgency, in 1791.[12] Furthermore, I have found no trace anywhere else of a church in Dominican history called Nuestra Señora de las Treinta Gracias, which could be an indication that the curé Sauvage and the notary Rozond both misread the Spanish of Romaine's baptismal certificate. It is more likely that Romaine had been baptized in a Dominican church dedicated to Our Lady of High Grace, Nuestra Señora de la Altagracia, patron saint of the Dominican Republic, whose cult dates to 1502 in Higuey, site of the cathedral that today bears her name, a saint who is popularly celebrated as "*Tatica de Higuey*." Whether he was baptized in Higuey or in some other Dominican town with a church consecrated to Altagracia, Romaine-la-Prophétesse was connected virtually from birth to the oldest form of Catholic devotion in the Americas, Iberian Marianism, and particularly to the cult of Altagracia in the very place where the Catholic evangelization of the New World began, (la Capitanía General de) Santo Domingo.

Whatever the true name of the church in which Romaine was baptized, it is Gallicized in the notarial and parish records as "Notre Dame des Trente Graces."[13] The names of the prophetess' deceased parents seem also to have been Gallicized, as they appear in four of the documents as Jean Rivière and Gabrielle Joseph, who were both deceased by the time of Romaine's wedding. It is not beyond the bounds of reason to suspect that the prophetess' parents' names were in reality Juan Rivera and Gabriela Jose, while Romaine might have been born with the name Román Rivera, although it is also possible that his parents were originally from the French side of the island and had immigrated to the Spanish side before giving birth to Romaine, which would mean that the names as recorded in the Léogâne parish and notarial records had been correctly spelled. Beyond this, there is not much else that one may glean about Romaine's biography from these documents, save for one reflection on his character. This was a man who evidently fell in love with a mulatta slave, a woman who fathered three of his children. By the time the eldest of them was 11, Romaine had managed to save enough money to manumit Marie Roze and their three children, from which point on they lived free with the prophetess up until the beginning of the Haitian Revolution.[14] Their ultimate fate will be discussed later, but here let it be said that Romaine's successful efforts over the course of 12 years to liberate his children and their mother and to provide a home for them at Trou Coffy bespeaks a kind of familial loyalty that really should inspire admiration and respect. These were, after all, disprivileged black people in an oppressive world of white power, a family of five, four of whom were born into slavery, and a father who liberated them and would then go on to fight to change that very oppressive world, leading thousands of others to join him in the cause.

"The respect that blacks have for their godfather and their godmother goes so far as to equal that which they have for their own parents," as M. L. E. Moreau de Saint-Méry observed toward the end of the eighteenth century.[15] "Godparenthood was a sort of social glue that held the community of people of color together," as Stewart King further explains,[16] and it was a role that Romaine Rivière assumed no fewer than nine times between 1785 and 1791,[17] while on at least four occasions his wife, Marie Roze, became a godmother (two of the occasions were with her husband standing as *"compère"*).[18] Baptism was something that free blacks and mulattoes actively sought to arrange for their children, both for religious and legal reasons, as baptismal records were crucial forms of proof of one's free status throughout life, and the resultant fictive kinship networks were important forces against social marginalization.[19] It is also the case that in Saint-Domingue becoming a godfather could "serve as a cloak for illegitimate fatherhood, and this was one of the signposts to determine who the father of a child was,"[20] meaning that at least one or two of Romaine's godchildren, if not all nine of them, may have been the prophetess' biological offspring. More certainly, the frequency with which Romaine appears in the parish and notarial records establishes that he was widely respected in the local free colored community and connected to numerous families in a kind of synthetic but meaningful religious kinship, and that he was well known to three successive curés of parish of Léogâne, Father Grulé, Father Sauvage, and Father Menetrier. It also helps explain how the prophetess was able to quickly amass his initial insurgent group when his feud with Joseph-Marie Tavet escalated in the summer of 1791; Elie Courlogne, Romaine's second-in-command at Trou Coffy, was, at any rate, likewise a godfather for a free colored child in the Léogâne parish.[21]

Beyond the notarial records and the Léogâne parish registry, which consistently state that Romaine was illiterate and unable to sign his name, there is one detail that sheds additional light on his family history. Ranking just below Elie in its high command, the prophetess' closest confidant in the Trou Coffy insurgency was his son-in-law, Soliment.[22] Unless, of course, Romaine had other children who do not appear in his wedding contract, this means that Soliment had at some point by December of 1791 married Romaine's youngest child, Marie-Jeanne, when she was just 14 or 15 years old, which by French law was too young to wed.[23] It would appear that the marriage of Soliment and Marie-Jeanne may have been illegal, but it was clearly recognized as legitimate by the prophetess, otherwise Soliment could not possibly have enjoyed the position of trust that he occupied in the Trou Coffy insurgency.[24]

Contemporary references to Romaine as being "Spanish" have caused some confusion over the prophetess' "national" or ethnic identity. George Eaton Simpson is certainly incorrect in calling Romaine a "Spaniard" in the nominal national sense of the word, as the prophetess was surely a Creole who had been born and raised in the Spanish colony of Santo Domingo, across the border from Saint-Domingue.[25] Even if he was identified in the notarial records as being "of the Spanish nation" and even if he was called "Spanish" in the nominal rather than the adjectival sense of the term by one of the only two contemporary observers on record who had actually met the prophetess in person, namely Abbé Ouvière, we should not take this to suggest that Romaine was from Spain.[26] To this day in Haitian Creole anyone from the neighboring Dominican Republic is referred to as a *panyol* (lit.: Spaniard), and this identifier extends to Hispanics in general.[27]

By virtue of the deep, ambiguous, and ever-shifting racism that defined and stratified people in Saint-Domingue, pinning down Romaine's racial identity represents something of a challenge. Father Blouët, the pastor of the Jacmel parish and author of one of the most detailed contemporary discussions about the prophetess and the Trou Coffy insurgency, was the first on record to refer to the prophetess as a "*grif*," meaning someone born to one black and one mulatto parent. However, a closer reading of the curé's "Report Made to the Colonial Assembly" reveals that he never personally met or even saw Romaine, casting doubt on his estimation of the prophetess' race. Though referring to himself as "an eyewitness and a victim of the atrocities committed by many brigands of all colors," Blouët's specific information on Romaine was secondhand, acquired "from the *nommé* Bergeron, Mulatto planter from the grande riviere of Jacmel, presently in chains aboard the state ship *le serein*, [a] mulatto raised in France for twelve years and who is not to be counted among the stupid dupes of this Romaine."[28] The Jacmel parish registry suggests, furthermore, that Blouët wasn't even in the area when Romaine's followers sacked the city, or at least he was ill and unable to perform baptismal, nuptial, or funerary services.[29]

Notwithstanding the secondhand nature of Blouët's information on the prophetess (which he had received, no less, from a man who for some reason had been placed under arrest), the curé's account was submitted to the Colonial Assembly and as such would be passed down as the authoritative historical register of Romaine's racial identity and his putative fanaticism and charlatanry. It was, for instance, picked in two of the most widely cited contemporary sources on the Haitian Revolution, Jean-Philippe Garran de

Coulon's official four-volume report on the *"troubles"* in Saint-Domingue and General Baron Pamphile de Lacroix's *mémoire* of events during the first years of the Revolution. And, so, *"grif"* or *"griffe"* has been used as a racial identifier in almost every other discussion of the prophetess ever since.[30] But the notarial and parish records, legally binding documents, consistently identified Romaine as a "free black";[31] a long report on events in the parish of Jacmel submitted to the Colonial Assembly at the beginning of March in 1792 also simply called him "black";[32] while parish and notarial records consistently identify his wife as a *mulatresse* and his children as *grifs*—and a black parent coupled with a mulatto parent would have, by definition, *grif* offspring. Prior to visiting Trou Coffy and meeting Romaine in person, Abbé Ouvière had been told that the prophetess was of mixed race, meanwhile, yet the priest found the prophetess to be "very black for a mulatto." Furthermore, Romaine "was a pretty man of average size, but quite stocky, with a broad chest, ovular face, smooth skin, little or no beard .... no negroid features, but on the contrary, was perfectly European."[33]

Further confusing matters in this regard, Saint-Domingue's complex system of racial classification allowed for no fewer than eight "mixed" racial parental combinations that could produce a *griffe*, as infamously calculated by Moreau. None of them permitted for a "purely" white father or mother. That putative disadvantage notwithstanding, the *griffes* of Saint-Domingue, who generally appeared to be "a bit browner than mulattoes, even though one sees some Griffes who are as clear as the dark mulatto," were "so favored by nature that it is quite rare to see one of them who doesn't have an agreeable face whose overall look pleases." However, "none of the combinations produced by the colonial mélanges can have an offspring that is as prone to amorous impetuosity than the Griffe." Because *griffes* were only "at best" one-third white, furthermore, "they offended the sense of smell."[34] Finally, Mayor de Villards, one of only two authors of any documents in the archive who actually met Romaine in person and visited him in Trou Coffy, never bothered mentioning Romaine's race at all. The other, the priest, initially simply called him "a Spaniard who is passionately devoted to the cult" without alluding to his race, though years later he would somewhat uncertainly refer to him as a "mulatto."[35] At any rate, the notarial and parish records are clear on this matter and should be the determining voice: Romaine-la-Prophétesse was a free black from the Spanish side of the island of Hispaniola.

This is perhaps why Mayor de Villards saw no point in indicating Romaine's race in the several letters to Abbé Ouvière in which he refers to the prophetess—it was simply too well known locally that Rivière was a free black. More interestingly, the mayor did make one intriguing reference to Romaine's appearance and demeanor that may shed light on his adoption (or reception) of the feminine title "la Prophétesse." In lamenting Romaine's erratic behavior in a letter written to the priest during the second week of 1792, thus very early in the prophetess' formal rule over Léogâne, the mayor condescendingly calls the prophetess "the hermaphroditic tiger," suggesting that Rivière's title reflected not only his religious vision and mediumistic role but also some measure of visible femininity in his demeanor and appearance.[36] The prophetess did dress rather flamboyantly, after all, according to the priest: "He was all adorned with ribbons, rosaries, and a cross on his chest ... covered with images ... with medals, and with gold chains." What's more, the prophetess wore "a turban topped with a plume on his head," thus giving him the appearance of "a prophet of the Roman religion" dressed in "the clothing of a Turk."[37] In a society in which many people of color, men and women alike, wore head wraps, there must have been something distinctive, besides the plume that topped it, about Romaine's that prompted Ouvière to refer to it as "a turban" that made him appear to be "a Turk." It should be admitted as possible that Romaine had some knowledge of Islam and perhaps recognized a turban, rather than a more culturally conventional headdress, as an adornment of prophecy, while, as Sara Johnson explains, "in addition to indicating a fashion or a social statement about the wearers' identity, a certain way of tying a head wrap, for example, also indicated belonging to a place where racial hierarchies had been turned on their heads."[38]

In light of all of this, in addition to affirming his rebellious challenge to Dominguan "racial hierarchies," one wonders whether Romaine-la-Prophétesse was transgender and thus challenged sexual ones. It is clear that he transgressed conventional gender norms in appearance and comportment, though to call the prophetess "transgender" would be to tempt anachronism, as this term and the valences that it inflects today were most likely unknown in his world or at best were known in quite different ways. That he was conventionally, heterosexually married and fathered at least three children would seem to rule out any homosexual identity (if not longing), though not necessarily a bisexual one, yet there is no evidence anywhere that he was ever intimate with other men. But one should not reduce the question of Romaine's femininity to sexuality, especially because this was an individual who was a religious specialist whose beliefs were at least in part African-derived, though among some Vodouists in Haiti today the prophetess is believed to have been gay.[39] Romaine's self-identification as "prophetess," rather than "prophet," certainly inverted his gender in ways reminiscent of Kongolese prophetic traditions, as reflected in the prophetess Beatriz Kimpa Vita's self-identification with Saint Anthony and the remarkable millenarian movement that she inspired in the Kongo at the turn of the seventeenth to eighteenth century.[40] By the sixteenth century in West Central Africa, after all, the spiritual power of gender-inverted male prophets was well established and highly influential.[41] Thus Romaine may very well have taken the feminine title "la Prophétesse" as a reflection of a feminized passivity that made him penetrable by the spirit world, thereby enabling his performance as a medium. Such a gender fluid state would have made his mediumship resonate in the religious habitus of both his Kongolese followers and those who hailed from West Africa, where male possession priests performing as females were (and remain) also prevailing.[42] Sacerdotal gender inversion was thus rather traditional in eighteenth-century Africana religious culture. In the case of the millenarian movement at Trou Coffy, furthermore, "the hermaphroditic tiger" effectuated such a recalibrated, gendered revitalization by masculinizing the Virgin Mary and thereby transforming her into the penetrator, or rider, with the prophetess serving mediumistically as her penetratee, or horse (*chwal*).

The Prophetess and Marronage

Some scholars, myself included, have associated Romaine-la-Prophétesse with marronage, or the culture and communities of escaped slaves, and not without reason, though the prophetess himself cannot be said to have ever himself been a maroon—an escaped slave—per se.[43] But during the very time that Romaine Rivière was working his coffee plantation in Trou Coffy, one of the most notorious maroon communities in Caribbean history was surging in his homeland across the border and wreaking havoc in the prophetess' adopted colony. By the middle of the eighteenth century, Bahoruco maroons had penetrated Saint-Domingue to menace planters near the towns of Jacmel and Mirebalais. With reinforcements from among the residents of Petit-Goâve, the colonial police force, *le marechaussée*, [44] acted to repel them, resulting in a 1786 treaty that formally granted the insurgent maroons amnesty in exchange for their disbandment and pledge to keep the peace.[45]

The mountainous stretch of the southern peninsula between Jacmel and Petit Goâve is precisely the region in which Romaine's insurgent band operated just a few years later, in 1791 and early 1792, furthermore. Ironically, Baudoin DesMarattes and his son led the efforts from the French side of the island to neutralize the Bahoruco maroons, and subsequent to their eventual success in doing so, their own planation would be raided and occupied by the prophetess' followers, or perhaps they offered it to their cause, as there is some evidence that the DesMarattes willingly joined the Trou Coffy insurgency.[46] Under the leadership of Alexandre Boursiquot, furthermore, the

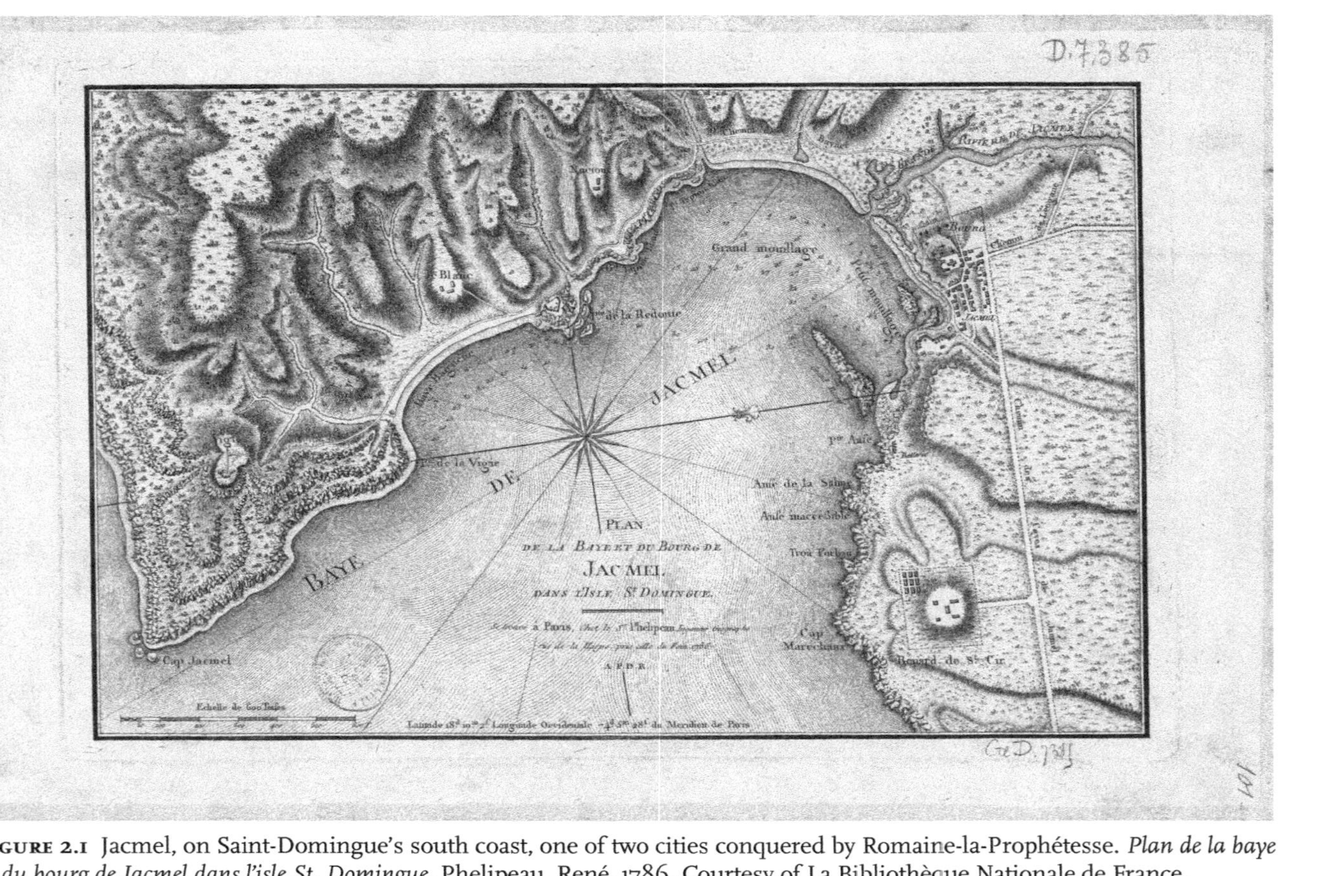

FIGURE 2.1 Jacmel, on Saint-Domingue's south coast, one of two cities conquered by Romaine-la-Prophétesse. *Plan de la baye et du bourg de Jacmel dans l'isle St. Domingue*. Phelipeau, René. 1786. Courtesy of La Bibliothèque Nationale de France.

DesMarattes plantation would serve as the insurgents' main camp for their strikes on the city of Jacmel in December of 1791 and likely for the bloody assault on Bainet early in 1792, as discussed in the previous chapter.[47] By then, thousands of slaves from Saint-Domingue had absconded across the border, many of them settling at Bahoruco, whose maroons' menace to the planters of Saint-Domingue's West Province would eventually be superseded by the menace of Trou Coffy.

The terms of the treaty that was eventually signed between the Bahoruco maroons and Saint-Domingue provided for 130 of the maroons, most of whom had originally been slaves in Saint-Domingue, to settle anew, now baptized and free, back on the French side of the island. This included their leader, a "Black Creole Spaniard from Banica [a small town on the border]" named Santiago, according to Moreau.[48] In language that would be resoundingly echoed in later French officials' accounts of Romaine's own insurgent movement, furthermore, Moreau wrote of Santiago's influence as follows: "Taking advantage of their superstition, he leads them by playing among them the role of a *padre*. He has taught them to pray in Spanish, and a small cross and a rosary in his hands are two weapons with which he readily subdues their weak reason."[49] It is quite likely that some veteran maroons from Bahoruco joined the Trou Coffy insurgency, though most of them had succumbed to smallpox by 1791. And while technically speaking Romaine-la-Prophétesse was not the successor to Santiago, Moreau rather prophetically warned that one would indeed follow: "Who would dare to confirm that whoever is the successor to Santiago will not be more formidable than he?"[50]

Some of the slaves who joined the Trou Coffy insurgency viewed the border as a conduit to freedom, attesting that short of achieving their political objectives as insurgents they would simply *"passer à l'espagnol."* It was more generally the case for slaves in much of Saint-Domingue that "the border came to signify freedom," as observes Eugenio Matibag. "Representing a threat from the outside, it also symbolized the dangerous discrepancies between the two colonies."[51] And though the insurgent camp at Trou Coffy did, in effect, become something of a maroon community, refuge to an untold number of absconding slaves, there is simply no evidence that Romaine himself had ever been a maroon,[52] save perhaps for Abbé Ouvière's referring to him as "a Spanish defector."[53] In considering this question, David Geggus points to Romaine's landownership as conclusive counterevidence, and to this we can add that the prophetess was freeborn and that he owned slaves, thus if he had indeed defected from Santo Domingo, it must have been from debt, an arrest warrant, or military service, rather than from bondage.[54]

Be that as it may, as news of Trou Coffy's power spread throughout the region, those slaves on the area's plantations who had ever contemplated absconding now had a viable destination on the French side of the border, and doubtless many of them wound up in the prophetess' lair, arriving there as runaways from plantations rather than as ones who had been liberated or abducted during insurgent raids on them. Surely many of them were Kongolese, furthermore, as we do know that Kongolese slaves were often reported to have escaped plantations around Léogâne. Take, for instance, Jasmin Barbe-Blanche, who "went maroon" (*al mawòn*), as is said in Haitian Creole, on August 17, 1774,[55] and Jolicoeur, who absconded twice in 1775, once on the Feast Day of Our Lady of the Assumption, and then again on Christmas Day. Jolicouer's owner wrote from Léogâne on January 4, 1776 that he wasn't at all surprised by his slave's multiple flights into marronage, "because for all of his life, he mastered no other craft than going *marron*."[56] Notwithstanding Gabriel Debien's reasonable argument that "the bands of insurgent slaves that assembled in the North and in the West beginning in August of 1791 appear to have nothing in common over a long period of time with the old bands of maroons of the North-East or West of the colony," it is certainly the case that many of Romaine's followers were, by Debien's own definition, maroons: "slaves who flee from the plantation or the house of their master."[57] For many, then, Trou Coffy surely must have served as a haven from bondage, and though Romaine had never been a maroon, marronage did play an important role in his rise to power and the success of his movement.

Thus, his free legal status, slave ownership, land ownership, and the fact that he had never himself been a slave or a maroon clearly distinguish Romaine-la-Prophétesse from the insurgent leaders in the North Province, like Makandal, Boukman, and Jean-François, who had been slaves. Among the free colored insurgent leaders in the West and South Provinces, furthermore, his national origins would also distinguish the prophetess, not to mention the extent to which religious vision fueled and marked his mission, as would his illiteracy. Though others among the free colored insurgent leaders were also landowners and slave owners, and some of them quite wealthy ones at that, their counterparts among former slaves who led the northern insurgency were not. As we've seen, by 1784 Romaine had purchased land that either already was serving as a plantation or on which he built one from scratch, seeking to make a living, if not a fortune, from the coffee boom then surging Saint-Domingue's West Province.[58]

Were one to ask Romaine Rivière to describe his own identity, it is most likely that this would be among the most defining descriptors that he would choose: Catholic. Not maroon, not Vodouist, not charlatan, not black, not *griffe*, not mulatto. Catholic. Let us now turn our attention to Romaine's religion and its influence on his followers at Trou Coffy. Seeing as at the height of the insurgency the prophetess' followers numbered in the thousands, mostly free coloreds and liberated slaves, doing so requires some consideration of their religious needs, over and above their political aspirations.[59]

The Religious Culture of the Trou Coffy Insurgency

Romaine-la-Prophétesse preached that Divine Will was expressed to him by the Holy Spirit and the Virgin Mary, his godmother, and he in turn channeled their messages to his followers. They were willing to kill and to die to carry out these deific injunctions, and indeed they did. For this reason Romaine either assumed or was given the title la Prophétesse. Communications from the Virgin compelled the prophetess to take up arms and muster an army to wage battle against those forces in Saint-Domingue that denied his people their full rights as French citizens and that threatened the reign of the king of France. While not disagreeing with the general statement made by Sidney Mintz and Michel-Rolph Trouillot that "it seems simplistic to make religion the linchpin of resistance" in the Haitian Revolution, for Romaine-la-Prophétesse it was clearly just that.[60] After all, he was a Catholic visionary who accepted extreme violence as a means to the ends that the Sacred had outlined for him and the Trou Coffy insurgency. Per Abbé Ouvière, furthermore, Romaine understood himself to be called to "some divine mission to bring forth the abolition of slavery."[61]

What more can be said about the religious content of the Trou Coffy insurgency? The most extensive contemporary descriptions of Romaine-la-Prophétesse and the religion that he and his acolytes practiced at Trou Coffy are found in the report to the Colonial Assembly written in March of 1792 by Father Blouët, the conservative curé of Jacmel, and a memoir about Trou Coffy that Abbé Ouvière wrote some 30 years later. Though brief, secondhand in nature, and obviously biased and hostile, Blouët's discussion of Romaine contains some of the most important information that we have about Trou Coffy's religious culture. Thus, I translate the most relevant passage at length here:

> [T]he one Romaine, Spanish griffe; this griffe married to a mulatresse has constructed a chapel, an altar, where he celebrates the mysteries in his own way. He puts his head in his tabernacle to listen to the replies of the Holy Spirit, made written by the Holy Virgin, and the Virgin's letters are found the next day in the tabernacle. He engages

> in meditations and preaches with a sword in his hand, teaching to his imbecilic proselytes a doctrine that has resulted in thefts, arsons, and murders. This villain, who does not know how to read, is also a charlatan. He composes remedies and has one sign his name as Romaine, so called prophetic. . . . Indoctrinated by one of these men, born to bring misery upon others, led by the ways of the crudest superstition ever invented but which, combined with stupidity, [he] covers its subtle dissimulation and has not missed his target.[62]

Once we have sifted through the curé's sanctimonious rancor, what is important to take from this passage is the image of a charismatic prophet whose homestead had been transformed into an insurgent camp and a veritable religious commune, replete with chapel, altar, tabernacle, icons, candles, and sacred vessels. From a different contemporary account, we may also surmise that somewhere in the chapel, perhaps on the altar, was a particular statue of the Virgin Mary that was especially revered and perhaps the conduit of the divine messages that her godson claims to have received. In one of his letters to Abbé Ouvière, Mayor de Villards mentions that it is "the little Virgin that speaks" to Romaine and relays prophecies to him. One could perhaps read the mayor's words as derisive, but they were written to a Catholic priest whom he deeply respected and with whom he had recently attended Mass in Léogâne. It is thus more likely that by "the little Virgin" Villards was referring to an icon of the Virgin Mary standing somewhere in Romaine's chapel at Trou Coffy, a place that both the mayor and Abbé Ouvière had visited in person. If indeed it was a statue of the Virgin that communicated with Romaine and his followers, it would be, at any rate, one of the first of several such politically charged Marian apparitions in Haitian history.[63] Abbé Ouvière, meanwhile, described the Trou Coffy chapel as "a long splendidly illuminated room, full of crude images, adorned by flowers and relics." In addition to its normal state of thus being "overloaded" with ritual paraphernalia, on Christmas Eve Romaine's chapel also housed "a grotesque model of the nativity scene or the birth of Jesus."[64] Surely thus the prophetess' godmother was iconically there, too.

Which particular cult of the Virgin Mary predominated at Trou Coffy is an interesting question, and though there is no clear evidence on which to base an answer, the possibilities were relatively few: Our Lady of the Immaculate Conception was the preferred Spanish devotion in colonial Hispaniola, while French Catholic missionaries sought to supplant it with Our Lady of the Assumption in Saint-Domingue;[65] meanwhile, being a devout Catholic from the Spanish side of the island, Romaine was surely a devotee of Our Lady of High Grace (Altagracia), whose cult would become widely popular in the

French colony of Saint-Domingue by the 1830s, and likely much earlier, as was pilgrimage to Higuey among Dominguan Marian devotees.[66] Given the proliferation of icons in Romaine's chapel that Abbé Ouvière described, it is safe to say that multiple forms of Marian devotion were practiced at Trou Coffy, just as it is easy to imagine that Altagracia was primary among them.

From Father Blouët's account, moreover, we have an image of the prophetess' retrieving written messages from his godmother, the Virgin Mary, on the days after he would place his head in the tabernacle, where normally the Eucharist is housed between Masses, to communicate through her with the Holy Spirit. In stating that the prophetess "celebrates the mysteries in his own way," the curé clearly implies that Romaine was saying Mass at Trou Coffy, and perhaps the prophetess was officiating over other sacramental rituals. And, of course, he preached there, "with a sword in his hand," emblematic of the potent fusion of religious and political inspiration that fueled the Trou Coffy insurgency and indeed the entire Haitian Revolution. Unfortunately, Abbé Ouvière did not describe any Mass that he attended while in Trou Coffy or over which either he or Romaine might have officiated. Besides his physical description of the chapel, the only religious practice that the priest mentions having observed in Trou Coffy was solemn prayer. The priest did note that the prophetess held a sword during his initial meeting with the prophetess, but not while at prayer before his altar or the nativity scene.[67]

Without exception, contemporary commentators and nineteenth-century historians alike take Father Blouët's denunciatory account to be trustworthy, either directly or secondarily, thus the earliest primary and secondary source literature about Romaine-la-Prophétesse is seasoned with similarly inculpative rhetoric. Blouët called Romaine a "villain" and a "charlatan," while other contemporary observers variously referred to the prophetess as an "adventurer," "profaner," "tiger," and a "maniac";[68] and Jean-Philippe Garran de Coulon's official report follows suit in lambasting Romaine for his "fanaticism." The term "maniac" is the conventional translation of the French *énergumène*, but the original is also used to refer to someone who is possessed by demons or someone who has become batty with old age. Nineteenth-century Haitian historian Thomas Madiou, who is the most commonly and often only cited source for subsequent discussions or mentions of this intriguing historical personage, explains that Romaine-la-Prophétesse "called himself the godchild of the Virgin Mary. He dominated through superstition the bands of slaves whom he'd led into the mountains. He said Mass, brought all kinds of torture upon the whites and pretended that this was according to the orders of the Virgin."[69] The account of the other nineteenth-century giant of Haitian historical studies, Alexis Beaubrun Ardouin, is equally dismissive of the prophetess.

Ardouin, who, as Trouillot notes, "is known for his hatred of Christophe and his harsh criticism of the dark-skinned heroes of Haitian independence,"[70] only mentions Romaine in passing as a "swindler who goes by the name of *Romaine la Prophétesse*, who, with the aid of religious fanaticism, led teams of slaves to commit all sorts of crimes."[71] In more recent scholarship, meanwhile, we find the following terms used to identify the prophetess: "backwardness," "sorcerer," "Voodoo priest," "charismatic," and "shaman."[72] Discounting the intellectual sanctimony of the first term, from C. L. R. James's classic *The Black Jacobins*, let us carefully consider the other four labels that historians have pinned on Romaine-la-Prophétesse.

David Geggus and Pierre Pluchon respectively employ the term "sorcerer" in identifying Romaine-la-Prophétesse, while Alfred Métraux implies as much in calling Romaine "one of the imitators of Macandal," although evidence in the primary source material to support this idea is scant at best.[73] Sabers, spears, guns, cannons, and torches and other incendiary devices were the instruments of Trou Coffy's destructive campaign, but nowhere in the primary source material is the chief instrument of sorcery in Saint-Domingue, namely poison, mentioned regarding Romaine's ministry and movement, something that otherwise receives considerable attention in the archive, including an entire folder in the Moreau papers.[74] Though not in Moreau's sorcery folder, his papers do contain one intriguing document that provides very important evidence that Romaine-la-Prophétesse manufactured amulets. Botanists and naturalists in Saint-Domingue often sent samples of their discoveries back to France for posterity and, presumably, for further scientific analysis. Some of their accompanying lists were published in the colony's chief newspaper *Les Affiches Américaines*, while Moreau thought it important to collect original or handwritten copies of them. One of especial interest is found in his "*Mineraux*" folder, dated only by the year 1788 and carrying no signature or other explanation of its purpose, save perhaps for its title, "*Curiosités de St Domingue.*" It lists a range of minerals collected before arriving at items 12, "A magnetism fetish," and 13, "A fetish by Romaine, the Spaniard," which is casually followed by notation of "a bunch of seeds."[75] Whether the complier of this list came into possession of a "fetish" from Trou Coffy by chance or set out to acquire one from the prophetess himself is unknown, but one does get a clear sense from the item's attribution to Romaine that by 1788 the prophetess had earned a reputation for the creation and employment of talismans or amulets, a full three years prior to the emergence of the Trou Coffy rebellion in all of its religious trappings.

By extension, one might suspect that Romaine-la-Prophétesse was a *féticheur*, a term usually associated in the Dominguan context with sorcery.

But on the evidence of a single mention by a white witness of a *"fétiche"* made by Romaine, one cannot reasonably infer that he worked destructive magic as a *bòkò* (sorcerer). All things considered, it is more likely that the amulet or talisman in question was designed for protective or curative ends, meaning that Romaine's *fétiche* may just as well have reflected his identity as a *kaperlata*, one of a class of religious specialists in Saint-Domingue defined by Karol Weaver as "practitioners of spiritual and natural medicine," and a member of "a Creole network of supernatural healers," many of whom were mistaken by Europeans to be sorcerers outright.[76]

Of course, Romaine's followers might themselves have practiced sorcery—and it is indeed difficult to imagine that none did—but they obviously had more than adequate material weapons to wreak the extensive havoc that they did. Sorcery, moreover, is a kind of destructive magic, though one that in Africana contexts usually employs material means, while as Emile Durkheim put it emphatically in his classic *The Elementary Forms of Religious Life*: "*There is no church of magic.*"[77] Romaine had a chapel, if not a church per se, one that he had constructed. His chapel housed an altar on which stood a tabernacle and mostly likely some statute of the Virgin Mary; more importantly, he led a *congregation*. This is not to deny the communal dimensions or social causes and effects of sorcery, but there is no clear historical evidence that Romaine was himself a sorcerer. More certainly, though not ordained, the prophetess was a priestly leader and a *kaperlata*, who employed physical violence against white oppression and a brutal colonial regime, all in the name of Church and king, all in a rather visionary effort to effect social healing.

Although Father Blouët's account indicates that Romaine said Mass at Trou Coffy, the prophetess was of course not formally authorized by the Catholic Church to do so. Thus, whereas one contemporary report mistakenly calls Romaine "a Spanish priest,"[78] and though the prophetess indeed exercised sacerdotal functions, it would be more accurate to call him a catechist. This was a position of Catholic ritual specialization with which his Kongolese followers would have been very familiar from their homeland, where more often than not catechists presided over Eucharistic celebrations in the absence of ordained priests, a practice that endures widely in the Congo today.[79]

In an earlier article than that in which he calls him a "sorcerer," Geggus also refers to Romaine as "a shaman," which is by definition a more accurate identifier of the prophetess's religious leadership role, even if the two terms are not, in certain cultural contexts, mutually exclusive.[80] The term "shaman" derives from the Russian Tunguz dialect, in which *saman* refers to a religious leader who is chosen by the spirit world and endowed with the gifts of vision, healing, mediumship, and magic.[81] It is the mediumistic dimension of shamanism that is especially manifest in the case of Romaine-la-Prophétesse, notably in his frequent reception of directives and prophecies from the Holy Spirit and the Virgin Mary. Thus far no historian has looked more closely at the archival sources concerning the Trou Coffy movement than Carolyn Fick, who concurs that Romaine "appeared to be a shaman," adding the somewhat dismissive suggestion that "[i]t is possible that he adopted a shamanistic pretense to reinforce his influence."[82] What is more important concerning both the shamanic and prophetic dimensions in this case, however, is that his followers believed Romaine to be in direct communication with the Holy Spirit and the Virgin Mary, the supernatural guarantors of their imminent victory, whose messages were for them the source of conviction and inspiration that led them to act out the prophetess "theodicy of compensation," to invoke Max Weber.[83] Nevertheless, it is not implausible that the prophetess might have suffered from some measure of megalomania, for at least one observer "claimed that his real intention, once the whites were defeated, was to become king of Santo Domingo,"[84] a claim that suggests that Romaine's abolitionist vision may well have been of the "transcolonial" kind outlined regionally by Johnson: "for black residents of the region and economically marginalized whites, the appeal of transcoloniality often contained an idealistic impulse to imagine another world that could result in improved material circumstances."[85]

Ever since Jean-Price Mars declared some two generations ago that "1804 emerged from Vodou," several scholars have somewhat dubiously appropriated Romaine-la-Prophétesse as an icon of this putative revolutionary emergence.[86] For instance, Serge Larose claims, without attribution, that "Roman the prophet . . . said the Mass before an inverted cross; he preached that God was black, that all the whites had to be killed; those who would die during the war would return to Guinea where they would enjoy eternal bliss."[87] While not explicitly calling him a *oungan* (male Vodou priest) per se, Michel Laguerre asserts that at least one Vodou priest "accompanied" Romaine on the battlefield," while identifying the prophetess as one of the "urban maroons" whose "public meetings . . . were the Voodoo dances and the markets." For good measure, Laguerre adorns the prophetess with an accoutrement that one might expect to find on such a Vodouist leader: "He always carried on his saddle-horse a *rangé* chicken (one having magical powers) as a talisman and went into battle scoffing at bullets and bayonets."[88] And while Abbé Ouvière's invaluable description of the prophetess and his chapel does offer an image quite reflective of Vodou, as in the ribbons, chains, and medals draped over Romaine's body (but not the plumed turban), and the multitude of icons in his sacred space, nowhere does the priest or any other contemporary observer say anything about a magical rooster tied to his saddle—in fact, none even allude to Romaine as ever being seen on horseback, or on the battlefield, for that matter.[89]

At least one other religiously inspired rebel camp in the West Province was designed to be inaccessible through supernatural means, being surrounded by African-derived occult obstacles, raising the question as to whether Trou Coffy might also have been. In February 1792, roughly one month before Trou Coffy was raided, the French colonel Malenfant and his troops stormed a band of insurgents in Fonds-Parisien, just east of Port-au-Prince, to discover the following:

> While approaching the camp, we were quite surprised to see, along the pathway, large, steep mounds of dirt on which were placed an assortment of dead birds, each arranged in a different manner. On some were herons ["*oiseaux crabiers*"—*Ardeolla ralloides*] and on others black chickens. In the path itself bird parts had been cut up and tossed here and there, encircled by carefully arranged rocks; finally, there were about broken eight eggs also round the large circles.[90]

Their dancing and singing suddenly disrupted by the raid, members of the Fonds-Parisien camp, including some 200 women and led by a "high priestess" described by Malenfant as "a very beautiful, well dressed black woman," were altogether puzzled by how the French colonel and his troops "were able to pass beyond the obstacles that the great female Vodou master had spread beneath our steps. That is the assurance that the *Negresse* gave them and gave them confidence and made them dance."[91] Tempting as it might be to imagine such rituals and ritual paraphernalia at Trou Coffy, there is simply no evidence of any in the archival documents, unless the severed head of a white planter named Deshayes affixed to the camp's gate could be taken for one. Deshayes had been killed by Romaine's troops when they raided his plantation in Grand Harpon in September 1791, to recall from Chapter 1, and his "head was exposed on the fence of the so-called Romain, chief of Trou Coffy."[92] Abbé Ouvière's eyewitness description of Trou Coffy does not allude to any kinds of supernatural "obstacles" that a "Vodou master" would have placed around the prophetess' camp. One other contemporary observer, meanwhile, the Léogâne native Bonnet, did recall that Romaine-la-Prophétesse combined "religious ideas with superstitions from Africa," though unfortunately providing no details on what these "superstitions" might have looked, sounded, felt, or smelled like.[93]

Except for the detail about the prophetess' saying Mass at Trou Coffy (with or without a sword in his hand), there is no evidence in the archival sources for most of the specific claims about Romaine made by Larose or Lageurre. Nonetheless, I would not go so far as to concur with Fick that "in all of the documentation surrounding these events, not one reference to this leader can be found that even vaguely suggests genuine African voodoo practices, unless his were in some way peculiar to cults in the Spanish colonies."[94] As seen above, Father Blouët's report notes that in addition to "celebrating the mysteries in his own way," Romaine-la-Prophétesse "composed remedies," which is evidently the statement on which Fick bases her own correct observation that he "practiced herbal medicine," though without affirming this to be one of Haitian Vodou's most fundamental aspects, herbalism. Surely this more than "even vaguely suggests" if not "genuine African voodoo practices" then some earlier Creole form of African-based religious practice that Romaine was incorporating into his Catholic practice, for herbalism was and remains central to both African and African-derived religions.[95] More importantly, Romaine's employment of herbal remedies defined him as a healer in the eyes of his African followers. And, of course, there is the amulet and the adornments that the prophetess wore, as well as Abbé Ouvière's description of the chapel and Trou Coffy, which could indeed just as well be taken to be a vivid description for any given Vodou temple in Haiti today.

In one sense, the question as to whether Romaine-la-Prophétesse preached or practiced Vodou is anachronistic, for the religion did not truly crystallize until the first half of the nineteenth century.[96] In an interesting essay in which he calls Romaine "a westernized mulatto," Drexel Woodson suggests as much, while questioning Fick's discussion of the prophetess for its "surrealism" and dichotomous framing, lamenting her perceivable distinction between "genuine voodoo practices" and "bizarre and dubious cults": "Romaine's amazingly syncretic cult was, she admits, subversive.... Yet the cult relied too heavily, it seems, on systematically inverted Catholic ritual paraphernalia and symbolism to suit Fick's taste for genuine Africana."[97] Woodson's criticism is in part valid, but it misses an important historical point, which is also lacking in Fick's consideration of Romaine-la-Prophétesse: That the "Catholic ritual paraphernalia" on display at Trou Coffy was itself a reflection of "genuine Africana," for many of Romaine's followers, hailing as they did from the kingdom of Kongo, were African Catholics who surely interpreted Romaine's ritual performances and sermons in African Catholic terms. The question as to whether Romaine practiced some form of "Vodou" is also somewhat obviated by the fact that there was then no unified religion to which one could, strictly speaking, refer to by the term. For, as Laguerre helpfully explains, "The various Voodoo traditions that developed in the colony were not standardized. Reciprocal acculturation and syncretism occurred; yet each Voodoo cult had its own traditions."[98]

That Romaine took part in some kind of "reciprocal acculturation" is indeed suggested by the historical accounts. But the prophetess' self-identification is somewhat glossed over by such considerations. Judging from the few letters that he left, by the contemporary eyewitness observations, and by his mystical allusions to the Virgin Mary, that self-identification was Catholic. Nevertheless, once we also take into account his garb, amulets, herbs, and chapel teeming with icons and candles, Romaine-la-Prophétesse may be reasonably suggested to have been a patriarch of Haitian Vodou, innovatively contributing to the emergence of the religion, even if his religious practice was in reality a form of folk Catholicism (which Haitian Vodou sometimes strongly resembles to this day). Most of the religious elements of Romaine's ministry and the Trou Coffy movement mentioned in the primary source data are Catholic, after all, and nowhere is there any mention in contemporary descriptions of Trou Coffy of such quintessential aspects of Vodou as drumming, dance, or animal sacrifice. That said, one should never lose site of the fact that in the world of Romaine-la-Prophétesse, for most Dominguans, Catholic also meant African, amounting in effect to a form of primeval Vodou, or as a splendid example of what Métraux calls a "veritable seizure of Catholicism by Voodoo"—or vice versa.[99] In any case, and here Fick is certainly correct, "it is true that as a leader of slave resistance, his influence over his following was as undisputed as any Vodou leader using the rallying powers of religion for political ends."[100] Let us now more closely consider the African dimensions of the Trou Coffy movement, some of which were clearly Catholic.

African Dimensions of the Trou Coffy Movement

Haitian Vodou is today loosely divided into several identifiable *nasyon* (lit: nations), or rites, the chief two being Rada and Petwo. Generally scholars view the former as being largely of West African origins and the later of Central African derivation, and the etymologies of the terms reflect as much: Rada derives from Arada, the name of a kindgom in Dahomey, while Petwo likely derives from Dom Pedro, the name of a feared maroon from the Spanish side of the island. Dom Pedro was likely a participant in a New World extension of the Central African cult of affliction called Lemba, and in parts of Haiti today the terms Lemba and Petwo remain synonymous.[101] There is evidence, furthermore, that the distinction between Rada and Petwo already existed in the colonial era, raising the question as into which rite, if either, one might place Romaine-la-Prophétesse.[102] Rather unconvincingly, Larose suggests that Romaine-la-Prophétesse performed Petwo rituals;[103] because many of Romaine's followers were Kongolese, it is certainly plausible that Trou Coffy might have been something of a cradle of Petwo religion in Saint-Domingue/ Haiti. It is more likely, however, that had Romaine indeed practiced Lemba he would have imported it from the Spanish side of the island, where the cult was evidently then more popular, or that he was part of a longstanding local manifestation of the cult in the West Province of Saint-Domingue.[104] It is also possible that Romaine was unfamiliar with Lemba but nonetheless benefited from the fortuitous resonance between his religious performance and the Lemba-inflected worldview of many of his African followers; the Virgin Mary, after all, held a place of great importance in colonial Lemba/Petwo religion in Saint-Domingue.[105]

If indeed Romaine had been influenced by Lemba, then he "drew more heavily on ... Kongolese elements than anything seen in the south since the arrest of Sim Dompête [Dom Pedro; also known in Haiti as "Jean Petro"] in 1782," as John Garrigus reckons.[106] Dompête was "a creole slave who had escaped from the Les Cayes area and was reported to be poisoning animals in the area around Nippes," and whose religious leadership was steeped in a "form of African spirituality strongly identified with Kongo slaves, the largest ethnic group in the southern peninsula," and which formed a cornerstone for the Petwo rite in Haitian Vodou. "It had first been identified in the 1760s near Léogâne, on the northern face of the southern peninsula." The Petwo cult was greatly feared in Saint-Domingue, furthermore, because it provided its adepts " 'access to magic to inflict their vengeance.' "[107] Like Dompête's, Romaine-la-Prophétesse's message resonated significantly with Kongolese religious culture in other ways. For instance, in his radical appropriation of the Catholic symbol of the Virgin Mary, Romaine was doing precisely what Kongolese prophets had done for generations,[108] which would help explain his appeal to Central Africans who participated in the Trou Coffy insurgency, who would have taken him to be a social healer (Kikongo: *nganga marinda*) and a prophet (*ngunza*). From the time of the Kongo kingdom's initial contact with Europeans in the late fifteenth century, Kongolese religious leadership was marked by healing and prophecy, after all, and for centuries prophets have had unparalleled and enduring impact on Kongolese religious life.

Romaine's very title of la Prophétesse would strongly suggest that many of his adherents interpreted his function in the traditional Kongolese sense of the term, just as some of them surely understood the function and message of Beatriz Kimpa Vita. Beatriz was an immensely popular millenarian prophetess whose movement became so alarming to local elites and Catholic friars in the shattered Kongo kingdom that she was burned at the stake in their homeland in 1706.[109] Romaine's mediating role involved his communication with the Virgin Mary, much as Beatriz's had involved her self-identification with Saint Anthony. There is also a striking element of gender inversion in the message of Makaya, a Kongolese insurgent leader in the North Province. Consider, for example, Makaya's inversion of the gender of the king of Spain by referring to him as "my mother." Makaya and Romaine thus each employed the inversion of gender in staking claims to the legitimation of their shamanic authority. Furthermore, like Makaya, both Romaine and Beatriz militated against slavery and endeavored to bring about the establishment or the restoration of some kind of a kingdom. It is worth adding that Beatriz appealed to the Virgin birth story to legitimate her influence, preaching that Jesus had actually been born in the Kongo and that her own pregnancy was immaculately conceived. Perhaps the most important comparison to be made between Beatriz and Romaine is that each envisioned her/his calling to be divine and his/her mission to be supportive of an earthly kingdom, all overseen by Catholic saints, respectively Saint Anthony and the Virgin Mary. Regarding ritual performance, meanwhile, "sacrilegious" acts were reported of each the prophetess and "St. Anthony" (as Beatriz preferred to be called): though not ordained to do so, Romaine celebrated Mass at Trou Coffy, while Beatriz burned the cross and other items of Catholic ritual paraphernalia, and they each answered a calling to seek to end slavery, a call that was also answered by Makaya.

Romaine's subversive appeal to the Virgin Mary and his claims to be both related to and in communication with the Blessed Mother held considerable sway over both the Africans and Creoles at Trou Coffy and its satellite insurgent camps between Jacmel and Léogâne. For the Kongolese Marian devotees among them, to have survived the horrors of the Middle Passage and endured enslavement and brutality on Saint-Domingue's plantations would have made any invocation or representation of the Blessed Mother most comforting, especially exhortations calling for a radical transformation of the harshly unjust social world in which they found themselves. They would have surely taken keen interest in one of the most striking assertions made by Romaine, that he was the Virgin Mary's "godson." Although appeals to Catholic saints or biblical personages was a common feature of Dominguan popular religion, assertions by religious leaders to be related to and in direct communication with them were not. Such claims were, however, sometimes made by Kongo prophets in Central African history, which further reflects Kongolese political and religious influences on the Trou Coffy movement. Romaine's military campaign against the white and free colored elites of Léogâne and Jacmel was, in any case, commanded by the Virgin Mary through the mediumship of her godson and by the Holy Spirit. Additionally underscoring their closeness, the title that Romaine adopted for himself, the prophetess, was also one that he applied to the Virgin—actually, he referred to her as "the prophetess of grace."[110]

As the human population diversified in Saint-Domingue with the forced arrival of ethnically varied Africans, so too did interpretations of the Virgin Mary. Many Kongolese slaves brought Marian devotion with them from Africa, while many West African slaves, whether ethnically Fon, Igbo, or Nago (Yoruba), interpreted the Blessed Mother through the lens of the veneration of female divinities in their respective homeland religions, like Oshun, Yemaya, and Oya.[111] Both of these African religious baselines helped the cult of Mary flourish in Dominguan and Haitian Catholicism, while also infusing notions of religious leadership with healing, prophetic, and mediumistic qualities. Scant though they may be for the period in question, missionary records do suggest that slaves in Saint-Domingue were especially fond of the Virgin Mary and found great appeal in the ritual paraphernalia associated with Marian devotion (medals, rosaries, candles, icons, etc.), which surely fertilized the Dominguan religious field for the development of a profound Marian dimension that helped inspire the Haitian Revolution.[112] In Trou Coffy, this element would crystallize around the charismatic figure of Romaine-la-Prophétesse, whose religious movement represents one of the most radically heterodox and effectively seditious example of symbolic appropriation in the illustrious annals of political Marianism and a kind of New World inversion of Catholic symbolism that had long featured in Kongolese prophetic tradition. And it is only logical to assume that Mary, as *Queen* of Heaven, would lend additional force to the royalism and ideologies animating insurgents in Kongo, Trou Coffy, and elsewhere in the revolutionary Atlantic world.

The Prophetess Who Would Be King: Romaine and the Question of Royalism

In crafting and/or receiving his charismatic authority, Romaine-la-Prophétesse drew upon an impressive array of power sources: the Church, the king, the Virgin Mary, the Holy Spirit, amulets, and herbs. Nothing is more reflective of the high esteem in which Romaine held the king of France than a passage in a letter that he wrote (or dictated for a scribe to write) to Abbé Ouvière on January 26, 1792. Here the prophetess assured the priest of his "inviolable attachment and love for the mother country" and affirmed that "our monarch and the national assembly are deserving of the esteem in which the universe views honest men." As for Romaine's followers, meanwhile, several months earlier, in September of 1791, they were overjoyed by the arrival in Trou Coffy of the king's appointed mayor of Léogâne, de Villards, crying out "Long live the king! Long live our sad king!"[113] As for the Church, Romaine was, according to Abbé Ouvière, "passionately devoted to the cult,"[114] and however syncretic that religious practice might have been at the chapel in Trou Coffy, the prophetess held the sacerdotal authority of the Catholic priesthood in deferential respect: When Abbé Ouvière first arrived in Trou Coffy he was received with something like a 21-gun salute (*Des salves de mousquetaire*).[115]

These communal gestures of esteem for Villards and Ouvière are very suggestive of the hybrid nature of black devotion in Saint-Domingue to Church and king. While on first glance, because they were expressed to white Frenchmen, they might seem to reflect merely a mimetic embrace of a white Church and king, they were in fact deeply inflected with experiences of an African Catholic Church and with nostalgia for African kings. "The enslaved recalled and sometimes called upon their homelands," writes Laurent Dubois. "In one Vodou song recorded in the 1950s, probably a relic from the days of slavery, a singer calls on the King of the Kongo to 'look at what they are doing to me.'"[116] Fused with European notions of kingship, this "ideological syncretism continued in Saint-Domingue even after the break between the Republic and the royalty was accomplished in France," soon spreading throughout the colony.[117] That Romaine would be identified as a future king was thus quite in keeping with aspirational notions of monarchal rule in other insurgent camps in the early years of the Haitian Revolution, like in the "kingdom of the Platons" in the South Province; in Acul, where Jean-Baptiste Cap was anointed as regent;[118] and in Petit Anse, where a Catholic priest, Father Cachetan, crowned Jean-François and Charlotte as the "king and queen of the Africans."[119]

Dubois further suggests that insurgent leaders in the North, like Biassou and Jean-François in Dondon, "had a powerful incentive to take a 'royalist' tone: the collaboration, and ultimately alliance, they developed with the Spanish across the border in Santo Domingo."[120] Could this have also been the case with Romaine-la-Prophétesse, who had the distinct advantage of speaking Spanish fluently? Léogâne was considerably farther from the border than Dondon (roughly 80 vs. 50 kilometers), however, and Romaine's letters cast doubt on that possibility, as they reflect a patriotic devotion to France. Although this could itself have been a form of "posturing" designed to secure the trust of Abbé Ouvière, the priest believed the prophetess to be sincere in this regard.

Among the other religious visionaries in revolutionary Saint-Domingue, none is more comparable to Romaine-la-Prophétesse than Makaya, a Kongolese rebel who once miffed Toussaint Louverture because "[e]very day he organizes dances and assemblies with the Africans of his nation and gives them bad advice."[121] Consider, for example, Makaya's remarkable declaration: "I am the subject of three kings: of the King of Congo, master of all the blacks; of the King of France who represents my father; of the King of Spain who represents my mother. These three Kings are the descendants of those who, led by a star, came to adore God made Man."[122] Here two points of comparison with Romaine's syncretic theology are particularly noteworthy: First, the evident infatuation with kingship; and second, both Makaya and Romaine placed themselves in positions of filial relationship with holy figures in the sanctification of Christ's birth: respectively, the Magi, or their "descendants," (Makaya's master, mother, and father), and the Virgin Mary (Romaine's godmother). "Kongolese ideologues had reworked Christian concepts in a similar way for many years," as John Thornton concludes, reflecting how profoundly important was Central African religion and culture in the Haitian Revolution.[123]

It should be affirmed that among the prophetess' African followers were counted many who were in fact not socialized by Kongolese religious thought or political ideology, as they hailed from other parts of Africa, especially the Bight of Benin. Though, even there monarchal ideas infused with notions of divinity permeated political consciousness and collective identity and forcefully shaped societies, as it obviously also did among Romaine's Creole followers.[124] Relatedly, Creoles and West Africans in Saint-Domingue held similar beliefs to those in the Kongo about the social dimensions of healing and prophecy, and, as victims and survivors of the transatlantic slave trade, they were animated by such beliefs in explosive places like Trou Coffy and they fully expected a divinely anointed king to usher in and safeguard a redeemed world.[125]

Conclusion

Romaine-la-Prophétesse's rise to prominence as an insurgent leader in 1791 owed a great deal to religion, in general, and to his close relationship to the Virgin Mary and the prophecies and injunctions that he received from his godmother in his chapel at Trou Coffy, in particular. This is quite a powerful example of what Deborah O'Neil and I mean by the term "liberation hagiography."[126] Although the prophetess was not Kongolese, the cult of the Virgin Mary in Saint-Domingue was certainly shaped in significant part by the Marian devotion and beliefs that people from West Central Africa brought with them across the Atlantic, and thus it is clear that the Trou Coffy movement was, to a certain extent, part of what might be called a militaristic form of transatlantic Kongolese Marianism. Exploring this in a different context, namely the 1739 Stono Rebellion in South Carolina, Mark Smith writes, "the Virgin Mary seeped into Kongolese historical memory, religious discourse, and spiritual ritual. Plainly, the Virgin Mary had military and religious significance." For the Kongolese, both in Central Africa and in the Americas, "she emerged as savior and holy warrior, protector and advocate"—this was in effect liberation hagiography actualized and militarized.[127] Nowhere in the revolutionary Atlantic world was this truer than in Trou Coffy in 1791 and 1792.

This is a suggestive conclusion, one that raises new questions regarding the role that religion played in the Haitian Revolution. Jean Fouchard and others have convincingly argued that it was not so much some theological message of a "precise idea of liberty" inherent to Vodou that allowed the nascent religion to play a meaningful role in the success of the Revolution, but rather its ability to inspire and to unify slaves and maroons, members of diverse ethnic groups, and to equip them with spiritual powers and supernatural weapons for material battles.[128] Add to this the intertwined-yet-antithetical Christian and French Enlightenment notions of human equality, reinforced by the lives of the dead-but-intercessory Catholic saints and African ancestors, and you have one powerful and revolutionary confluence of religious and philosophical ideals.

The potency of the messages preached by the likes of Beatriz, Boukman, Makaya, and Romaine-la-Prophétesse depended largely upon the religious needs and interests of their audience, of course, in this case one of world history's most oppressed peoples. As Weber compellingly argues, in addition to pining for the alleviation of their suffering, subjugated classes often demonstrate "a need for just compensation," which "serves as a device for compensating a conscious or unconscious desire for vengeance."[129] Moreover, the "theodicy of compensation" that is reflected in both Boukman's celebrated but largely mythological Bwa Kayiman sermon and Romaine's Mariology (that God and the Blessed Virgin Mary frowned upon the whites and would ensure the turning of the tides) was essential to the prophecy of each.[130] If, for the sake of argument, Romaine had indeed been something of a "self-styled prophet,"[131] mixing and marketing "salvation goods" from various religious traditions, it could be reasonably ventured that it is precisely the expression of such a "theodicy of compensation" wherein lies the fundamental explanation of religion's effective role in the Haitian Revolution. It was not so much out of Vodou that 1804 issued, then, but out of the transaction between religious leaders like Boukman and Romaine and the laity around the marginalized free coloreds' and slaves' desire for revenge and compensation, as well as their desire for freedom and justice; that is, for social healing. Other religious or quasi-magical elements certainly played a role, such as the belief in immortality in Africa for martyrs and in the power of talismans as protection against bullets and cannon balls, but religion's effectiveness in the Revolution relied above all on the theodicy of compensation. Evoking the Virgin Mary, the prophetess served to rally the Trou Coffy insurgents around the vision of this theodicy realized and his social healing ministry. The rest is history.

Who, then, was Romaine-la-Prophétesse? Concerning the religious dimensions of the Trou Coffy insurgency, Romaine was a medium, prophet, catechist, *kaperlata*, and social healer. Although many contemporary observers and even some historians have doubted the sincerity of the prophetess' sense of calling, Romaine's followers clearly did not, nor did he; to many of them, he was indeed both a *ngunza* and a living Catholic saint, a shaman and even a savior. Judging from the archival evidence, or lack thereof, meanwhile, one cannot soundly call him a sorcerer, a magician, or a Vodou priest per se, though one may realistically call him a forefather (or even a godparent) of Haitian Vodou, Haitian Catholicism, and Haitian independence. And though he was a free black Creole from the Spanish side of the island and not an African, that he practiced herbalism and manufactured amulets clearly connects him to two quintessential forms of Africana spirituality in the Americas.[132] Another quintessential form of Africana spirituality at the heart of Romaine's practice, finally, was mediumship, and the prophetess himself understood this in decidedly Afro-Catholic terms.

For all of the violence, death, and destruction that his followers wrought, meanwhile, Romaine-la-Prophétesse, godson of the Virgin Mary, was a mediumistic, prophetic catechist who took divinity to be conducting through him a war to be waged for a better future ruled by church and king—a future in which no one would be a slave. For all of the things that the prophetess has been called ever since, it is well worth noting here that the priest considered him to be "not in the least bloodthirsty," but rather a "sober and brave" man on a "divine mission" to abolish slavery, and that Romaine should therefore "one day receive some gratitude and some honors in the name of his tyrannized nation."[133]

3

Abbé Ouvière

A bowl rotates faster at the top than the bottom.

—AMINU KANO[1]

Overview

FEW PEOPLE LIVE to experience two political revolutions, especially when menaced by the prospects of being beheaded, hanged, or otherwise executed in both of them, and fewer still live to also experience the aftermath of a third. Abbé Ouvière was one such rare person. He was about 27-years-old and somewhere in his native France, perhaps Marseille, when the Bastille fell in Paris in 1789. Two years later the priest found himself in the midst of the devastating slave and free colored insurgencies in Saint-Domingue that marked the beginning of the Haitian Revolution, where his dramatic encounter with Romaine-la-Prophétesse would occur, at Christmas in Trou Coffy. In 1793, meanwhile, misfortune forced Ouvière to flee the Caribbean by ship for yet another land, the United States of America, whose own revolution had concluded just 10 years prior. A Catholic cleric, physician, scientist, diplomat, visionary, and Freemason, the priest's life story is a powerful case in point of what Alison Games means in stating that "Atlantic perspectives deepen our understanding of transformations over a period of several centuries, cast old problems in an entirely new light, and illuminate connections hitherto obscured."[2] This chapter sketches the first three decades of Abbé Ouvière's life to illuminate such connections and help us understand the man who would one day become advisor to Romaine-la-Prophétesse.

Early Life in France

The priest was born in 1762 in Aix-en-Provence and his full name was Félix Alexander Pascalis Ouvière.[3] Both of his parents, Jean François Ouvière, a surveyor, and Anne Françoise Pascalis, were said to be of "honorable" and "respectable" families, and there was some relation to the famous royalist jurist Jean Joseph Pierre Pascalis (1732–1790), who was executed in Aix-en-Provence during the French Revolution, his head impaled on a spike and paraded through the city streets.[4] At least one side of his family, likely his mother's, was of Armenian descent and had been in the country since the reign of King Francis I (reigned 1515–1547).[5]

We know almost nothing about the priest's early days, save for two passing references that he makes much later in life to childhood memories, both of which relate to religion. In the first, a letter from 1810, Ouvière recalls that his father had received from a Jesuit missionary in India a bean, a St. Ignatius bean, and that it was found to be effective in controlling fevers produced by "toxins."[6] In the second, the priest recounts a religious procession "for the holy host" (perhaps his First Holy Communion) in which he was horrified to discover that part of the elaborate vestments in which he was adorned for the occasion had been torn. The garments had been made "by noble ladies . . . rich and pious women," and Ouvière, who "was about twelve years of age" at the time, despaired over the expense this could bring upon his family, for "my father was not rich."[7] The bean that the Jesuit gave to his father may have been a source of enduring inspiration to the young Ouvière, at any rate, for he would go on in life to be a Catholic priest, scientist, and physician. In due course the priest was educated at the university in Aix, and "[w]hen he graduated he took the first prize of honour, which distinction introduced him to the celebrated Professor Darluc, a botanist and professor of natural history"[8] and a devout follower of the great Swedish naturalist Carl Linnaeus, rightly known as "the father of taxonomy."

One of the priest's descendants in America recalls hearing stories about how as a young man Ouvière "travelled a lot" and combined his wanderlust with his keen scientific curiosity:

> He was one of the first persons to cross the Alps. He traveled in Asia Minor a lot. While in Asia Minor he heard about magnets. . . . In Asia Minor there is a range of mountains, named Magnesia, that runs north and south. There is a lot of rock and metal in the range. The rock is magnetized and we call it loadstone. He got some of the rock and made a magnet out of it. He put it in a box made of brass and glass. He fixed it so he could hold it up and measure how much (weight) it would pick up. I have that magnet.[9]

His American descendants also recalled that Abbé Ouvière had at some point been a friend to Napoleon Bonaparte, but the correspondence between the two

Frenchmen that the family once possessed had "unfortunately been lost in the shifting sands of time."[10]

Because in eighteenth-century France many physicians and scientists were also Catholic priests, it is unsurprising that Ouvière's studies would follow a confluence of science, medicine, and religion, with especial devotion reserved for naturalism. Few, if any, French naturalists were more passionate or influential in inspiring this "botanophilia" than Abbé Noel-Antoine Pluche (1688–1761), whose tome *Le Spectacle de la nature* was widely read in France at the time.[11] Despite the fact that Ouvière "studied divinity for three years ... still his partiality for medicine was so strong, that his mind was occupied with the thoughts of this science while on a tour in France and Italy,"[12] and so as a young man he enrolled in medical school at Montpellier and completed his studies there sometime in the late 1780s. His intellectual preference for the former subject notwithstanding, both science and religion held a lifelong fascination for the priest, who took the ultimate purpose of scientific endeavor to be the deepening of our understanding of God, the wonders of God's creation, and the divinely instituted and unchangeable laws of nature. In this respect, Abbé Ouvière may be placed in a lineage with Abbé Pluche in what one might call the French botanical theology of the era, in whose "discussions we get repeated assurances that we see, in plants, the work of God. Quite clear is the implication that the new science supports religious truth."[13] Ouvière's own scientific work later in life would also clearly reflect his training at Montpellier, whose influential faculty wed philosophy and medicine, developed a vitalist understanding of the human body, turned to nature for curés, and spearheaded enthusiastic explorations of the impact of vapors on human health and behavior, thus playing a key role in what Anne Vila calls "the medicalization of the Enlightenment."[14]

A contemporary of two of the most famous Catholic priests in modern French history and key political figures of the French Revolution, Abbé Henri Grégoire (1750–1831) and Abbé Emmanuel Joseph Sieyès (1738–1836), Abbé Ouvière was a brilliant, ambitious, mysterious, cunning, and mercurial man of strong (and opportunistically shifting) faiths and ideologies, which he voiced in print throughout his adult life.[15] In 1789, for instance, after failing to obtain a state license to start a newspaper in Marseille, Ouvière "went on to publish two editions of *Spectateur provençale en divers discours* from Avignon, outside direct French jurisdiction. Still wanting to publish from Marseille, he then put in a second request to the *directeur de la librairie* but received no reply."[16]

The next year, Ouvière published a political editorial in Marseille, "Adieux d'un cosmopolite aux Marseillois,"[17] in which the priest "even justified the gap between the very rich and the rest."[18] Though he praises

Marseille for its industry and riches, and though he cites Abbé Raynal at one point, who was then believed to be a leading abolitionist, in "Adieux" Abbé Ouvière never alludes to the fact that Marseille's rise to prominence as "the Kingdom's second city" owed much to the labor of black slaves in Saint-Domingue. And though the author waxes poetic about human suffering under despotic political powers, and despite his objections to Paris' politically centralist exploitation of Marseille, nowhere in this rather pedantic essay does the priest mention the suffering of the tens of thousands of African and Creole slaves whose forced labor helped make Marseille the great city that Ouvière so admired.[19] But soon enough he would get to witness that misery firsthand, which evidently inspired an abolitionist turn in the priest's ideology.

By the time he published "Adieux," Ouvière was already in touch with free colored Dominguan elites in France and was—or at least he pretended to be—supportive of their cause. Thereby the priest managed to ingratiate himself to them and gained their trust. The source of his connection to the *gens de couleur* was almost certainly his relationship to the great Creole general André Rigaud, one of the founding fathers of Haiti, whose own father was a wealthy Frenchman whose "legitimate" (read "white") son (André Rigaud's half-brother) was married to the priest's sister.[20] However deep those political and family ties might have been, Abbé Ouvière's emigration from France to Saint-Domingue was a matter of urgency, as sometime during the summer or autumn of 1790 his theological writings provoked the ire of the archbishop of Paris and placed his life and liberty in danger:

> His active mind could never be quiet, and he dashed out into the literary world, in a work, on the celibacy of the clergy. The essay made a great noise, and the Archbishop of Belloi [*sic*] excommunicated the young ecclesiastic, who had dared to speak his mind on such a delicate subject. In a few days, the Reverend Prelate was obliged to fly his country. The subject of this sketch now determined to make medicine a profession, and on acquaintance with a surgeon of the army, he went with him to Port-au-Prince.[21]

Ouvière's own recollection is that he was defrocked by the archbishop after having himself first renounced his title as abbé, though it must be said that the former priest was then writing more than 30 years after these events in a memoir explicitly designed to defend his reputation against some rather serious partisan attacks.[22] A different version of the priest's dramatic escape from France is recalled by his progeny in South Carolina, one rooted in politics rather than in theology, suggesting that Abbé Ouvière had multiple reasons to flee his native country:

> Dr. Pascalis was a young Frenchman who was a graduate of the University of Paris and had practiced Medicine in the Royal Families—we know that—he was also friendly to the poor people down the river—he used to deliver their babies and one thing and another and they thought a lot of him. The revolution came about and the movement was on to behead those loyal to the French (King?). These poor people found out that his "number was up" and they took him down the river to a bayou, from which he escaped to Santo Domingo and later to Maracaibo.[23]

Just how Abbé Ouvière occupied himself during his entire first year in Saint-Domingue is something of a mystery, but by the end of November 1791 the priest had been appointed as a member of the Administrative Council of the free colored Confederate Army, based in Croix des Bouquets, and a month later he would find himself in heart of one of the most notorious insurgent camps of the Haitian Revolution, in the chapel of Romaine-la-Prophétesse in Trou Coffy.

Ouvière as Abbé

The term *abbé* literally translates as "abbot," and originally in French Catholicism it connoted a cloistered monk who exercised administrative authority in an abbey or monastery. But by the eighteenth century in France the title was also given to secular priests with no connections to institutional monasticism. (There is in English no such valence to the term "abbot" like that subsequent meaning of the word in French). Secular priests emerged in medieval Christianity as a body of clerics who did not train to be members of a particular religious order, like the Benedictines or Franciscans, or to submit to such an order's "Rule," instead taking on a vocation in and a ministry to the "secular" world. That said, secular priests have always been considered to be under the authority of a bishop or archbishop. Abbés also underwent the Rite of Tonsure, a rite of passage in which the crowns of the initiands' heads were shaved as a symbol of "their separation from the laity and renunciation of the world, a demonstration of their willingness to wear the crown of thorns, to suffer with Christ."[24] From then on it was assumed that those thus tonsured—*les tonsurés*—would continue on the path to clerical ordination. As Joseph Byrnes explains, on this path "they received the four minor orders, then subdiaconate with the obligation to continue on to the diaconate and priesthood,"[25] though in rare cases some French abbés did not take that step. Either way, secular priests in eighteenth-century France, as always and according to canon law, were expected to honor a vow of celibacy and to perform daily the Liturgy of the Hours, which consisted of a series of prayers said at various times of the day and readings from the Psalms and other biblical and doctrinal passages.

There were some 770 abbés in the French Catholic Church in Ouvière's day, and reasons behind their assumption of the position varied greatly, as did their material remuneration.[26] Given that in eighteenth-century France most abbés secured incomes that entailed virtually no commitment of labor, that brought prestige, and that opened doors to ascendant careers in the Catholic Church, it is unsurprising that the position held much appeal for young French males, and not just for the religiously inspired. Parents thus sought canonries or benefices (Church-subsidized appointments as clerics), and sometimes their sons received them and secured the title of abbé at as young an age as nine years. The great *philosophe* Diderot found himself to be an abbé by age 13, for instance, and dressed the part for two years before having "a crisis of faith" and "realizing his unsuitability" for the priesthood.[27] In the case of Abbé Ouvière, he "accepted a clerical benefice which was then in the gift of his family," meaning that the priest had been tonsured while an adolescent and "raised in the ecclesiastic state."[28] Then, following his three years studying theology (much more than the average of "sixteen months"),[29] the young abbé "was now licensed to preach and delivered several eulogiums, and charity discourses; but he was drawn, however, from his clerical pursuits, by attending his older brother's lectures on physical science."[30] Abbé Ouvière had also at some point secured a chaplaincy in a noble household, that of a count who was Lieutenant General et Commandant en Provence.[31] This perhaps deepened his royalist commitments; more certainly, it afforded him a degree of privilege that irked more democratically minded clerics, who in their "ordinary enthusiasm for revolutionary propaganda pronounced themselves in pamphlets as opposed to the privileged, like Abbé Ouvière."[32]

The clerical position of abbé often required little, if any, service to the church, no curé of souls, and no ministerial obligation to any given parish. Still, many eighteenth-century abbés were of course active as parish priests, both in France and in the French Caribbean colonies, while some, like Ouvière, used their canonries as platforms for scientific endeavor. There was thus an entire range among abbés in their sense of vocation, and, although rare, there were some cases in which a tonsured novice would not go on to seek ordination as a priest, like a one Abbé Chamfort, who liked "repose, philosophy, women, and honor too much"[33]—and, of course, like the aforementioned Diderot.

In Abbé Ouvière, clearly we have a character whose sense of vocation was shaky, at best. As an *abbé* rather than a *curé* (parish priest), furthermore, Ouvière seemingly fits very well what John McManners ascertains to be the "stereotype" of "abbés on the margin of the Church" as "dubious and opportunistic adventurers."[34] The position of abbé brought him some measure of respect and an income, at any rate, and like a number of other members of his clerical brood, Ouvière took advantage of the liberty that it afforded him to embark on scientific and literary pursuits—and political pursuits, none more adventurous than his journey to and machinations in Saint-Domingue. It is clear that Ouvière took the Sacrament of Holy Orders and was thus ordained, as there is documentation from Saint-Domingue in 1792 in which he explicitly refers to himself as a "priest."[35] At least three other archival sources, two of which he wrote himself, suggest that he occasionally said Mass in Saint-Domingue in late 1791 and early 1792, furthermore, perhaps twice in Croix-des-Bouquets and once in each Léogâne and in Trou Coffy.[36] However, prior to ever going to Saint-Domingue, the priest had either renounced his vows or was defrocked: "As for the title of Abbé . . . I am not ashamed of having abandoned the Sacred Calling into which I was cast, but in which more piety and sincerity is required than I could ever have mustered."[37] Celibacy was also an insurmountable challenge for Abbé Ouvière, as there is unambiguous evidence that prior to departing for Saint-Domingue in 1790, the priest had married a young woman from Marseille.[38]

Though lapses in their commitment to celibacy were not at all unheard of among Catholic clerics in eighteenth-century France, that an abbé who had been ordained as a priest would marry in 1790 was quite scandalous and clearly in violation of both canon and civil law.[39] While I have not found Abbé Ouvière's publication on celibacy that seemingly led to his defrocking and his flight from France for Saint-Domingue, it is not unimaginable that the brash, young priest announced therein that he was not only opposed to clerical celibacy, but that he also had defiantly wed. In stating such opposition, Ouvière was not alone. In May of that year, for instance, Maximilien de Robespierre delivered a speech to the National Assembly promoting a series of Church reforms, like having bishops elected by the people and clerics paid by the state rather than through tithing. However, given "all of the trouble that it would cause with the pope in Rome," he evoked especial outrage when he proposed that their vow of celibacy be optional and that priests be allowed to marry.[40]

In light of the timing of these developments, it is clear that Abbé Ouvière's decision to marry was quite premature, politically speaking. Still, Robespierre's speech of May of 1790 helped promote this theretofore fringe idea in revolutionary France and probably struck a chord with Ouvière or any other abbé whose sense of vocation might have been ambivalent or challenged by heterosexual desire. Ouvière surely knew that the marriage of priests had not yet been formally legalized, although legislation was passed that year to protect any espoused cleric from miffed bishops who might otherwise take action to sanction and/or defrock them.[41] So the priest, who had evidently fallen in love with a young woman in Marseille, acted upon the idea that one might be both a Catholic priest and a husband, and Monsieur et Madame Ouvière married sometime between the day when he heard news of Robespierre's May 1790 speech and the day when he fled France in late August or early September of that year, thereby becoming one of the first married Catholic priests of the French Revolution.

The timing of Abbé Ouvière's illegal marriage is quite intriguing, as it seems to have taken place just after the approval of the Constitutional Clergy by the Constituent Assembly, on July 12, 1790, and just before the Assembly's ratification the following month of a requirement that "all clerics sign an oath of allegiance to the Civil Constitution."[42] This means that even if he would have intended to do so, Ouvière could not have formally then become a member of the Constitutional Clergy, unless, of course, some arrangement had been made for him to sign the oath from Saint-Domingue, which had been the case for at least two prelates in the French Caribbean colonies.[43] Though now defrocked, he may have clung to some hope of one day being formally reinstated as a priest in France as he left his new wife back in Marseille and sailed across the Atlantic to the New World, bolstered by the optimism that Robespierre would eventually succeed in legislating priestly marriage. For, on September 7, 1790, the priest wrote a letter to Robespierre from Saint-Marc with the following pressing inquiry:

> The marriage of priests, is it decreed? Your patriotism, has it been crowned by a success that would be forever memorable? Ah, monsieur, if you were in this country here, you would see how important it is to bring an end to the license, the prevarication, and the fornication [alluding here to the clergy that he had just begun to encounter in Saint-Domingue].[44]

Abbé Ouvière's letter to Robespierre also demonstrates that the two men had known each other prior to the priest's departure for Saint-Domingue, and it is likely this document that Jean Fouchard had in mind when writing that the priest "had relations with Robespierre."[45] Furthermore, this letter's content and tone suggest that Ouvière was expected to report back to Robespierre on the state of the Church in the colony, or at least that the priest took it upon himself to do so in yet another of his attempts to gain political influence on a grand scale. Intended to be read as "the witness or the confirmation of a French patriot," the letter opens: "Having arrived in a distressed colony, I hasten to write you to give you some instructions and some details that are not unworthy of a legislator." After denouncing the "shameful defection" of many whites in the colony and updating Robespierre on a number of recent political developments, Ouvière offered the following observations on the state of the Church in Saint-Domingue:

> It needs a new organization of the clergy. There exist here two missions, one of the Capuchins and the other of the Dominicans. Both of them are led by apostolic prefects, monks, who distribute to them about 52 *curés* and 100 positions of *vicaires*. Because the monks are detractors, isn't it time for France to establish two bishops or two ecclesiastic prefects who would form an establishment of a seminary that would produce priests who are a bit more legitimate? All I see here are whites who are clueless about such arrangements.[46]

The next line of the letter is very hard to decipher but seems to suggest that such an arrangement should be proposed to the National Assembly for "all individuals of the clergy in France." Given Ouvière's lifelong track record of proposing initiatives of national (and even global, as we'll see later) proportions and envisioning himself as their orchestrator, it is plausible that the abbé had one of the proposed bishoprics for Saint-Domingue in mind for himself. Being a newcomer in the colony and an ordained (albeit defrocked) Catholic cleric without a parish, his economic prospects were likely not the greatest, so such an idea might indeed have been appealing. The idea would ultimately prove to be pie in the sky, however, yet Ouvière's position as an abbé would still immediately help him gain respect in his new world, which, along with his considerable education and natural talents, he would later employ to great effect. Thus, though the colonial bishopric that he had proposed to Robespierre would never happen, during his ensuing year and a half in the colony many dramatic things would, and Abbé Ouvière soon found himself surrounded by cadavers, flames, and political intrigue; and, in the latter, he would manage to carve out a place for himself of some measure of influence and prestige.

Abbé Ouvière's Arrival and Settlement in Saint-Domingue

Why did Abbé Ouvière go to Saint-Domingue in the first place? In part, seemingly he had to flee France because of his controversial publications, but certainly there was more behind his emigration than that. That he was a Catholic priest involved with insurgents might suggest that his presence in Saint-Domingue was due to some relationship with the influential French abolitionist organization the Société des Amis des Noirs (Society of the Friends of Blacks). Rightly or wrongly, white planters in Saint-Domingue blamed the Société for fomenting revolt among their slaves, and thus they burned in effigy the leading Catholic priest in the Société, Abbé Henri Grégoire.[47] Because of his position as a Catholic priest and his association with one of the colony's most notorious insurgent leaders, Romaine-la-Prophétesse, one might reasonably suspect that Abbé Ouvière could indeed have been an agent of the Société. General François Joseph Pamphile de Lacroix, a French military officer who partook in General Leclerc's expedition to attempt to reconquer Saint-Domingue for Napoleon's France in 1802 and lived to write about it, offers, for example, that Ouvière "was suspected" to be a member of the Société,[48] while Jean Fouchard claims that "Abbé Pascalis Ouvière was in relations with Robespierre and the *Société des Amis des noirs*."[49]

By the time of Ouvière's arrival in the colony, French Catholic opposition to slavery had become increasingly boisterous both in the metropole and in Saint-Domingue. Abbé Grégoire's abolitionist writings and those incorrectly attributed to Abbé Raynal circulated widely throughout the empire and contained ideas that found a receptive audience among the enslaved. Rightly striking fear in the hearts of plantation owners, Grégoire's pamphlets and letters, along with their accompanying engravings,[50] exhibited "a very extraordinary tendency ... promising protection and support" and declaring that "'*the day will come when the sun will shine upon free people only*'.... *The beams of the morning shall no longer shine on slavery*."[51] So inspiring was Grégoire's message that he was in effect canonized by the rebel slaves, who turned his likeness, or something intended as his saintly likeness, into battlefield amulets:

> Abbé Grégoire, to whose good office this benevolence was imputed, was immediately considered as the patron of all the mulattoes and negroes in the island.... The above conjecture is confirmed by the following circumstance: "In the first of the engagements, one of the chiefs of the rebels being killed, there was found about his neck a medal of San Gregorio, a Saint in the Romish calendar; and it appeared in evidence

> that this medal was worn by a negro as a portrait of his patron, the abbé: the familiarity of the name giving countenance to the conceit . . . . It has this description: SAN GREGORIO MAGNO P.M."[52]

I had long suspected that Abbé Ouvière must have been a member of the Société who had been sent to Saint-Domingue as something like Abbé Grégoire's emissary, and in an earlier draft of this book I made that association a centerpiece of a larger argument about the pivotal yet underappreciated impact of Catholic antislavery in the Haitian Revolution.[53] While I remain convinced that the Catholic contribution to the Revolution has thus far been underemphasized in scholarly and popular literature, there is no clear archival evidence connecting Ouvière to the Société. He is not listed in the Société's 1789 membership roll;[54] furthermore, though he was surely aware of their initiative and influence on politics and popular opinion in France and was perhaps once sympathetic to their cause, which was aimed at curtailing the slave trade, if not at the outright abolition of slavery itself, in the priest's papers in the Archives Nationales in Paris, there is not a single piece of correspondence with any leading members of the Société, which is not even so much as mentioned in any of the dozens of letters to and from Ouvière that have been preserved. It is thus highly unlikely that he was among the unnamed priests who had been "sent over . . . from France by M. ________ to teach the negroes to revolt," as was reported in the *Philadelphia General Advertiser* on October 10, 1791.[55]

Despite having been defrocked or having abandoned his vocation in France prior to his dramatic flight to Saint-Domingue in 1790, Abbé Ouvière continued to assume the title, function, and appearance of a Catholic priest in the colony and was always addressed there as "Abbé," even though he was never appointed to serve as a priest in any parish there. He seemingly did say Mass at least a few times, however, he certainly preached there, and he publicly referred to himself as a "priest." In addition to incorrectly suspecting him to be a member of the Société, Lacroix was also mistaken in his assertion that Ouvière once served as "*curé* of Léogâne,"[56] as the abbé from Aix-en-Provence is nowhere listed in the St. Rose de Lima parish registries for 1790–1792, the years of his residency in Saint-Domingue.[57] Insofar as they exist, these ecclesial records seem to be fairly complete and list baptisms, marriages, and funerals, with each entry signed by the officiating priest, but not a single entry is signed by Ouvière. On the occasions that he may have said Mass in Trou Coffy and in Léogâne, Abbé Ouvière was a visitor and then residing in Croix-des-Bouquets where he seems to have also said Mass though never functioned as a *curé* or *vicaire* (assistant pastor), and the same holds for the parish records in

Port-au-Prince.[58] I thus agree with Church historian Adolphe Cabon's conclusion that while in Saint-Domingue "the one abbé Ouvière ... did not belong to the parochial clergy."[59]

Without mentioning the turmoil in France that initially drove him to seek refuge in the colony, the priest explicitly and publicly declared another, far less controversial, reason for his immigration in a long advertisement that he placed in the *Gazette de Saint-Domingue* on January 21, 1791: "I have come to Saint-Domingue, like so many others, to employ the fruitful part of life to right the wrongs of fortune."[60] Ouvière claims here that his principal motive for being in the colony was to make money, plain and simple, and his first attempt to do so took the form of launching a newspaper, the *Journal de Port-au-Prince*. This did not go very well, however, to say the least. The first editions of the newspaper, which are evidently lost to history, provoked such outrage that the abbé was briefly forced into hiding.[61] He eventually would resurface in Port-au-Prince, however, and seek to operationalize an ambitious backup plan to find a way to make a living.

Putting into action one of the many grandiose ideas that would possess Ouvière throughout his adult life, the priest set about designing and founding a boarding school in Port-au-Prince for the children of elite families. He also wanted to enter a line of work that "would be suitable to my tastes," one that would garner for him a livelihood while also contributing to the betterment of Dominguan society and family life, which both suffered from the long absence of the colony's most promising youth in France: "I have heard fathers and mothers moan over a cruel separation in which the objects of their affection are tossed two thousand leagues away from them. Nothing is more painful than the regrets and fears that they endure to provide an education." Furthermore, the six years in France required for most elite Dominguan children to gain an acceptable education risked eroding their sense of "filial piety," for many of them returned to Saint-Domingue as ingrates who no longer "recognized that their fathers and mothers were the authors of their fortune." Better that they remain in Saint-Domingue and attend the priest's proposed school, and, if they needed "to see and know the mother country," they should simply wait until after their studies in the colony to make their maiden voyages to France: "It is thus not until between the age of 18 and 20 that a young man can travel usefully."[62]

Enthusiastically promising to provide a high quality education that would steer children away from "ignorance" and "vices," the proposed curriculum of Ouvière's boarding school included the following subjects: "Readings, writing, commerce, orthography, arithmetic ... everything relative to banking.... Latin, French, English, Italian, history, mythology, and rhetoric." Also to be taught "without any additional cost" would be "natural history," along with "the arts" and *"belles lettres."* Furthermore, because the school was envisioned as a form of "national" French education, the priest promised "to provide a teacher of *tactique civile*" and to require each student to wear a "national uniform." Instruction in religion would be left to Abbé Ouvière himself, whose "state and character rendered" him ideally suited for the position. The school was to be located in a large "well ordered house" and promised to provide "a hair dresser, a wig maker, and daily baths." Each resident student (nonresident students *[externes]* could also enroll) could expect to enjoy a "full bed, their robes and national uniform, a trunk with a silver cover, linens and a bath, a table."

By the time that he placed the ad for his boarding school in Port-au-Prince, Abbé Ouvière had been in Saint-Domingue for nearly half a year, surely long enough to understand that tensions between whites and mulattoes in the colony were on the rise. It was perhaps such an awareness of the boiling racial hatred surrounding him that prompted the abbé to affix to the ad the assurance that as its director he would "be rigorously exacting in admitting only whites" into the school. The ad indicates an address on Rue Royale for Ouvière, the home of Abbé Peyré, *"médecin du roi"* (royal physician), "or chief medical officer in the colony."[63] This is the same sending address that Ouvière indicated in his letter to Robespierre the previous September, meaning that the priest had been living with Abbé Peyré in Port-au-Prince during the interim months. It also suggests that he had secured his initial lodgings in the colony through connections in the Church, or that perhaps he had known Peyré previously in France, either/or both as a priest and/or a scientist. Peyré had evidently already been in Saint-Domingue for quite some time by 1790, but it is quite possible that he was in France on furlough that year and returned to the colony accompanied by Ouvière. The *médecin du roi* had resided in colony long enough, at any rate, to have published by 1789 a study of quinquina based on research he conducted at the royal military hospital in Port-au-Prince, of which he was the director.[64]

Living with one of the colony's royal physicians, a kindred abbé *cum* physician, might have provided Ouvière with opportunities to either work at the military hospital in Port-au-Prince or to engage in the kinds of botanical research that Catholic priests had been conducting in Saint-Domingue for over 100 years. But by 1790 secular researchers on the crown's payroll had largely supplanted the clergy in French colonial science.[65] Furthermore, there is no clear indication that Abbé Ouvière ever practiced medicine or conducted scientific research in Saint-Domingue. However much that their shared identity as physicians, priests, and scientists might have informed his relationship with

Abbé Peyré, the activities for which Abbé Ouvière would go down in history as an actor in Saint-Domingue were mostly political in nature, and not in the least medical or scientific. If indeed he had harbored ambitions to become either a bishop or a scientist in Saint-Domingue, moreover, neither was ever realized.

For the period of time between the publication of the priest's ad for his boarding school in January of 1791, which also never materialized, and when he reemerges in the historical record as a member of the advisory council of the Confederate Army in Croix-des-Bouquets in November of that year, the archive offers no clues about Ouvière's activities or whereabouts, save for a receipt for a horse he purchased in Croix-des-Bouquets in June.[66] Seeing as he was related to André Rigaud and had known the general during his education in France, it is possible that the abbé had arrived in the colony with letters of introduction to key figures of the free colored civil rights movement, like Pierre Pinchinat. Pinchinat, the mayor of Mirebalais and the Confederate president, was a mulatto attorney who had been raised in France and who had fought in the Battle of Savannah during the American Revolution, and Ouvière would work closely with him in diplomatic efforts from late November 1791 until April of the following year. Whatever the conditions of his arrival in Saint-Domingue, politically speaking, the priest would soon find himself in the eye of the storm, and he was catapulted there by some of the most catastrophic violence yet witnessed in the West Province, the horrific November massacre of free coloreds in Port-au-Prince.

A Priestly Adviser to the Confederate Army

The mercurial priest had only been in the colony for a couple of months when his brash publishing efforts in Port-au-Prince incited something of a riot that nearly cost him his life. In his evidently short-lived *Journal de Port-au-Prince*, the ever opinionated Ouvière "couldn't keep himself from writing a bit more liberally than before and revealed some of the operations of the enraged and the brigands. Meanwhile, he never ceases to erode any circumspection that might be necessary to avoid irritating the spirits and provoking the ill-intentioned." Sure enough, the priest provoked them, sparking such an "uprising" in November of 1791, when "persecution had redoubled" against the "honest citizens" of Saint-Domingue, that soldiers from the Confederate Army had to come to his rescue and place him in protective custody.[67] Subsequently, it didn't take long for the priest to insert himself into their cause:

> Escaped from the massacre and burning of Port-au-Prince on November 21, 1791, I found myself the next day at Croix des Bouquets among all the

> leaders of the reunited citizens whom the National Assembly had vindicated by the decree of March 11 of the same year. It should be recalled that this faction consists of all of the wealthy landowners, solemnly united with the people of color thus combined to prevent the insurrection of the slaves that the revolutionary frissons of the demagogues never ceased to encourage.[68]

On that very day, November 22, the free colored leaders at Croix-des-Bouquets appointed Abbé Ouvière as a member of their army's advisory council, along with three white planters, whose first task together was "to instruct the general and the parishes of the horrible catastrophe" and to endeavor to get "all honest whites to unite with the people of color."[69] His political stature soon rose to a high enough level for the colony's governor general, Philibert François Rouxel de Blanchelande, to write to Ouvière personally on November 28 to inform him, and presumably the Confederate leadership thereby, of the arrival in Cap-Français of the three national civil commissioners, Mirbeck, Roume, and Saint-Léger.[70] From then on while in Saint-Domingue, up until April of 1792, Ouvière lived with the Confederates in Croix-des Bouquets and in Saint-Marc, save for a brief period during which he resided at the Foucault plantation, near Léogâne.

Clearly his hosts in Croix-des-Bouquets recognized Abbé Ouvière to be a man of many talents who could serve their cause very well. So, after appointing him to the Confederate Army's advisory council, they named him a "conciliatory commissioner" and later a deputy of the people of color of Saint-Marc.[71] It was in the latter capacity that the priest would make his return trip to France in April/May of 1792, which is the subject of Chapter 7. But in the interim, Ouvière was entrusted by Pinchinat with several important missions to fulfill. One of the most pressing of these assignments was to, as a Catholic priest, help curb some of the excessive acts of violence being committed by certain members of the Confederate Army based in Croix-des-Bouquets. Toward that end, on December 20, 1791, Ouvière seemingly said Mass for the army and delivered a long and impassioned sermon that, rather than offering any extensive religious reflections, went to great lengths to denounce the "monsters" in their midst who were responsible for the recent wanton murder of a white planter, someone who was actually an ally to the Confederacy, a one Monsieur DuTerte:

> Ah, well! My friends, my comrades, you are reunited, for a second time, for a religious ceremony, for a new oath, to hear of terrible threats ... to see finally the terrible spectacle of the Pain and

> indignation carved on the faces of your leaders and of the honest citizens who have declared themselves to be your friends, who have availed themselves as your comrades in arms. Remember everything that I said, some time ago . . . at the tomb of an honest man who fell victim to the fire of murderers, who was wantonly attacked in his own home, which was pillaged, his blood spilled. Alas! Tasked with conveying the displeasure of the army chiefs and parish representatives, I alert you to those principles that are violated by such attacks and robberies . . . . the revolution that has brought you equality as French citizens would be shameful if your rights are built upon murders and crimes.[72]

The priest was in his element, pontificating to a captive and tearful audience whose applause assured him that there were before him "many honest, sensible, and generous souls worthy of the name French citizens." He implored those guilty of murdering DuTerte—"more atrocious than savages, who at least respect friends"—to hear the "cry of nature" and submit to the "laws of justice and of reason" by stepping forward and confessing to a "horrible and desperate crime" that rendered its perpetrators "unworthy of the name people of color" for having

> brought dishonor on your cause, soiled your rights, and cast blame upon the army . . . and dishonor the army in the eyes of all of our brothers in the other provinces, in the eyes of the entire colony, in the eyes of the national commissioners, in the eyes of all of France, in the eyes of the king himself.

Inasmuch as the national civil commissioners would soon offer amnesty to insurgents throughout the colony who had committed much more horrific crimes than this, it is hard to imagine that DuTerte's killers would have been compelled to confess upon hearing Abbé Ouvière bellow that "before God . . . the crime of murder cannot be expiated but by the death of the murderer." Probably the priest was hoping that his sermon would instead inspire some of the "honest" citizens in the army who had knowledge of the crime to come forward and share it with the Confederate leadership, or that remorse more terrifying than "bolts of lightning that burn the night and interrupt nightmares" would "rip apart their hearts and consciences" and indeed induce the guilty parties to own up. There was, after all, "an enormous difference" between "the destruction of one's enemy on the battlefield and that of honest and peaceful citizens relaxing at home," and so the abbé exhorted his audience "to purge your army" of such "cruel people" who failed to understand and respect that difference. He then proceeded to squelch rumors of a crushing defeat suffered by Rigaud and his troops in Port-au-Prince, where in fact they had not lost "an inch of land or a drop of water," before waxing poetic with the following question: "Ah, what interest would any just and honest whites have in not sincerely supporting your rights?"

Ouvière's protracted, exhortative sermon wound down by calling upon members of the Confederate Army to never fall prey again to the kind of "indiscretion" that led to DuTerte's death and the theft of some 30 animals from plantations surrounding Croix-des-Bouquets. "Remain at your posts, obey your leaders, demonstrate by the correctness of your service that you are worthy of being free, as Frenchmen, and to enjoy the rights that you reclaim as Frenchmen." Their leaders were, after all, "only united" with them "by honor," an "honor that formed the combined army, which is all about the rights and justice that are to the Frenchman inseparable." The priest made one final plea to his audience that someone turn in DuTerte's murderers so that "all of France will applaud your rights, your success, our zeal, and the reunion of all true citizens." Though the speech is largely devoid of religious references, Abbé Ouvière concluded by invoking the name of God in DuTerte's honor:

> *Messieurs*, there is but God almighty who reads the conscience and hears the prayers of the honest soul; it is thus necessary to act in order to satisfy natural justice, which has been violated, in order to restore the Frenchman, who has been soiled... and thereby the tomb of an honest man avenged could become a monument to the glory of the combined army of the West.

Rousing and fascinating in its clarity, content, and tone, Abbé Ouvière's sermon to the Combined Army is also striking for its reflection of the Confederate leadership's decision to use religion to frame a renewed oath of allegiance for their troops. Moreover, the sermon foreshadows Ouvière's next opportunistic turn and his eventual falling out with Pinchinat and company. For, in lauding the equality with white "Frenchmen" that free colored citizens should enjoy, the priest conveniently glossed over his promise to "rigorously" restrict entry into his proposed boarding school only to white children. But evidently the Confederate leaders were unaware of or unconcerned with the priest's compromised understanding of their rights and citizenship, which would also manifest in Ouvière's vision for how the colony should henceforth be governed. With the backing of General André Rigaud, they were about to task the priest with his most important mission in Saint-Domingue yet, one he designed and they "unanimously approved": to travel to Léogâne to "tranquilize" the region, which would bring him into the eye of the storm, to the prophetess' insurgent camp at Trou Coffy, as we shall soon see.[73]

4

Trou Coffy and the Léogâne Insurgent Theater

L'esprit même du château fort
C'est le pont-levis
—RENÉ CHAR[1]

Overview

IN ANY EFFORT to understand such a complex historical saga as the Haitian Revolution, conventional categories of analysis, like race, religion, or region, tempt misrepresentation, gloss, or anachronism. Differentiating between events in the North Province and those in the South and West Provinces in 1791–1792 thus runs some risk of obfuscation. For example, although the massive slave insurrection that broke out in the North in August 1791 was indeed primarily the initiative of enslaved black Africans and Creoles on plantations, it was contextualized by the brewing civil war between whites and free coloreds throughout the colony and by revolutionary political events in France.[2] Furthermore, there were also at least some mulattoes, free and enslaved alike, involved in the slave insurrection in the North, as well as some white royalists and Catholic priests, not to mention Spaniards across the border who provided many insurgents with weapons. The motives of those who risked their lives in the uprising were also varied, and it would take several years for some semblance of unity of purpose to congeal among them under the able leadership of Toussaint Louverture. As for the South and West Provinces, though the simultaneous 1791 "*troubles*" there may be categorized at the outset as insurrections led by free people of color, mostly mulattoes, slaves were quickly drawn or forced into that insurgency, while one of the most influential insurgent leaders in the Jacmel theater, as we saw in Chapter 1, was a white man, a *petit blanc* named Delisle de Bresolle. Here, too, the motives and objectives of the insurgents varied.

Thus, before turning our attention to the tumultuous events of the insurgent Léogâne theater, which were orchestrated by Romaine-la-Prophétesse out of his rebel camp at Trou Coffy, it should be affirmed that slaves needed no signal from free colored militants—let alone from the *Declaration of the Rights of Man*—to rise up on their own to strike out against the racism and brutal injustices of French imperialism. Nor did they require connections to the powerful and organized insurgent movements led by the likes of Boukman in the North or Romaine-la-Prophétesse in the West. Carolyn Fick details one largely independent slave uprising that occurred among conspiring slaves from several plantations in the Cul-de-Sac, for example, between Port-au-Prince and Croix-des-Bouquets, in June and July of 1791. Just prior to the slave insurrection in the North and free colored rebellions in the South and West, some 50 slaves from five plantations in all rose up and attacked their oppressors. Some from *habitation* Fortin-Bellantien "assassinated their *commandeur*, whom they considered overly loyal to the whites and therefore dangerously untrustworthy." Though putting up resistance that demonstrated "unrestrained courage," when the *maréchaussée* stormed one of their meetings, the insurgent slaves of the Cul-de-Sac were defeated and nine of their attackers were killed.[3] Many who survived the struggle absconded, becoming maroons and/or eventually joining the Confederate Army based in Croix-des-Bouquets.

Even before the tragically ill-fated 1790 Ogé rebellion, free people of color had resorted to violence in pursuit of their civil rights as French citizens. In the South Province, for instance, as John Garrigus explains, free coloreds revolted in 1769 in response to military reforms that sought to extract increased service from them and effectively "locked free men of color into a kind of second class citizenship they had never known before." Twenty years later it was also the South Province, specifically the parish of Port Salut, that would become "the site of Saint-Domingue's first revolutionary slave conspiracy." Slaves there "gathered on the Duhard plantation to discuss the reforms they believed had been decreed in France" but were being denied them by white and colored elites in the colony, like having three days off a week rather than just one. More than 200 slaves amassed on the plantation in the early morning darkness of April 25 and "decided to recruit other slaves to join them in demanding three free workdays per week from their masters.... If whites refused, the conspirators would kill them."[4]

Meanwhile, another band of militants had emerged in the region with only loose ties, if any, to either the insurgent camps around Jacmel and Léogâne or the Confederate Army, one called Camp Robiou, near La Rivière Froide, between Port-au-Prince and Léogâne. Not much is known about this camp, but there is at least one shard of evidence of a connection to insurgents around

Jacmel, as several of the Robiou militants were said "to have gone down to La Gosseline," a river near Jacmel, and thus there was quite possibly, too, a Trou Coffy link. Formed by early October 1791 and led by a group of free men of color and mulatto slaves, this particular uprising was among the earliest in the West Province that year. Details about Camp Robiou's raids on several plantations in the area are thus especially interesting for our purposes because they took place precisely around the time when the Trou Coffy insurgency was gathering steam about 25 kilometers to the west, and because they shed light on some of the motivations and strategies employed by mulatto-led insurgent camps, as well as on their accomplishments and crimes. We also gain insight into the weaponry employed by insurgents; firearms were in relatively short supply, as in Camp Robiou insurgent slaves were mostly armed with machetes and sugarcane knives, but they also attached knives designed for cutting indigo to the ends of batons, creating a kind of spear that was likely reconstructed out of some insurgents' previous military experience in civil wars in West and West Central Africa.[5]

A rebelling slave by the name of Pierre Louis was taken into custody for his part in the Camp Robiou uprising and brought before local authorities for interrogation on October 11, 1791.[6] Such interrogations often began with biographical questions about the suspect, like where he lived, when he was born, and what religion he professed, as in the case of Joseph Blek in the South, discussed in Chapter 1. But, perhaps because Pierre Louis was a black slave, the preliminary interrogatory phase was in this case foregone, or at least it went unrecorded, and it seems instead that the accused just quickly raised his hand while swearing an oath of truth, and then his captors cut right to the chase. Asked first if he was aware of any insurgent slaves on plantations neighboring that of his master, Pierre Louis listed four: "the plantation of Sieur Du Chemin, that of Sieur Brouet, that of Anglade, and that of Dicourt." Who incited these slaves to revolt?

> Mulattoes, under the weight of the liberty of the slaves ... advised the revolt ... [namely] Charlemagne, owned by Sieur Cotineau; and another mulatto named Jean Baptiste, belonging to the Du Chemin plantation; François of the Bois Martin plantation; Saurnom, a free mulatto who resides with Sieur Ferté; the so-called Lali, a mulatto from Camp Robiou; Jean Louis Duplessi, a free mulatto living at la Charbonniere; to his knowledge it was they who incited the revolt of the Blacks.

It is noteworthy that the Robiou insurgency was launched by both free and unfree mulattoes, and yet the investigators referred to it as a "Black revolt," even though when they asked about the camp's racial composition Pierre Louis explained that "there were many people, but mostly mulattoes and not a single white." Mulattoes, furthermore, were clearly the instigators of the revolt, and they enticed black slaves to join them in the conspiracy by making some fantastic promises:

> Interrogated if in order to engage the blacks in the revolt the mulattoes employed certain methods of seduction, or what kinds of promises that they made.
>
> Responded that the mulattoes had promised freedom to the slaves and told them that they, the mulattoes, would become masters of the country and that the blacks would only have to answer to them, and in the case that the whites continued to be masters of the country that they would consent to serve them and to make peace insofar as henceforth they would only have to work three days a week.

The promises that Charlemagne and his co-conspirators made to black slaves like Pierre Louis were as idealistic as they were deceitful. If the revolt were to have failed and whites remained "masters of the country," slaves, they claimed, would still have enjoyed the victory of having the number of days that they labored for them cut in half. In reality, however, in Saint-Domingue, as in colonial plantation societies throughout the Americas, slaves arrested during uprisings were usually executed, often in quite torturous fashion. And even if the revolt were to have succeeded, Pierre Louis and his ilk would only enjoy an ambiguous kind of freedom in which they would no longer have to answer to whites but to mulattoes.

In addition to torching several plantations and pillaging their *"grandes cazes"* (big houses), the Camp Robiou insurgents killed numerous whites. Pierre Louis explained that both "some mulattoes and some blacks" were responsible for the murders and named six of the victims: "Sieur Coutelier, a manager . . . of the Aubagne plantation; M. Gateau, manager of the La Mardelle plantation; Monsieur Langlade, that plantation's surgeon; Sieur Francois, M. Laval's treasurer; M. Caron the shoemaker." The captive added that the manager of the La Mardelle plantation "was killed by the very slaves of that plantation." And what did they do with the victims' bodies? "[T]hey were thrown into the bushes after having their heads cut off, with the exception of M. Coutelier, and the heads were taken to Camp Robiou and placed in a row on a glacis." During other raids around La Rivière Froide, he added, the insurgents "cut off many heads," which also were brought to Camp Robiou on the backs of donkeys and added to the grisly collection on display.

Displaying severed human heads had a rich history in Saint-Domingue, and one could reasonably assume that at Camp Robiou they were arranged in a row on a low stone wall to strike fear in the hearts of any unwelcome parties harboring designs to enter the camp without invitation and/or to attack the insurgents holed up there. It is also possible that the militants placed them there for spiritual purposes, perhaps as protective charms or receptacles of supernatural power; to this day in Haiti skulls are commonly found on Vodou altars.[7] As for Pierre Louis's own head, we'll probably never know what happened to it after he was summarily hanged at five in the evening on the day after his interrogation, having been sentenced at four that morning.

Also uncertain is what happened to Camp Robiou and the rest of its insurgents, as I have found no other mention of these events or Pierre Louis in either primary or secondary source literature, apart from his interrogation docket. This would suggest that the camp was short-lived and neither as organized nor defensible as Camp Prou or Trou Coffy, whose leaders carried military titles, whose holdouts were guarded by carefully positioned sentries, and whose raids were strategically orchestrated and ultimately aimed at the capture of cities: Les Cayes, in the case of Camp Prou, and Léogâne and Jacmel, in the case of Trou Coffy. Though causing immeasurable devastation, killing an untold number of mostly innocent people, and bringing for a time the local economy to a grinding halt, the Prou insurgency ultimately failed to conquer Les Cayes, however. By contrast, this is one of the things that makes the Trou Coffy insurgency so remarkable in the history of Saint-Domingue and indeed all colonial New World history: it succeeded in conquering the cities of Jacmel and Léogâne and forced whites to submit to the rule of its notorious black leader, Romaine-la-Prophétesse. Though Jacmel saw its fort fall to insurgents, authorities there nonetheless managed in the end to force the rebels in Camp Pasquet to disperse, just as authorities in Les Cayes had overthrown the menacing Camp Mercy; however, during the tumultuous months of September 1791 through February 1792, they contemplated but never mounted an attack on Trou Coffy. In fact, the royalist mayor of Léogâne, de Villards, counseled against it.[8]

Trou Coffy's Conquest of Léogâne

To recall, the Trou Coffy insurgency emerged in the summer of 1791 out of a simmering, racially charged feud between Romaine Rivière and a neighboring white planter named Joseph Marie Tavet.[9] For organizational purposes, I have chosen to split my discussion of this insurgency into two theaters of operation, Jacmel and Léogâne, though admittedly this categorization risks obscuring certain dimensions of the conflict. For instance, though Tavet's plantation, like Trou Coffy, was closer to Léogâne than to Jacmel, the planter himself was named a representative of Jacmel during negotiations of peace treaties with free coloreds in Port-au-Prince in October of 1791, and he became the mayor of the city around the same time.[10] Episodes of violence did not occur sequentially in the one theater and then the other, furthermore, but with a sometimes intermittent simultaneity, thus the two theaters overlapped spatially and temporally. Nonetheless, Léogâne fell to the insurgents first and would remain under Trou Coffy's control longer than Jacmel, while Jacmel and Léogâne were (and are), obviously, two different coastal cities on opposite sides of Hispaniola's southwestern peninsula; this latter simple fact and his obsession with conquering them both would contribute to Romaine-la-Prophétesse's eventual undoing. Academic apologies aside, once the prophetess' coffee plantation was transformed into an insurrectional base camp in late summer 1791, over the next several months Trou Coffy launched raids on plantations in the mountains and plains surrounding Léogâne and Jacmel and on both cities. As we saw in Chapter 1, one of the first plantations to be targeted, on September 24, was Tavet's, located adjacent to Trou Coffy in a place called Coq Qui Chante.[11]

As for the city of Léogâne itself, by November of that year an alliance formed by Pierre Pinchinat, the leading statesman of the free colored Confederacy in Saint-Domingue, and André Rigaud, it's leading general, had brokered an agreement with local elites and, from afar, exercised joint control of the city, with the royalist mayor, Villards, still holding some semblance of municipal authority and now assuming a critical mediatory role. This tenuous alliance amounted to a caretaker agreement between Léogâne's whites and the confederated free coloreds, as the drama of other concordats and treaties between their respective peoples in the West and South Provinces played out and as the entire colony awaited the arrival of the national civil commissioners from France, to recall, Ignace-Frédéric de Mirbeck, Philippe-Rose Roume de Saint-Laurent, and Edmond de Saint-Léger.[12] The alliance's hopes rested on the shoulders of local free colored leaders who were "distinguished by their morality, like la Buissonnière, la Fleur-Viala, Alvarès, Lemaire, Brunet, etc.," and Villards, who represented Léogâne's leading white voice, one that, most importantly, held sway with Romaine-la-Prophétesse.[13] Those hopes were short-lived, however, as the Trou Coffy insurgency swelled and sacked more and more of Léogâne's surrounding plantations, some of them owned by the likes of Brunet and Lemaire. That Romaine's troops would siege the city before the commissioners could exert any concrete influence over events in Saint-Domingue now seemed like a foregone conclusion. Many people fled Léogâne and the plantations throughout its surrounding plain, while those who remained knew that they would be outnumbered and outgunned should Trou Coffy mount a full-scale offensive.

In the interim, they lived in constant fear. In an October 19, 1791, letter to his friend Monsieur Bauchin in Port-au-Prince—a city that was itself on the brink of being nearly annihilated by the escalating conflict between whites and free coloreds—a Léogâne resident by the name of Duchemin implored Bauchin, someone recognized to be "knowledgeable of these affairs,"

> to tell me whether, if one raids this town, we'll have guns ... otherwise I would find myself in a very critical scenario. My health, on the one hand, would normally force me to stay here, but the desire to take part in the work of my brothers, on the other hand, to muster all of the energy I can from my too weak position ... if we must take up arms, nothing will stop me.[14]

Meanwhile, Labuissonnière, a wealthy "general captain of the free coloreds of Léogâne,"[15] now a refugee who had been forced to abandon his own plantation, lamented how his once prosperous existence on the Plain of Léogâne was no more, thanks to the "the infernal Trou Coffy, receptacle of villains," who had left hundreds of dead in their wake by the end of 1791.[16]

As was the case in the Jacmel theater, in and around Léogâne, as Fick explains, Romaine's power grew by spreading "insurrection throughout the countryside from one plantation to the next" and by sweeping up into his religiously inspired insurgency more and more "proselytes by liberating those slaves detained in prison or condemned by their masters to chains, and by threatening to kill, and sometimes even killing, those slaves who would remain loyal to their masters."[17] Their raids on Léogâne and surrounding plantations were devastating for colonial rule and commerce, as famine ensued and shipping to the port ceased altogether.[18] Travelling to Léogâne from Croix-de-Bouquets in late December 1791, one Frenchman described the "vestiges of the devastation" he observed: "I saw many sugar plantations burned; I came to realize that all those that were not yet ruined were daily pillaged for their provisions and animals, that work had come to a halt, the owners and managers now fugitives or dispersed."[19] Sixty people convalescing in the city hospital were allegedly murdered by Romaine's followers sometime that month, while reportedly "other accounts of their treatment of matrons, virgins, and infants, would make a Nero blush."[20]

Help could not arrive soon enough, so the leading citizens of Léogâne saw no recourse but to negotiate with Romaine-la-Prophétesse, ultimately signing a concordat with him that effectively named him ruler of the city. The treaty formally declared Romaine to be "Commander of the Reunited Residents, that is to say of both whites and the *gens de couleur*,"[21] effectively ceding to him and his troops dominion over the city of Léogâne. By another account, Romaine's title as ruler of Léogâne was "Commander of all the assembled citizens." Under the terms of the treaty, the prophetess was thus empowered to give "orders to all whites and persons of color. . . . and it is by virtue of his orders alone that the slaves work and are led to abandon their masters' plantations to join the camp that he established near Jacmel."[22] Furthermore, they were required "to welcome . . . one of Romaine's lieutenants, who was every bit as ferocious as him, and blindly subject themselves to his tyrannical domination and fulfill all requests for requisitions."[23] Now feeling very much like "hostages" in their own homes, whites were forced to surrender their weapons and were now prohibited by "attentive guards" from assembling.[24]

Throughout revolutionary Saint-Domingue, when treaties were signed between whites and free coloreds, it was common to have the occasion solemnized by celebrating Mass in a local Catholic church, ideally a *Te deum*, which in the case of Léogâne occurred just days after the treaty's signing in the Church of St. Rose de Lima, with the curé, Père Menetrier, presiding. Peace in Léogâne following the signing of the treaty was short-lived, however. In one of the rare documents in the archival materials from Saint-Domingue written by a black woman, Marianne Valde lamented to her sister in Port-au-Prince that throughout January both white and free colored "brigands" in Léogâne were killing people "every day."[25] It is thus understandable that after his initial elation over the peace treaty Villards saw that "it might require more art to handle Trou Coffy," as Romaine's followers soon dishonored the terms of the accord and recommenced terrorizing the city and surrounding plain.[26] For example, sometime during the second week of January "20 men from Trou Coffi" broke into the home of a French official, "demanding that he turn over his weapons, and to find them they tore his house apart for three hours—the furniture, the clothes, even the pockets of his overcoat. This little adventure, sir, shames . . . the honest citizens of color."[27] At around the same time, Romaine's insurgents demanded of Villards that he arrange to furnish them with cannons and shoes, while the prophetess himself ordered that another Mass be celebrated at St. Rose in honor of "the prophetess of Grace," his godmother, "the little Virgin."[28]

A much larger adventure threatened to turn occupied Léogâne into even more of a killing field when sometime in early January a French naval vessel arrived offshore escorting several cargo ships carrying flour destined for the famine-threatened city. The lead ship in her naval class, *La Galathée* was a 32-gun frigate that by 1791 had amassed an impressive battle record in the American Revolution, and it was the very ship that had brought the national civil commissioners from France in November of that year (pictured in Figure 4.1).

Whether Romaine knew any of this nautical backstory, his godmother might have, as she alerted the prophetess that the illustrious corsair was a threat to his rule over the city. "The prophet Romaine had predicted that once arriving within striking distance of Léogâne this frigate would not leave until bombarding the city, and his predictions, spread by the spiteful, caused a great uproar."[29]

In addition to escorting the cargo ships, *La Galathée* had been tasked with the mission of picking up any sick or wounded residents of Léogâne for care, but none of the objectives of its voyage was achieved because "52 men came from Trou Coffy to ward off the frigate."[30] One of the ship's officers, who had come ashore via canoe to explain that "the mission of the frigate was the protection of commerce and tranquility," was beaten, and several other officers were abducted, though the ship soon disembarked without further incident. The three days during which *La Galathée* was anchored off of Léogâne were tumultuous enough, however, to cause the city's white residents "the cruelest of anguishes," as they surely believed that upsetting the prophetess could lead to their extermination.[31] As for the bombardment of Léogâne that Romaine had prophesied, "that might happen some other day," scoffed Villards, "because the Virgin cannot tell a lie" (he was right about this, actually and unwittingly!).[32] Or was it "that the little Virgin changed her mind? Yes, undoubtedly. Just know that the prophetess calls his little Virgin, quite simply The Prophetess. But I am running out of paper, so I had better just stop there." For his part, once the ships had lifted anchor, hoisted sail, and departed, Romaine ordered that another Mass be celebrated at St. Rose.[33]

The mayor's evident satire aside, and soon acquiring more writing paper, Villards must surely have been relieved that the January frigate affair did not provoke a riot or the ethnic cleansing of his city's remaining white population. He attributed this sarcastically to Romaine's failed prophecy, while more realistically he reasoned that because Trou Coffy was comfortably (and formally) in control of Léogâne, the prophetess was now turning his attention more

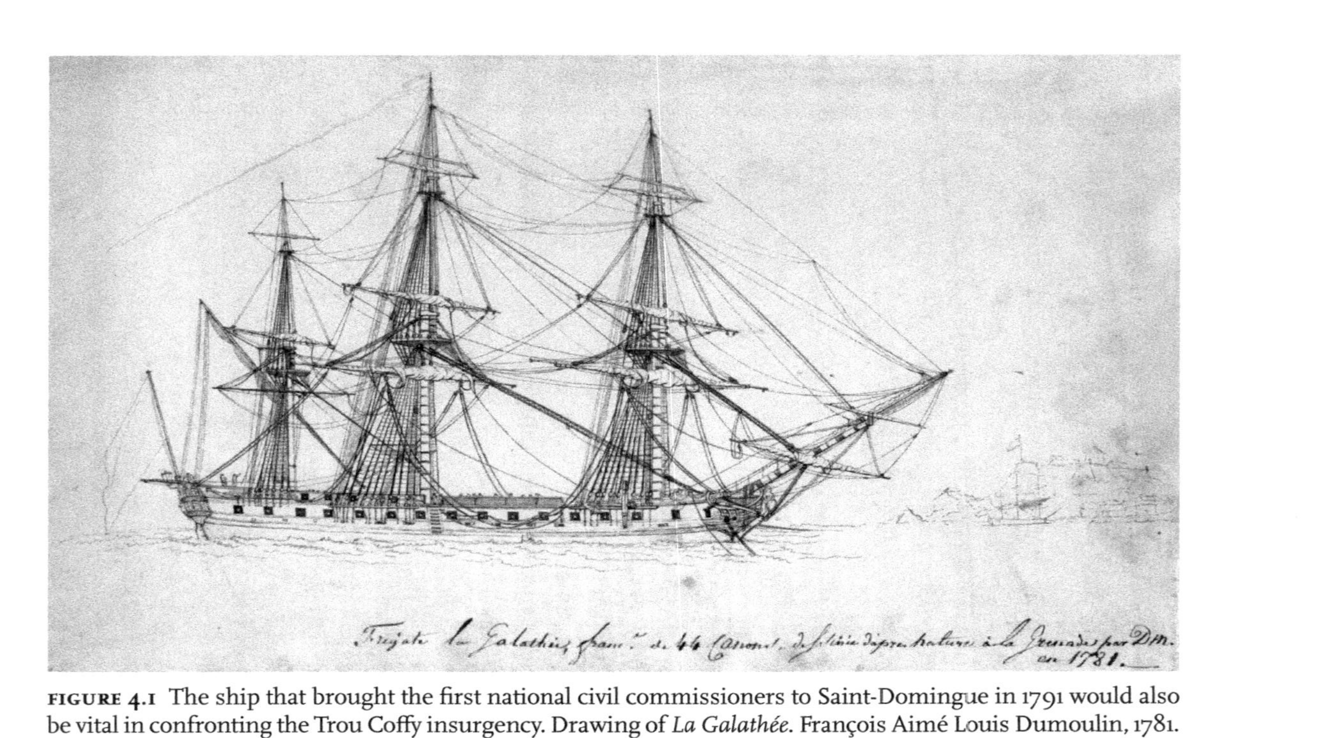

FIGURE 4.1 The ship that brought the first national civil commissioners to Saint-Domingue in 1791 would also be vital in confronting the Trou Coffy insurgency. Drawing of *La Galathée*. François Aimé Louis Dumoulin, 1781.

fully to the Jacmel theater. Villards rightly sensed that this meant that Jacmel would, like Léogâne, soon fall altogether:

> It is said that when shepherds bring their herds to graze in the pasture, they are careful to first ask if there is any carrion in the ravines. If they are told yes, they go back to sleep and leave their sheep attended; if they are told no, the sheep dogs and shepherds all put their eyes and ears on the lookout. Trou Coffy is in Jacmel, and while it is there, it is not here. That much is very clear. What do you say? Jacmel is the carrion, we are the herd, and Trou Coffy is the . . . that is also very clear. Allow my parable to complete itself.

By sending most of his forces to Jacmel, Romaine was spreading himself thin and losing control over the situation in Léogâne, with some of his troops now evidently deserting. Emblematic of his deteriorating authority, on the very evening that the prophetess was at prayer in his chapel at Trou Coffy, contemplating the mystery of Christ's birth and preparing to sign the peace treaty, insurgents were amassing on the DesMarattes plantation to prepare their assault on Jacmel.[34] Worse yet, during the New Year's Day *Te deum* Mass at St. Rose in Léogâne to solemnize the treaty, insurgents from Trou Coffy burst into the church and disrupted the priest's homily, an act that would surely have mortified the pious Romaine.[35] Furthermore, the prophetess and his inner circle knew that things were spinning out of control, as reflected in two letters written during the second half of January by Trou Coffy's second-in-command, Elie Courlogne, to Abbé Ouvière. In the first, Elie noted, "We have done everything we can to maintain Léogâne, and we still maintain it, but the number of outcasts has been inconceivable, and they are indomitable."[36] A week later, Elie added, "There are some brigands in our parish who continue to make threats, They have nothing but their breath, and they profit from dissension, apparently believing that they intimidate us, but we remain firm in our resolutions and in the spirit of the laws."[37]

It is of course possible that Elie was trying to distance Romaine and himself from the ongoing crimes then being committed daily in both Jacmel and Léogâne, for they knew that the national civil commissioners were now in the colony and destined to confront them. Abbé Ouvière had written to Trou Coffy about the commissioners on January 13, after all, and Elie and Romaine were quick to respond, on the 16th, assuring the priest that "we await with impatience the arrival of the national civil commissioners, being equally well

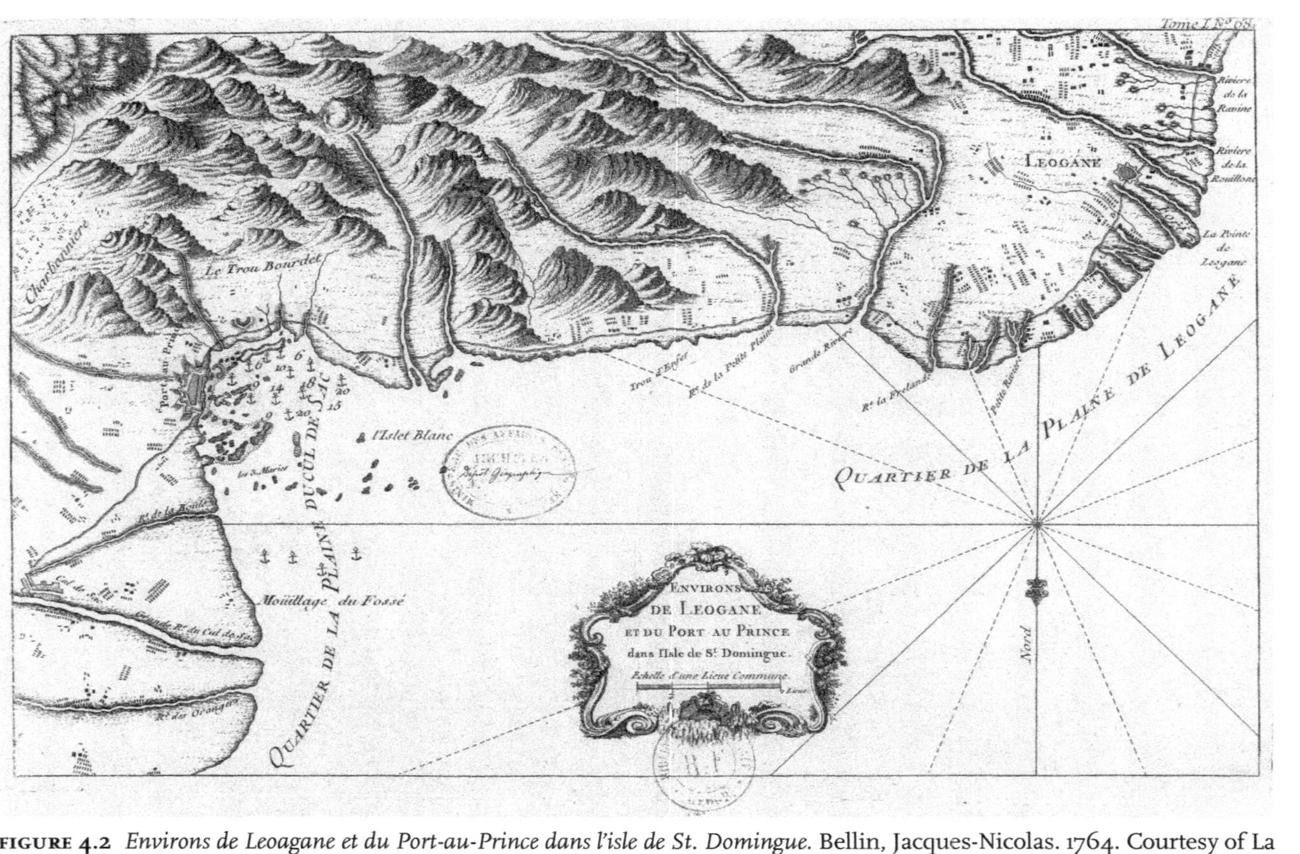

FIGURE 4.2 *Environs de Leoagane et du Port-au-Prince dans l'isle de St. Domingue.* Bellin, Jacques-Nicolas. 1764. Courtesy of La Bibliothèque Nationale de France.

persuaded of their intention, with feelings for public affairs."[38] A week later the prophetess again wrote to the priest, in similar vein:

> The news that you have given me of the national civil commissioners is to me as equally agreeable as it is interesting, for it carries the balm of the new regeneration that can do nothing but aid us and engage us to unanimously take part in the union, concord, and peace. Even if the prosperity of Saint-Domingue experiences misfortune, the inviolable attachment and the love that we have for the mother country equally obliges us to employ with all of our powers everything necessary to save for France this so flourishing island, and to prove ourselves trustworthy of our king and the national assembly of the esteem merited by wise men in the sight of the universe.[39]

This was a climactic moment for the prophetess. He had just been declared ruler of one city and was about to conquer another, and he now possessed more power over a large swath of the West Province than any single man on the "so flourishing island" ever had. It was all faced with pending doom, however, as Commissaire Nationale Edmond de Saint-Léger made his way from Saint-Marc to Port-au-Prince and eventually mustered troops to bring to Léogâne and confront the Trou Coffy insurgents (see Figure 4.2). With his own troops now deserting him, and with his reputation as a violent charlatan now cemented in the minds of not only whites but also many free coloreds as well, Romaine endeavored to cast his lot with the Confederate Army, perhaps with the hopes of consolidating forces with them and/or being commissioned as an officer. This could very well be why he required of the whites in Léogâne "to send munitions, clothing, and food supplies to Camp Bizoton," near Port-au-Prince, where Rigaud and his battalion were stationed. Some of Rigaud's free colored soldiers in Bizoton, meanwhile, esteemed Romaine's troops in Trou Coffy "to be among the most valiant" in the entire war, troops "in whom they had the most trust." [40]

But sending supplies to Bizoton and scripting ornate letters professing loyalty to King Louis XVI could simply not undo the extensive harm that Romaine-la-Prophétesse had already done. Too many innocent victims lay dead in his wake, too many plantations burned, and too much "superstition" had been inspired among his "gullible" acolytes for the leaders of the Confederacy to share Rigaud's soldiers' admiration for and trust in Trou Coffy. Rigaud evidently acted to communicate this to Romaine, as on January 24, 1792, emissaries from Bizoton arrived in Trou Coffy. Mayor de Villards was miffed that he only learned of this after the fact, so he stormed off to Bizoton to demand an explanation a few days later, also writing to Ouvière in Croix-des-Bouquets to inquire: "Some have assured me that the goal of this visit was to complain about Léogâne. Others say that they went there to ask for support."[41] Either way, the visit could not bring about any lasting reconciliation between Trou Coffy and the Confederacy. Realizing this, Romaine-la-Prophétesse looked to escalate matters by gearing up to launch a major offensive, as reflected by Gauthier, a Léogâne resident, in a February 2, 1792, letter, just as news of Saint-Léger's arrival in Port-au-Prince had reached him:

> We are fully convinced that he [Saint-Léger] will restore the peace, but our prophet continues to abduct people and muster troops, and in the parish of Grand Goave he has ordered entire plantations to prepare themselves to march at any moment. They have gathered the strongest among them. Romaine would not dare to do such a thing unless he was pushed into it by someone on whom he counted, and this suspicion weighs heavily upon me. There will be so many scoundrels. What does he want to do with these armed soldiers? One holds us here disarmed and he is arming our slaves. This is the height of horror and the height of the shame that the council of Croix-des-Bouquets leaves us here in such a state. [42]

Gauthier and his ilk were indeed in a horrible state, and they feared that ultimately Trou Coffy's "intentions were to kill all the whites, and if they lost hope they would just escape across the border."[43] In a February 2 letter to her sister in Port-au-Prince, the aforementioned Marianne Valde, a free black resident of Léogâne, seconded the impression that Romaine's intention indeed amounted to what in the twentieth century would become known as "ethnic cleansing," for "the citizens of color kill some [whites] every day, and soon there will be none remaining."[44] If indeed Romaine's followers had intended for his troops to "kill all the whites" in either or both the Léogâne and/or Jacmel insurgent theater(s) (a dreadful objective that they quite possibly could have achieved), once the prophetess arrived at the peak of his power he had either changed his mind or his followers decided to spare certain unallied whites against his orders, for some remained alive, if not well, in and around Léogâne as of February 1792. And, as we have already seen, one of the prophetess' closest collaborators was a *petit blanc*.

Clearly, thus, Romaine-la-Prophétesse had nothing against white people per se, but against what he perceived to be injustices in the forms of racism, antiroyalism, and anticlericalism. Under his rule, after all, some white *habitants* were allowed to keep at least a few of their slaves and even to work them, and evidently not all whites were prohibited from circulating in the area.

Such is reflected in a January 25 letter from one city resident named D'Audard, who indicated his intention to return a borrowed slave to his rightful owner in Léogâne, but he was unable to because one of his horses was injured. Writing to Abbé Ouvière, Monsieur D'Audard went so far to request a letter of recommendation from the priest to "the prophet Romaine so that he could take confidence in me, who desires nothing more than to serve public affairs and ward off evil, even among my enemies, whom I forgive most willingly."[45]

Yet, over all, the lives of those whites and free coloreds unallied with Trou Coffy who had not managed to leave Léogâne by the turn of the year had become unbearably difficult, with the possibility of abduction, torture, execution, and eventually famine gripping them daily. "We are very unhappy," as one resident summed things up, "and left with no means to make any money."[46] Writing in late January, Villards estimated that "[w]ithin two weeks, there will be no more cows and we are running low on food and drink .... Famine threatens us ... and I uselessly ask myself ... how can we oppose the torrent of these flaming hordes?"[47] Elimination by violent death or starvation would indeed be "the height of horror" for a people who had just lost their right to prosper, the very things that their new rulers were themselves fighting to obtain. On February 7, 1792, one beleaguered French planter wrote of the nature of the occupation of Léogâne and environs by the Trou Coffy insurgents:

> We have done everything ... that Romaine has asked, and nonetheless the pillaging, murders, and arsons have not stopped. They hold us as prisoners to the point where we cannot leave town without a permit from them, which are very difficult to obtain. We are surrounded by camps which we are obliged to furnish with all the supplies and munitions that they need. Over and above all that, our homes have been pillaged, vandalized, and threatened with arson. Very many homes along the mountain have already suffered this fate, and others on our plain, also. All of the animals have been taken. We are left with just a few mules with which to make a living; but even then, just when our work seems to be regaining a bit of traction, yet another band of brigands of color shows up to shut down our mills and keep the blacks from entering them. There is no more than a single white left in any of our homesteads, be it on the plain or in the mountains; they have all been killed.[48]

As unbelievable as it may sound, the planter who authored this letter might have in fact considered himself to be relatively fortunate, for upwards to 400 insurgents then occupied the city of Léogâne, where they held 260 white prisoners, all with "support of the miscreants of Trou Coffy under the orders of the leader of the assassins, the so-called Romaine Rivière, who immolate more and more victims and seek to take slaves, a great number of whom have joined them."[49]

Another plantation's manager, Bérouet, wrote the following account to its absentee owner in France:

> From November 21, 1791 until March 1, 1792, I lived with my wife in the midst of 30 villains that the infamous Romaine Rivière, chief of the murderers at Trou-Coffi, had sent to our homestead as if to establish a command center from which they could dominate the entire plain. I managed to keep the homestead intact through to the first of March. That very day, at 6:00 in the evening, I was tipped off that Romaine had planned to have my throat slit that night, along with that of my wife, her child, and two other whites who were then staying with us. I barely had enough time to hitch up a ride and flee.... By 7:00 fifty rebelling slaves had occupied the big house, interrogating the maids, whom they accused of helping me escape. I thus managed to avoid their furor, and they avenged my escape by pillaging the place.

A few days later, on March 12 at about three o'clock in the morning, some 5,000 slaves swept through the city of Léogâne "intent on killing all of us, leaving one neighborhood a pile of ashes." Slaves who remained loyal to their masters or who refused to join Romaine's legions were killed, like five that day on Bérouet's plantation, "Lafleur, Tranquille, Antoine Congo, Sans-Façon, and Jupiter Congo." The following day the Trou Coffy insurgents "spread throughout the plain and torched virtually all of the sugar cane."[50] It's hard to believe that by then there were any crops left to burn, but such was the once remarkable productivity of France's colonial crown jewel, Saint-Domingue.

Conclusion

The signing of the peace treaty between the city of Léogâne and Romaine-la-Prophétesse was unprecedented not only in Saint-Domingue but also in the entire revolutionary Atlantic world. In effect, by virtue of its signing, a black religious visionary and warlord now ruled one of the colony's most important cities, and his followers were on the verge of seizing another. In the end, however, Romaine's rule over Léogâne would be short-lived, due largely to the insurgents' excesses and to a spectacular breakdown in discipline at Trou Coffy. But this should not obscure the fact that the prophetess' triumph on behalf of his oppressed people was altogether remarkable, an achievement unparalleled in the colonial history of the Americas. Thus, given the treaty's great historical importance, it remains for us to carefully analyze its drafting and negotiation, and the key role that the priest, Abbé Ouvière, played in these dramatic affairs. But first, let us carefully consider the actions of several other Catholic priests who found themselves in the midst of rebels when the 1791 insurgencies broke out, both in the slave insurrections in the North Province and the free colored civil war in the West, toward outlining the context in which the priest and the prophetess developed their own intriguing relationship.

5

Sacerdotal Subversion in Saint-Domingue

As we come to know the seriousness of the situation, the war, the racism, the poverty in our world, we come to realize that things will not be changed simply by words or demonstrations. Rather, it is a question of living one's life in a drastically different way.

—DOROTHY DAY

Framing the Questions

IT IS A rather stunning fact that certain Catholic priests in the Haitian Revolution, all of them white and French, not only supported the rebel slaves' cause but also deeply immersed themselves in it and sometimes went so far to participate in campaigns to rape, pillage, and burn their enemies. From the very moment that the 1791 insurgencies began, in the North Province rebel slaves coveted the collaboration of Catholic priests. This was also the case in the free colored uprisings of 1791–1792 in the South and West Provinces, nowhere more so than in the Trou Coffy insurgency. Trou Coffy's leader, Romaine-la-Prophétesse, was a man of deep Catholic faith who was overjoyed by news that reached him in late 1791 that Abbé Ouvière sought to visit his insurgent camp. In response, he scrambled to secure ritual items from the Church of St. Rose of Lima in Léogâne to enable the priest to say Mass at the private chapel in the prophetess' mountain lair. Romaine even prepared an honor guard for Abbé Ouvière's reception in Trou Coffy, their muskets' firing in the air a salute to the esteemed visitor. Although Ouvière would only stay with the prophetess for a few days, Romaine deeply trusted him, despite some objections from his subordinate officers. The priest and the prophetess were also in contact via written correspondence over the span of about three months, and the tone of their letters is one of mutual respect. But what was the true nature of their relationship? What motivated each man to seek out the other? In the following chapter I analyze in detail the relationship between the priest and the prophetess toward answering those very questions; meanwhile, the present chapter provides important context for that analysis by exploring the various ways in which other Catholic priests related to, collaborated with, and/or denounced subversive and/or insurgent free coloreds and slaves in Saint-Domingue, beginning with the first Jesuit mission (1704–1763).

The Jesuit Legacy in Revolutionary Saint-Domingue

Although the Jesuit mission was expelled from Saint-Domingue 28 years before the 1791 insurgencies, and although it was geographically limited to the North Province of the colony, it provides a number of interesting examples of both the ways in which Catholicism appealed to slaves and the ways in which certain priests' actions were perceived of by planters and administrators as seditious. The Society of Jesus was also a cornerstone of the Catholic Church in Saint-Domingue and a taproot of Dominguan Catholic culture. That there is no evidence of more specific connections between the Jesuits, Abbé Ouvière, and Romaine-la-Prophétesse should not belie the fact that they all belonged to the same Church in the same colony or that the Jesuit example offers relevant background for exploring questions about the relationship between priests and insurgents in 1791 in general and Ouvière and Romaine in particular. The Jesuit mission had been responsible for ministering to a massive number of slaves in Saint-Domingue, after all, and their influence on Catholicism was surely still resounding in the colony by the time of the Revolution, where neither the priest nor the prophetess—both of them immigrants—stepped into a religious vacuum, as it were.[1] Despite the exit of the Jesuit order from scene, there nonetheless clearly reverberated a Jesuit spirit in the drama of the Haitian Revolution.

Thus before moving on to an analysis of the various motives and roles of specific Catholic priests in the slave and free colored insurrections of 1791, a brief review of certain relevant aspects of the Jesuit mission in Saint-Domingue is in order, though not without losing sight of the important fact that the Jesuits themselves owned many slaves and three prosperous plantations in the colony. Furthermore, even the most compassionate or progressive missionaries among them cannot be counted as abolitionists per se. In

1743, for example, the Jesuit Father Margat wrote in homage of the late Father Pierre-Louis Boutin, "the apostle of Saint-Domingue" for 37 years and the order's influential and beloved superior there,[2] describing Boutin's theological rationalization of slavery:

> [T]hese people [enslaved Africans] are unrefined, of dense intellect, don't express themselves but with the greatest difficulty in a language that they barely understand and never speak well. But the holy missionary [Boutin] ... viewed these poor souls to be the elect that Providence had torn from their homeland in order to have them make it to heaven by way of the misery and the captivity that their condition entailed.[3]

Boutin obviously loved slaves and labored for their fullness of life within the social boundaries in which they had been cast, but he still understood and accepted their bondage to be in keeping with the will of God.

As the number of slaves in the colony skyrocketed, some Jesuits became increasingly uneasy with the blatant moral contradiction between Christian notions of human equality and slavery.[4] In response, they allowed their churches to be transformed into spaces where slaves could develop "hidden transcripts," to adopt James Scott's term.[5] Alarmed by this, on numerous occasions colonial authorities formally admonished the Jesuits for granting slaves extraliturgical use of sanctuaries and for harboring fugitive slaves.[6] We thus see how quite early in Saint-Domingue's history planters and administrators saw the subversive potential of Catholicism among slaves, and they took measures to curb it.

Such restrictive measures in fact were already being implemented in Saint-Domingue as early as 1710. In what was obviously a growing climate of concern regarding Catholic feast days, and in response to the "remonstrance" of the colony's governor general, the Council of Petit Goâve expressed its "surprise" that local missionaries, members of the Order of Friars Preachers, had added a feast day to the liturgical calendar, the feast of St. Dominic, and circulated notice to local planters and slaves alike that it entailed a new day off from work in the parish. Seeing as the Friars Preachers are part of the Order of St. Dominic, from one perspective the missionaries' initiative made perfect sense. However, they had forged ahead without state approval, thereby "doing much wrong to the Colony." The feast was thus suspended, and the Friars were ordered to provide papal explanations of the nature and need of the celebration.[7]

Nine years later, an agreement was signed between the Jesuit superior and his mission's most influential priests, Fathers Louis Olivier and Pierre-Louis Boutin, and secular church wardens in Cap-Français. It stipulated

- that the Jesuits must gain the wardens' approval before installing any icons in the Church of Notre Dame or burying deceased clerics in the sanctuary;
- that once the new church construction was complete it would be owned entirely by "the Residents, Parishioners, and Benefactors" and not at all by the Society of Jesus;
- and, most importantly, that the feast day celebrations would be restricted to the Jesuits' private chapel and not be held at Notre Dame for the public to attend (which would have entailed days off from labor for slaves, which planters and administrators alike resented for economic and political reasons).

Several months later, in July, another decree modified the terms of the agreement, permitting the celebration of feast days at the city's Notre Dame parish church, but "without allowing for the people to celebrate them in any way that would disrupt their manual labor."[8]

Although these concerns with Catholic feast days in Saint-Domingue seem to have been driven primarily by economics—the more feast days, the more days off for slaves—elsewhere in the French Caribbean colonies they also were rooted in fears that they were occasions for slaves to conspire to revolt. On September 25, 1722, for instance, one colonial administrator in Martinique wrote a memorandum to the crown's Conseil de Marine to encourage that legislation be passed to reduce the number of feast day celebrations in the colony, for fear that there

> could be total revolt when there are several feasts in a row, when they can develop their conspiracies.... The excessive number of feasts that should serve toward the sanctification of Christians, are the object of abuse and disorder for these miserable slaves, for they only use them to throw themselves into vice and come up with ideas and means against the state.

The best way to deal with this menace? Either greatly reduce the number of feasts or "limit all but Christmas and Easter to free people."[9] If on the parish level any priests were turning a blind eye to slaves' volatile "abuse" of Catholic feast days, however, the colonies' apostolic prefects and fathers superior were not. In a letter written within days of the one just described, they lament "the disorder that reigns among the slaves, mulattoes, and Indians," especially on feast days, despite the signers' "constantly preaching that they are only free from working for their masters on Sundays and feast days, to use them for the service of God and the sanctification of their souls." They add with alarm that as many as 400 slaves sometimes gathered on feast days to engage in "plots of mutiny."[10]

In Saint-Domingue, feast days were soon, too, identified as being dangerous occasions for slaves to rise up—if they hadn't been already—over and above the toll that they took on planters' profit margins. On November 14, 1729, the apostolic prefect and superior of the Jesuit mission, Père Larcher, decreed a reduction in the number of feast days, "whose multitude has thus far allowed for the desertion and thievery among the blacks, neglect among whites to observe them, the former using them for debauchery and pleasure and the latter for labor and commerce." The feasts, he tellingly adds, had become a "pretext . . . of disorder among blacks."[11] Thus Larcher decreed that there would theretofore be only 13 feast days observed during the calendar year; others were not necessarily eliminated but would be observed at Masses on the nearest following Sunday.

From the perspective of the elite in the French Caribbean, Catholic feast days thus needed to be reined in because they caused a loss of revenue for planters and allowed blacks time to gather en masse to let loose and plot revolt. And even though evidently few slaves were actually going to church to celebrate the feasts (nor were many whites, for that matter), they nonetheless generally esteemed Catholic priests as healers and mediums who were on other occasions due their respect. This is most likely why state authorities were alarmed in 1737 when Père Boutin had the audacity to celebrate a requiem Mass for a female slave whom they had just hanged for some unspoken crime, most likely sorcery/poisoning. On October 22 authorities circulated a letter that read in part as follows: "In the affair that transpired during the burial of the tortured negress, conducted with some measure of solemnity by P. Boutin, the Jesuit, the behavior of this Religious would never be approved." The judges "at the same time warned the Jesuit Superior to prevent such a thing from ever happening again," dreading the thought of any "similar adventure."[12] The judges' fear was surely rooted in their recognition that such a burial service for a slave who had been executed might send the message that salvation awaited those who died as martyrs in the struggle against white oppression.

Meanwhile, broader complaints about the Jesuits' ministry to slaves that Boutin had founded, la Curé des Nègres, were loud enough and, from the perspective of colonial authorities, valid enough that the Superior Council of

Le Cap emitted a decree in February 1761 carrying the ominous title "On the Abuses in the Matter of Religion." The decree opens by expressing concern that slaves were using "the veil of darkness and that of Religion" to mask gatherings that had ulterior, subversive motives. It proceeds to admonish the Jesuits for, among other things, allowing the "Temples of God" to become "the temporary refuge of fugitive Blacks" and "often the theater of prostitution," places where "Black Slaves" were allowed "to assemble . . . after sunset."[13] Among other things, the decree outlawed the entry of slaves into churches at night and prohibited them from evangelizing or serving as churchwardens or beadles, with "the pain of the whip" awaiting any transgressors.[14] Despite being tacked to church doors, the February decree seemingly had little effect and thus "abuses in the matter of religion" raged on, prompting the Council to request copies of the "Constitution, Statutes, Bulls, Rights, and generally of any acts concerning the Regimentation, Institution, and Governing of the so-called Company of Jesus" in October of 1762, and then to emit another edict aimed at further restraining the order, two months later.[15]

If the writing on the wall wasn't clear by then, it surely was when the Council produced another missive that opened with the sweeping observation that since its inception in Europe and its establishment in most "Catholic States," one could find "a host of condemnations, of censures by Popes, the French clergy, the Bishops, the Sorbonne and other lesser Faculties of Theology" of Jesuit doctrine and morality. "If the doctrines of this society are dangerous in Europe, they are only more gruesome and to be feared in this Colony," where "the disorders and crimes of the slaves are in part derived from the doctrine and the conduct of members of this Order."[16] Another decree followed in June of 1763 that prohibited Jesuits from wearing their habits or serving as parish priests, and then the coup de grace a few months later: On November 24, 1763, the Council ordered the expulsion of the Jesuits, giving them six weeks to pack up their things and leave the colony.[17]

Of course, colonial authorities realized that a wholesale deportation of the Society of Jesus from Saint-Domingue would leave some parishes bereft of any priests. So, to compensate, the expulsion order allowed for such parishes to be served by any Jesuits who volunteered to stay, provided that they undergo a security clearance. In relation, another decree was passed by the Council indicating that the colony would provide funds to "itinerate" priests, such as Fathers Dusaunier and Desmarets.[18]

Other Jesuits may have remained in the colony out of sheer defiance, like an intriguing and nameless prophet of doom who appears in the historical record in 1770. That year, a massive earthquake devastated the colony, described in a letter by a French settler named des Rouaudières as "one of the most horrible events through which divine rage can terrify the human being." Port-au-Prince, Léogâne, and Petit-Goâve were leveled, an ensuing tsunami surged over the crushed cities, and hundreds, perhaps thousands, died. "On the plain, the earth jolted upward, leaving the land sliced up into mounds. In the end, there has never been anything more frightening." It is an altogether gripping letter. That the earthquake happened to strike on the Feast of Pentecost was surely interpreted by many—white colonists, free people of color, and black slaves alike—to mean that this was an event of divine, perhaps even apocalyptic, proportions.[19] Many Africans in the colony had experienced prophetic messages and participated in millenarian movements in Africa prior to their enslavement, moreover, as with the Antonians in Kongo. Now, further conditioned by the Jesuit ministry's liberal ecclesiology in Saint-Domingue, their religious habitus inclined them to consider the earthquake to be either theologically restorative or apocalyptically destructive, and either way as being of serious divine moment.[20] Thus when one unnamed Jesuit priest began preaching about the divine will behind the 1770 earthquake, he found a receptive audience and nearly caused not only a riot but a revolution:

> And that's not all, dear sister: an imposter has endeavored to take advantage of this situation to add furors of fanaticism to the chaos of the elements. This man, dressed in the habit of a Spanish Dominican friar, exhorts the masses to repent and to be absolved of their sins through almsgiving, the proceeds from which he makes sure to pocket himself. The slaves and the free blacks give him everything that they own; in return, he prophesies that the island "was going to be destroyed, but that only the whites would perish." These gullible people, superstitious and roguish as they are, began to gather and initiate the kinds of disturbances that could very well have led to the prophecy's realization. Several of them were arrested, along with the preacher himself, who was discovered to be an ex-Jesuit of the Dijon residence, and for this reason he was locked up.[21]

Whether the *dijonais* Jesuit was on the crown's payroll to minister to a parish subsequent to his order's expulsion or he remained as something of a renegade, disguised "as a Spanish Dominican," his preaching following the earthquake compellingly underscores the subversive potential that Catholicism possessed in Saint-Domingue, a potential that was often realized.

Although the Jesuits were the only religious order to be banished from Saint-Domingue, colonial authorities also later considered expelling the Capuchins for, among other things, having "claimed that children born to

Christians should not be slaves. And they baptized them as freepersons." As Joseph Janin points out, "[g]iven that all of the Blacks were Christians, at least by way of baptism, this would have brought slavery to a rapid end and overthrown the entire colonial system."[22] When compared with other priests engaged in the 1791–1792 slave insurrection, especially Abbé Cachetan, meanwhile, the Jesuits seem to have operated in keeping with some unspoken principle of nonviolence. Despite their order's having been expelled from the colony, no Jesuit in Saint-Domingue was ever deemed by colonial authorities to be so criminal to deserve capital punishment, at any rate. And, to be sure, throughout the history of the colony priests from other orders and some secular priests were deported. To end this section with just one more example, in 1777, seven years after the Jesuit earthquake prophet of doom was himself arrested and sent back to France, "a Capuchin priest, in Cap-Français, in Saint-Domingue, Father Michel de Vesoul, preached openly from the pulpit against slavery," per Janin. "Already revolt was spreading in among Black slave gangs. They had to expel him, too."[23]

There is thus little doubt that certain Jesuit priests in Saint-Domingue not only advocated for slaves' rights but also laid part of the foundation for later slave insurrections that would eventually culminate in the Haitian Revolution."[24] The Jesuit mission of Saint-Domingue should therefore be viewed as an important precursor to the Catholic radicalism of Romaine-la-Prophétesse and, despite the order's expulsion in 1763, as a reverberating force in the religious and political fields in which he and the Trou Coffy insurgency arose in 1791, and more so to the massive slave uprising in the North Province that year.[25] In a similar vein, closer to the present era, we may allude to liberation theology and the base church communities that it inspired in the 1970s and 1980s throughout Latin America; though the movement that once politically radicalized the popular church had lost most of its force by the 1990s, there is no turning back to a time when the Catholic hierarchy was unquestionably allied with the state, the military, and the elite. Hence, liberationist legacies remain and continue to inspire even after the utopian visions out of which they were born have been shattered, just as the struggle for justice remains.[26]

Catholic Priests and the 1791–1792 Insurgencies

The relationship between Abbé Ouvière and Romaine-la-Prophétesse is a clear example of the allure that Catholic priests held for insurgent leaders in the

Haitian Revolution, among both rebelling slaves and insurrectionary free coloreds.[27] Far from rejecting Catholicism, most key figures of the 1791–1792 slave and free colored uprisings in Saint-Domingue were themselves Catholic and they associated so closely with Catholic priests that there was a general sense among elite colonists that the priests themselves were fomenting insurrection, thus generally they held them in contempt.

Laënnec Hurbon estimates that "the majority of priests in service in the North of Saint-Domingue *chose* to be in solidarity with the insurgent slaves."[28] This might not be entirely correct, however, as at least one of them was, for all intents and purposes, held hostage by the rebels and was thus not among them by *choice* per se. Understanding the intentions of historical actors like French Catholic priests associated with insurrectionary groups in Saint-Domingue is of course difficult; their association likely reflected a whole spectrum of motivations, some of them spiritual and compassionate, others material and vengeful. Even in the case of Abbé Delahaye, the pastor of the parish of Dondon who stated under questioning his reasons for remaining among the insurgents in his occupied parish, the priest's "answers must be read with some skepticism," as Jeremy Popkin cautions: "he initially tried to minimize the extent of his cooperation with the rebels and then tried to argue that it had been involuntary."[29] It is likely that some priests found themselves without a choice in the matter, while others were opportunists who seized upon the chaos of the 1791 insurrections to pursue positions of Rasputinian power and influence. One must therefore avoid any romantic temptation to categorically canonize these priests as revolutionary saints or to portray them as prototypical liberation theologians who actualized the social implications of the Gospel out of sincere Catholic piety. Some may have been, to be sure, while others fell far short of such ideals, as we'll see momentarily.

Whatever ambitions or ideals that might have animated them, such clerical alliances with rebels cost Abbé Philémon, the pastor of Limbé, and at least two other priests their lives,[30] while earlier another Catholic priest may have been executed for his role in the ill-fated Ogé rebellion of 1790.[31] It is important to note, furthermore, that these priests were killed by white colonial authorities, and not by insurgent slaves or insurrectionary free coloreds.[32] A wealthy French planter and commissioner named Pierre-Victor, baron Malouet lamented, "What pierced the heart with pain was the thought that most of the parish priests had only remained among them [the rebels] to profit by their ignorance or to place it at the mercy of wild fantasy."[33] Setting Malouet's obvious biases aside, Catholic clerical support of insurrectionary slaves in the French colonies demonstrates "that while Catholic Christianity could and did support the institution of slavery, some missionaries used their independent authority, founded in their exclusive right to administer the sacraments, to challenge the absolute powers of the mature plantation regime," as Sue Peabody expounds. "These were not isolated interventions on the part of individual priests but part of a cultural and social system that undermined the hierarchies of the material world with the tenet that all souls are equal in the eyes of God."[34]

Let us now examine the involvement of eight Catholic priests in slave uprisings and free colored insurgent movements in Saint-Domingue in 1791–1792 on a case-by-case basis, before proceeding in the following chapter with an analysis of the specific case of the relationship between Abbé Ouvière and Romaine-la-Prophétesse at Trou Coffy: Abbé Philémon, Père Cachetan, Abbé Guillaume Silvestre Delahaye, Abbé Bienvenu Amonet, Abbé Aubert, Abbé Jêrome Blacé, Père J. P. M. Bloüet, and Père Menetrier. Taken together, their stories as Catholic priests in Saint-Domingue in 1791 provide an illuminating background for our understanding of the priest and the prophetess. As we'll see, with the possible exception of Aubert, all eight priests were pastoring local parishes when the insurrections broke out and found themselves with the opportunity either to support the rebels, who invariably sought their sanction and aid, or to invest their religious capital in efforts to thwart them.[35]

Abbé Philémon

Abbé Philémon's was the first Catholic priest to be executed during the Haitian Revolution, at four o'clock in the afternoon on November 11, 1791, near the Cathedral of Our Lady of the Assumption on the city square of Cap-Français, La Place d'Armes. During or after Philémon's hanging, Boukman's head was placed adjacent to the priest's dangling corpse on the galleys "to parody the intimate liaison that had existed between him and this leader."[36] Upon his arrest in the first French counterattack on the rebelling slaves, the curé "admitted to having supported the blacks in the revolt, and to having corresponded with their different leaders, as well as with the Spanish." In planning his military response to the slave uprising, Governor General Blanchelande decided that wresting control of Philémon's parish of Limbé from the insurgents was a priority, so he dispatched Lieutenant Colonel Anne-Louis de Touzard to lead a detachment to take back the town. The governor general had "considered attacking Limbé for a long time" because he deemed it to be the "first hotbed of the revolt and one of the principal boulevards of the brigands."[37]

By Blanchelande's account, Touzard's detachment, which consisted of 600 to 700 men, made quick work of reconquering Limbé for the colony, suffering only few casualties while "killing many enemies" and taking prisoners. But "the height of the victory" was their liberation of "about 100 white persons," mostly women and children, whom the rebel slaves had abducted and who were found by Touzard in custody at Abbé Philémon's presbytery and church, where "they had languished for two months" and were "exposed to the cruelest treatment, and expecting but death at any instant."[38] Though Philémon might have tried to argue that they were providing sanctuary to these white refugees, at least one witness offered testimony that was quite to the contrary:

> [T]he supreme insurgent leaders of the quarter were most intent on rounding up all of the unfortunate women scattered and isolated on their plantations. They brought them to the presbytery of the parish where Father Philémon was appointed as their guardian. But what did these unfortunates not suffer, whether at the hands of the brigands or of the villain Philémon? Each one of them was the object of their vile recreation, the young girls not being exempt from this abominable servitude! After making them work all day in the fields or the kitchen, commanded by black women, they locked them up in the church, where Father Philémon, as if in a harem, arrived in the evening to choose which one he would spend the night with and to bring the others to the brigands. This disgraceful trade, tolerated as it was by a religious minister, lasted for some two months, that is to say up until the liberation of these victims on the day that M. de Touzard finally raided the area.[39]

In Abbé Philémon, we thus have an example of a Catholic priest who clearly sided with the insurgent slaves and stayed with them of his own volition during the rebellion. His motivations for doing so are not entirely clear, however. The option of fleeing to safe haven prior to creating his "harem" in Limbé was very likely open to this priest and could well have saved his life, but for whatever reason he did not avail himself of it. The allegation that he transformed his church into a prison full of female sex slaves would seem to rule out the possibility that the priest remained in Limbé out of any sense of vocational devotion to his parish, furthermore. It is more likely that Philémon—and in this he wouldn't be alone—believed that the insurgent slaves would one day rule the island and that he had a bright future as their spiritual adviser.

Père Cachetan

Like Abbé Philémon, Père Cachetan, the pastor of the parish of Petite Anse, was arrested in late 1791 during Touzard's counteroffensive against the insurgent slaves in the North Province. As in Limbé, some whites who were alarmed by the "imminent danger" found themselves in the presbytery at Petite Anse when the uprising swept through their plantations. In the latter case, initially "they were forced to flee to the shore where boats were awaiting them," meaning that the whites found at the Petite Anse presbytery and church when Touzard's troops arrived were not refugees but people who had been captured while trying to escape the insurgents' raids. In particular, they discovered that "some white women and children wound up being prisoners at the residence of Father Cachetan, who was ministering to the rebel camp." Three French sailors were also among the prisoners; the insurgents enlisted them in the resistance to Touzard's raid, putting them in charge of the cannons and instructing them to fire upon the enemy, but they deceitfully "aimed high enough so as to do no harm."[40]

Among all the Catholic priests in Saint-Domingue at the outbreak of the Revolution, Father Cachetan alone held the distinction of having presided over a coronation, having "solemnly crowned the Negro Jean-François and the Negress Charlotte king and queen of the Africans, and leaders of the revolt."[41] In keeping with such a regal moment, Cachetan is said to have "preached the gospel of faith" to the rebel slaves in an effort "to bolster them in an insurrection that was holy and legitimate in his eyes." It is thus unsurprising that this priest, "who should have, like all of the *habitants* of his town, made way to *le Cap* at the very start of the insurrection, preferred to stay among the rebelling blacks."[42] Cachetan thus had to be brought to the city "by force."

The curé's actions led one anonymous French eyewitness to lament that "it was not only the aristocracy that should be blamed for our disasters; the clergy cause the woes of France and contributed to ours. You can judge by the conduct of one minister of religion, Father Cachetan." More specifically:

> So when the army overan [*sic*] the camp, seeing that he would soon be punished for his crimes, he didn't want to leave his presbytery. He had the nerve to say that he would be fine in the midst of his parishioners (the blacks) and that if anything had been damaged at his place, it was only by the whites. This unworthy minister of religion, according to the testimony of the white women and sailors who were rescued, was imprisoned the day after his arrival in Le Cap.[43]

For reasons unknown, Cachetan was spared the fate that awaited Abbé Philémon in Cap-Français. As Philémon languished in the city jail, Cachetan, "in order not to scandalize the public and above all the blacks . . . was sent back to France."[44] Why executing Cachetan would have been more scandalous than executing Philémon is a good question. Was he more revered among the rebelling slaves? Was he a "better" priest? Short of additional documentary evidence, we just cannot say.

In any event, a better priest surely would not have indulged in the kind of sexual slavery that Père Philémon reportedly orchestrated in Limbé. One contemporary observer, Monsieur Monchet, "*instituteur des enfants de M. de Castellane*" (private tutor of the children of Mr. de Castellane), claimed that, like Abbé Philémon in Limbé, Cachetan prostituted the women and girls who had been taken prisoner in Petit Anse, alleging that the curé "encouraged this horrible Vendée and persuaded these tigers, who were already enough predisposed to cruelty and lechery, that everything that they were doing was agreeable to God, and that the most abominable debauchery was just recompense for the services that they rendered to God and King." According to Monchet, accompanying two of the captives, "Madam N... and her daughter," was a letter from Cachetan to the black rebel leader Georges Biassou in which the priest rejoiced, "What a happy hand for you, brave Biassou, what joy! The little one will put up some resistance no doubt but the whip will make her give in." Monchet's account adds, "It was another priest who had the horrible audacity to assist in the torture of the ill-fated Berchois and his unfortunate companions, after having delivered their sentence with these terrifying words: 'You must die. Jesus Christ is forever on our side'!"[45]

Abbé Delahaye

In addition to being a Catholic priest, Abbé Guillaume Silvestre Delahaye was a botanist who conducted extensive research on Saint-Domingue's flora, some of which he published.[46] He was also a gifted artist whose illustrations appeared in his own and other botanical studies.[47] As with most of the Catholic priests in Saint-Domingue, we know little about his life prior to his appearance in the colony, where he had already been for 23 years when the 1791 uprisings broke out. It does seem, though, that Delahaye was a native of Rouen, where he had at one point served as a deacon in the parish of St. Jean; he had also studied law in Caen. Long before his extraordinary adventures in Saint-Domingue, the priest was accused of "debauchery" in 1757 in Paris after he was once discovered by police "lying naked and without a nightgown" in bed with a woman named Marguerite Desmarais, "nude and nude." The lovers were both 23-years-old at the time. Despite this youthful indiscretion, the priest was released without further ado, and within a few years he would find himself in Saint-Domingue.[48]

Up until the outbreak of the slave insurrections of 1791 that led to his demise, Abbé Delahaye had enjoyed a long and storied career in the colony.

He had arrived in Saint-Domingue in 1765 and published in Cap-Français, 16 and 24 years later respectively, his botanical treatises. Meanwhile, Delahaye served as "assistant pastor of le Cap, curé of Quartier-Morin and finally curé of Dondon, where for twenty years he much occupied himself with extensive research on the use of plants in tropical zones."[49] But, when the insurrection broke out, as one planter recounts, "the curés were divided between the two camps. Those who found themselves in areas controlled by whites sided with the whites, while the others followed bands of rebelling slaves." Among those who "followed" the rebels, as another observer explains, was "the execrable abbé de la Haye, curé of Dondon, the most ardent apostle of the liberty of the blacks, writer of the news of the *Daily Letter* [*Feuille du jour*]."[50] Delahaye's newsletter seems to have caused quite an uproar when it prematurely announced that slavery had been abolished in Saint-Domingue. "In Le Cap, the daily Letter wrought terror and dread for five weeks running in the souls of the owners [of slaves]. . . . [T]his ferocious priest didn't cease to further douse us with chalices full of venom and to deepen our wound with such inhumane comments."[51]

As pastor of the parish of Dondon in 1791, Delahaye had a front row seat for the outbreak of the Haitian Revolution. He was taken captive by Jeannot Bullet when the notoriously violent former slave seized the town on September 10 of that year, as was Abbé Philippe Roussel, parish priest of Grande Rivière, a nearby town that Jeannot had seized two weeks earlier, on August 27, and the parish in which the insurgent leaders established their principal camp, La Tannerie.[52] Both priests were spared the torture and execution that befell many of the other whites in their respective parishes. In fact, Delahaye was allowed to live relatively well in occupied Dondon and eventually would exercise considerable sway over three of the Revolution's most influential leaders, Biassou, Jean-François, and Toussaint Louverture.[53] Among other French prisoners in Dondon, meanwhile, the priests were greatly feared. One of the prisoners, an attorney named Gros, author of an important eyewitness account of the 1791 slave insurrections in the North, described his dread upon the arrival of Abbé Roussel to the place where he was being held:

> About five o'clock in the afternoon arrived the curate of Grande-Riviere. Fresh room for panic trepidation. Thought we to ourselves: "Tis only to confess us, and we shall be dispatched this evening." What refuge had we to fly to? What alternative to partake of? What a miserable existence this was to drag on? Let but the reader reflect upon it. After all, however, our fears were ill-grounded, as nothing of the kind happened: He came purely and simply to pay his court to the generals.[54]

Throughout Saint-Domingue, when Catholic clergy were absent from their camps, insurgent leaders actively sought their counsel via written correspondence. Jeannot even once wrote a letter to Delahaye offering to pay him for celebrating Mass.[55] Yves Benot has analyzed another exchange in 1792 between Delahaye, Biassou, and "Fayet, the free black commander of Dondon," in which Biassou "asked the cleric to draw up a sort of constitution for him," at a time when the priest still owned several slaves "with the acceptance of Biassou. Only toward the end of the year, when the military situation had grown worse, did he free them." Fayet, for his part, "was concerned about a rumor that accused Delahaye of having preached to blacks that they should not work—which was no doubt false."[56] Delahaye himself explained that his participation in the rebels' constitutional project was fueled by "the most terrible anarchy and the greatest disorder among the brigands" and that in reality he did little more than to contribute "counsels of peace and humanity."[57] In addition to its further illustrating the nature of Catholic clerical support for insurgent leaders, this exchange is noteworthy for at least three reasons: (1) its reference to Delahaye's ownership of slaves demonstrates that in the revolutionary Atlantic world abolitionism did not necessarily preclude slaveholding; (2) its indication that insurgent leaders like Fayet esteemed Catholic religious capital as crucial not only to the struggle for liberation but to the creation of a more just political order as well; and 3) its reflection that motivations for slave insurrections were diverse and sometimes unconcerned with questions of abolition.

When news of the execution of Abbé Philémon reached him, Abbé Delahaye quite understandably feared that he would be the next to fall, and the priest expressed as much to Jean-François in writing, receiving words of comfort from the rebel leader in eloquent reply:

> I do myself the honor of responding to your second letter in which you indicate to me your worries, that you greatly fear to be in this place here; I beg you that you not allow the least worry enter your mind, seeing as I wrote to you that I would spill my last drop of blood to defend our rights and yours; as such, if you fear something, you can put yourself at ease. If misfortune dictates that we be attacked and the enemies be the victors, I will do everything possible to get you out of there because I would say that I am quite anxious . . . about the subject of the reverend Father of Limbé and of Petite Anse. Know for sure that I will never abandon you.[58]

Despite Jean-François's promises, eventually Delahaye was indeed arrested, and in December of 1792 he was interrogated by Léger-Félicité Sonthonax, a

French envoy who had arrived in Saint-Domingue in September of that year as a member of the Second Civil Commission. During his interrogation, the abbé gave multiple reasons for which he had remained among Jean-François's insurgents, who occupied his parish, though he obviously could have retreated to Cap-Français, even as of September 10, 1791, when Dondon was first captured by the rebels. At first he claimed that the attack surprised him and "his fellow citizens, surrounded and besieged by a troop of five or six thousands brigands." The next day, upon "being struck by the horrible spectacle of the murders committed by these brigands," the priest requested of Jeannot that he be allowed to conduct funeral services for them. "Jeannot, motivated to respect the clergy because of his fear and superstition, responded positively to this request," only later to have the bodies removed before the priest could do so. In other words, "the deponent would have considered it dishonorable and a dereliction of his duty if he had thought of abandoning his parishioners," adding that he was also waiting to help any white counteroffensive that would follow "because he had taken on the responsibility of transmitting the signals he had agreed on with the leaders of the plantation owners' army."[59] Delahaye also claimed to have been documenting the insurgents' abuses, though he was forced to burn these records for fear of their being seized by the rebels.

Intent on finding "evidence that he had colluded with the blacks," Sonthonax pressed on with his questioning, while Delahaye dug in:

> He was asked why, when he was with Jeannot, he busied himself with burying the dead rather than saving these pitiful victims from these abominable cruelties, why he did not use all the resources that his clerical garb and his personal reputation must have given him with the superstitious Africans to save the whites from being sacrificed.

The priest responded that he had been threatened with death by decapitation were he to "involve himself in things that were none of his business," though he had managed to save one child. Delahaye further rejected the suggestion that he might have been serving the rebels as some kind of "counselor," insisting that "he never had any relations with them other than those that he was forced into because of personal need."[60] In the end, the interrogation of Abbé Delahaye was neither damning enough to have him executed nor exonerating enough to secure his release, and he was sent to jail in Le Cap, languishing there until insurgent slaves torched the city in June of 1793.[61]

It appears that Abbé Delahaye may have been the only Catholic priest to have been killed by insurgents rather than by the state, though this is in dispute among historians.[62] Jean-Marie Jan alludes to conflicting reports regarding the priest's fate: one has it that he drowned, or was executed by drowning, in Le Cap in 1803, while Adolphe Cabon indicates that he "was killed in 1802 by the blacks out of fear that he might betray them."[63] It may be that Delahaye was murdered during the ensuing chaos as Cap-Français burned in June 1793, as seemingly rumor soon spread that he was killed at the hands of whites in the city, for, as Cabon adds, the putative event so angered the insurgents in Dondon that they exacted revenge "by the massacre of 116 whites."[64]

Whatever his fate, during Delahaye's tenure in Saint-Domingue he had come a long way from the night in Paris in 1757 when, as a young priest, he was found naked in bed with a woman. In addition to his pastoral and scientific work in Saint-Domingue, the abbé was elected *procureur syndic* (local magistrate) of Dondon and he had worked in that capacity to aid not only the pursuit of escaped slaves but also French resistance to the 1791 slave uprisings prior to Jeannot's siege of Dondon. Although Delahaye has long been portrayed as "one of the apostles of the rebellion," these were hardly the acts of a radical abolitionist priest.[65] As Benot therefore explains, it is "without doubt by accident and not by intention that he remained among the insurgents, who, as we know, far from being anticlerical, publicly claimed to belong to the king and the Catholic church. It appears though that Delahaye was above all concerned with his personal comfort and wanted to be served and respected."[66] And at this the priest was successful, for among the rebel slaves he was indeed highly respected and comfortably enjoyed a position of some authority in their midst.

The case of Abbé Delahaye thus demonstrates that at least some priests' affiliations with insurgent camps in Saint-Domingue were not so much driven by abolitionist ideology or Catholic humanism, but by the sheer will to survive. Delahaye at first had no choice but to remain in Jean-François's fold, and he quickly adapted as well as any white person possibly could have to life in occupied Dondon, abandoned his earlier procolonist stances, and soon assumed a privileged position as chief counselor to the Haitian Revolution's most important early leader. Times had been hard for the colony's Catholic clerics, so garnering favor with rebels who actually esteemed them, as opposed to the contempt in which white planters and administrators held them, clearly had its material advantages.[67]

Abbé Bienvenu Amonet

Abbé Bienvenu Amonet was the pastor of the parish of Marmelade, located roughly 15 kilometers due west of Dondon, when the Haitian Revolution began. His entry into the insurgent fray differed from those of the priests discussed above in the sense that his parish was left unscathed during the initial phase of the 1791 slave insurrections, and in that his white and free colored parishioners evidently remained tenuously in control of their property. However, they greatly feared that the slave rebellion would soon spread to Marmelade, thus prompting them to seek to enter into negotiations with Jean-François and Biassou. Just who would risk their lives to go to Dondon to do so? In light of the rebel leadership's deep reverence for the Catholic Church and high respect for its priests, this question seemingly answered itself, judging by Abbé Bienvenu's explanation in a deposition that he wrote soon thereafter:

> On Sunday, September 25, we the undersigned, curé of Marmelade, after having celebrated our parish Mass at the usual time, it was proposed to us by the municipal officers to go to Dondon, then occupied by rebelling slaves, in order to work with the curé of that parish to try, by the voice of pain and persuasion, to produce some good effects in the ferocious and bloodthirsty hearts of the rebels. Animated by the public good and empathetic about all the misfortune and the pending invasion that threatened Marmelade, we accepted, at the almost certain risk of our lives, the proposed mission, which was delivered to us ad hoc in writing and signed by members of the said municipality.[68]

Reluctantly accepting the assignment, Abbé Bienvenu was escorted that very day to Dondon, carrying with him the written proposal from Marmelade, "just in case." Upon his arrival, the priest was startled by "cries and threats of an approaching death," which he surely thought would be his own. However, "thanks to Sieur Ogé, Dondon's *majeur de place*" and a relative of the late Vincent Ogé, the curé was brought to "the residence of Monsieur Abbé Delahaye, where we were fraternally received and welcomed." Evidently that was enough for Bienvenu, who indicated that he wished to return to Marmelade the next day, despite the unfulfilled objectives of his mission. In the interim, he proposed to Delahaye that the two say Mass together, which they did. Ogé agreed to allow Bienvenu to leave, "but the other leaders were opposed to this, so we were constrained and forced to stay in spite of everything, and thus became prisoners." The curé understood that he was suspected of being "a spy" and before long found himself surrounded by 40 rebel slaves. "It is in such a critical moment that the most sinister and distressing reflections swarmed our imagination—spears, arrows, and other weapons that surrounded us were very much the instruments that would sacrifice us."

Thus with his "soul agitated," Bienvenu thought of writing to Jean-François and Biassou "to probe their intentions for us," only to be quickly transported to a second place of captivity. At this juncture, the curé decided that, should he survive, and short of succeeding in entering into any meaningful negotiations with Jean-François or Biassou, he could best serve his Marmelade constituents by taking mental notes of everything he observed while among the rebels in Dondon. Jean-François and Biassou were not in Dondon at the time, and those left in charge of the camp were indecisive as to what to do with the priest, despite Bienvenu's "solicitations . . . made in the name of humanity, of religion." For his part, Abbé Delahaye was either unable or unwilling to intervene for Abbé Bienvenu's release, even though he had "fraternally" welcomed his fellow priest the day before and said Mass with him that very morning. Things took a turn for the better, however, when Jean-François returned to Dondon: "Our surprise was as great as agreeable when the supreme leader (jean francois) came to make us take an address back to Marmelade, a happy occasion that procured our deliverance."

In addition to returning to Marmelade with Jean-François' address to the municipal authorities there, Abbé Bienvenu also brought military intelligence, which he put into writing in his deposition. It included the following six observations:

1. The rebels possessed Spanish firearms and swords.
2. A white prisoner told him of having seen Spaniards bringing weapons and ammo on mules to the camp.
3. He saw Spanish soldiers in the camp and even spoke with them, and that they came to deliver and pick up mail.
4. The chiefs often go to the border to meet with the Spaniards, who share with them intelligence about the French.
5. The rebels trade sugar with the Spanish for weapons, and everyday sugar is brought to the camp on donkeys for this purpose.
6. The Spanish trade unfairly.[69]

During his captivity in Dondon, Bienvenu became acquainted with another white prisoner, the aforementioned French attorney Gros. When Gros first met Abbé Bienvenu, the priest was "stretched at his length upon a sofa" and entranced in "the profoundest silence." The pastor "was glad of a favorable opportunity" to speak with the attorney, and he did so liberally:

> He mentioned that he had been made a prisoner of, and treated exactly as we were; that his fate, like ours would have been irrevocably fixed, had not an end been put to *Johnny*'s [Jeannot's] existence. He informed us that he was the person who exhorted the monster previous to his

> death; that after his preparation for the execution, he even solicited by all that was most sacred, his pardon from *John Francis* [Jean-François], offering (a matter inconceivably mean, and which proves that ferocity is not real courage) to be chained and accept the most abject occupation; that he felt no inclination to relieve the wretch, but seeing his sentence could not be recalled, he upbraided him with his barbarity, pointing out the scattered carcasses of the unhappy citizens of *Dondon* massacred by his order. He told him that his end was but proof of the divine wrath, which permitted no act, frequently inhuman, to pass unpunished; and added that he died afterwards with the most despicable pusillanimity and cowardice.[70]

In the French original the passage "exhorted the monster previous to his death" reads "*avait exhorté ce monstre à la mort*," which could also be interpreted to mean that, in spite of his imprisonment and the suspicion in which the rebels held him, Abbé Bienvenu may have been instrumental in Jean-François's decision to have Jeannot executed for his excesses. It is clear anyway that the priest quickly gained the confidence of Jean-François, for he was able to compel him to accept certain "important truths." Comparably, Abbé Delahaye mentioned in his interrogation that Bienvenu served as something of a scribe to the rebels as they drafted "a memorandum to the whites, proposing conditions under which the slaves and the freedmen who were with them would lay down their arms."[71] Thus, like Delahaye, Bienvenu assumed the function of counselor to Jean-François and worked with the rebel leader on "plans that would ensure to the colony a state of universal tranquility."[72]

Visions of "universal tranquility" for Saint-Domingue were highly idealistic, of course, but at least Abbé Bienvenu succeeded in convincing Jean-François not to attack Marmelade. Something of a treaty was written up, and Bienvenu, with Gros's urging, was charged with the mission of presenting it to Marmelade. The curé promised to soon return to Dondon. He never did, however, instead sending word back to Gros that "he had been detained by his parishioners; but that the address had met their approbation, and they felicitated themselves upon its success."[73] For his part, and knowing full well the great suspicion with which colonial authorities viewed Catholic priests, Gros was sure to underscore that Bienvenu was above reproach: "This virtuous pastor had braved all dangers . . . and we can attest his conduct to have been an example of moderation, patience, and firmness. Indeed, the nature of his mission among those plunderers is sufficient to efface every suspicion that evil-minded persons or the misinformed could have entertained to his prejudice."[74] In other words, Bienvenu was a far cry from another priest who had earlier in his captivity declared to Gros and his fellow prisoners, "My children, we should all know how to die: Our savior, Christ, died for us on the cross . . . you must know how to die."[75]

Abbé Aubert

Scholars who have thus far analyzed the activities of Catholic priests in the early stage of the Haitian Revolution have understandably focused their attention on the 1791 slave uprisings in the North Province, discussing the activities of the likes of Fathers Philémon, Cachetan, Delahaye, and Bienvenu, as I have thus far in this chapter. In the quite different but equally tumultuous free colored insurgency in the West Province, meanwhile, there were at least four Catholic priests who were centrally involved in the struggle, engaged in various alliances and animated by various ideologies, and a fifth who endeavored to keep his distance and remain more or less neutral. Among them, Abbé Aubert, a priest who was evidently unaffiliated with any parish in Saint-Domingue, was clearly the most radical and the most convinced that being a Catholic priest in the Haitian Revolution meant exercising "a preferential option" for the insurgents, to evoke the language of twentieth-century liberation theology, even if it also meant participating in the killing of white people and in the destruction of their property. The others were Father Bloüet, curé of Jacmel; Abbé Jerôme Blacé, curé of Cayes Jacmel; Abbé Ouvière, who, as we've seen, was a secular priest without a parish in Saint-Domingue; and Père Menetrier, curé of the parish of Léogâne when the 1791 insurrection broke out.

Though he goes unnamed in Father Bloüet's detailed report about the 1791–1792 free colored insurgency around Jacmel and is nowhere mentioned in Abbé Ouvière's papers, Abbé Aubert was perhaps the most audacious of all subversive and militaristic Catholic priests in Saint-Domingue. Reporting in mid-January 1792 that there were "several whites" embedded in the leadership of the insurgent camps near Marigot and Cayes Jacmel, municipal authorities identified Aubert as being "without a doubt" the chief instigator of the revolts.[76] In a letter written by a *habitant* of the Jacmel parish named Cussan to the Colonial Assembly a few weeks later, a clear case is made for Aubert to be arrested because "it was he who obtained the cannons and who made the devices that were used to commit arson in the city. All of the testimonies show that this abbé was commander of the artillery. The city has conclusive evidence against him."[77] The Municipality of Jacmel further detailed the effects of Aubert's leadership: "It would be very difficult to paint an accurate portrait of the crimes, robberies, and arsons that the mulattoes have committed. . . . They killed almost all of the whites within their reach . . . [and] burned many plantations and take the blacks from them," their "rage" seemingly fueled by "the proclamation of the Civil Commissioners." With Beaudoin Desmarattes and Abbé Aubert "without a doubt directing them in their revolts," the marauding mulattoes also "armed many blacks" and "stole all of our livestock as well as our horses and draught animals." To make matters worse, the city's "ammunition supply is very insufficient and the gunpowder that we have is very old," plus "we are running out of flour and wine."[78]

Abbé Aubert was closely tied to one of Romaine-la-Prophétesse's satellite camps in the Jacmel theater, Camp Pasquet, though it is unclear if this priest had any direct relationship to the prophetess himself or if he ever visited Trou Coffy in person. Camp Pasquet was commanded by a notoriously violent free black who went by the name Gros Poisson (Fat Fish), and his troops were seemingly quite swayed by Aubert. One witness overheard a mulatto acolyte of Aubert stating, for example, "they wanted to roast all of the whites and that the country was now theirs, and that they could easily destroy any armed forces coming from France." Furthermore, "Abbé Aubert was a brave man who was working to dislodge the cannons from Marigot and who implored them to have courage, saying that they would soon manage to destroy all of the whites and that there would be a procession on every plantations that would bring blacks to recognize them and to restore order."[79]

With such a stated vision of a future Saint-Domingue in which mulattoes would rule over blacks and however few whites that remained standing, Aubert's subversive role in the free colored insurgency thus went beyond those of the Catholic priests among rebel slaves in the North Province. He also distinguished himself from other priests in the Haitian Revolution by taking on the function of not just political adviser and moral counsel but of military commander and armorer as well. One insurgent, Lamy Lartigue, testified that Aubert had instructed Gros Poisson "to ready the artillery" and that the priest had "unhitched the cannons, which he had taken from Marigot, loaded them with powder charges and balls, and forged their loading rods in the furnace at the Cyvadier plantation, then he returned to Poisson's camp where he busied himself with making incendiary devices."[80] Once positioned within firing range, the Marigot cannons would prove to be devastating for Jacmel during the insurgents' bombardment of the city in January of 1792.

The harrowing results and the insurgents' eventual sack of the city, detailed in Chapter 1, underscore how decisive Abbé Aubert's influence on the insurgency in the Jacmel theater was. Not only did he manage to seize and transport the cannons, three in all, it seems that he also dictated where they were to be positioned and when they would be used to bombard the city. It is likely that Aubert did all of this in collaboration with Delisle de Bresolle, a violent and radical *petit blanc* who is denounced in the same sentence in which Cussan calls for Aubert's arrest as "the principal chief of the excessively cruel brigands; it is very important that the assembly take precautions that he be arrested in the case that he crosses the border [*passer a l'espagnol*], the priest Aubert requires the same."[81] I have not uncovered any documentation concerning the fate of Aubert; had he been arrested and executed, there would likely have been some notation to this effect in the archives or in Jean-Philippe Garran de Coulon's official *Rapport*, and it is of course quite possible that I simply have not found it elsewhere. It is equally possible, though, that the priest indeed "passed over to the Spanish"—that he crossed the border and evaded the juridical consequences of his complicity in the insurgency.[82]

Père Jérôme Blacé

A Franciscan and "former professor of philosophy," Père Jérôme Blacé became the pastor of the Cayes Jacmel parish in May of 1785. He replaced Father Dom Joseph Constans, who had died on March 3 of that year and was buried on the same day in the parish church. The first entry in the parish registry signed by Blacé is for the funeral of a surveyor named Antoine Guibert, who died after "a fall from a horse" on May 15. During the rest of the year, the new curé would preside over 7 weddings, 15 baptisms, and 17 funerals for people besides Guibert, including a three-year-old boy named Julien Isidore on July 9, two poor souls who drowned in a flooding river on August 16, and one who drowned in "the swollen seas" (*des grosses mers*) on September 11; the latter three deaths likely resulted from tropical storm activity.

Parish records for Cayes Jacmel between 1787 and 1793 are lost, though those for 1785 and 1786 were kept by Blacé and are extant, and from other archival sources we know that he still occupied the position of curé during the Trou Coffy insurgency. From May of 1785 until the end of 1786, Père Blacé presided over a total of 39 baptisms, 14 weddings, and 35 funerals. All but one of the burials were performed in the parish cemetery; the other, that of a one Mathurin on April 23, 1786, took place "in the savannah." Blacé's registries also record one Act of Abjuration, dated January 15, 1786, for Stephen Charles (Stêve), a free mulatto from Port Royal, Jamaica, who was renouncing his former religion, "the heresies of Luther and Calvin," and converting to Catholicism, evidently as a necessary step toward marrying a local *"griffe libre"* named Marie Magdalene Lavocat a few weeks later.[83] Blacé wed the couple on the sixth of February.[84]

Like Abbé Aubert, Blacé had close ties to Delisle de Bresolle in the Jacmel insurgent theater. Somewhat like Abbé Delahaye, meanwhile, Blacé is a deeply curious figure in that he was both associated with a violent insurgency aimed at overthrowing white rule in Saint-Domingue and was an elected deputy to the illegal Colonial Assembly of Saint-Marc (General Assembly of Saint-Domingue);[85] the Assembly had been formed in April of 1790 by white planters, whose representatives, as Laurent Dubois explains, "declared flatly that they would never share political power with a 'bastard and degenerate race'—the free-coloreds."[86] In a letter to the Colonial Assembly dated March 1, 1792 and sent from Jacmel, Lamothe-Vedel, "major of the district of Jacmel," strongly denounced Blacé as being a "decided enemy of the [French] Revolution." Blacé, Aubert, and Delisle, furthermore, "never ceased to be the leaders of the movement and bringing this cursed class of mulattoes to employ fire and all of the most barbaric things invented by hell to concoct demands, thinking that the desolation and the troubles that they incite will need the *ancien régime*" to pacify the colony and restore it to its former glory.[87]

Père Blacé "usurped a reputation for civility," whereas in reality he was allegedly linked to "these villains" who "committed murder, arson, and all of the evils that we have experienced" and that "drove peaceful citizens to abandon their homes to save themselves from their barbarous ferocity." Not all the peaceful citizens succeeded in doing so, however, as Blacé and his charges allegedly "killed six people who were trying to take refuge among the reunited brothers in Jacmel."[88] Furthermore, whereas Blacé should have remained among "his citizens" in the midst of such a calamity, instead "he quickly went to Marigot to join the brigands and then on to the Garreau plantation," which had evidently been taken over by the insurgents and transformed into yet another rebel camp.

In addition to alleging Père Blacé's complicity in such crimes, Vedel also expressed his horror that the priest had illegally and heretically administered the sacraments of baptism and marriage to slaves. By law, such rites required that the petitioning fiancés or the parents of the newborn child produce documentation to prove their free legal status. When Blacé arrived at *habitation* Garreau, he brought with him the parish registry from Marigot to record weddings that he was about to sanctify between "many whites and the slaves of the *nommé* M. Garreau." Vedel seemed as concerned with the illegal weddings and baptisms as he was with the arsons and murders that he tied to the priest or the meeting he described in which Blacé rallied free colored insurgents to storm the city of Jacmel:

> Father Blacé, no less deceitful [than the insurgents]; I beseech the respectable assembly to promulgate a decree attesting to the infamy of

> all whites without exception who are proven to be part of the mulatto faction, and to declare that those serving in public functions, notably Father Blacé, curé of Cayes Jacmel, unworthy of them ... and to also declare the certificates of baptism and marriage made outside of the *chef lieu* of the parish and contrary to the decree of the provincial assembly to be null and void.[89]

In effect, Père Blacé was, at one and the same time, breaking the law in consecrating these marriages and manipulating the law to free slaves, for at the time in Saint-Domingue, marriage to a free man was a path to manumission for enslaved women, and one that was tax exempt to boot.[90] The marriages also signal that Delisle de Bresolle was not the only *petit blanc* participating in the Trou Coffy insurgency, for surely some of the other "white men" whom Blacé married to slaves were also lower class malcontents who were swept up into Romaine's rebellion, further fueling it with subaltern rage.

Blacé managed to escape arrest for his involvement in the Trou Coffy insurgency. Evidently the Franciscan also managed to keep news of it from reaching Church authorities in the wider Catholic world. For, by 1797, he had made his way to Havana and later that year was appointed pastor of the parish of Pensacola by Bishop Luis Penaver y Cardenas of the Diocese of Louisiana and the Floridas. Penaver also directed Blacé to minister to the Louisiana Third Battalion.[91] All told, that is quite a remarkable resumé for a Catholic priest in the revolutionary Atlantic world.

Père J. P. M. Bloüet

On April 3, 1788, Père J. P. M. Bloüet assumed the position of curé of the Jamel parish, replacing, for reasons that are unknown, Père Lemaire, who had held the post for about three years. On that very day the new pastor officiated over the marriage of Jean-Baptiste Hyacinth, a free mulatto who resided on Jacmel Mountain, and Rose Seraphine, "*mulatresse*." Between then and when the 1791 insurrections in the West Province radically disrupted life as usual in Jacmel, starting in November of that year for city dwellers, Père Bloüet had baptized at least 344 children, married 86 couples, and buried at least 265 deceased parishioners (a couple of pages are missing in the parish registries for this period).[92] In addition to thus being a busy priest, Père Bloüet was an ardent supporter of white privilege in Saint-Domingue and a fierce denouncer of the free colored cause. In a long report that is one of the most important sources of information about Romaine-la-Prophétesse and the Trou Coffy insurgency, Bloüet waxes poetic in trying to make sense of the unspeakable devastation then unfolding all around him and literally destroying the French colonial enterprise that was Saint-Domingue:

> Equality is but a dangerous chimera throughout the colony, whose existence rolls on a pivot so essentially different from this, such that to preach this system to the varied castes that comprise our population, is not so much to remind them of their supposed rights as to incite them to murder, pillage, and arson.[93]

By January 1792, Jacmel's supply routes had been cut off by insurgents led by Delisle and Gros Poisson, as we've seen, and many of the city's buildings had been reduced to ashes, having been torched by incendiary devices created by Abbé Aubert. Surrounded on all sides by insurgents, and bombarded by the cannons that Aubert had stationed in the hills above, it was only a matter of time before the whites would be forced to surrender their last stronghold, Jacmel's seaside fort. As Father Bloüet lamented, "condemned by this imperious series of circumstances, and wanting to reduce the effects of the threats, the murders and fires, we accepted the petitions we adhered to the conditions of the concordats, we gave up our fort." To mark the occasion, the insurgents demanded that Bloüet say a Mass for them and that the city prepare a feast for 50 of their representatives. The curé does not indicate whether the likes of Boursiquot, Delisle, Charpentier, Gros Poisson, Elie, Soliment, or Romaine were in attendance at the "sumptuous feast," only regretting that the rebels came in much greater numbers than had been stipulated in the treaty. Worse yet from the curé's perspective, Père Bloüet had to "conduct the service without distinction of color," while the insurgents were especially "filled with pride over our humiliation" when the city had to "render military honors for their deceased officers."[94]

In Père Bloüet we thus have a seemingly rare example of a French Catholic priest who stood in vehement opposition to the 1791 insurgencies in the West Province, and one can well imagine what he thought about the simultaneous slave insurrections in the North. When the possibility of amnesty for the insurgents was raised, upon the arrival in the colony of the national civil commissioners Roume, Mirbeck, and Saint-Léger, the curé bristled and railed against the idea, calling instead for aggressive punishment for "the ferocious tigers" because "the measure of their crimes must be the measure of the vengeance . . . our blood cries . . . the law speaks . . . may that it condemn them . . . that its gavel weigh down upon their outcast heads . . . that it cast this denatured race into an abyss."[95] Père Bloüet would later express similar outrage upon learning that

Saint-Léger had reported that whites were partially to blame for the devastation of the city of Jacmel and the parish's plantations.[96]

Somewhat curiously, although Bloüet submitted his report detailing insurgent activity in his parish to the colonial assembly in March of 1792 and signed as "curé of Jacmel," he did not sign a single entry in the parish registry that year. It is difficult to say why—perhaps he had departed or was infirm. Be that as it may, at some point thereafter Bloüet returned to France, where by 1796 he had assumed the post of *"garde de chapelle"* at the Church of Saint Anne, in Auray, Brittany, one of France's most important Catholic pilgrimage sites.[97]

Père Menetrier

Serving as pastor of the parish of Léogâne when the Trou Coffy insurgency broke out, Père Menetrier differed from the other priests under discussion here in that he remained rather neutral throughout the 1791 insurrections, neither joining forces with rebels, seeking to broker peace treaties with them, nor denouncing them. Menetrier became curé of Léogâne in September of 1790, with his first act in this role being the performance of funerary rites for a deceased man from Coq Qui Chante named Lesestieux, on the 20th of that month.[98] He replaced Père Duquet, apostolic prefect, who had served as curé on an interim basis only since June of 1790, following the brief tenure of Father Sauvage and the long tenure of Father Grulé, who had himself occupied the post as of October of 1777.

Fathers Grulé and Sauvage had known Romaine Rivière personally, as the prophetess stood as godfather for several children that these two priests baptized; for example, a *"quarteronne"* (quarteroon) child named Marie Elizabeth, on August 15, 1788, and for a *grif* named Jean Baptiste on June 12, 1789, both born to free mulatta mothers.[99] As we saw in Chapter 2, furthermore, Sauvage had officiated over Romaine's marriage to Marie Roze,[100] while Grulé also knew Romaine's wife personally; on February 15, 1790, the priest baptized a free black child named Pierre Louis François (b. July 2, 1789), with Marie Rivière standing as the godmother.[101] Later that year Marie Roze would become the godmother of another child, Pierre Gédeon, who was baptized on October 18 by Menetrier.[102] It is unclear whether Romaine was in attendance, but in his record of Gédeon's baptism the curé identified the godmother as "wife of Romain Riviere, free black." Clearer evidence that Menetrier knew Romaine personally is found a few months later in the parish registry, where, on February 8, 1791, the prophetess served as a witness at the wedding that the pastor officiated for Dimba, "Creole from Port-au-Prince," and "Rosette, *griffe libre.*"[103]

Seeing as he presided over a total of 168 baptisms, 41 weddings, and 149 funerals from September 1790 until the end of the following year, a period of just over 15 months, carefully recording details of each one into his parish registry, it is safe to say that Père Menetrier was a dutiful priest. It is impossible to read anything about the curé's politics in the registry, however, and beyond its pages I have not found a single document written by, to, or about him in the archival material. There is one letter signed by Romaine-la-Prophétesse that does offer some clue of his neutrality vis-à-vis the insurgency, though. Late in 1791, with the insurrection in the West Province then in full bloom, the prophetess requested that Menetrier send ritual paraphernalia from Léogâne's St. Rose Church to Trou Coffy so that Mass could be said there in his ornate chapel,[104] which Menetrier had at some point visited and considered to be "very pretty."[105] That the curé quickly acquiesced suggests either he was supportive of Romaine or he feared the consequences that any refusal of the prophetess' request might provoke; a similar fear might have compelled Menetrier to say Mass in Léogâne at Romaine's behest on at least two other occasions.[106]

One might also infer some sense of Père Menetrier's political posture from things that he either did *not* enter into the Léogâne parish registry or that he crossed out. It is imaginable that he could have enjoyed a position of great privilege and influence as of January 1, 1792, the day that the treaty went into effect that formally ceded rule of the city to Romaine-la-Prophétesse. Being curé in a city ruled by the Virgin Mary's godson, after all, would surely have been an attractive option to some of the other Catholic priests in revolutionary Saint-Domingue, but evidently not for Menetrier. The curé was on hand in Léogâne to perform one baptismal rite on January 1 and two more on the 2nd. However, the following day he crossed out all three entries in the registry, declaring "all acts nullified. *End of register.*" It was a perplexingly troublesome decision, to be sure, one that suggests that Father Menetrier might have seen an opportunity to flee occupied Léogâne and he seized it. It is unknown what became of him beyond that and, in any case, there are no extant parish records for Léogâne for either 1792 or 1793.

Thus, one may situate Père Menetrier at the middle of the Catholic clerical spectrum in revolutionary Saint-Domingue, neutrally placed between the violent radicalism of Abbé Philémon and Abbé Aubert and the racist conservatism of Père Bloüet. And just where, we may now ask, should one locate Abbé Ouvière on this spectrum? It is to this important question that our attention now turns.

6

The Priest, the Prophetess, and the Fall of Trou Coffy

Bel dan pa di zanmi; dan pa kè.

—HAITIAN PROVERB[1]

Overview

THIS CHAPTER CONCERNS itself chiefly with the question of the relationship between Abbé Ouvière and Romaine Rivière, the priest and the prophetess, and with the eventual fall of the Trou Coffy insurgency, purporting to answer the following questions: What was the nature of this relationship? What motivated each man to seek the other out? What was the priest's role in the Trou Coffy insurgency? What distinguishes Abbé Ouvière's connection to Trou Coffy from the connections of other Catholic priests to other insurgent camps during the outbreak of the Haitian Revolution? How and why were the prophetess and his Trou Coffy rebellion ultimately defeated?

The great Haitian scholar who in a single sentence inspired this entire book, Jean Fouchard, is one of only two historians to have thus far commented on the relationship between the priest and the prophetess, between Abbé Ouvière and Romaine Rivière, albeit briefly, and he is correct in stating that the priest served the prophetess as "his advisor."[2] In this capacity, the priest's relationship to the prophetess was similar to that of Abbé Delahaye to Jean-François in Dondon. Also like Delahaye, Ouvière was a scientist and a naturalist who would leave to the world publications on his research, as we'll see in Chapter 8. Like Abbé Bienvenu, the curé of Marmelade who found himself amongst the rebels in Dondon, meanwhile, Ouvière was sent by local elites to negotiate with insurgents, whereas all the other priests profiled in the previous chapter were already among the rebels or surrounded by them when the respective insurrections broke out, and they remained in the camps either of their own accord or they were forced to do so. But, the similarities end there.

The other priests, Fathers Philémon, Cachetan, Bienvenu, Delahaye, Aubert, Blacé, Bloüet, and Menetrier, were not newcomers to Saint-Domingue when the 1791 insurrections exploded in the colony, as they were each serving as local curés, except perhaps for Aubert, as the calamitous events spilled into their parishes and swept their parishioners into the vortex of revolution. Their spiritual and material ties to their respective parishes would go far in shaping their particular affiliations with the insurgencies, while their respective political ideologies would determine which cause or causes they would advocate or even take up arms for, and in some cases die for.

Abbé Ouvière had no parish in Saint-Domingue. Furthermore, he had few connections in the colony, but the ones that he did have were very powerful and placed him, too, at the heart of an insurgent camp, the most notorious in the West Province in 1791–1792, Trou Coffy. Both in person and in correspondence with Romaine, the priest clearly served the prophetess as a trusted adviser, a trust that was rooted largely in his station as a Catholic priest. That, however, is only part of the story, and his underlying motives come to light through a careful analysis of one of his letters from 1792 and an 1821 memoir that he wrote about his experience at Trou Coffy: Though the priest and the prophetess were each abolitionists in their particular ways, their brief time together in Trou Coffy was not in the least a summit to promote the liberation of the slaves of Saint-Domingue; rather, it was a religiously inflected political entente aimed at resolving the spectacular crisis of violence and anarchy in and around Léogâne. This chapter explains the events that led to the priest's visit with the prophetess in Trou Coffy in December of 1791; the objectives of his mission as a representative of the Confederates headquartered in Croix-des-Bouquets; and the terms of the treaty that he presented to Romaine, the treaty that placed the Virgin Mary's godson in formal control over Léogâne and all of its residents, whites, blacks, and mulattoes, free and enslaved alike.

Abbé Ouvière as Conciliatory Commissioner

To recall, the priest had arrived in Saint-Domingue by the summer of 1790. Being related to André Rigaud and having gotten to know the future Creole general during his studies in France,[3] Ouvière had ties to leading absentee free colored elites in Paris, like Julien Raimond,[4] and he may well have been sent to Saint-Domingue by Raimond himself.[5] The priest made short work of operationalizing these connections to take on a number of important roles in the free colored civil rights movement, which, as we've seen, was then mushrooming into an all-out civil war. Soon after this movement formed a Confederacy and elected Pierre Pinchinat as its president, in August of 1791, and mustered a "combined army" of some 4,000 mulattoes and free blacks from throughout the South and West Provinces (hence the moniker "combined"), Ouvière became a member of its "advisory war council."[6] This context is key to understanding his relationship to Romaine-la-Prophétesse, a relationship that Ouvière cultivated on behalf of Pierre Pinchinat, André Rigaud, and the "United Citizens" of the Confederacy toward achieving their immediate aims of neutralizing Trou Coffy and their broader political objectives of securing full civil rights in Saint-Domingue for free coloreds.

Shortly after the horrific November 1791 massacre of free coloreds in Port-au-Prince, two men, "one white and the other a man of color," arrived in Croix-des-Bouquets "on behalf of the citizens of Leogane to explain the frightful situation in their region and to ask for help," bringing with them dreadful tales of "pillage and murders" committed by the "brigands who gathered in the high elevations in a land called Trou Coffy." Romaine's followers had simply run rough shod over the surrounding area and effectively seized the city, forcing "the citizens" to provide them with "massive amounts of money, food, and munitions of war, and they had also kidnapped a few respectable citizens." The insurgents also emptied the local prison of their allies, barred anyone from leaving the city, and "established a garrison" in town.[7]

The Confederate leaders in Croix-des-Bouquets debated what to do about the unruly Trou Coffy insurgency, meanwhile, and two plans were proposed. The first called for the "entire evacuation, women, children and movable possessions, from the city," with some of the evacuees to take refuge in Croix-des-Bouquets and others on ships anchored offshore at Port-au-Prince. The second "proposed the partial uprising of as many slaves as necessary for defeating Romaine's troops," which in retrospect could have been altogether disastrous had it been implemented. While the various "committees" were deliberating these matters, Abbé Ouvière devised his own plan, "along with the measures" that the priest "had already taken for assuring its success." In short order, his plan was "unanimously approved," and Ouvière was given the title of *commissaire conciliateur* and formally tasked with the mission of traveling to Léogâne "to bring forth the reestablishment of public tranquility in the name of the United Citizens and by the authority of their permanent council."[8]

The priest wrote to Rigaud of his proposed mission and, understanding that Romaine greatly respected the general, offered to serve him as "the bearer either of his orders or of his prayers to General Romaine in order to bring about a better order of things."[9] As soon as Rigaud's approval of the plan reached Croix-des-Bouquets, it was launched, and on the night of December 22 the priest departed for Léogâne with an escort and with Pinchinat's blessing "to reestablish the tranquility" there. For his part, Rigaud was especially

FIGURE 6.1 The leading military officer of the free colored Confederacy, and a relative of Abbé Ouvière, André Rigaud was the conduit that brought the priest and the prophetess together. Portrait of André Rigaud. 1914. Courtesy of the New York Public Library.

concerned that the Trou Coffy insurgency would soon spread to the South Province, his native region, which likely amplified in his mind the need to act soon and with urgency;[10] in relation, Romaine's title of "commander general" was not self-assumed but had been bestowed upon him by Rigaud in an effort to mollify the Virgin Mary's godson. To the extent that Trou Coffy never launched excursions into the South Province, which Rigaud thus managed to preserve "in the most perfect tranquility," Rigaud's diplomatic efforts to contain Romaine's influence in the West were successful.[11] In any case, all of this clearly reflects the faith that Rigaud had in Ouvière, which Pinchinat then obviously shared.

Abbé Ouvière thus left the relatively safe confines of Croix-des-Bouquets just two days after he had delivered an impassioned sermon to the Confederate Army there.[12] Clearly this was a most perilous journey, but the priest was confident that in the event of trouble or uncertainty he could turn to Rigaud, who "could help me infinitely in this occasion with his advice and could become my safeguard when it came to the redoubtable Romaine," and who provided Ouvière with a get-out-of-jail-free card in the form of "a personal letter for my personal protection as his relative and his friend, for whom he himself assumed responsibility."[13] Though the distance between Croix-des-Bouquets and Léogâne is just more than 32 miles, it took the priest's party two days to get there "because of the secret routes that it was necessary to take."[14] It is unclear how many people accompanied Ouvière on this hazardous journey, but one presumes that he would have enjoyed the protection of at least a small armed escort.

Once arrived on scene in Léogâne, Abbé Ouvière was "struck with shock" by "an air of pain and consternation among all of the white men there." The priest was well received by the beleaguered townsfolk, though they must have been dismayed to learn that the Confederates "had neither a single man nor a single bayonet to give them."[15] He was also alarmed to see that "[f]ew citizens would go out into the streets, where Romaine's brigands rode about on their horses, acting as if they were the police there." With the priest being their only hope, they, the leading white and free colored citizens of Léogâne, embraced Abbé Ouvière in confidence and told him everything that he needed to know to take the next step in his mission:

> I spent the entire day listening to painful stories of disastrous scenes that went on and on, on the plain and in the hills.... After having applied myself toward knowing the true causes, after having interrogated many wise persons, among the citizens of colors of the city, I readily discovered that all of this disorder emerged primarily out of an unfortunate division that existed between the reunited citizens of Léogâne and the men of color camped at Trou Cophy, in the *dependance* of this very parish.[16]

The plucky priest's next step was to meet with the notorious prophetess in person.

The Christmas Treaty at Trou Coffy

From the moment when he heard the plaints of the planters and townsfolk of Léogâne, it was clear to Abbé Ouvière that any effort to bring peace to the region would require meeting and negotiating with Romaine-la-Prophétesse. Toward this end, he was introduced to the prophetess' son-in-law, Soliment, whom he asked to take a letter to Trou Coffy requesting permission to visit the infamous insurgent camp, which by then had long been "rendered inaccessible by terror," and to arrange for him to meet with the prophetess in person. In two sentences of a letter in which the priest describes his subsequent mission to Trou Coffy are revealed his true intentions in visiting the insurgent camp, as well as his true opinion of the prophetess: "I took care to announce my departure for Trou Cophy and above all to promise to solemnize the feast of Christmas by the celebration of Mass. This circumstance had to be of some advantage with a Spaniard passionately devoted to the cult and to his charades."[17] Abbé Ouvière thus exploited Romaine's religious devotion and invested his own religious capital as a Catholic priest to gain the prophetess' trust and to gain entry into Trou Coffy and personal access to one of the most feared insurgent leaders of the 1791–1792 insurrections that sparked the Haitian Revolution.[18] In this sense, his strategy was somewhat like that which Abbé Bienvenu had employed in his visit to Dondon, though Ouvière did so under the cover of Christmas, and whereas Bienvenu was quickly suspected by the insurgents as being a spy and taken into custody, Ouvière would be warmly welcomed in Trou Coffy.[19] It also helped, of course, that he carried a letter of introduction from General Rigaud.

Soliment delivered the priest's letter to Romaine and quickly returned to Léogâne with his father-in-law's reply in writing, which I translate here in full:

> Camp of Trou Coffy 24 December 1791
>
> Monsieur Labbée
>
> We receive with much pleasure your letter of the 23rd of this month and [would be] even more charmed when we can see you in person which will be nothing but advantageous to that which we hope for, by the trust that we have, and that we will place in you. In advance, you may count on our inviolable attachment to the love of country, to our union and to order.
>
> To this effect, we have addressed a letter to sir Reverend father menetrier of the parish of St. Rose of Leogane to acquire for you all that will be necessary to you, all that you will need for the Holy Sacrifice of the celebration of tomorrow's Holy Mass.
>
> We all salute you, and we have the honor, Sir Father, to be your very humble and very faithful parishioner,
>
> Romaine Rivière
> the Prophetess
> and
> Elie
> Colonel General[20]

Thus, while Romaine had dispatched emissaries to Léogâne to request that Father Menetrier provide sacred vessels from the St. Rose de Lima Church in order for Christmas Mass to be said at Trou Coffy, he also sent Soliment

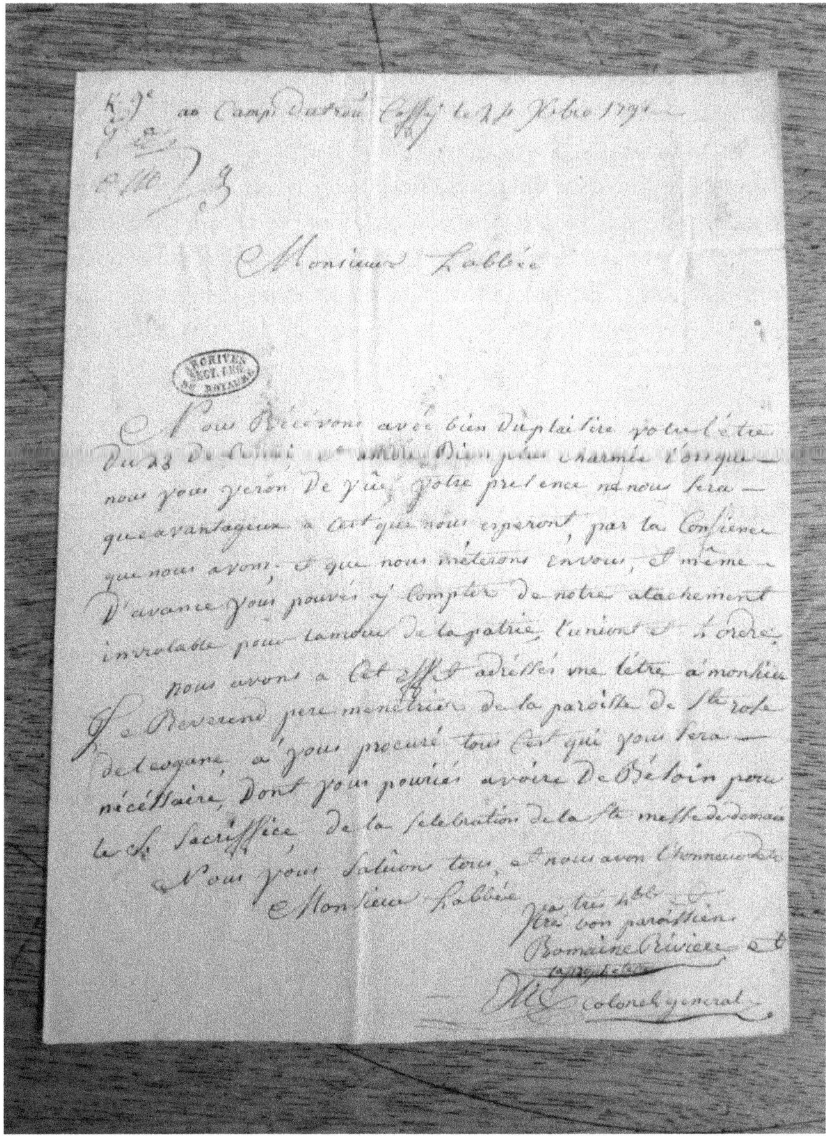

au Camp du trou Coffy le 24 Xbre 1791

Monsieur Labbée

Nous Recevons avec bien du plaisire votre lettre du 23 de [illegible] nous charmés lorsque nous vous verons de yeux, votre presence ne nous sera que avantageux a cet que nous esperons, par la Confience que nous avons, et que nous meterons en vous, et même d'avance vous pouvés y compter de notre atachement inviolable pour lamour de la patrie, l'unions et l'ordre.

nous avons a cet effet adréssés une lettre a monsieur le Reverend pere menetrier de la paroisse de Ste rose de Leogane, a vous procuré tous cet qui vous sera necéssaire, dont vous pouriés avoire de besoin pour le St Sacriffice de la celebration de la Ste messe de demain

Nous vous saluons tous, et nous avons l'honneur d'etre

Monsieur Labbée

vos tres humb[illegible]
tres bon paroissien
Romaine Riviere et
[illegible]
colonel general

FIGURE 6.2 A letter from Romaine-la-Prophétesse to Abbé Ouvière dated December 24, 1791, indicating that the prophetess had obtained ritual paraphernalia for the priest to say Mass during his pending visit to Trou Coffy. Courtesy of les Archives Nationales de France, La Bibliothèque Nationale de France.

to present his letter to Abbé Ouvière and instructed his son-in-law to escort the priest to Trou Coffy that same day. It was a flurry of activity, reflecting an obvious excitement among the prophetess and his followers over Ouvière's imminent arrival, as well as the desperate hope among Léogâne's planters and townsfolk that *monsieur l'abbé* could somehow perform a miracle of peace.

Surely with much enthusiasm, Romaine-la-Prophétesse expected Abbé Ouvière to say Christmas Mass at Trou Coffy, and he hastened to arrange that everything be provided for the priest so that he might indeed preside over "the Holy Sacrifice." Both his response to the priest's letter asking permission to visit Romaine's insurgent camp and the priest's initial letter to the Confederates in Croix-des-Bouquets after their entente unambiguously indicate that Ouvière had indeed promised to do so. In his 1821 memoir, however, Abbé Ouvière—as Doctor Felix Pascalis—claimed that it was the idea of the curé of Léogâne, Father Menetrier, that he wear vestments during his trip to Trou Coffy, but that he was actually offended by the suggestion and thus refused:

> The parish priest strongly encouraged me to employ the sacerdotal function in my approaching expedition and that he would wash the robes and vestments for me; this way I could be assured of greater respect among the brigands and from Romaine.... [But] I did not believe that I had any need at all of an act worthy of an imposter in order to accomplish the good that I had hoped to do.... *Monsieur le Curé* seemed satisfied and excused himself for the inappropriateness of his proposal.[21]

Ouvière's 1791 letter and his 1821 memoir thus clearly contradict one another concerning the question as to whether he in fact said Christmas Mass at Trou Coffy, though neither document offers conclusive evidence either way. The memoir should be read with a hermeneutic of suspicion, however, as it was written three decades after the fact and under the duress of having been accused of not only aiding Romaine-la-Prophétesse but also of ordering the massacres of French citizens and the mutilation of white corpses on the prophetess' behalf, so there were surely more than a few details that Abbé Ouvière would have wanted to leave out of the document. In all likelihood, the priest did say the Christmas Mass at Trou Coffy; after all, to promise Romaine that he would do so and then to renege on that promise would have gravely imperiled his entire mission.

Whether or not the priest was dressed in clerical garb, with "a large escort,"[22] Abbé Ouvière and Soliment set out for Trou Coffy on horseback "at 5:00 on Christmas Eve [1791] . . . in a procession through lines of mountains . . . about 20 miles away," reaching the camp "by midnight or 1:00 in the morning." The backdrop could not have been more dramatic, nor the journey more perilous: "We were shrouded in a thick cloud as thousands of thunderbolts streaked at every instant, threatening us with torrents of rain that could well have thrown us down to the deep valleys below."[23] But the torrents spared the priest and his escort, no one was cast into an abyss, and the party made it to Trou Coffy without further incident.

Upon their arrival at the edge of the camp, Abbé Ouvière and company were met by "an avant-garde of six men commanded by a new lieutenant-general . . . a soudan."[24] With Soliment at his side, the priest was guided to his lodging, where "[a] twenty-one gun salute [*salves de mousqueterie*] honored my entry into a large house that looked to me like a colony in which women and children alone constituted a very large population."[25] Once settled into the "sparsely furnished" room that he would share with Soliment, Ouvière asked to be taken directly to meet the prophetess, but this request was initially denied, for Romaine was "at prayer in the chapel in commemoration of the birth of the Savior."[26] Abbé Ouvière persisted:

> I responded to Soliman that recollections of Christmas Eve were deeply engraved in my memory and that from a young age, in my father's family I had been raised in the cult and religious sentiments that worship inspires, and besides, I believed that we only managed to escape certain dangers on our trip but by the watchful eye of Providence and so I would like to go straight away to tender my humble confessions to the Supreme Being, sole commander of the destinies of men.[27]

It worked. Though reluctant, Soliment led the priest to the "superbly illuminated" chapel, where they found a number of people, more women than men, at prayer with Romaine, who was "superbly dressed and kneeling before a kind of altar." The prophetess soon got up and took the priest by the hand to welcome him to Trou Coffy, promising a meeting at noon on the morrow. This was the first time that the priest and the prophetess actually encountered one another in person, and the two men spoke in Spanish, on Abbé Ouvière's initiative. As the priest would later recall in his memoir:

> I have already said that Romaine was Spanish and that it was in my situation quite well that I address him in that language, which was by then very familiar to me and in which I could exchange some observations

> without offending him and which could hint to me his dispositions toward me.

After this brief exchange between the priest and the prophetess in Romaine's sanctuary, Soliment and Ouvière retreated to their room for the night, evidently in a nearby large house, though not in the *grande caze,* which the priest never had the chance to enter. The prophetess, meanwhile, returned to his nocturnal yuletide prayers.[28]

One can well imagine the emotions that gripped Abbé Ouvière when he awoke on Christmas morning 1791 in Trou Coffy. Surely he was relieved that the prophetess had greeted him cordially the night before, and he must have been animated by thoughts of the task that lay before him—to negotiate with Romaine-la-Prophétesse in person. With time to kill before his noon meeting with the prophetess, the priest told Soliment that he wanted "to take some air," and thus the two roommates went for a walk about the camp. Along their way, Ouvière "encountered between the camp's huts and around Romaine's residence a number of whites wandering about there who appeared to glance at me with expressions of distress, and Soliman informed me that they were some of his father's prisoners." In explaining this to the priest, Soliment "appeared to be most laconic and ashamed."[29] Though later in life the priest would forget (and perhaps change) certain details about his time in Trou Coffy, the looks on the prisoners' faces would ever remain etched in his memory:

> Oh, how I regretted not being able to respond to their glances, to signal that I could soon deliver them from their suffering and from their terror, and thus they had perhaps indeed lost the hope of being delivered from the evils in which they could say, as in Dante's inferno, *"O voi ch'intrate Lasciate ogne speranza."*[30]

Following their stroll, the priest and Soliment were treated to "a robust breakfast," after which Abbé Ouvière passed the rest of the morning doing a bit of writing. Then noon struck, and he "was imperiously summoned to Romaine's chapel." The priest might have been expecting a warmer greeting there:

> He stood before a table on which he had two pistols, holding a long saber in his hand, with which he seemed to be saluting me. Brandishing it, he directed me to a place before him.... Besides him were aligned some eight to ten black or colored officers, and many others appeared armed surrounding the chapel.... First he spoke somewhat angrily of the mistreatment to which the colony's whites always subjected his

> people of color. This obliged him to offer himself as their leader for their protection.[31]

Standing before the slightly agitated, saber-rattling prophetess and surrounded by his armed guards, the priest took care to "limit myself to speaking only of the object of my mission and express myself in ways to inspire trust, and to make clear the reasons and benefits" thereof.[32] Invoking the name of Romaine's "friend, General Rigaud," and reassuring the prophetess that he had been sent to Trou Coffy "as delegate of the General Council of Croix-des-Bouquets," the priest galvanized anew the prophetess' trust in him and outlined the following terms of the treaty:

> [T]hat the residents of the town of Léogâne commit themselves to peace, to forgetting the past, and to the works of agriculture on the condition that General Romaine's forces would be considered the national guards of the Parish under the authority and orders of the military commander of the city; that they recognize the orders of the latter without taking themselves to be the city police; that all of the initial measures taken by General Romaine for maintaining order and peace on the plantations be legal as long as he answers to the commander and that he release from his camp and commit to the authority of laws every slave or maroon and then liberate the prisoners that he had held in the city prison or anywhere else without any opposition to the ordinary legal process; and finally that otherwise the Parish would provide . . . food, munitions, and uniforms, as well as the wholesale surveillance of the region; that all of Romaine's prisoners would be freed; that all of the past wrongs be forgotten; and that the general could in the name of his assembled troops send a representative to the General Council of Croix des Bouquets . . . that the jurisdiction of General Romaine was a recognized fact, equal to that of the military commander of the parish; no act of his armed forces could be tired other than by a military court that he himself would form.[33]

It is not entirely clear whether the treaty, for all the power that it tendered to the prophetess, intended to place Romaine, "as military commander of the parish," under the authority of a Confederate-appointed "military commander of the city." This question is somewhat immaterial, though, in light of the fact that none of his troops could be subjected to judgment before any "military court" other than one that the prophetess would himself assemble. And though a couple of Romaine's officers, "doubtless the most criminal" among the "marauding brigands," objected to certain provisions in the treaty, the prophetess pulled rank and accepted them all. Interestingly, the priest would later note that Romaine himself "signed" the document "rather graciously," though notarial and parish records uniformly indicate that "Romain Riviere" was unable to write or even to sign his name. As for the treaty itslelf, save for Ouvière's detailed recollections thereof, it seems to have been lost to history; I have uncovered no extant copy, at any rate.

Having thus met the "difficult challenge" of visiting Trou Coffy and gaining the prophetess' acceptance of the terms of his treaty, and marveling at how quickly it was achieved, Ouvière "felt perfectly happy" and "completely out of danger." The priest was, furthermore, confident that Romaine, "though he was the leader of brigands, he would keep his word" and would be able to neutralize the most violent of his officers. For his part, Soliment "expressed a great deal of joy at all that had just happened." The priest hoped he would be able to share supper that evening with the prophetess, but Soliment indicated that Romaine never dined with anyone besides his wife and children. So, the abbé took the time to write a letter to Rigaud to "inform him of the success of my mission under the auspices of his good recommendation," and later he visited with a "mulatto neighbor," one known as "a respectable man," accompanied by Soliment.

Before departing Trou Coffy for good the next day, after "a rushed breakfast," the priest went to say goodbye to the prophetess at the door of his *grande caze*. "He was in the same outfit that I have already described, he touched my hand, tracing with his finger the cross of salutation in the Catholic style of the Spaniards; he wished me much happiness and assured me that he was not as bad a man as people had made him out to be."[34] Abbé Ouvière then bid farewell to Romaine-la-Prophétesse and came down from the mountain to present the Christmas treaty to the free citizens of Léogâne for ratification.

Aftermath of the Trou Coffy Treaty

This was a remarkable turn of events and the apogee of the Trou Coffy insurgency in the Léogâne theater. In addition to returning to Léogâne on December 28 or 29 with 22 liberated prisoners and getting about 200 of Romaine's troops to lay down their arms,[35] Ouvière brought with him important military intelligence that was surely to be employed in Saint-Léger's ensuing raid of Trou Coffy in March of 1792, which is described below; he offered, for instance, that "2000 men would not suffice to form a cordon on the hills that surrounded" the insurgent camp,[36] and boasted that despite being taken to Trou Coffy on a circuitous route to confuse him, he could nonetheless recall how to get there.[37] And, of course, the priest brought with him the terms of the treaty that he had negotiated with the prophetess. His return to Léogâne was altogether triumphant:

> Several miles from the town, I was greeted by a number of citizens who had learned of the success of my mission and who had come to meet me, and who the delay of a single day had already rendered anxious. Among them I soon had the pleasure to recognize Monsieur de Viller [de Villards], who actually burst into tears of joy; the closer we got, the larger my escort increased in number and became altogether glorious, right up to the house of Monsieur Gaviche, from which I had departed four days earlier. Soon some musicians were at the door to play a beautiful serenade that went on late into the night.[38]

Though Abbé Ouvière had been well treated in the prophetess' lair at Trou Coffy, he returned to Léogâne exhausted from both the journey and the drama of his negotiations with Romaine. The priest reveled in his reception as a hero:

> I went to rest where there stood a table sumptuously covered with everything that one could want and with gifts that had been sent to me from all over, and nearby there was a hot bath, and finally a bed in which I could sleep with the idea and the sentiment of happiness beyond expression.[39]

The careworn residents of the city and the region's remaining planters probably saw no option but to agree to the terms and accept the treaty, and on the last day of 1791 Abbé Ouvière read it aloud and they signed it in the presence of "four of Romaine's officers."[40] To mark the solemnity of the occasion, on the following day Mass was said at the Church of St. Rose de Lima, with Abbé Ouvière delivering the homily. There is no evidence that Romaine was in attendance, and it seems that during the entire insurgency he may have never left Trou Coffy, though many of his followers were in the pews that morning. In an act that Romaine surely would never have impelled, and perhaps demonstrating that the prophetess was not entirely in control of his charges, the priest's "good sermon" was interrupted when a "horde of armed men" loyal to Romaine, "who really needed to hear it," stormed the church. No one in attendance was physically attacked, though, and whites in the city were deeply grateful to the priest for having "inspired peace and reunion," as one citizen put it.[41] With his mission as *commissaire conciliateur* having been accomplished, the priest soon returned to Croix-des-Bouquets. Romaine-la-Prophétesse was now at the peak of his powers, and he and Elie Courlogne wrote to Abbé Ouvière a thank you note ebullient in its praise: "Monsieur l'abbée [*sic*] your virtue, your talents, will always merit for you in the eyes of men the praise merited by a man who is worthy of the public trust."[42]

News of the treaty between the municipality of Léogâne and Romaine-la-Prophétesse quickly spread throughout the colony. Free colored leaders in Aquin, in the South Province, for instance, wrote to Abbé Ouvière on January 3, 1792, to congratulate him for his successful efforts "for the good cause of the law" and to invite the priest to serve as their liaison to the Confederate leadership in Croix-des-Bouquets.[43] Two days earlier another correspondent, a planter named Richallet, wrote of having heard news of the treaty from Léogâne residents then taking refuge in Port-au-Prince, and reported that they were "overjoyed" with his work as conciliatory commissioner and that heaven smiled upon the priest: "should the Divinity find our wishes worthy, you will enjoy perfect prosperity" and have "all that you desire." Richallet added that the citizens of Jacmel also displayed "veneration" for the priest and praised him for the "talent" and "zeal that you employed . . . to fulfill the title of a true conciliator."[44] A few days after the priest had returned to Croix-des-Bouquets, Mayor de Villards wrote a word of gratitude from Léogâne "for the peace that you have given us. . . . Thanks to you, we are happy."[45] Soon the mayor again wrote to the priest to implore him to return to Léogâne to become the city's "patron," while another resident did the same, saluting Ouvière as the city's "titular angel."[46]

Far from sharing in such heady elation over Abbé Ouvière's diplomatic triumph, however, Confederate leaders in Croix-des-Bouquets received the news from Léogâne with shock and outrage, as the treaty with Romaine "filled our hearts with consternation and despair." Ouvière had written to Pinchinat about the treaty on December 28, and the next day a copy of the terms reached Croix-des-Bouquets. An incensed Pinchinat wrote an urgent reply to the priest on December 30, lambasting him for overstepping the boundaries of his mission and desperately imploring him to undo what he had done:

> You were charged with reestablishing the calm and the tranquility in the quarter of Leogane. You could do so without making a concordat. Your mission having nothing left to fulfill, I implore you in the name of everything that is most Sacred to return at once to Croix de Bouquets. I implore you above all to not communicate with anyone about the project you have sent to us. In case you have given any knowledge to someone, you must employ all means within your power to destroy the impressions that this would produce. If your plan would be carried

> out, it is from then on that we could say that you have been, without knowing it, the cause of all of our misfortune. I arduously desire your return.[47]

Mortified by the treaty, surely in part because it put a "fanatical" black immigrant in charge of one of Saint-Domingue's most important cities and surrounding fertile plain, an immigrant who had theretofore proven difficult to manage and bring into the Confederate fold, Pinchinat even considered concealing it from his advisory council. But had he possessed any hopes that his letter of December 30 might reach Abbé Ouvière in Léogâne early enough for the treaty's ratification to be aborted, they were dashed the very next day when it was signed by Villards and other Léogâne dignitaries in the presence of the priest and four of the prophetess' delegates from Trou Coffy.

Although it wouldn't last long, for the first time since August peace did descend upon occupied Léogâne following its civic leaders' signing of the Christmas treaty with Romaine-la-Prophétesse. With their surrounding plantations now mostly in ruins, cautiously relieved local white residents heaped praise upon Abbé Ouvière for having achieved his goal of "tranquilizing" the region, but the terms of the treaty were unlikely to hold in his absence. A few days after its signing,[48] the priest returned to Croix-des-Bouquets, whence he remained in frequent contact via written correspondence with Villards, Léogâne's mayor, and the others he had left behind, including Romaine and Elie. On January 13, for instance, the priest wrote a letter to the prophetess concerning the mission of the national civil commissioners. Perhaps because Romaine was sick at the time, Elie alone responded that they were "waiting with impatience the arrival of the national civil commissioners, being equally well persuaded of their intention, with the sentiments for the public good." Included in this letter were bits of news about events in and around Léogâne and Jacmel since the priest's departure and the assurance that "Monsieur Romaine and his son-in-law [Soliment] embrace you with all their heart."[49]

The priest followed up with another letter on January 21, and the prophetess' response of five days later reflected his enduring trust in Abbé Ouvière: "I remain with inviolable attachment, assuring you of my sincere friendship, wishing you perfect health." The prophetess had evidently been ill but notes, "my health has begun to improve, thanks to the Lord." He adds, "Messieurs Elie et Soliment are well and miss you. They express to you their sincere attachment." Romaine signed off as "Your most humble and obedient servant, Romaine Riviere, prophetess, commander general." Written in the hope that their efforts would "save for France" and "our monarch" their "flourishing island," the letter also carried a promise to fully cooperate with the commissioners upon their arrival in Léogâne.[50]

The Fall of Trou Coffy

Romaine-la-Prophétesse would continue to reign over the city and plain of Léogâne until mid-March 1792. But the fate of his movement was pretty much sealed when he began losing control over his troops and when the region's free colored elite, many of whom had never really embraced him in the first place, would "come to regret their initial alliance with this self-styled prophet and religious zealot, whose reign of terror had gone beyond their control and now merely cast discredit upon their cause."[51] Thus they turned on the prophetess and collaborated with Commissaire National Edmond de Saint-Léger in his campaign "to divide, to neutralize, and to extinguish the fanatical gathering at Trou Coffi."[52] A man described by one of his French contemporaries as being "not in the least initiated into the cult of negrophilia,"[53] Saint-Léger left Port-au-Prince on March 6 for Léogâne, making several stops along the way and eventually arriving before dawn on the morning of the 12th by sea aboard *La Galathée.*[54] Although spurned in Port-au-Prince by potential recruits for his mission, many of the *gens de couleur* in the city of Léogâne and others from Grand Goâve would join the French commander in confronting Trou Coffy, along with the 100 troops from Croix-des-Bouquets that Pinchinat had commissioned to Saint-Léger, who brought with them some cannons. Sailors from from *La Galathée* would also participate in the offensive against Trou Coffy, along with a battalion of local free coloreds under the leadership of a young mulatto named Guy-Joseph Bonnet, who had "cried tears of blood over the deaths of Ogé and Chavannes."[55] Saint-Léger also appointed Bonnet to command his honor guard.[56]

Because it is by far the most detailed account of the fall of Trou Coffy, I summarize at length here the relevant passages from Saint-Léger's own report on his mission, whose objectives were to "enforce the decree of February 11, 1791, maintain order and public tranquility, to ensure that the national will is respected, and to assure, under the shade of peace, the prosperity of one of the richest parts of the empire."[57] Furthermore, the commissioner "endeavored to promote peace accords, and to arrange for the safety of everyone by restoring the rule of law in the West province, where the situation was even more distressing, marked just about everywhere by murder, pillage, and arson."[58] Successful slave uprisings in Jacmel had "rallied" other slaves who had been "imprudently" armed by their masters for their own self-defense, furthermore, drawing ever more numbers—and weapons—into the rebellion. Being "exposed on all sides," Léogâne was especially defenseless, and by November 1791 the whites had been "disarmed by the *hommes de couleurs*, and lived in a constants state of alarm."[59] Of course, so much of this alarm was caused by Romaine-la-Prophétesse:

> Above the Plain of Léogâne, there had been formed a formidable gathering comprised almost entirely of slaves who had been seduced or taken from their plantations . . . they had been moved by the wishes of a Spanish *griffe* named *Romaine*. This leader, allying fanaticism with ferocity and ignorance, gave himself the ridiculous title of prophetess, called himself the godson of the Virgin, melding pious ceremonies to the *ordres de sang* that he made them execute. It was in the name of Heaven that he ordered murder and pillage; it was through the cachet of crude superstition that he ruled over these unfortunate slaves, as gullible as they are ignorant. In promising them freedom and certain victory over the whites, and assuring them that they would be sheltered from their attacks, he stirs them up to commit atrocities, the recounting of which is glazed with horror.[60]

As already noted, the relentless raids on Léogâne orchestrated through "the audacity of Romaine and his cruel mignons" probably left the city residents with little choice but to sign the Christmas treaty with the prophetess, in which "the fanatical leader was recognized as the commander of the reunited residents of Léogâne" whose "tyrannical orders they had to obey without complaining."[61] The *hommes de couleur* were of divided opinion, some siding with the whites, others secretly allied with Romaine and "always ready to help execute his deceitful plans."[62] In the midst of such "cruel extremities,"[63] Léogâne was left to fend for itself, with no more ships arriving from France or American or Caribbean ports. The situation was one of total lawlessness and destruction. Saint-Léger would first try to restore order and the rule of law through diplomacy, which had been successful in other parts of the West Province, as "delegations from Grand Goave and Petit Goave, and from Bayenette [Bainet] and other nearby parishes came in the name of their fellow citizens to pledge their absolute submission to the rule of law." "Shocked" to learn that Saint-Léger had so quickly managed to muster considerable forces,[64] Romaine sent Elie to lead a delegation from Trou Coffy to negotiate with the commissioner in Léogâne:

> One delegate came to me from Trou-Coffi, the place where *Romaine* was camped out. Elie Courlogne, *his colonel général*, assured me that henceforth

> all of Romaine's efforts and his own efforts would go toward reestablishing order. Fearful of inciting the fierce nature of this villain and his cruel companions were I to mention the horror that their crimes instilled in me, I resisted, endeavoring instead to engage him with sweet talk to lay down their weapons and make all the slaves return to their work.

The result of the Elie-Saint-Léger summit was an agreement "to make the slaves return to the homesteads of their masters within three days."[65] In a separate letter to the mayor of Léogâne, Saint-Léger indicated that Elie had come with a treaty already prepared in writing, "a pact to no longer act against the law" and a promise to instruct all the maroons among them to "return to their duties" as slaves.[66]

Elie and Romaine had no intention of honoring the agreement, however. Instead, they hoped that it would lull Saint-Léger into a false sense of security, and they tried to catch the French civil commissioner with his guard down. "We were waiting for the three days accorded to *Romaine* and Elie to pass and had pinned our hopes on seeing peace restored to the area; but the most dreadful event occurred to crush those hopes for good. A troop of blacks descended from Trou Coffi, taking the city by surprise the night of 11/12 March";[67] more precisely according to another account, on "the 12th, at about 4 o'clock in the morning, their whole force entered the town of Leogane, and began to plunder and destroy," armed "mostly with sharpened sticks,"[68] descending from Trou Coffy "like a flood swollen by storms."[69] The insurgents quickly overpowered sentries and commandeered the cannons that had been stationed to defend the city. Allegedly they "slit the throats of many citizens and many *hommes de couleur* in their beds, and massacred others in the streets, broke into homes and pillaged them, and announced with deranged screams that they would spare no one."[70] Much of the city was also torched, according to Abbé Ouvière, "by rebelling blacks and by some whites."[71]

The valiant Saint-Léger fought back, summoning his troops to repel the insurgents and rallying local whites and free coloreds to join them in the frantic defense of the city. Bonnet was nearly killed in the attack, but a former slave of his father named Télémaque whisked him out of harm's way on "that fatal night" and delivered him to join in leading the defense side-by-side with Saint-Léger.[72] The commissioner's call to arms was answered by Romaine's enemies throughout the city, and they fought back with reported bravado:

> I exhorted all the citizens around me to march against the blacks who were gathered in the city plaza, and to do everything in their power to ward them off; my exhortations were successful: the 100 *hommes de*

> *couleur* advanced with a number of whites and with the *hommes de couleur* of Léogâne; combat ensued and the blacks, who were soon forced to flee, abandoned the center of the city and settled in to surround it, only to be soon repelled by the cannon fire from the ship.[73]

As the Trou Coffy insurgents retreated, the battle moved outside the city walls, and

> one party set off and began to set fire to the plain—the negroes immediately revolted and joined the Trou Caffee [*sic*] gang in great numbers, and continued fighting all day in the savannah out of town. . . . the 13th at 4 o'clock in the morning the enemy attacked the town again, but the town party repulsed them and killed great numbers.[74]

The swiftness with which the attack was repelled was rather surprising, leading Abbé Ouvière to report, with some measure of exaggeration, that Saint-Léger had "taken back the city in an instant."[75]

The March 11–13, 1792, assault on Léogâne was in effect a last-ditch effort by Romaine-la-Prophétesse to prolong his reign and to achieve his higher objectives of seeing through the will of the Virgin Mary, his godmother, by abolishing slavery and establishing some kind of kingdom on the island, perhaps with himself on the throne. Though by comparison with "the enemy," the force that Saint-Léger had hastily assembled to defend the city against the assault was outnumbered by at least ten to one, they were much better armed than the insurgents, whose homemade spears and torches were in the end no match for their opponents' cannons, muskets, sabers, and bayonets. Despite the fact that during the second day of the assault absconding slaves "joined the Trou Caffee gang in great numbers," they suffered devastating casualties, and with that, Romaine's religiously inspired insurgent movement would now be grounded even more quickly than it had taken flight in August of the previous year.

Evidently, many of Romaine's troops who had been repelled by the cannon fire from *La Galathée* never returned to Trou Coffy, where it seems that dissent had already been spreading. Some may have returned to the plantations on which they once had previously labored, though that is unlikely given the widespread destruction and the flight or death of most white planters. More likely, the Trou Coffy deserters joined the Confederate Army, settled in other insurgent camps, or embarked on lives of marronage, perhaps to be swept up as rebels anew in later stages of the Haitian Revolution. By one estimate, some 2,000 people were reported to have been killed during the battle, and 56 more plantations were torched by the retreating insurgents.[76]

Meanwhile, although the prophetess had lost the city of Léogâne and many of his followers, it remained for Saint-Léger to pursue Romaine himself and launch an assault on Trou Coffy:

> Léogâne had nothing left to fear from Trou-Coffi, which still remained: I thus enlisted the leaders of the *hommes de couleur* of Léogâne, and the commanders of the detachments from Grand Goave and Petit Goave to destroy it. Under the command of Singlar, a free black whose upright conduct merits distinguished praise. They set out with the four gunners from the ship against *Romaine*, broke up his camp, arrested his wife, his daughter, along with the one Boursicot, the most infamous *homme de couleur* who had massacred in the parish of Daynette [Bainet] 30 whites in a single day. They brought them to Léogâne, where I had them put on board a merchant ship to remain there as hostages for the security of the area. During the same expedition, once having seized weapons and shut down the cannons, the blacks were disarmed and sent back to their various plantations. I knew that they had only been misled [by Romaine], and I had prevented a massacre.[77]

Led by Singlar and another free black named Baptiste Boyer, Saint-Léger's detachment raided Trou Coffy on March 25 or 26. The detachment consisted of "foot soldiers and sailors from *La Galathée*, and reunited whites of Légoane, of Grand Goave, and of Petit Goave."[78] They stormed the insurgent camp from two sides, with one unit of troops "passing through the Formy plantation and the other passing through the Peyrot plantation." Considering how large and formidable that the Trou Coffy insurgency had been, it is remarkable how easily that it was, in the end, snuffed out. According to Antoine Dalmas, the rebels in fact dispersed as soon as they were attacked, and "[t]he post was taken without resistance."[79] A number of insurgents were arrested, while a bounty of 400 gourdes was placed on the head of a mulatto named Gros Poisson, who was considered to be "the chief lieutenant" at Trou Coffy. In an act of deception that outraged many in and around Léogâne, another mulatto named Lemaire, a friend of the fugitive, arranged to meet with Gros Poisson in confidence, only to stab and decapitate the insurgent officer, bringing the Big Fish's head to the city to collect his bounty.[80]

Ever intent on congratulating himself for his success and valor—and it should be affirmed that his efforts were indeed courageous and largely successful—Saint-Léger coyly left out one important detail from his *Rapport*: he failed to capture the prophetess. Though Romaine's wife and one of his children were arrested in Saint-Léger's raid on Trou Coffy, the prophetess escaped, abruptly disappearing from the historical record. By noon of March 25, Boyer and Singlar's battalion of some 400 men had "destroyed Trou Coffi, but Romaine escaped."[81] The earliest press account of Saint-Léger's raid on Trou Coffy, a letter dated April 12, 1792 (and likely authored by Abbé Ouvière) that was published in the *Mercure de France* six weeks before Saint-Léger delivered his own report, likewise indicates that Romaine indeed did escape:

> Léogâne was invaded by an eruption that M. *de St. Léger* fought off with the Gens de Couleur and with those from the frigate la *Galathée*. All of the buildings and vast cane fields had been burned down, giving the impression that all had been destroyed. The Chief of this enterprise, who distinguished himself by his cruelty, called himself *Romaine*; his residence was in trou Coffi, above Léogâne: he led his horde, composed of free blacks and slaves, pell mell, by superstition, to the most unspeakable lengths; he was indiscriminate, furthermore, with regard to age or sex; he mixed them all in his predictions. M. *de St. Léger* was nearly assassinated by one of his Emissaries, who may have come from further afield, an homme de couleur gave his life to save him, just like the Chevalier d'assas à Clostercamp. This very class refused the proposition of the Blacks of Romaine to unite with them to massacre the Whites; on the contrary, they marched in concert with the Whites to trou Coffi, which was sacked, along with a number of satellites of Romaine, who escaped, and who continues to preach his infernal doctrine. Prior to his departure, M. *de St. Léger* reestablished order among the Blacks of the plain.[82]

Noteworthy is that the success of Saint-Léger's campaign against Trou Coffy relied on part upon local *gens de couleurs* who had only recently supported Romaine, as Garran indicates: "These *hommes de couleur* of Léogâne and neighboring parishes were quite guilty or quite blind in their resentment toward the whites, in taking sides with this villain in turn consenting to his leadership ... atrocities worthy of cannibals."[83] As put more recently and soberly by Carolyn Fick, furthermore, Romaine "certainly represented a far left-wing fringe that would eventually jeopardize the credibility of his fellow confederates of Léogâne and Jacmel, who had formed an alliance with him, causing them later to break of their ties with Romaine."[84]

Romaine-la-Prophétesse was indeed in some respect representative of a "far left-wing fringe." He was, after all, an illiterate immigrant who claimed to receive messages from the Virgin Mary, his godmother. Although ethnically

Romaine was not Kongolese (though his parents certainly might have been, as surely were many of his followers), the prophetess both crafted his prophetic ministry and managed to silence his own defeat and his own death in rather Kongolese ways. In escaping pending execution during the Saint-Léger raid on Trou Coffy, the prophetess simply disappeared, much like the Kongolese insurgent leader in the North Province Makaya, and much like Kongolese prophets past and present have proven capable of doing, escaping certain death, like his godmother in ways reflective of the Catholic Doctrine of the Assumption.[85]

Conclusion

After all the triumph and destruction of the Trou Coffy insurgency, and despite all the confidence that the prophetess had in the priest, in the end Romaine-la-Prophétesse was betrayed by Abbé Ouvière as 1791 gave way to 1792, and the extraordinary Citoyen Rivière would indeed then disappear from the historical record. As for the extraordinary priest, soon after his betrayal of the prophetess he departed for France on the very ship that, as the Virgin Mary had prophesied, bombarded Romaine's troops in Léogâne, *La Galathée*, with the very man who defeated Trou Coffy, Edmond de Saint-Léger, and brought the prophetess's rule to an end. Far from the killing fields of Saint-Domingue, the two Frenchmen would dine together later that spring in Paris.[86]

Thus Abbé Ouvière and Romaine-la-Prophétesse were no match made in heaven, even though they respected one other and shared in the hope that peace and justice would ring and reign in Saint-Domingue and for all French citizens. Their brief union was prompted by the prophetess' violence and destruction and was realized through the priest's cunning and deceit. Echoes of the legacy of Jesuit subversion in Saint-Domingue do reverberate in the cliffs between Trou Coffy and Léogâne, which for a long time inculcated in me the belief that the story of the priest and the prophetess was at heart one of liberation theology and radical Catholic abolitionism. It may well have been for Romaine-la-Prophétesse, but not for Abbé Ouvière. That, like most other insurgent leaders in 1791, Romaine-la-Prophétesse coveted the presence of a Catholic priest in his camp, and that he was so "passionately devoted to the cult," ultimately contributed to his demise, on the contrary.

Just as the prophetess had warmly welcomed the royalist mayor of Léogâne, Villards, in the notoriously inaccessible and inhospitable Trou Coffy, so too did he trustingly receive Abbé Ouvière there, who in reality had no interest in genuinely collaborating with Romaine beyond his mission on behalf of the Confederacy to pacify the prophetess and his followers. The priest was merely exploiting the prophetess' ardent Catholic piety to gain his trust, and though Abbé Ouvière did deliver an entire city to the prophetess, he also covertly delivered dooming intelligence to Romaine's enemies. Admittedly, there is no clear evidence that Ouvière's description of Trou Coffy was used by the Saint-Léger detachment in its raid on the Romaine's camp, but one can hardly imagine that it would not have been, as the priest had previously been in contact with the national civil commissioner. Even if it wasn't, however, it is inescapable to perceive that the priest betrayed the prophetess, a man whom he would later denounce as "the Muhammad of Saint-Domingue" who preached an "infernal doctrine" and "did nothing for the public good."[87]

Abbé Ouvière's conception of "the public good" motivated his intriguing work in Saint-Domingue. He had left his homeland with a hopeful vision of the Saint-Domingue of the likes of Julien Raimond and André Rigaud—an emergent mixed-race elite who could genuinely contribute to the glorious French empire and then the ideals of the French Revolution. But the priest's commitments were ever undulating in the stormy seas of the revolutionary Atlantic world. Witnessing the November 1791 slaughter of mulattoes by whites in Port-au-Prince surely dampened the hopefulness of Ouvière's vision, however, and his visit to Trou Coffy and his meeting with Romaine-la-Prophétesse brought him close enough to the suffering of slavery and the divisiveness of class and race in Saint-Domingue to abandon all hope for the French colonialist project. Romaine was, after all, very different from the mixed-race men whom the priest befriended, admired, and worked closely with, and though devoutly Catholic, the prophetess was steeped in all sorts of mysticism and religious paraphernalia at a time when Abbé Ouvière was clearly abandoning both his clerical vocation and allegiance to the Church. He was once again embarking on a different path.

7

An Abbé's Atlantic Adventures

If you do not change direction, you may end up where you are heading.

—LAO TZU

Overview

THE YEAR 1792 was one of tumult and transition for Abbé Ouvière. It began in Léogâne with the signing of the peace treaty that he had negotiated with Romaine-la-Prophétesse at Trou Coffy. A few months later the priest was sent as a delegate by Saint-Domingue's free colored Confederacy to represent them before the National Assembly in Paris. On a more personal level, it was also a year that promised to reunite him with his wife, who had been left behind to live with her abusive father in Marseille while Ouvière sought fame and fortune in Saint-Domingue, at a time when the colony was on the verge of revolutionary war. This chapter traces the events of the priest's life during the period of time between his divergence from the prophetess and his eventual settlement and illustrious scientific and medical career in the United States, which will be the focus of the next chapter. It is a remarkable story of a mercurial, talented man tumultuously adrift in the unpredictable currents of the revolutionary Atlantic world. One dense chapter of this story is comprised in a single year, 1792, during which the adventurous abbé would twice cross the ocean, and at least twice evade almost certain execution for his cunning politics and opportunistic, sometimes duplicitous, machinations.

Why Did the Priest Leave Saint-Domingue?

Brokering the peace treaty with Romaine-la-Prophétesse on Christmas Day 1791 was the single most influential thing that Abbé Ouvière did while in

Saint-Domingue, which should also be counted among the most stunning political twists in the first year of the Haitian Revolution. Pierre Pinchinat, the leader of the free colored Confederacy who had enlisted the priest to negotiate with the prophetess, had serious reservations about the Trou Coffy accord, however, which in effect placed a radical black shaman in formal control of the city of Léogâne and its surrounding plantations.[1] Nevertheless, Pinchinat kept enough faith in Ouvière not only to retain him on his advisory committee but also to later appoint him as one of three emissaries to Paris to represent the Confederate cause before the National Assembly, the others being Messieurs Dubourg and Viart.[2] The deputation was formed by the third week in January 1792, and Ouvière worked closely with Pinchinat in its planning.

For reasons that are unclear, the priest left Croix-des-Bouquets early in 1792 and took up residence on the Foucault plantation, located roughly 40 miles west-southwest of Léogâne. On January 26 Pinchinat wrote to summon the priest from Foucault to either Mirebalais or Croix-des-Bouquets to "give you some important things." The tone of this letter was urgent, and Pinchinat warned that he would be "very angry" if the priest did not come within the following few days and especially if he left for France without at least once more meeting with him. Pinchinat had been urged by a one Monsieur Savary to prepare a *"mémoire circonstancié"* (a report of recent events), and being himself a self-professed man of "little talent," he needed the priest to assist him with its research and composition. There was also "very satisfying" news to share of Pinchinat's recent meeting with Edmond de Saint-Léger, one of the national civil commissioners who were in Saint-Domingue to endeavor to bring some semblance of order to the colony. Though encouraged by Saint-Léger's achievements during the commissioner's adventurous five months in the colony, above all the defeat of the Trou Coffy insurgency, Pinchinat still cautiously rued, "but when will we finally have peace? God only knows."[3]

By the end of February 1792, Abbé Ouvière had once again managed to provoke Pinchinat's ire by writing him to register complaints for having not been accorded the respect that his "talents would demand." For Pinchinat, this was more of an annoyance than a concern, at least when compared to the horror with which he had received news of the Trou Coffy peace treaty. On March 1, he responded by suggesting that "the calumnies that had spread over" the priest were, on the one hand, the fault of his enemies, who "knew not otherwise how to avenge themselves," and, on the other hand, his own fault: "I thus think that you are correct in one sense, and wrong in another."[4] Pinchinat did not go into further detail as to what the "calumnies" were precisely, except for a passing allusion to a letter that Ouvière had written to the national civil commissioners; reading between the lines, one gets the impression that the letter had not first been cleared by Pinchinat.

With the departure date of the Confederate deputation for France fast approaching, Pinchinat added that he would soon be completing the *mémoire* that he and Abbé Ouvière had begun in late January and sending it to the priest to take with him to Paris, destined for Julien Raimond and the National Assembly. He invited Ouvière to edit their *mémoire* with his "sage and patriotic pen," while also offering him the option of forgoing the voyage and returning to work with him further in Croix-des-Bouquets: "As for me, my dear abbé, I am not rich; but I believe that I have a few friends, and if you should come to renounce the project of this trip to France, I offer to share everything that I own with you; if, however, your resolution is invariable, I would only regret not having the chance to see you again before you leave." The two men would never meet again.

The priest set sail from Saint-Marc for France on April 9, 1792,[5] along with the two other "Deputies of the People of Color of St. Marc," Dubourg

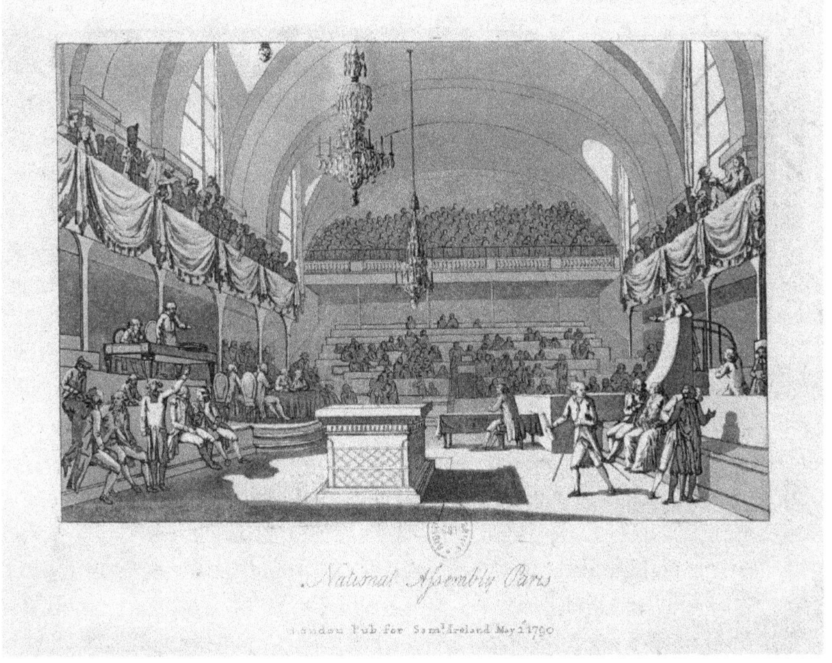

FIGURE 7.1 The famous Salle de Manège, where Abbé Ouvière addressed the Assemblée Nationale in the summer of 1792. *National Assembly Paris.* Collection de Vinck. 1790. Courtesy of La Bibliothèque Nationale de France.

and Viart. Arriving in Nantes on May 28,[6] they soon made their way to Paris to deliver urgent news to the National Assembly. Among the papers that Abbé Ouvière carried with him was a letter from Pierre Pinchinat to Julien Raimond dated April 9, 1792, which stated that the purpose of the deputation's mission in France was "to explain to you the state of the colony . . . it is essential that they be well received."[7] Carrying with them "the first cry that thirty thousand citizens of color will have the French nation hear," the deputation arrived in Paris early in June and at some point met with Raimond to begin carrying out their mission and to deliver to him Pinchinat's *mémoire*, among a host of other documents, and to address the National Assembly.[8]

The Abbé's Ailing Wife

The priest had survived the violence and conflagration that raged all around him in Saint-Domingue during the 1791 insurrections, and next he faced the additional challenge of returning to France in a diplomatic capacity, in the spring of 1792, as a delegate for the free colored Confederacy. By now his commitment to their cause had been seriously wavering, perhaps because of what he had witnessed at Trou Coffy—white prisoners uncertain of their fate at the hands of the unpredictable free black warlord Romaine-la-Prophétesse—and his political ideology was slowly but surely reverting to conservative royalism. Ouvière would have seven weeks to ponder it all as he sailed back to France, and it's not difficult to imagine his being altogether stupefied by a range of emotions. Among the anxieties and uncertainties caused by the revolutionary whirlwinds in which he had inserted himself, the priest was also surely thinking of the wife he had left behind in 1790, of how she fared, and of what their reunion might entail.

In what can only be seen as an astonishing twist of events, prior to leaving the priesthood altogether, Abbé Ouvière had gotten married, as already mentioned, perhaps around the time that he published his ill-fated diatribe against priestly celibacy, which seemingly outraged church authorities and may have led to his defrocking. However clandestinely, the priest wed a seemingly younger woman from Marseille, probably sometime in 1790, before initially leaving France for Saint-Domingue. Thus it had been nearly two years since Abbé Ouvière and Madame Ouvière had seen one another. Upon his arrival in France in late May, from Nantes the priest first travelled to Le Havre, for some unknown reason, before making his way to Paris, on June 1, to fulfill the duty for which he had been sent.[9] During the few months that he then resided in Paris, Ouvière wrote and received numerous letters, and three that are preserved in his papers in the Archives Nationales in Paris were written to him by his ailing wife in Marseille.

Sadly, the priest did not manage to see his wife during his stay in France in 1792, though clearly he had intended to send for Madame Ouvière so that the couple could reunite in Paris.[10] The signature on each letter from his wife is unfortunately illegible and thus her name is unknown. Reflective of the couple's intimacy, meanwhile, in all of the extant French correspondence that is addressed to the priest (several dozen letters in all), these are the only letters that employ the informal second person *"tu"* pronoun and corresponding verb tense, and the only ones that call him by his first name, Félix. They are also heart-wrenching, written by a forlorn yet faithful young woman living under the "domination" of a father whom she despised as "a tyrant," all the while suffering from some grave illness, mourning the recent death of her adored mother, and beseeching her wayward husband to rescue his wife from her living hell:

> My very dear friend ... I have done nothing but cry for the last two months since the death of my mother. I have nothing but you, Felix you are my everything. It is only for you that I live. You tell me in your letter that I should say to you if I want to go with you. I would like to wait until certain matters are settled ... then I would fly to you, my angel, my good friend, my life, my husband, finally, my all. What greater happiness than to be married and to be with you, it's all that I desire ... these two years I have suffered the harshest, most horrendous torments, like you could not imagine ... all that consoles me is that I belong to you.... I hope that you will come yourself to get me, I would be so happy to return into your arms of Felix.... You are ever in my heart and ever shall be until my last breath.... I assure you of my eternal love and faithfulness.... [and hope] that I not be forgotten for your business. I need your advice and again I send with my letter all of my love and the strongest of vitality until the moment I can kiss you, dear husband.[11]

Abbé Ouvière soon responded to his wife's morose, suppliant letter, for on July 24 she wrote to him again about the joy that his response had brought her: "My dear friend, I have just received your adorable letter, which has filled me with tears." The "matters" that needed to be settled before she could rejoin Félix evidently were being tended to, as she notes that "we are going to sell our property in the country that my aunt left us." Though much shorter than her letter of 20 days prior, it is likewise sprinkled with expressions of deep affection and fretful longing: "Be sure of my pure love for you"; "I send with my letter the purest and most faithful love."[12] In passing, Madame Ouvière adds that her neighbor, Monsieur LaRoque, was upset with her husband, though in two letters that LaRoque himself wrote to Abbé Ouvière at around the same time there is no rancor registered; LaRoque does, however, lament "the total ruin . . . of the beautiful colony of Saint-Domingue."[13]

Five days later, on July 29, 1792, Madame Ouvière again wrote to the priest, only now with much greater urgency. With her health having evidently taken a turn for the worse, the pen fell repeatedly from her hand as she expressed fear that she might not live to ever see her beloved husband again. "If I had the wherewithal to go and join you . . . but I have no strength":

> And such are the prayers that I say every day to the Lord . . . to see you again, but my days have flowed by and I only have the strength to say that I really need a change of climate . . . the sun bakes, and that it is in the name of the most faithful love that I tell you the truth. . . . Nothing has been worked out with my family, but I will let you know as soon as there is anything. I await your advice as to what I should do. . . . I know that you have always regarded me to be your woman. . . . The time has come that God could call me to him. . . . If I get worse I will be the testament to you, my heart. Forgive me that this letter is short, it's just to say a thousand times that I am for life entirely yours until death. *Adieu, mon couer.*[14]

It is a most heartbreaking letter, one that surely gave Abbé Ouvière the strong impression that his distant wife was dying. There is no indication that they would ever see one another again, nor that she ever recovered, while soon the priest would suffer more misfortune in the form of a political twist of fate that could very well have cost him his own life. Within weeks of receiving from his wife her last letter of *adieu*, the abbé would once again find himself on the run.

A Duplicitous Diplomat: Paris, Summer 1792

Once securing lodging in Paris and getting settled in, as of June 21, 1792, Abbé Ouvière launched into a flurry of mysterious correspondences with parties in Nantes, Marseille, and Rouen. The seemingly alternating pseudonyms used in these exchanges strongly suggest that their authors and recipients had something to hide and were fearful of retribution in the event that their letters might be intercepted. This was revolutionary France in the summer of 1792, after all, the king was about to be arrested, and the Reign of Terror was about to leave tens of thousands of politically suspicious persons dead, so those with "unpatriotic" agendas had good reason to operate clandestinely. Dating May 31 to August 22, a series of the letters in Ouvière's seized papers carry code names and are often sarcastic in tone. The pseudonyms employed in these exchanges alternated, furthermore, making this body of literature very difficult to make sense of. Evidently Ouvière is often addressed here as "Algonquin," though sometimes also as "Batiment" or "Caraïbe." For instance, one letter dated June 29 and received by Ouvière in Paris, with no sending location indicated, proclaims, "Bravo, dear Algonquin, you are now advancing in a political career, and I do not despair that you will not soon be a fantastic Jacobin." Several of the letters convey news from Saint-Domingue, particularly about the arrival of a ship called *La Borée* in Saint-Marc, and/or acknowledge reception of the *Journal de Saint-Domingue* that Ouvière wrote and circulated in France (now seemingly lost to history). One particularly ominous letter to the priest dated August 7, 1792, and sent from Rouen, meanwhile, stands out for its decidedly "unpatriotic" tone and strong denunciation of the French Revolution:

> I received, the day before yesterday, your last latter, and yesterday the fourth edition of your newspaper .... in which you did not fear to state some major truths.... Thank you for inviting me to stay with you in Paris, all of this infinitely flatters me ... but at the moment when I received your encouragement to make the trip, three families arrived [from Saint-Domingue with news of] ... a general massacre of property owners. I confide in you, my dear founder, without being attacked by excessive fear, that it is among the crimes of Paris that our kingdom is danger... such a great crime has France committed.... AH! Tremble, you monsters. Your blood one day will water the tomb of an unfortunate monarch ... how many anxieties must by now have crippled the royal family? ... you appear poised to wage war on Brissot and his negrophile projects ... this monster doesn't thus see that he has done enough? He wants to make the very last white person perish ....
>
> God holds you, monsieur Algonquin, in his Holy guard.[15]

Somehow Julien Raimond caught wind of the tenor of such letters, while also reading the priest's royalist newspaper, which was more than enough to shatter his trust in Abbé Ouvière. Had he seen the above letter, Raimond certainly would have interpreted it as evidence that the priest was an imposter who was acting in accordance with a white royalist agenda that was antithetical not only to the free colored cause in Saint-Domingue but also to the very principles of the French Revolution. At least one other observer also suspected that Ouvière was possessed by "hatred for the revolution."[16] In denouncing Jean-Pierre Brissot, the leader of the Société des Amis des Noirs and one of the Dominguan free coloreds' most important and influential white allies in France, meanwhile, and in lauding the priest for going to "war" against Brissot the "monster" and his "negrophile project," Ouvière's correspondent, "Caraïbe," indicated in the strongest of terms that the priest was no true friend to Raimond or the cause for which the Aquin native so brilliantly militated. Abbé Ouvière had been exposed as a traitor, such that within two weeks Caraïbe wrote to Algonquin of his fear of further correspondence with him.[17] At around the same time, Ouvière received a letter from his brother in Nice, François Pascalis Ouvière, expressing concern that his publishing initiative "could compromise your life . . . I implore you, take good care of yourself."[18]

Raimond might also have gotten his hands on a copy of the "Constitution for the French Colonies" that the priest had drafted, which would have likewise shockingly revealed that the priest was no true advocate of the free colored cause. Ouvière's Constitution is undated and does not indicate where he had drafted it or to whom he intended to address it. Of all the lavish plans that Ouvière devised during his remarkable life—from the boarding school for white children in Saint-Domingue to the global health care network that he would propose much later in life—none was more impolitic or duplicitous than his constitution. The structure of government envisioned by Abbé Ouvière for Saint-Domingue was conventional and in itself innocuous, featuring a governor general, 31 elected officials in an administrative chamber, and a justice of the peace for each parish. The devil was in the details, however: "But the *affranchis* cannot be permitted to serve in the administrative chamber unless they own at least 65 slaves," which would have excluded the likes of Romaine Rivière and Jean-Baptiste Chavannes.

Two items in this stipulation would have especially caused Raimond concern: (1) the patent inequality between white and free colored representation in the chamber; and (2) Ouvière's choice of the word *"affranchi"* for any free mulatto or free black in the colony who might be elected to the chamber. As the term means "ex-slave" (more literally, "liberated one"), it imputed an enslaved past among those identified as *affranchi*, and yet many *gens de couleur* in Saint-Domingue, like Raimond and Pinchinat (and Romaine and Chavannes, for that matter), in fact had been born free. There was thus much more at stake than semantics.[19] Raimond called this appellation "a humiliation,"[20] while in November of 1789 "more than 40 free men of color in the North Province's Grande Rivière parish had signed a petition to their Provincial Assembly in Cap Français" in which they, among other demands, "requested 'that it be expressly prohibited to call us *affranchis*.' "[21] Being an *affranchi* in Saint-Domingue, whatever one's color or past, meant being possibly subjected to enslavement or re-enslavement.

Whether in reviewing Caraïbe's correspondence with Algonquin, Abbé Ouvière's draft of a constitution for Saint-Domingue, or some other documents, Raimond became altogether alarmed by the priest's "incendiary and counterrevolutionary" ideas and his "most aristocratic newspaper," and he quickly set out to "unmask" the abbé and expose him as being in reality a foe to *liberté, fraternité, egalité*. He also concluded that Ouvière's chief and true objective for the colony was "to establish the [ancien] regime and military government in Saint-Domingue,"[22] thus alerting authorities in Paris and arranging for an arrest warrant to be issued and for the abbé's papers to be seized.[23] Had the warrant been effectively executed, Ouvière's life would have been gravely imperiled. But the ever crafty priest somehow managed to evade capture and to once again flee France. Meanwhile, an alarmed Raimond hastened to send word to Pinchinat back in Saint-Domingue, imploring him that Abbé Ouvière was to no longer be trusted. In turn, Pinchinat and dozens of *gens de couleur* signed the following decree, dated October 15, 1792:

> Considering that Sieur Ouvière never had the power to consider himself a member of the delegation, that is to say as having a deliberative voice but only a consultative one, it is decreed:
>
> That the delegation revokes, in their entire content, the powers that it might have accorded; mortified at having been led to error by the falsehood of Sieur Ouvière, whose *duplicity of character and perversity of heart* in his addresses to M. Pinchinat and M. Savary it recognizes; . . . [the delegation] prohibits him from any involvement in any of their affairs whatsoever. *it deems this vile and contemptible libeler, and his execration of all good French citizens, to be an enemy of the nation, which he attempts in his public and personal writing* TO DETACH FROM THE COLONISTS OF SAINT-DOMINGUE.[24]

In equally urgent tone, Raimond also wrote on July 19 to Chanlatte and Viart, two of Ouvière's deputational "colleagues" from Saint-Domingue, who in turn thanked Raimond for having "unmasked such a dangerous traitor," one "possessed to a supreme degree of the perfidious and contemptible art of disguising himself."[25] For their part, Chanlatte and Viart had already begun to doubt the priest's motives since their arrival together in France from

Saint-Domingue, toward the end of May; shocked to read in one of his letters that Ouvière regarded Raimond and all free coloreds to be racially inferior, for example, "with sorrow" they disbelievingly asked him, "have you switched countries [i.e., allegiances]? We cannot believe this."[26]

By the time of the October 1792 decree in which the free coloreds of Saint-Domingue denounced their once beloved and esteemed confidant, Abbé Ouvière was in London, having fled France because of the "troubles" there and awaiting the opportunity to return to Saint-Domingue, evidently unaware of the decree.[27] That more than 75 prominent men of, or with ties to, the free colored Confederacy signed this anathematic document surely left the priest with few, if any, allies in Saint-Domingue. He certainly could not have resumed service as an adviser to Pinchinat or taken him up on his earlier invitation to live with him in Croix-des-Bouquets. The same would have been the case with Romaine-la-Prophétesse, for that matter. By then, Pinchinat and Romaine surely understood that the priest had betrayed them, and they both probably would have liked to see him killed. Where, then, for the priest to turn? His ship disembarked from the Thames on January 25, 1793, not bound for Saint-Domingue, however, but for Jamaica.

When Abbé Ouvière reached Jamaica he was likely unaware of either Raimond's denunciatory letter to Pinchinat or of the free coloreds' resultant decree that stripped him of his powers to represent their cause. Thus the priest still envisioned his eventual return to Saint-Domingue and believed he would once again enjoy the trust and good graces of his old friend. In that spirit, Ouvière wrote to Pinchinat from Kingston on March 8, 1793, indicating that his stay in France had lasted from May 28 to September 2, 1792, and that he had sent to Saint-Domingue four copies of his report on his activities as the free coloreds' emissary there.[28] Ouvière's letter offered the harrowing news of the beheading of the king in France and provided a few details of his journey to London. He had lingered in London for a while, eventually finding passage to Jamaica to wait for the "dangers" in Saint-Domingue to subside and for "order and peace" to be restored in the colony before returning. In the meantime, he needed money:

> I do not fear to indulge your kindness for the first time because I need it now, and your friendship to me has always accorded me certain rights to your favors. I already sent you in my previous letter receipts for the sums that I earned by virtue of my powers. 50 *portugaises* on the one hand, 50 on the other . . . that is all that I had, despite the care that you took to provide the deputation with funds. It required much more than that . . . and I have wound up completely out of money. I thus beg of you,

> sir, dear friend, to send me some money, and you will see that is only in the name of friendship that I will receive it. I imagine that it will be easy for you to do me this service, of which I have the greatest need.[29]

It was wishful thinking, and one can only imagine Pinchinat's reaction to the letter. But the mercurial priest would never return to Saint-Domingue. Perhaps he had come to the realization that he was now persona non grata among free coloreds in the colony. If so, then Abbé Ouvière probably sensed the need to once again cross the sea and seek out a new life in a new land—a new outpost in the revolutionary Atlantic world. This would indeed be his next move. Where else to turn, but Philadelphia? The relatively young city was home to a large and thriving French exile community, after all, one into which he could slyly blend and recreate himself without insurmountable fear of arrest, ridicule, or social marginalization.

The Priest's Dramatic Passage to America

Thousands of French colonists and refugee *gens de couleur libres*, some bringing selected slaves with them, were forced to flee Saint-Domingue following what Jeremy Popkin calls "the most spectacular episode of the Haitian Revolution—the burning of the main city of the French colony of Saint-Domingue and the simultaneous issuance of the first emancipation proclamation in the French empire in June 1793."[30] Many sought safe haven and new lives in Philadelphia, and all but one of the biological sketches or obituaries of Abbé Ouvière (as Doctor Pascalis) that I have found assume that he had been among these French and Dominguan refugees. However, this is not entirely true. The priest did indeed arrive in Philadelphia at around the time in question, a bit earlier actually, but not from Saint-Domingue, rather, as previously stated, from Kingston, Jamaica:

> The commissioners [of the Saint-Marc deputation] arrived at Paris just two months before the arrest of the king. They were introduced to the Assembly, but soon the flood of Jacobism overwhelmed everything, and Pascalis felt fortunate in effecting his escape to London; and from thence he sailed to Jamaica;—here he was suspected and underwent a rigid examination which resulted in his release and honor. The governor, understanding his whole course, found [him] a passage to the United States in an English brig.[31]

The Jamaican newspaper *Royal Gazette* of May 18, 1793 indicates that Ouvière left "On the Catherine, for Philadelphia," to be precise.[32]

An 85-ton British merchant ship carrying a cargo of "rum, ginger, and pimiento," *The Catherine* did not quite make it to Philadelphia, however.[33] Britain and France were now at war once again, and the first theater of their renewed conflict was the Caribbean, with naval battles and privateering spilling into the Atlantic along America's seaboard. Thus, unsurprisingly, a high seas drama unfolded three weeks into the voyage, when "a French Republican frigate" took chase after the English brig carting spirits, spices, and the renegade priest.[34] Seeing as the French vessel, *L'Embuscade*, was a 36-gun corsair whose name ominously translates as "The Ambush," *The Catherine* stood little chance of evading or resisting her pursuer.[35] Captained by Jean-Baptiste François Bompart, on June 8 *L'Embuscade* caught up to and captured *The Catherine* "about one half mile off the coast of New Jersey,"[36] but not before Abbé Ouvière "stepped into an open boat, with a few articles of clothing and food, and left the brig."[37] Probably this drama occurred somewhere in the Delaware Bay, where *L'Embuscade* had previously captured at least one other British vessel, the *Grange*, the month prior, on May 8.[38] By the following day,

FIGURE 7.2 Replica of a portrait of Dr. Felix Pascalis Ouvière, believed by his descendants to have been painted by Charles Wilson Peale circa 1822. Whereabouts of the original are unknown. Photograph by Todd Lista. Image provided by the Aiken County Historical Museum, Aiken, South Carolina.

Ouvière and evidently a few other escapees in the "open boat" had managed to row all the way to Philadelphia, which would have been nearly impossible in such a short period of time had their escape begun instead somewhere in the ocean off of New Jersey, much farther than any number of points "off the coast of New Jersey" in the bay would have been.[39]

Terrified by the thought of being captured by the French and having another collection of his incriminating correspondence and essays seized, and with good reason, before making his dramatic escape and rowing up the Delaware to safe haven in Philadelphia, the priest "destroyed his papers," which clearly suggests that he was by then an avowed royalist. Save for at least one letter, that is: a letter of introduction to President George Washington, written in Kingston on the priest's behalf by Madame Guyot Ve De Mauduit, the exiled widow of Thomas-Antoine, chevalier de Mauduit du Plessis, who had been "killed at Saint-Domingue in March 1791." Because of its great historical significance and the light that it sheds on Ouvière's flight to, and settlement in, America, I transcribe it here in full:

Kingston Jamaica 8th May 1793

Sir,

The widow of Colo. Mauduit duplissis, the french Officer who fought victoriously under your orders, and merited your eulogies, charges M. Pascalis Ouviere with this letter for your Excellency. This is not only to give him a title to your high protection, but it is likewise to have the opportunity of presenting to you my respectful homage. I flatter myself that this tribute will be acceptable to your Excellency, to whom is due the admiration & gratitude of all the family of Colo. Mauduit Duplissis.

M. Ouviere who has been unfortunate in France & in St Domingo—who had the friendship of my unfortunate husband—who has been a witness to his last efforts to preserve the Colony—who has acquired all our esteem by his talents and merits—is obliged by the circumstances of the war to go from Kingston to Philadelphia. If I dared to contribute to that which he has the honor to present to your Excellency, I would leave it to your beneficent Virtues & to his own worth to obtain more.

As to myself, a refugee at Kingston with my uncle the Chevlr d'aulnay, I wait for some event to put an end to the troubles of St. Domingo & permit us to return to our own estate. If this hope should be frustrated, Illustrious General, I think it best to go the dearest Country in the world—that great Nation over which Your Excellency presided, that in which the life of my husband was so honored & his

> death regretted. I am, with the most profound respect Your Excellency's most Hbe & Obet Sert.
>
> Guyot Ve De Mauduit[40]

It was a great letter for a French exile to bring to America, especially at a time when such documents "structured travelers' lives," and this one would indeed open doors for the priest.[41] Just two months prior, on an unseasonably warm late-winter day in Philadelphia, Washington had been sworn in to serve his second term as president, and he lived in the city, which was then the young nation's capital. It is unknown which particular doors Washington might have opened for Ouvière, though Madame Mauduit's letter was surely instrumental in helping the priest to transform himself from Abbé Ouvière into Doctor Pascalis.

And just who was her late husband and what might his relationship with Abbé Ouvière suggest about the priest's politics? Colonel Mauduit was among the French military officers who joined the Continental Army during the American Revolution, where he amassed a distinguished reputation for bravery and valor. As a lieutenant colonel and commander of artillery, he had fought in the Battles of Brandywine, Germantown, Monmouth, and Red Bank, while also training some of General Washington's beleaguered yet stalwart soldiers during the legendary winter at Valley Forge. His conduct during the French Revolution was decidedly counterrevolutionary, however, and cost him his life. After taking leave from Washington's army he was appointed commander of the French military regiment in Port-au-Prince in 1787, soon becoming one of the colony's staunchest and most outspoken royalists. He refused to implement decrees emitted by the revolutionary National Assembly in Paris, railed against free colored reclamations for their civil rights, denounced abolitionism, arrested members of the local colonial committee, and disarmed his battalion and created in its place a new brigade of volunteer royalists dubbed *les pompoms blancs*, so called because of the white epaulettes sewn to their shirts. When, in March of 1791, fresh batallions had arrived from France, confusion and upheaval ensued, and Mauduit was turned upon and hanged by his own troops,[42] who then "mutilated his body, sparing it no indignity."[43]

In Mauduit's widow's letter to Washington we find clear evidence that while residing in Saint-Domingue Abbé Ouvière had become friends with the repressive commander, further suggesting that the priest's deepest ideological commitments were not in the least truly allied to the people of color whom he had represented before the National Assembly in Paris in 1792, but to the ancien régime. In one sense, the two friends were similar in their opportunism, for just as Mauduit could fight in one nation's revolution against monarchal rule while fighting against revolutionaries in another in support of monarchal rule, so, too, could Ouvière feign to support the free colored cause in Saint-Domingue while also dining with the a man who was arguably the colony's most notorious royalist. The 1791 killing of Mauduit surely gave Ouvière good reason to curb or at least conceal his own royalism while in the colony, for a while anyway, and he would soon take on his role as an adviser to Pinchinat and the free colored Confederacy. Among those who had been arrested by Mauduit was André Riguad, furthermore;[44] because Rigaud continued to trust Ouvière throughout the rest of the priest's residency in Saint-Domingue, confirming his selection as the "conciliatory commissioner" for negotiations with Romaine-la-Prophétesse, one is led to believe that the priest had indeed managed to either downplay or keep his friendship with Mauduit secret during the rest of his dramatic months in the colony. But when need arose for the priest to make his way to the United States, Ouvière was able to secure proof of that very friendship in writing from Mauduit's widow in Jamaica. Desperate times call for desperate measures, after all.

Although the next phase of his extraordinary life would be nowhere as dramatic as his machinations in Saint-Domingue and Paris, or his flight up the Delaware River in a boat clinging to life and clutching Madame Mauduit's letter to President Washington, Pascalis would face a number of challenges to remake himself in the young United States of America, a nation just a few years removed from its own revolution and its securing independence. One of those challenges was to downplay and distance himself from his growing reputation as a political opportunist, a turncoat, and a royalist, while another took the form of rumors that would soon circulate in his new homeland that he had actually participated in the mutilation and murder of white French citizens in Saint-Domingue.

As should be abundantly clear by now, the priest was decidedly not an accomplice to the prophetess; however, he was soon to be accused of having not only abetted the Trou Coffy insurgents but also of orchestrating their "barbarity" altogether. In 1797 Louis Marie Prudhomme, "one of the French Revolution's best-known journalists and publishers," published a six-volume "reading of the Revolution that was simultaneously morbid, fragmentary, hallucinatory, and terrifying." Its second volume includes a scathing attack on Ouvière, accusing him of having been the "chief" of Trou Coffy, without so much as mentioning Romaine-la-Prophétesse.[45] Prudhomme was as misinformed as he was "hallucinatory" in his partisan diatribe, claiming that under Ouvière's direction the rebels committed

> the most revolting acts that rage and barbarity can invent. Infirm whites were massacred in hospitals, houses pillaged and destroyed,

> their owners' throats slit in the midst of the cruelest of torments . . . such were the curses that signaled the rebels' retreat that also flooded the entire province of the West. The base camp of this region, the local capital of the murderers, was in the hills surrounding Léogâne, in Trou-Cassé [*sic*]; it is from there, every day, that fifteen or twenty *hommes de couleurs* embarked at the head of a company of blacks, and mercilessly shot all of the whites they came upon, men, women, children. They [upon their return] would not be well received by the chief of Trou-Cassé [*sic*], l'abbé Ouvrière [*sic*], unless they brought with them the ears of the whites they had massacred.[46]

Fortunately for Ouvière, however, Prudhomme's account would never trump Jean-Philippe Garran de Coulon's "official" report on the 1791 insurrections in Saint-Domingue. A French lawyer and member of the Estates-General in Paris, Garran was sent to Saint-Domingue to investigate the causes of the destruction of France's colonial crown jewel. Like Pinchinat before him, Garran found cause to criticize Ouvière for some fleeting moments of "imprudence," though he seems to have slightly misinterpreted the priest's connections to the prophetess, failing to mention that the priest's "relations" with the prophetess were endorsed by Pierre Pinchinat and André Rigaud:

> It is no less true that Villars [*sic*; Léogâne's mayor] and abbé Ouvière had relations with Romaine around the time when the residents of Léogâne threw themselves into his arms no doubt before the scope of the atrocity of his character was made clear. But what is also seen in their correspondence is that they did not hesitate to repent for their imprudence, and then felt great satisfaction after learning that he [Romaine] was driven out of Léogâne.[47]

In the end, Garran lauded the priest as someone possessed of "the purest morality" who expressed "the most vigorous denunciations of those *hommes de couleur* who had soiled their cause with murder or other crimes."[48]

Garran's exoneration of Abbé Ouvière notwithstanding, some later commentators evidently believed Prudhomme's version of events, and its influence endured for quite some time in at least one scientific circle. Twenty-five years after he had left the Caribbean for good in 1793 and settled in the United States, where in the ensuing years he cemented his distinguished reputation in American science and medicine under the name Doctor Felix Pascalis, Ouvière was denounced in a French medical journal by scholars named Fournier and Begim for his allegedly incendiary "religious quackery" in Saint-Domingue:

> [T]he so-called doctor Pascalis . . . this *quidan* is without a doubt less in fact a good judge of medical thought than of matters of religious hypocrisy. . . . As for Monsieur l'abbé Ouvière-Pascalis, we will not do him the honor of responding to his diatribes. . . . We will only add that he is incontestably abler to preach insurrection than to define true political and individual liberty; he should just go back to trou-coffy and the company of the pious RÓMAIN.[49]

But Abbé Ouvière would never return to Trou Coffy, instead finding himself among hundreds of French refugees who arrived in Philadelphia from the Caribbean in 1793. Fournier and Begim's slanderous attack of the priest/physician were ultimately of no avail, moreover, for Abbé Ouvière, as Doctor Pascalis, would effectively refute them and continue his remarkable ascent to the highest peaks of influence in early American science and medicine.[50] It is to that long and storied chapter of his remarkable life that our attention now turns.

8

Dr. Pascalis and the Making of American Medicine

I can see how it might be possible for a man to look down upon the earth and be an atheist, but I cannot conceive how a man could look up into the heavens and say there is no God.

—ABRAHAM LINCOLN

Overview

IN EFFECTIVELY DISTANCING himself from his checkered political and religious past, the priest underwent such a radical personal transformation in the United States that connecting the two chapters of his life is rather difficult, amounting to a perfect example of what Pierre Bourdieu refers to as "the biographical illusion."[1] Reflecting this, although a few historians of the Haitian Revolution have taken note of the priest's activities in Saint-Domingue as Abbé Ouvière, and although a few historians of American science and medicine have taken note of his illustrious professional career as Doctor Pascalis in Philadelphia and New York during the first three decades of the nineteenth century, that *Abbé Ouvière and Doctor Pascalis were actually one and the same person* has until now been lost on scholars.[2] Between the time of his arrival in America in 1793 and the remaining 40 years of his life, Pascalis' voice is recorded amply in numerous publications and letters, but in them he very seldom mentions politics in Saint-Domingue or France. Pascalis would have much to say instead about race, slavery, religion, and science. It is on these matters that the present chapter focuses attention, touching along the way on his impressive and varied scientific and medical achievements, after first considering the abbé's extraordinary journey to and settlement in the United States and the priest's blazing foray into the young republic's yellow fever epidemics.

Coming to America: How Abbé Ouvière Became Dr. Pascalis

In 1793 Abbé Ouvière arrived dramatically in Philadelphia, a refugee from the Caribbean, as did some 2,000 of his French compatriots. Historians like H. Carrington Bolton have long assumed, and reasonably so, that the priest fled Saint-Domingue in the summer of that year when "a revolt among the negroes compelled him to take refuge in the United States."[3] It is indeed the case that Ouvière may be counted among *les français* who were "swept along on the tidal wave of the three revolutions washing over the Atlantic world" and who landed in Philadelphia that fateful year, surviving what was often a harrowing journey replete with disease, storms, pirates, and multiple stops along with way.[4] Though Ouvière sailed not from Saint-Domingue but from Jamaica, his journey was no less dramatic than that of those fleeing Cap-Français, a once impressive city that was then pillaged and burned by insurgent slaves. He certainly related to his refugee compatriots, as reflected in a letter he wrote to one of them much later in life: "Who would have been able to believe and to say that after having broken bread with you in the midst of war when the skies of Saint-Domingue burned, among a number of friends among whom perhaps none should have survived, and after an interim of 35 quite resolute years, that you and I are still alive and well?"[5]

Surely thanks in large part to the letter of introduction that Madame Mauduit had written in Kingston on the priest's behalf to George Washington and to Ouvière's innate brilliance and medical training, we may certainly count the priest among the few French refugees who found something resembling good fortune in Philadelphia, even if at times he did struggle financially.[6] It also helped, of course, that the priest already knew some of the city's Frenchmen, and he soon secured a letter of recommendation from several of them.[7] Though the document is torn and the date partially illegible, it appears to be from 1793 or 1794 and attests to his good character and observes that Pascalis was "presently residing in Philadelphia where he practices medicine." Testimony to his flourishing professional reputation and the kinds of lofty social circles in which he was soon moving, a few years later the priest would secure another letter of recommendation from Thomas McKean,[8] the governor of Pennsylvania, while his descendants in America believe that at one point he also corresponded with Benjamin Franklin,[9] a man that Pascalis greatly admired for having "wrestled the lightning from heaven and the scepter from a tyrant."[10] Later in life he would also befriend the great Creole naturalist John James Audubon.[11]

Excepting the likes of Stephen Girard and Charles-Maurice de Talleyrand-Périgord, one would be hard pressed to identify many among the roughly 10,000 Frenchmen who came to the United States in the 1780s and 1790s who would achieve a place of greater prominence or influence in early republican America than Félix Alexander Pascalis Ouvière.[12] He would spend the rest of his long life in the United States, only not as a priest, but as a physician and scientist—as Doctor Pascalis, not Abbé Ouvière—first in Philadelphia and then in New York City, where he moved initially by 1806 and permanently by 1811, four years after having formally become an American citizen.[13] Though that he waited 14 years before taking American citizenship might suggest that Pascalis had designs of doing so, returning to France was not likely an attractive option. The anticlericalism of the French Revolution would have made resuming pastoral duties there nearly impossible, especially because Abbé Ouvière had been defrocked by the archbishop of Paris in 1790. He may even have faced criminal charges and possibly execution in France for the writings that led to his falling out with the free colored Confederacy in Saint-Domingue, though years later he was able to visit Paris and Bordeaux without incident.

Philadelphia was the perfect place for the priest to remake his life. With the arrival of the refugees from Saint-Domingue, Philadelphia's French community had swelled to comprise "between six and eight percent of the entire population of the city."[14] This community was concentrated along the Delaware riverfront around Spruce Street, and it is possible that upon arrival Pascalis resided at either one of the French pensions at Second and Spruce, one of them "a hotel filled with Dominguean refugees."[15] He surely spent some time in the bookshop owned by Médéric Louis Élie Moreau de Saint-Méry at 84 South Front Street, which was a hub of French intellectual life in the city, though Pascalis clearly disliked Moreau, someone he criticized for being "a great and rapid talker, full of arrogance and of contempt for anything belonging to this country."[16] Not far from Moreau's *librairie*, the priest lived for some time at 70 South Street, just a few blocks from Second and Spruce, where his closest neighbors were "Christian Scott, huckster"; "Thomas Matthias, hatter"; D. Canizares, tavern keeper"; "Jacob Durang, bleeder"; "Susannah O'Neal, gentlewoman"; and "John Douglas, cabinet maker."[17]

The timing of the priest's arrival in Philadelphia combined fortuitously with his expertise as a physician and a scientist. Dr. Pascalis quite ambitiously and effectively positioned himself in a then "growing exchange between American and French scientific bodies; for instance the American Philosophical Society had nominated twenty-one Frenchmen to its ranks (out of a total of fifty-three members), French scientific magazines were being distributed to American scientific societies, and some French scientific textbooks were in use in some

American colleges."[18] The priest took full advantage, and thus Abbé Ouvière became Doctor Pascalis, one of the most shining of French luminaries in American science and letters.

Although religion was of considerable influence on the formation of early American politics and culture,[19] the Catholic religious capital that Pascalis, as Abbé Ouvière, possessed in Saint-Domingue would have been of relatively little worth in Philadelphia and would have had little transubstantive value, either as political or social capital, in a society where deism, Anglicanism, Freemasonry, Lutheranism, Presbyterianism, Quakerism, and Enlightenment philosophy were the dominant religious and ideological influences on the intelligentsia and cultural and political elite. Other French Catholic priests who settled in Pennsylvania at the same time seem to have abandoned their ministries.[20] As for Doctor Pascalis, he had lost his sense of "Sacred Calling" years prior.[21] When the priest first arrived in Philadelphia in 1793, the city had only two Catholic churches, furthermore, St. Joseph's, founded by the Jesuits at Third and Walnut Streets in 1733, and St. Mary's, founded at Fourth and Locust in 1763.[22] Philadelphia was not then a Catholic diocese, and the city counted only about 2,000 Catholics out of a total population of 55,000. These Catholics were hardly unified, furthermore, as the Germans among them then clamored for their own ethnic parish.[23] And though initially the Dominguan refugees might have added significantly to Pennsylvania's Catholic population, many of the whites among them were notoriously irreligious, while others converted to Protestantism in the United States, due in part to a need to integrate and to American prejudice against French Catholics, which was at "a high pitch" in Pennsylvania following the French and Indian War.[24] And whereas the involvement of French officers like Lafayette and Mauduit in the American Revolution had a positive impact on American views of the French in general, anti-Catholic attitudes and "fear and hatred of Catholic France" persisted in the new republic, such that conversion to Protestantism would become a common response among French immigrants like Pascalis.[25]

Thus did Pascalis have good reason to distance himself even further from his sacerdotal vocation as Catholic abbé in America, so the priest became an Episcopalian doctor. Cementing this transformation once and for all, he soon took an American wife, Elizabeth Harris McKlintock, "a very beautiful woman" 20 years his junior,[26] a "young lady" of "refinement," "keen intellect," and "youthful charms."[27] Félix and Elizabeth were married on March 12, 1801 by Reverend James Abercrombie at Christ Church in Philadelphia, arguably the nation's most storied church, whose worshippers included Benjamin Franklin, George Washington, John Adams, and Betsy Ross, and whose cemetery holds the remains of Franklin and Benjamin Rush, as well as three other signers of the Declaration of Independence.[28] There is, however, no record in Christ Church's archives of Felix or Elizabeth Pascalis' membership there, nor that of the baptism any of their three children, who were all born in Philadelphia, Francesca Anna Pascalis, in 1803, Félix Pascalis, in 1805 or 1806, and Cyril Ouvière in 1810.[29]

Another notable shift in the priest's stateside transformation was the de-emphasis of his second surname: "Ouvière" quickly slipped into the background, and he became known in America as "Pascalis;" the title "Abbé" disappeared entirely, meanwhile, and was replaced by "Doctor." *Who's Who in American History* explicitly states that he was "known as Félix Pascalis after 1801."[30] Another source indicates that the priest consciously and strategically "changed his paternal to his maternal name" upon arrival in the city in 1793, after having destroyed his papers for similar reasons, to distance himself from his suspicious political past.[31] An altered name, a new country, and a change in profession—in a matter of a few short years the eclipse was complete: Abbé Ouvière vanished under Doctor Pascalis.

These shifts in name, profession, and politics did not amount to any wholesale concealment of his identity, however, as Pascalis did not change his name entirely, and in his English-language scientific publications, all of them authored and published in the United States, he made occasional observations about people and plants in Saint-Domingue. In rare instances, he did use the name "Pascalis Ouvière" in his writings in the United States, furthermore, and his younger son carried the surname Ouvière. But after 1793 rarely did the priest provide any glimpse into his political activities in Saint-Domingue or France, knowledge of which in Philadelphia and New York medical circles certainly could have blunted his career ambitions. These ambitions were immediately set on the path to their realization, though, when just a couple of months after the priest's arrival in Philadelphia from the Caribbean on a British merchant ship called the *Catherine*, yellow fever arrived on a British merchant ship from the Caribbean called the *Hankey* and quickly swept the city with suffering and death.[32]

Dr. Pascalis, Yellow Fever, and Ideas to Heal the World

The timing of the priest's arrival in Philadelphia was uncanny, for later that summer Philadelphia was devastated by a yellow fever epidemic, positioning Doctor Pascalis to ingratiate himself to the overwhelmed local medical community by treating the afflicted, thereby gaining the confidence of no less a luminary than Benjamin Rush. It also helped that another French physician who had served for a time in Saint-Domingue as "chief surgeon for the national troops of the Northern Province at Cap Français," Jean Devèze, had been placed in charge of Philadelphia's Bush Hill Hospital in the battle against the epidemic.[33] Bush Hill was a mansion transformed into a hospital by another French émigré with important ties to Saint-Domingue, Stephen Girard.[34] Though it is unclear whether Pascalis had known either Devèze or Girard in Saint-Domingue, Devèze invited Pascalis to Bush Hill to work with him, but Pascalis declined, claiming a lack of experience with the disease; instead, Pascalis treated patients at Benjamin Rush's home on Walnut Street. Devèze and Rush differed on how to treat yellow fever patients, and Pascalis clearly sided with Rush in their debate, employing massive bloodletting and calomel as the treatments of choice, over tree bark and wine.[35]

The summer of 1793 was a very busy time for Pascalis' neighbor Jacob Durang and the rest of Philadelphia's bleeders. For some idea of how widespread the treatment of bloodletting was in the city, a process in which the bleeder employed a lancet to slice open an artery in the patient's arm, we only need envision the scene in front of Rush's house at Third and Walnut Streets, then transformed into a clinic overflowing with the sick and his medical students: "[W]hen there were not enough bowls for his pupils to use, the young men would take patients out to the front yard on Walnut Street and bleed them as they stood in the open air. The blood flowed freely on the ground, dried, and putrefied there, stank hideously, drew flies and mosquitoes."[36] In fruitless efforts to ward off the dreadful disease, people doused their homes and clothes with vinegar and wore tar-soaked ropes and rags if they needed to go outside. The bitter smell of vinegar and the pungent odor of tar, combined with the stench of putrid blood and rotting corpses, were ubiquitous reminders to anyone still standing that she could be next to fall. Philadelphia in 1793 was thus a city in dire need of medical assistance, affording a prime opportunity for Abbé Ouvière to remake himself as Doctor Pascalis.

Thus would yellow fever set the priest on a path to the highest summits of American science and medicine. Among his closest collaborators were some of the new republic's most distinguished physicians and scientists, including Rush and Samuel Latham Mitchill, with whom Pascalis founded the nation's first medical journal, *The Medical Repository*. For a brief time at least, Rush was also Pascalis' personal physician, at one point treating him with calomel and "six successive bleedings" for complications from a liver abscess. The abscess had caused the patient "horrid feelings of an impending suffocation . . . and violent delirium and fever," a dramatic event that Pascalis saw fit to write about in a medical journal.[37] Another source suggests that Rush bled Pascalis 15 times,[38] though it is unclear whether the priest's teeth and hair fell out as the result of Rush's excessive use of mercury in treating a whole range of ailments, side effects that many of his other patients endured.[39]

By February of 1799 Pascalis had been elected a member of the College of Physicians of Philadelphia's "committee on correspondence," with Rush then being elected to the College's "committee on revision."[40] Their association also helps explain how Pascalis became one of the most influential of the city's 85 doctors,[41] in large part, too, because he began to write with relative authority and some measure of license on a wide range of medical subjects, from mania and rabies, to venereal disease and, of course, yellow fever.[42] On the latter subject he soon became the world's leading expert, as his book on the 1797 yellow fever epidemic in Philadelphia was highly influential and widely debated.[43] In *An Account of the Contagious Epidemic Yellow Fever, Which Prevailed in Philadelphia in the Summer and Autumn of 1797*, Pascalis' intellectual genius and medical authority—not to mention his rich imagination and ornate diction—are most impressively on display. Motivated by the twin objectives "to promote medical knowledge" and make "some improvements to the healing art," he quite originally argued against the then prevailing opinion that yellow fever was transmitted to Philadelphia on human bodies carried by ships from the Caribbean—from Saint-Domingue, in fact.[44] Pascalis allowed for the importation of the disease on ships, but he argued that its path of transmission was miasmic, passing through wood and air rather than through people. While thus not denying the possibility of foreign importation, the priest opined that yellow fever, which in 1797 killed 3,500 or more Philadelphians,[45] could also have "domestic origins," deriving as well from the wood of many wharves on the city's two rivers, whose "exhalations" of "putrid air" while drying emitted the contagion.[46] For this reason he suggested that wooden wharves be replaced by "[s]tone wharves; and their owners obliged to cover them once a year with a coat of tar."[47]

The fact that Pascalis actually remained in Philadelphia to observe both the 1793 and 1797 epidemics and to treat the sick is noteworthy, as many physicians fled the city out of fear of contracting the dreaded disease. Pascalis stayed out of a sense of sacred duty: "in the midst of a pestilential havock, they [physicians] should, like soldiers, remain on their breach; or *that, like sacred ministers, they had a God, and altar, and a sanctuary, within the precincts of which, if it is necessary, they must fall the first victims.*"[48] Most people weren't so hardy, and those who had the means to do so, including "President George Washington and most of the federal government," left the city.[49] Pascalis also saw the epidemics as vastly exciting research opportunities. Thus, when news reached Philadelphia of an outbreak of yellow fever epidemic in southern Spain in 1805, Pascalis hopped on a ship and sailed yet again across the Atlantic Ocean, a trip that may have been financed by the Jefferson administration.[50] Visiting Cadiz and Gibraltar, the epicenter of the epidemic there, the trip was fruitful for the enterprising scientist, for "the data that he collected and the observations that he himself made in these two towns confirmed his opinion that it wasn't at all a contagious disease."[51]

In one of the numerous ambitious "schemes that he never carried out,"[52] shortly after his trip to Spain, Pascalis wrote to Jefferson "to lay under your examination the plan of my intended work on the yellow fever" in the hopes that it would "bespeak interesting views."[53] The idea was to write a massive tome on the global history and course of the yellow fever epidemic, a magnum opus to be entitled *Pyrroloimoglia*, and he sought Jefferson's endorsement of study. The president responded positively: "Thomas Jefferson returns to Dr. Pascalis his subscription paper, to which he has with pleasure subscribed his name. he believes the doctrine which Dr. Pascalis proposes to support, is founded in fact; and sure that it is of great interest to the American commerce. he salutes him with respect and esteem."[54]

Being thus driven to eventually write the definitive tome on yellow fever, here considered geographically, Pascalis was surely energized when an epidemic of the disease struck New York City in 1819, where he then lived. The epicenter was on the Lower East Side of Manhattan, and the priest plunged into the eye of the storm to do the research behind his second short book on the subject, *A Statement of the Occurrence during the Malignant Yellow Fever, in the city of New-York, in the Summer and Autumnal Months of 1819*. In this study the French scientist reiterated his position that yellow fever had miasmic origins and thus was not spread from infected humans to other humans, but was instead "produced by impure and deleterious exhalations from putrid substances."[55] Here the priest's ornate diction is perhaps at its best where he expresses relief that just prior to the outbreak of the epidemic a number of residents had been evicted from an especially densely populated neighborhood, around Front and Water Streets, that otherwise would have been "a shocking theatre of pestilential devastation."[56] Though by the middle of the nineteenth century his theory on the origin of yellow fever would be discredited, Pascalis' studies of the disease are considered pioneering efforts in the fields of epidemiology and medical cartography, especially his New York study.[57]

The reputation as a medical and scientific authority that Pascalis gained was surpassed by very few people in early republican America. One of his first essays on yellow fever won a prize from the Medical Society of Connecticut in 1795, two years before the priest published his first major study of the disease in Philadelphia in 1797.[58] By 1801, he had been elected vice president of the Chemical Society of Philadelphia, reflective of Pascalis's growing enthusiasm for chemistry as being "the very root of the tree of knowledge," as Thomas Apel puts it.[59] Over the course of 20 years, he published several books and dozens of scientific essays; edited the young nation's leading medical journal; was secretary of the City Health Office of Philadelphia;[60] belonged as an officer to the world's first ever association of chemists; was a medical licensing authority; and held positions in a long list of medical and scientific bodies, including the Board of Health of the Commonwealth of Pennsylvania, the Medical Society of Philadelphia, the Medical Society of the State of New York (as "censor"), the College of Physicians and Surgeons (as "lecturer"), the Society of Medicine of Paris (as "special foreign correspondent"), and the National Academy of Medicine of Mexico (also as "foreign correspondent").[61] In one publication he is identified as "Permanent Member of the New-York Medical Society; Member of the New-York State and County Med. Soc.; Mem. Med. Soc. of Connecticut, Philadelphia, Charleston, New Orleans, Mexico; of Paris, Bordeaux, Marseille: Official Correspondent of the Med. Fac. of Paris; Mem. Linn. Soc. Paris; Mem. Agricultural Society New-York, Cincinnati, Havana, etc., etc., etc., etc."[62]

Asserting his ascendant medical authority, Pascalis implored the cities of New York and Philadelphia—though it is certainly feasible that he likewise envisioned this project for the entire civilized world—to help curb the spread of communicable diseases by making drastic changes in how humans buried their dead. In the most extensive scholarly study to date of Pascalis' medical career, William Middleton alludes to the French doctor's "pervading obsession" with the noxious effects of decaying corpses in city graveyards, which emit toxins that seep into wells and spread disease.[63] Pascalis' stated intention was to devise "a plan that would protect the dead without endangering the living." To allow for mourners, a *Polyandrium* with solid, high walls would be constructed outside the city, complete with "sextons" to ward of gravediggers and a washing station to be used by the living before departing the "*city of the dead.*"[64]

The very year that he published his treatise on burial, Pascalis, along with two coauthors, presented to the Medical Society of the State of New York a "System of Medical Ethics," which they had been tasked to write two years prior as the Society's committee on ethics. Reflecting a point that Pascalis had underscored some 25 years earlier in equating physicians with "sacred ministers," the System first and foremost insists upon the religious quality of the doctor's calling:

> A physician cannot successfully pass through his career without the aid of much fortitude of mind, and a religious sense of all his obligations

> of conscience, honor, and humanity. His personal character should therefore be that of a perfect gentleman, and above all, be exempt from vulgarity of manners, habitual swearing, drunkenness, gambling, or any species of debauchery, and contempt for religious practices and feelings.[65]

They also called the Hippocratic oath a "sacred obligation" for physicians, while their commitment to patient confidentiality was comparable "to the Catholic Confessional," citing case law in making the latter point.[66] The "System of Medical Ethics" is an example of how in the United States some leading figures in the field were "scientizing" medicine in that the document "relied on exclusively on physician authors as its ethical authorities," as Robert Veatch explains, whereas others working in the realm of medical ethics, including Benjamin Rush, "freely cited philosophers such as Locke, Bacon, Newton, Reid, Beatty, and (occasionally) Hume."[67] It remains for a medical historian like Veatch to further analyze Pascalis' scientific and medical writings and to assess more fully his true place as a pioneer of medicine in the United States, while a historian of science would be much better suited than I to explain the priest's contributions to science and naturalism in America, and a few have indeed begun to do so.[68]

Though by then his reputation as a medical authority had been cemented, things could have gone horribly wrong for the priest when word of his relationship to Romaine-la-Prophétesse and the Trou Coffy insurgency began to circulate in American scientific circles and threatened to derail and/or unmask the esteemed Doctor Pascalis. In an evidently partisan attack on both Pascalis and Rush, two French medical researchers, in fact, set out to expose his dubious political and religious past in Saint-Domingue. In their caustic 1818 article, Fournier and Bégim bemoan "the insignificant and injurious tirades of the so-called doctor Pascalis, who has never really been a doctor at all, and who did not mine the ordinary sources on the elementary notions of healing." The authors take it as their task, furthermore, "to repel his aggressions . . . to refute his impertinent paradoxes, his inane remarks about the contagion of the plague and of yellow fever. . . . M. l'abbé would deign to understand us and provide us with some ulterior biographical details."[69] They conclude their tirade by explicitly mentioning the priest's association in Saint-Domingue with "the pious RÓMAIN" and the Trou Coffy insurgents, impugning the priest for overseeing the massacre of innocent whites and the mutilation of their corpses.

Pascalis bristled at the accusations and launched a furious rally to safeguard his reputation against "the malicious attack of the mulatto Fournier,"[70]

FIGURE 8.1 Standing second from the left, Pascalis is lampooned with other New York medical officials for misdiagnosing a vomiting patient. "A Case of Infectious Fever". Political Cartoon. 1820. Courtesy of the Medium Graphics Collection, Historical Society of Pennsylvania.

going so far to demand a hefty sum of $2,000 in damages.[71] To set the record straight, he also wrote in 1821 a long memoir about his experience with Romaine-la-Prophétesse at Trou Coffy, "Anecdote historique," which is one of the most valuable primary source documents that we have about any of the 1791 insurgencies in Saint-Domingue, one that has heretofore been unknown to scholars of the Haitian Revolution.[72] This memoir was among the documents that Pascalis sent from New York to Devèze in Paris in a successful effort to secure from the distinguished physician an affidavit clearing his name. Doctor Devèze obliged: "I thus declare, in the sincerity of my soul and with unbridled pleasure, that it has been demonstrated to me that Mr. Pascalis maintained, in Saint-Domingue and during the Trou Coffy affair, conduct that, far from meriting reproach, was one deserving of glory."[73] Pascalis also endeavored to defend the honor of Benjamin Rush against Fournier and Bégim's charge "that on his death bed, he had retracted his professional and public opinion on the non-contagion of yellow fever."[74] Devèze's testimony on his behalf was evidently enough to exonerate the priest, as nothing further was ever made of the accusations that he was a murderer, imposter, and charlatan—accusations that his one-time advisee Romaine-la-Prophétesse endures to this day, unjustly, in my view, a subject to which we shall return in the next chapter.

Pascalis on Race and Slavery

Felix Pascalis Ouvière never owned a slave, and deep down he thought that slavery was a bad thing. However, while living in Philadelphia he did own the contract of at least one indentured servant, a young mulatto named Joseph Brown. Indentured servitude in colonial and early republican America was a "bondage servant system" that "ranged in severity from a voluntary act to involuntary slavery," extracting labor from whites, Native Americans, and blacks alike, whose terms of servitude ranged from a few years to a lifetime. Because indentured servants' contracts could be bought and sold, they had little recourse to state protection from mistreatment, and they were subject to tortuous forms of physical punishment, which included whippings and the severing of ears.[75]

Unlike other French refugees from Saint-Domingue, who in many instances brought slaves and servants with them, Pascalis certainly purchased the contract of his indentured servant in Pennsylvania. We only know that he owned Brown's contract while living in Philadelphia because he allegedly stole money from the doctor and absconded, prompting Pascalis to place a runaway advertisement to that effect in the *Gazette of the United States*, which appeared on October 14, 1800:

> Stop Thief!
> THIRTY DOLLAR REWARD.
>
> RAN-AWAY from Subscriber, on Sunday 28th last, late in the evening, an indented Mulatto Boy, aged 17 years, engaged by the name of Joseph Brown, saying himself to be from Lancaster of that neighborhood; he is stiff set, has a round face, short hair, large mouth, smiling countenance, dull speech, big hands and feet and he has no beard. He may dress himself with a genteel coat of light drab colour, white buttons, and black caps, He wears a good round black hat. He has stolen from the subscriber upwards of 100 dollars in cash and value of other objects. Whoever will apprehend and secure him with as much value about him will receive the above reward, and 10 dollars if the young villain can only be brought to condign punishment.
>
> FELIX PASCALIS
> No. 70 Sonth [*sic*] Street
>
> Sept. 29[76]

Noteworthy is the speed with which Pascalis penned and placed the ad, just one day after Brown's disappearance, and how the priest was willing to increase the amount of the bounty should his capture lead to "condign punishment."

Somewhat ironically, the very year that he placed the runaway ad in an effort to track down and have Joseph Brown punished, Pascalis was elected a member of "the nation's most energetic antislavery organization,"[77] the Pennsylvania Society for Promoting the Abolition of Slavery.[78] Was his election in keeping with the fact that Pascalis owned the contract of an indentured servant?[79] Abolitionism would seem to oppose such arrangements, but the priest certainly was not the only abolitionist in early nineteenth-century Philadelphia to have an indentured servant or to own a slave. For instance, although "Anthony Benezet convinced the Quaker meeting to condemn slavery in 1757 . . . in the decade before the Revolution whites freed only 18 of nearly 1000 slaves in Philadelphia."[80] Nor did abolitionism in the revolutionary Atlantic world necessarily imply antiracism, for even the Quakers, the religious sect that spearheaded the American abolitionist movement, rarely admitted blacks as meetinghouse members in late eighteenth-century America and "definitely discouraged such action."[81] Pascalis' certificate of election to the Society was signed by a Quaker, at any rate, James Pemberton, then the organization's president, in 1800.[82] It may be, furthermore, that the priest's election to the Society had something to do with his relationship to Benjamin Rush, who, in addition to being the city's leading physician, was one of its leading abolitionists and was elected the Society's president in 1803.[83]

It should be underscored here that although Pascalis owned the contract to an indentured servant in Philadelphia and seemingly to two others later in New York, he never owned a slave. At some point in his life, the priest came to view slavery not so much as objectionable to God but as an obstacle to universal freedom and the progress of civilization. In a 1796 letter to Joseph Hawkins lauding his manuscript *A History of a Voyage to the Coast of Africa*, we find the priest's clearest written statement of opposition to the enslavement of Africans:

> The hospitable and generous treatment that you have received from the *Ebo King* and Nation, are sufficient proofs of the advantages which many celebrated philosophers have promised to all powers on earth, if, instead of trafficking with slaves and prisoners of Africa, and keeping, consequently, those nations in their customary ignorance, barbarity and warfare, they would exert themselves in civilizing and colonizing the numerous tribes of those immense countries.[84]

The racist ideas on parade here—that Africans required European colonizing and civilizing interventions to liberate them from their "customary ignorance, barbarity, and warfare"—were quite in keeping with the prevailing social and pseudo-scientific thought on race of the day.[85] Pascalis reflected them in other places as well. In an article entitled "Desultory Remarks on the Cause and Nature of the Black Colour in the Human Species," for instance, the priest *cum* doctor advanced a rather bizarre theory as to why members of "the African race" are black.[86] All humans have in their bodies the same quantity of "black matter," which consists chiefly of carbon in our blood, but white bodies secrete very little of it, while black bodies secrete so much of it as to be covered with it dermatologically. For, carbonic acid in the lungs forces the "black matter" onto the skin, making some people black. There is one advantage to this, however: "owing to the great employment of the black matter to clothe the whole surface of the African, no carbonic gas or very little of it remains to be elicited from his pulmonary organs, and that his breath must always be purer or less offensive that that of the white man." But there is a tradeoff: "in a state of perspiration, the black race emit always a most unpleasant sour and smoky-like odor, which results from the black matter of the skin."[87]

With writings such as these, Pascalis earned a reputation as an authority on race. In this capacity, the priest was called in as an expert witness in a paternity case in New York in 1808, one in which a central question concerned whether the child in question was of "mixed race." A "yellow woman" named Lucy Williams bore a female child out of wedlock on January 23, 1803, and claimed "that Alexander Whistelo, coachman to Doctor Hosack, is the reputed father of said bastard child."[88] In her testimony, Williams implies that Whistelo, "a black man," may in fact have raped her, though this seems not to have been a matter of concern to the court:

> I refused [to marry him]; for I did not choose to have him—I did not love him. He then carried me to a bad house, and locked the door—I scuffled with him a long time, but at last he worried me out. He went after that to sea, and after he came back I told him I was with child.[89]

From Williams' sexual history, which seemingly included incidents of prostitution, the examination turns to the question of her own race: "My father was white, a Scotchman, a servant; and my mother was a dark Sambo." Whistelo, for his part, denied the paternity charges, testifying "[t]hat the said child appeared to him to be the child of a white man."[90] Whistelo's opinion on this count was seconded by Dr. Joshua Secor, who had delivered the child, and "at the time when the said child was born, he had supposed the said child had been begotten by a white man" (interestingly, Secor had forgotten what the child's sex was).[91]

"Dr. Pascalis, sworn and examined, said that the child in question appeared to him to be three-fourths white and one-fourth black—that was his impression.

But he pronounced with diffidence upon such subjects, as he knew how easy it was to err where there was a want of certain *data.*" That diffidence notwithstanding, in his testimony Pascalis confidently alludes to data such as the "crispness of hair," "the *rete mucusom* which gives the black hue to the skin," and "the conformation of their legs and feet."[92] As in some of his medical publications, in his legal testimony Pascalis here draws upon examples from Saint-Domingue:

> One example which he cited out of numbers which he had noticed, was the French general, Rigaud. He was the son of a white man, a relation of the witness, by a black woman. He was so dark as to differ little from the true African complexion; but in return for that, he had the features and form of a white man—was very handsome and well made. If this principle of nature is not universal, it is, as repeated observations had proved to him, very general. The last symptom of the negro blood which disappears, is the crispation of the hair and the setting on of the ancle [*sic*], which he described in technical language amount ing [*sic*] to this, that the leg was inserted more forward on the foot, and consequently the heel longer.[93]

Based on these considerations, Pascalis offered his expert opinion that the child in question was "a perfect mulatto," meaning that she could not have been fathered by a black man. Note here how Riguad's laudable physical features, being "very handsome and well made," are associated in the doctor's testimony with his whiteness and not his blackness. This element of Pascalis' testimony seemingly had a catalytic evidentiary impact on the case, for the child in question, in part because of her perceived beauty, was adjudged to have not been fathered by the black man under examination, Alexander Whistelo. In other words, because she was beautiful, she could only have been fathered by a white man.

The court lauded Pascalis for having "fortified his opinion by some very able remarks," placing him on equal footing with another medical expert called in to testify: "James Jay, a physician of great respectability, and of the longest standing in the city, has given a decided opinion to the same effect, and has particularly indicated the want of crisped hair as a conclusive circumstance against the testimony of the woman."[94] In the end, the mayor of New York saw fit to site Horace in delivering his judgment: "*Nic Deus intersit nisi dignius vindice nodus, Inciderit*":

> But the mother has reluctantly attested, and explicitly admitted, that she had connection with a white man as well as with the defendant. We can, therefore, even upon her own testimony, be justified in dismissing

> the present complaint; and we accordingly order, that the application to charge the defendant as the father of the illegitimate child be overruled, and that he be discharged from his recognizance.[95]

Thus the case was dismissed and Alexander Whistelo was exonerated.

Pascalis on Religion and Science

That the priest had lost his faith in the Catholic Church even before meeting the prophetess in 1791 should not suggest that he ever became an atheist. It appears instead that the erstwhile abbé eventually adopted something of a deistic worldview, like so many intellectuals in the revolutionary Atlantic world, along with a strong dose of utilitarianism, as reflected in one of the final sentences of one of his last publications: "But without endeavouring to penetrate into the secret views of Providence, let us study the means of employing advantageously the powers offered with infinite goodness to human industry; for in the end, practical utility will be found to be the best part of philosophy, and the only one which we may cultivate with pleasure and profit."[96]

The deism of Félix Pascalis is discernible as early as 1801, in his address to the Chemistry Society of Philadelphia, where he writes: "You know, Gentlemen, how numerous are the branches of universal Philosophy! they form like a beautiful tree, which often has been drawn by the hand of genius."[97] A few pages later one finds further evidence of Pascalis' religious thought that reflects a kind of evolutionist view of polytheistic religion, and perhaps a premonition of secularization theory: "The supreme laws of existence . . . without the knowledge of its laws, Philosophy would be mute at the view of the stupendous works of nature, *or she would be obliged to conceive as many deities as there are prodigies in the creation*."[98] The address concludes on a note that reflects both his Enlightenment faith in science and his lingering belief in a distant creator God, something akin to Aristotle's "unmoved mover." In closing, Pascalis dedicates the address to the influential English religious dissenter and scientist Joseph Priestley, the man who discovered oxygen:

> [T]o whom our science is so much indebted: Priestley, the persecuted friend of Liberty, of Religion, and the model of all social and private virtues. Honoured is our Society with such members: congratulated is the Republic, with such citizens, and happy is the rising generation with such philanthropic examples, which have already opened to you the Golden Aera of SCIENCE and LIBERTY.[99]

Ultimately, Pascalis understood science, and especially natural science, more so than religion, to be the source of human understanding of "the only order in which the Almighty Creator of the world has performed all its wonders."[100]

By far the greatest insight into the religious thought of Félix Pascalis Ouvière is found in three letters that he wrote to his daughter in 1813 and 1814, which were lessons he scripted as a supplement to her schoolhouse education. At the time, the priest was living in New York City and trying to establish his medical practice and secure a house for his family there, while his wife and three children lived in Hanover, New Jersey, in some financial distress.[101] Dated December 13, 1813, December 31, 1813, and January 26, 1814, the letters respectively compare and contrast Judaism and Christianity, summarize classical Greek and Roman mythology, and critically discuss the Prophet Muhammad and Islam. It is some reflection of Francisca's (Francesca's) genius that her father wrote these long and rather sophisticated lessons for her when she was but 10 years old, just as it is noteworthy that Pascalis' theorization about religion features key ideas that would later be expressed by such giants of the classical history, philosophy, and sociology of religion as Ludwig Feuerbach, Karl Marx, Émile Durkheim, Max Weber, Rudolf Otto, and Mircea Eliade.

In the first of these letters, Pascalis speaks generally about religion before launching into his comparison of Judaism and Christianity. All religions are characterized by three basic things, namely "tenets," "worship," and "a sense of piety to God." Nevertheless, "the Christian religion is better than that of the Jews or any other" because it alone engendered justice and civilization. The problem with Judaism, for Pascalis—over and above his belief that Jews crucified Jesus as "an imposter"—was its theocratic inability to separate religious law from secular law, and here the priest quotes Jesus: "My kingdom is not of this world." Jews, furthermore, are prone to "fraud" and "addicted to traffic and commerce," while Jewish law is anachronistic, for "how is it to be obtained, if the law given once in the land of Palestine should not be fit for the people of America who certainly could not abstain from eating pork. Especially in Virginia."[102]

As for "the Heathen or the Pagan religion, it was very ancient and nearly universal." Calculating human history in biblical terms as being 5,813 years long, Pascalis lamented that Pagan beliefs were "a very shocking circumstance in the history of man," reflecting "darkness and ignorance" of ages and empires bereft of the Christian Gospel. It was, however, only natural for non-Christian peoples to be religious, for

> man in a state of nature is inclined to acknowledge a power or supreme being that overvales this world, and fills it up with wonders in the heavens as well as on the surface of the earth, and in the depths

> of the seas ... everything in the world is for ourselves prepared by that supreme power who takes care of us, which we sometimes dread, sometimes cherish, and must always supplicate. Hence mankind are inclined to assimilate God to themselves or to elevate their own species to all the great attributes which they can bestow on a deity or a supreme being they do not see but whom they assume present in everything that encites their admiration or their gratitude.[103]

Islam, meanwhile, although not as great as Christianity, enjoyed certain advantages over Paganism. The Prophet Muhammad, for one thing, was "an extraordinary man," while the Quran "in many ways is full of sanctity and good things." Muhammad was deluded, however, and perhaps an epileptic who mistook his seizures to be calls from the Archangel Gabriel, while "the splendid promises he made to his followers for future happiness in heaven was quite enchanting and seducing." For Pascalis, the true measure of prophecy was the ability to perform miracles, and in this Muhammad fell short, while the true measure of religion lies in its civilizing effect, and in this Islam fell short: "It is rather humiliating to see that the Mahometan religion, that of the Hindus and Chinese exist over a larger population than the Christian, yet ... almost all the Christian nations are civilized and enlightened, while the others are still semi-barbarians and savage-like tribes."[104]

At the time he was writing his letters on religion to his beloved 10-year-old daughter, the priest could not have imagined that nine years later she would be stricken with a fatal disease. In 1823 Francesca Anna Canfield (*née* Francisca Anna Pascalis) contracted tuberculosis, at the age of 19, and in effect spent the next 10 years dying.[105] Born in Philadelphia in 1803, Canfield was a tremendously gifted person. By her teenage years she was translating into English sophisticated literature from French, Italian, Spanish, and Portuguese, and she was a talented, if underappreciated, poet of "fine and promiscuous powers" who actually wrote some of her original poems in Italian and published in literary journals under various pseudonyms.[106] She was also an accomplished painter and musician, though the bankruptcy of her husband, Palmer Canfield, a man that Pascalis had distrusted and considered to be "too sly," left her destitute.[107]

Eventually Francesca's illness would drive her father to abandon his medical practice and transform him into something of a recluse, quietly awaiting his own death. Overwhelmed by her suffering, in the end the priest placed his faith not so much in Christianity or in the abolitionist cause, but in science, though even from science he would, too, become somewhat alienated in part for its failure to deliver Francesca from the scourge of consumption. Because

Pascalis took up a pen with much less frequency as of 1823, it is very difficult to tell if his daughter's suffering triggered any wavering in his religious faith, though a tone of sadness and a dip in the priest's trademark Enlightenment enthusiasm is notable in his writings thereafter.

With his daughter now seriously ill, on May 24, 1823, Pascalis gave an invited lecture before a distinguished gathering of scientists, doctors, scholars, politicians, and foreign diplomats in Flushing, New York, united in commemoration of the birth of Linnaeus. It was a grand affair, at which a congratulatory letter from Thomas Jefferson was read aloud to a crowd of hundreds of New York's most distinguished residents and visitors, including the French prince Achille Murat, erstwhile King of Naples, and both the French and Swedish ambassadors to the United States. There were 500 people in all, many having made the two-hour trip over from lower Manhattan on the steamboat *Fanny* to great fanfare: "On leaving the shore, a band of music, which had been provided for the occasion, struck up a lively air, and continued at intervals to regale the company with several favorite tunes till the boat reached its destination just before 11 o'clock."[108] Being now himself 80-years-old, Jefferson's letter was an expression of gratitude for the invitation and a salute to "Doctors Mitchill and Pascalis with sentiments of respect and the highest esteem."[109] Upon the completion of his speech on his "pure and energetic sentiments on recent advances in botany," meanwhile, Pascalis articulated what we may take to be his parting message to the world, even though he still had "ten disconsolate years" left to live:[110]

> Dr. Pascalis observed that he would take the liberty of adding one remark. In this age of revolution and contentious forms of respecting national government, of armed political alliances, and of sanguinary wars, from the ancient Bosporus, to the trans-Atlantic American shores, was it not a matter of congratulation that science *alone* was peaceably progressing in the adoption of a uniform language, and of principles of our welfare and happiness, thereby establishing a universal brotherhood in the great family of mankind?[111]

In science, the priest thus kept the faith, and science he never criticized. He refuted the scientific theories of others, to be sure, but he never explicitly offered any criticism of science itself. Criticism of religion, meanwhile, does occasionally surface in Pascalis' writings, even of Christianity, and one speech that he had delivered in Philadelphia in 1801 provoked an angry editorial in a local newspaper that accused him of being involved, along with the likes of Diderot, Jefferson, and Voltaire, in a "destructive conspiracy against the

Christian religion."[112] In one particularly outlandish passage from an essay on venereal disease, for another instance, Pascalis credits the emergence of the vow of celibacy in Catholic history with a rise in syphilis and other sexually transmitted ailments among monks and nuns; for, "the more numerous such institutions for celibacy were, the greater became the danger of that kind of immorality which insinuated itself into the solitary cloisters of virgins, overleaped the barriers of connubial beds, and exposed every female to promiscuous connections; thus multiplying the impure sources of virulent disease."[113]

Less speculatively than the priest's historical ruminations, his medical and scientific work often positioned him to keenly observe the function of religion in the face of human suffering. For example, Pascalis' treatment of many yellow fever patients over the years gave him occasion to witness firsthand the function of religion in negotiating the epidemic, which was not always, in his view, positive. Reflecting upon responses to the outbreak of the disease in Spain, while ruminating over his own observations on the 1805 outbreak that he went to Cadiz to study, he writes:

> Instead of resignation and comfort, religion did but administer despair, with the awful scene of a last judgment; for, with every case of death a funeral procession was instituted; and while holy images, relics, and sacramental objects were incessantly offered to the eyes of dejected people, thundering preachers were solemnly warning every one of his approaching and final destination.[114]

In a later study of an outbreak of yellow fever in New York, Pascalis makes careful and informed mention of the Catholic practice of one sick woman named Mrs. Kavanaugh, and "the sacred rites" that were administered during her last days. The first victim of the epidemic in Pascalis' study, Kavanaugh succumbed to the disease at her home near Fulton Street, after which, "according of the customs of the Irish nation, and to the rites of the Roman Catholic profession, there has been a repetition of night wakes, administration of the sacraments, and crowded meetings of friends and religious people."[115] Furthermore, Kavanaugh had received Extreme Unction two days before her death: "The Rev. T. W. French, a Catholic priest, administered the sacred rites on the evening of the 27th of August; after which she remained in a kind of agony, and died on the 29th."[116]

There are 65 other patients discussed in Pascalis' short book on the 1819 yellow fever epidemic in New York, yet religion is only mentioned in the Kavanaugh case. We read nothing of Protestant responses to the disease, despite New York's being a predominately Protestant city at the time: nothing of faith healing, of pastors visiting the sick and dying, of people turning to the Bible for solace, prayer vigils, or of funerary sermons. This is additionally curious in light of the fact that Pascalis himself served as a "lay delegate" to the 1817 Convention of the Protestant Episcopal Diocese of New York, which was held that year at Trinity Church in New York City, where presumably he was a member,[117] and that at least two collections of sermons by distinguished Protestant preachers were part of his library.[118] Protestantism is also absent from Pascalis' 1813 letters on religion to his daughter and from his most extensive published discussion of religion, which is found in his 1823 treatise on burial. Here he devotes many pages to describing funerary rites among the ancient Greeks and Romans, "the Hottentots," the Chinese, Hindus, Jews, "the Germans, Gauls, the inhabitants of Lithuania, the Tyrians and the Phrygians: the Ethiopians, Goths,"[119] and Catholic Christians. Still, there is not a word on Protestants. It would seem that the priest's Catholic religious habitus predisposed him to silence Protestantism in his oeuvre, just as his Catholic religious capital had allowed him to contribute to the fall of Romaine-la-Prophétesse and the Trou Coffy insurgency.

Thus was Doctor Félix Pascalis a stout embodiment of the central Enlightenment debates about science and religion. Though once a Catholic priest, at a time when many Catholic priests also engaged in scientific inquiry, and though later a deistically inclined Episcopalian and evidently also a Freemason,[120] Pascalis never abandoned belief in God and was a lifelong practicing Christian, and he leaves us with nothing that could be considered an outright rejection of religion. Ever aspiring to scientific rigor and objectivity, and being an astute observer of the past as well as the present, he did view some forms of religious leadership as being rooted in madness—that charisma could ultimately prove to be, in certain cases at least, rooted in delusion—or, as with the Prophet Muhammad, convulsive disorders. One has to wonder if Pascalis might have had Romaine-la-Prophétesse in mind when he wrote the following opinion in 1823, for example:

> It has also been clearly ascertained, that the greater number of victims of mental derangement are predisposed with the idea of superior attributes: and many conquerors of old, and religious sectaries, who disturbed the peace of the world by asserting that they were privileged beings, prophets or divine messengers, are now accounted nothing more than illustrious madmen.[121]

Such criticisms notwithstanding, in some of his letters to Benjamin Rush, Pascalis indicates that he remained a man of prayer at least as late as 1812.[122] As mentioned above, by the time that he married Eliza at Christ Church, in 1801, the former Catholic priest had become a lay Episcopalian. This conversion may have been a prerequisite to Pascalis' marriage, as his wife seems to have been of a deeper religious conviction than he, even though she would not take her first communion until very late in life, at age 70, in 1848.[123] Her prayerfulness is reflected in a March 8, 1812, letter that first thanks Rush for his suggestions for treatment of some unnamed illness that had afflicted Eliza, and then offers prayers to Pascalis' old colleague and friend:

> I am happy to inform you that Mrs. Pascalis continues enjoying of the best State of Health and not the least . . . remaining of her former complaint. She begs to be remembered to you offering her incessant prayers to heaven for health and happiness of all that belong to you, her prayers might be more worthy but not more fervent than those of your, respectfully
>
> Obedient and Humble Servant
> Felix Pascalis[124]

In an earlier letter informing Rush of his pending 1805–1806 trip to Europe to study the yellow fever epidemic there, meanwhile, Pascalis' words likewise reflect an enduring faith in God, though one whose definition was for him then perhaps blurring:

> The succeeding winter will see me in Paris and the ensuing spring in America again with my family if Providence protects my life and if it is not deemed that I must alter my projects. . . .
>
> May the Supreme ruler preserve your Health prolong your domestic happiness and entreat his blessings upon every individual of your family.[125]

A careful analysis of Pascalis' writings thus reveals changes in his religious thought over the course of his life. In light of his radical changes in character and the devastating tragedies that he knew so intimately—slavery, violence, and revolution in Saint-Domingue; yellow fever epidemics in multiple places; the terminal illness of his beloved daughter between her nineteenth and twenty-ninth years—this is to be expected. It is not inconceivable that the erstwhile priest had harbored deistic ideas even while he was a practicing Catholic priest, but my sense is that they are more the product of his own development as a thinker and his associations with leading scientific figures in America. All the same, for Pascalis scientific pursuits were sacred endeavors that ultimately shed light on the handiwork of the Creator: "The capacity to acquire a sufficient knowledge of the laws of nature, is a gift bestowed upon us by our Supreme Ruler, to the end that we may derive from it all those blessings which it is susceptible of yielding."[126]

Nearing the End

In his very last research paper, published in 1826, Pascalis chose to write on something that "mars the enjoyment of life," namely pain, perhaps driven to tackle the subject by the personal sorrow that had shrouded the priest in his waning years. In first reading the essay I couldn't help but wonder if in his ruminations on the nature of pain the priest had the prophetess and his victims in mind, or the sufferings of slaves in Saint-Domingue and the eventual triumph of the Haitian Revolution, when he ended his last essay with the following long quotation from Pierre Jean Georges Cabanis, a French contemporary who was renowned as a physiologist for his materialism:

> [I]t is, however, necessary, that pain should be assisted by a proportionate degree of reaction, and that nature should always be roused from depression, with a degree of vigour: thus it is that new afflictions can increase the power of the soul, provided it does not prostrate it in despondency and despair. Misfortune not only assists us in judging, with more truth, of all things, and men, in life, but it raises and sharpens our courage, that we could always find in it, when required, a firm support against the evils of human life.[127]

Though seemingly transformed into something of a recluse once his daughter fell ill, perhaps caring for her constantly at home, desperately unable to curé her, Pascalis did make an occasional public appearance in his waning years, all of the pain and suffering be damned. The most notable of such occasions was on October 15, 1831, when the New York City and County Medical Society invited him to deliver at City Hall a memorial address upon the death of his close friend and colleague Samuel Latham Mitchill, one of the towering figures in early American medicine.[128] Because it reflects some measure of sustained religious belief, and because it suggests that Pascalis viewed science as the handiwork of God, I cite here the entirety of the concluding paragraph:

> O sacred and revered shade! We are now parted forever in this mundane scene—but thou shalt still be with us in thy writings, in thy virtues, thy services to thy country and thy kind; still present to us in the

> work of Creation, which thou didst labour so earnestly to describe and arrange. O that I who am now allowed to dedicate this humble tribute to thy memory,—I though who wishing to tred in thy footsteps, have still ever found myself detained far behind,—tu autem longe vestigia sequere,—O that I might be permitted to climb by thy visible garments and fly with thee to immortality! Then should my faint and feeble tribute to thy praise be embalmed in thy glory, and might bear to be inscribed:— Exegi monumentum aere perennius!![129]

With his own health failing and the years of hard work and adventure eventually catching up with the priest, now overcome with grief, he wrote in a September 7, 1832 letter that he was "seriously indisposed and unable to go out."[130] Resigned to the inevitable, six months later Pascalis hastened to write his last will and testament, bequeathing his estate to his son Cyril in a handwritten document dated May 31, 1833, which opens with the line "In the name of God—Amen."[131] Perhaps thus flying to Mitchill in immortality, embalmed in like glory, the priest died seven weeks later, in New York City, on July 22, 1833.[132]

But even in death Pascalis would remain a part of the slave system that rocked and shaped the revolutionary Atlantic world and that largely financed modernity itself. For, in 1835, Cyril and his mother, the priest's widow, Eliza Pascalis, invested whatever fortune that Abbé Ouvière had left them in the purchase of a 790-acre plantation in the slaving state of South Carolina, naming the big house "Pascalina."[133] The priest's life, death, and postmortem trajectory may thus be traced to etch out a veritable map of the revolutionary Atlantic world as created by "the peculiar institution" of slavery: from Marseille, a city that flourished in large part through the French enslavement of hundreds of thousands of Africans and Creole blacks in the New World; to Saint-Domingue, "what was then the wealthiest colony in the world" owing entirely to slavery,[134] where Pascalis joined forces with the insurrectionary free coloreds in the Haitian Revolution; to Pennsylvania, where in 1780 the Atlantic world's first abolitionist legislation was enacted; to New York, a city whose population at the turn of the century was 20 percent enslaved";[135] and finally, postmortem, to South Carolina, where the priest's fortune was invested in a slave plantation deep in the American South. It had been quite a journey indeed, in life and in death, though in closing it should be affirmed that, unlike the mysterious prophetess, and unlike the priest's own beautiful wife, Félix Pascalis Ouvière never owned a slave.

9

The Prophetess in Fantasy and Imagination

Timoun fwonte grandi devan Bawon.

—HAITIAN PROVERB[1]

Overview

"TOUSSAINT LOUVERTURE, DESSALINES. Pétion, Christophe, as much as Dom Pèdre, Makandal, Romaine-la-Prophétesse, have furnished legend with an abundance of material. Popular imagination has pulled fantastic fables from them, some of which are the stuff of our wildest superstitions."[2] Such is the assessment of Jean Price-Mars, stated in his classic book *Ainsi parla l'oncle*, and he's right. From Vodou priest to female maroon;[3] from fanatical charlatan to bloodthirsty warlord; from "hermaphroditic tiger" to a hero of the Haitian Revolution—Romaine-la-Prophétesse has certainly "furnished legend with an abundance of material." In light of all the historical evidence presented in this book, it should be clear that some representations of the prophetess in historical memory and popular imagination deviate distantly from empirical fact, as is the case with the recounting and recalling of the lives of most historical actors who were quite literally larger than life. Romaine-la-Prophétesse's concrete achievements during the 1791–1792 insurgencies in Saint-Domingue were indeed as spectacular as they were violent, and they were indeed rooted in his extraordinary religious vision. And although I have found no clear evidence of what precisely became of the prophetess after the fall of Trou Coffy in March of 1792, it is quite likely that, over and above his conquest of Léogâne and Jacmel and his destruction of the region's plantations, Romaine served to radicalize an entire generation of slaves and politically-alienated free coloreds around him, thereby priming much of the West Province for triumphs by later, more celebrated heroes of the epic saga of the Haitian Revolution, like Toussaint Louverture and Alexandre Pétion.

One historian suggests as much; that is, after the defeat of the Trou Coffy insurgency some of "the disciples of Romaine Rivière, aka Romaine-la-Prophétesse," reorganized and participated in subsequent battles of the Haitian Revolution. Leslie Péan offers that Romaine's followers, along with other unruly warlords, "were gunned down on the orders of Dessalines and Christophe in 1802."[4] Péan's source for this intriguing claim is Claude Auguste's article "Les Congos dans la Révolution Haïtienne," but he seems to have misread it. Though Auguste briefly mentions both Romaine-la-Propétesse and Abbé Ouvière, later in the essay he discusses an insurgent leader in the North Province named "Romain," one of the "Congo farmers" whose followers "sacked the plantations around Limbé and Acul" in 1802.[5] Romaine-la-Prophétesse and the Romain discussed by Auguste, however, were surely two different people, and though he was a farmer, Romaine Rivière, as we have already established, was clearly not Kongolese.[6]

Scholars who work in biblical studies and Christology distinguish the *Christ of History* from the *Jesus of Faith*, to paraphrase the title of a David Friedrich Strauss classic in the field.[7] Without intending to draw comparisons between the Christian savior and Romaine-la-Prophétesse—however tempting it might be—methodologically, the same distinction may be made about the historical Romaine Rivière and the prophetess of desirous or desultory imaginings of the past. That they may be imaginings does not imply a lack of consequence, for their contributions to their bearer's very sense of identity are often deep and thus quite real, much like religious faith that is rooted in not the slightest shard of evidence in primary sources or archaeological artifacts. Though conservative historians might reject this short chapter as an unnecessary detour from the strongly evidence-based chapters that precede it, I believe that the book would be incomplete without the present exploration. As suggested by Michel-Rolph Trouillot, one of the real challenges of writing history, especially of writing history of political revolutions, is striking a balance between banalization and romanticization.[8] In part this chapter is rooted in an awareness of that challenge and an effort to rise to it, for slavish devotion to positivism in the quest to write history tempts banalization, while explorations of fantasy and imagination tempt romanticization. Just as those are two different kinds of distortion, so too are fact and fantasy both real, and they each beckon analysis toward striking that balance.

Visions of the Prophetess, or the Lack Thereof

Were this book about Toussaint Louverture, Henry Christophe, or Jean-Jacques Dessalines, it would carry a lavishly illustrated chapter analyzing their representations in the history of Haitian art. Unfortunately, I have never found a single representation of Romaine-la-Prophétesse produced by any Haitian painter. To be sure, some of them have quite imaginatively portrayed the most celebrated *léogânaise* in history, the Taino queen Anacaona, who has even appeared on Dominican and Cuban postage stamps, but not the city's most important revolutionary in the person of the *léogânais(e)* Romaine-la-Prophétesse.[9] Thus I am bound to commission one as soon as finances permit, but for now I can only comment on his invisibility, and his spirit, in Haiti's otherwise virile visual culture, especially its Vodouist visual culture, one born, as Karen Richman reports, out of mimesis, as in a real sense was Haiti itself: "Mimetic interplay has shaped all encounters between European colonizers and the colonized."[10]

Haiti's is among the world's most celebrated national artistic cultures, and rightly so. As colorfully as anyone, the French surrealist writer André Breton reflects upon its power: "Haitian painting will drink the blood of the phoenix. And, with the epaulets of Dessalines, it will ventilate the world."[11] Breton especially had in mind the work of legendary painter and Vodou priest Hector Hyppolite, a native of Saint-Marc, the very town from which Abbé Ouvière would leave Saint-Domingue forever in 1792. Like most of the Haitian masters, Hyppolite painted the great revolutionary heroes of his nation, along with a whole host of Vodou spirits and many other things. But also like all other Haitian masters and the legions that paint in their honor, never did he paint Romaine-la-Prophétesse. This strange fact has long puzzled me, for why should one of the most heroic figures of the Haitian Revolution, someone deeply devoted to the saints and the cause of liberty for which Haiti stands, someone who in a real sense was a patriarch of Haitian Vodou, be perpetually ignored by the nation's extraordinary artists? While living in Port-au-Prince, I marveled to see the founding fathers on murals, on tap-taps, and the walls of ubiquitous beauty salons, along with the likes of Jean-Bertrand Aristide, Jesus Christ, Bill Clinton, Bob Marley, Malcolm X, Muhammad Ali, Michael Jackson, and the French footballer Bixente Lizarazu, but nowhere Romaine-la-Prophétesse. Why is this?

Perhaps the answer to this question lies in the fact that there is no extant contemporary portrait of Romaine-la-Prophétesse from which painters may work, although such a reality has never prohibited Haitian artists from painting the *lwa*—or Makandal or Boukman, for that matter. Perhaps the absence of the prophetess in Haitian visual culture has to do with his relatively brief appearance in the earliest phase of the Haitian Revolution, as one finds few, if any, images of Jean-François or Biassou, but Boukman's appearance in the epic saga was brief, if not briefer, and that hasn't stopped many Haitian artists from painting him. Though there is no way of verifying this, another possibility is that because he may have been eliminated by one of the most popular historical figures in Haitian art, Jean-Jacques Dessalines, Romaine-la-Prophétesse may also have been banished from the easels of the nation's artists; the same could also be suggested for pages and notes of Haitian poets, novelists, and musicians.

The eventual desertion of Romaine by the *gens de couleur libres*, as well as their fighting for the French commander Edmond de Saint-Léger to defeat the Trou Coffy insurgency, reflects deep racial and class divisions within the free black community of Saint-Domingue; that, from the standpoint of the likes of mulatto elites who had obtained their education in Paris, Marseille, and Aix-en-Provence, Romaine-la-Prophétesse was simply too black, too un-French, and too uncivilized. As such, the prophetess might have been a victim of what Trouillot refers to as "the war within the war," an unpleasant sociocultural reality in Saint-Domingue that racially complicated and exacerbated the struggle of the Haitian Revolution:

> [A]n amalgam of unhappy incidents that pitted the black Jacobins, Creole slaves and freedmen alike, against hordes of uneducated "Congos," African-born slaves, Bossale men with strange surnames, like Sans Souci, Makaya, Sylla, Mavougou, Lamour de la Rance, Petit Noel Prieur (or Prière), Va-Malheureux, Macaque, Alaou, Coco, Sangalou—slave names quite distinguishable from the French sounding ones of Jean-Jacques Dessalines, Alexandre Pétion, Henry Christophe, Augustin Clervaux, and the like.[12]

In itself, that he took the title "Prophetess," just like Petit Noel Prieur seems to have taken the title "Prior," as in a monastic superior, as well as "Christmas," places Romaine in the former class of revolutionary actors; even though Romaine was not African born, he was indeed uneducated, black, and the leader of a violent "horde." He was also an immigrant "Spaniard"—a *panyol*—who, despite his stated, mimetic allegiance to the king of France, was illiterate and rather ignorant of the French culture with which the economically and politically powerful in Saint-Domingue identified, whites and free coloreds alike. Short a postcolonial optic and careful attention to the function of "power" in "the production of history," we are indeed left with a silenced Romaine, the Romaine of Edmond de Saint-Léger's heroic tale of the Fall of Trou Coffy, a "Congo," if not a "Kongo": "That many of these Congos were leaders of the 1791 uprising . . . [and] staunch defenders of the cause of freedom has been passed over."[13] Could it be that Romaine has thus far been passed over by Haitian painters for similar reasons?

There are signs in the blogosphere that Romaine-la-Prophétesse has recently been recast as a genuine hero of the Haitian Revolution. Take the following suggestion by Péan, for instance, which in effect flips the war within a war on its head:

> Let us also remember that the black generals of the army of Toussaint Louverture gave themselves up to [the French general] Leclerc in 1801 and that Dessalines butchered the black insurgents who never laid down their arms against the French. Let us finally remember that it was the farmers/soldiers *Lamour Dérance, Courfolles, Sans Souci, Macaya, Romaine la prophétesse, Mavouyou, Va-Malheureux, Petit Noel Prieur, Gingembre, Trop Fort, etc.* who were the true artisans of national independence, contrary to the history texts written by elites and their like who tell us that they merely amounted to "leaders of hordes."[14]

Here Romaine is celebrated as one of the "true artisans" of Haitian independence, while Dessalines is unceremoniously knocked off his pedestal on the Champ de Mars, the promenade in Port-au-Prince where his statue reigns supreme, the great warrior riding triumphant on horseback in an image that surely conjures Ogou, as Sen Jak Majè, for many Vodouists—and he appears again, additionally, just down the road on the Champ de Mars, only this time afoot, his sabre raised to the sky. Along with Dessalines, meanwhile, the prophetess becomes a muse for at least one Haitian poet, Jean Métellus, who celebrates Romaine in a poem for "the hero of the cause of Blacks in America," Mumia Abu-Jamal.[15] The dreadlocked activist/journalist Abu-Jamal was convicted in 1982 for the killing of a white Philadelphia police officer, Daniel Faulkner, just about 12 blocks from where Abbé Ouvière once lived; since then the accused has been internationally elevated to the status of a martyr, rightly or wrongly.

Elsewhere in the blogosphere Romaine is celebrated as a maroon in a lineage tied to native Indian chiefs like Anacaona. Without considering the deep Marian dimensions of the Trou Coffy rebellion, for instance, Daniel Daréus lumps Romaine-la-Prophétesse together with the likes of Makandal among the "Ancients" who employed Vodou as "the tool with which ... [they] had demolished the colonial slave order established by the Christian West in Saint-Domingue."[16] While Daréus obviously has some historical facts wrong, his effort to valorize Romaine-la-Prophétesse, along with that of Péan and others, will hopefully be embraced by Haitian artists toward inspiring them to visualize and to paint him, and toward inspiring more poets like Métellus to turn to him as a muse.

Or perhaps he is already there, even ubiquitously, in subtle ways. To evoke Thoreau, "The question is not what you look at, but what you see."[17] For those who know of him, Romaine-la-Prophétesse may well appear anytime they see an image of Our Lady of Czestochowa, the patron saint of Poland, who is widely revered in Haiti, a black Madonna with two scars on her cheek that are believed by some today to have resulted from wounds she suffered during the Haitian Revolution, perhaps even at Trou Coffy.[18] Or when they see other revolutionary heroes or Vodou spirits parading across the canvasses of the great Haitian masters, or Saint Jacques—Ogun, brandishing a sword, much like Romaine did on Christmas Day in 1791 when he held his historical meeting with Abbé Ouvière, and much like Dessalines does to this day on the Champ de Mars in Port-au-Prince.

Though the prophetess is seemingly absent from the scene, in these ways of seeing he may well still have his place in multivalent acts of "visual piety" among those who believe in him.[19] Though he may never become a Vodou spirit like Dessalines, nor his name become synonymous in Haitian Creole for something so fearsome as poison, as with Makandal's,[20] perhaps Romaine is already there, a part of it all, just preferring to remain a bit more mysterious than the more celebrated heroes and the mysteries themselves. "And that *Aha!* that you get when you see an artwork that really hits you is," writes Joseph Campbell, "'I am that.' I am the radiance and the energy that is talking to me through this painting."[21] Radiance and energy were two things that the dramatic, Virgin-intoxicated Romaine-la-Prophétesse certainly possessed in abundance, as reflected in both his charisma and the brief but remarkable description that the priest wrote about his chapel at Trou Coffy, and they surely shine through in Haitian visual arts even where the prophetess is not looked at, only to be seen.

In recently bringing up these issues in a lecture at Temple University, one of my students raised the possibility that Romaine-la-Prophétesse has not been embraced as a hero in statue or painting because he is thought to have been gay.[22] This is plausible, for there is a clear strain of hetero-masculinity in the statues of Dessalines on the Champ de Mars and the Neg Mawon before the Presidential Palace in Saint-Domingue. Unlike the common images of Toussaint, Christophe, and Dessalines, furthermore, who are/were adorned as military officers, Romaine dressed in a robe covered in rosaries, ribbons, and religious (not military) medals, and he wore a turban topped by a plume, rather than a tricorne. Haitian society is quite homophobic, so maybe Romaine-la-Prophétesse has been closeted in the nationalist registry of heroism because he is widely assumed to have been gay, even though in reality he probably wasn't, however much this really shouldn't matter.[23]

The prophetess' gender-bending, however, is in itself heroic, especially when we consider its time and place. Just as those who are reconsidering the narrative of the Haitian Revolution to situate him on the pedestal of political liberation and negritude, so too are some historians beginning to set the foundation stones of his monument as a hero of sexual liberation. Omise'eke Natasha Tinsley, for instance, interprets his feminine title as "prophetess" to mean "not only that Romaine had feminine identifications, but that he felt that those feminine identifications led him to do divine battle." To recall from Chapter 2, Romaine's femininity was indeed consistent with African notions of the penetration of feminized male human bodies by the spirits, raising the radical imagination of the prophetess' being penetrated by his virgin godmother, who indeed inspired him to take up arms and lead thousands of insurgents to conquer two cities and strike a serious blow against some of the worst human oppression that the world has ever known. Though historically we may never be able to verify such a connection, it is not a stretch to tie Romaine, by way of the Virgin Mary, to Ezili Dantò, the fiercest female divinity in the Vodou pantheon. Tinsley thus provokes us to read Dantò as "our mother of black independence . . . a lesbian mother" and "to love black women's queerness as if it gave birth to the possibility of freedom, because it did. . . ."[24] Why indeed shouldn't Romaine-la-Prophétesse thus serve as an icon of LGBT pride? Or freedom?

The Prophetess in Fictional Literature: Victor Hugo's Bug Jargal and Maya Montero's In the Palm of Darkness

Whatever worldly fate that might in the end have befallen him, and despite his being celebrated in some circles as a true hero of Haitian independence and in others as an icon of gay liberation and black power, history for the most part has been unkind to Romaine-la-Prophétesse. So, too, has fictional literature. News of the violence and destruction that he inspired out of Trou Coffy, for instance, did not go unnoticed in France, where it was sensationalized in the work of Louis-Marie Prudhomme and subsequently referred to over 15 years later in a medical journal.[25] Romaine-la-Prophétesse' white-written tale was then picked up by none other than Victor Hugo, "one of the shining lights of French Romanticism," in his 1826 novel *Bug Jargal*, which one critic called an "anti-Haitian diatribe" reflective of its author's "negrophobia,"[26] while another laments it as a "mixophobic text."[27] Léon-François Hoffmann locates the novel's inspiration in the "reactionary juvenilia" of its author's "royalist conservatism," for at the time Hugo "lamented the loss of France's richest colony," blaming "it on the cynical ambition of bloodthirsty native leaders and the misguided ideology of revolutionary France."[28] Hoffmann further suggests that the rebel leaders in *Bug Jargal*, like Romaine-la-Prophétesse, serve in the structure of the novel as "[a]n indispensable stock character of French melodrama ... the villain, who, in contradistinction with the hero, is the incarnation of all evil traits."[29] Meanwhile, Chris Bongie, translator of *Bug Jargal* into English, convincingly argues that "Hugo learned about this intriguingly named rebel leader from Lacroix,"[30] for elements of Hugo's description of Romaine are clearly derived from Joseph-François Pamphile Lacroix's contemporary account (which itself cites Father Blouët's *Rapport* in a footnote), one of the most influential sources for later commentaries on Romaine:

> A Spanish griffe named *Romaine-Rivière*, more widely known as *Romaine-la-Prophétesse*, had come and settled in Trou-Coffi with a fanatical band of blacks and men of color. From the midst of his camp, where he profaned the holy mysteries, he called the gangs of slaves from the hills and the plain of Léogâne to murder and carnage. He proclaimed himself to be inspired by the Virgin Mary, whom he consulted by placing his head into the tabernacle. He himself transmitted her answers; they always promised certain victories and easy pillages. This was more than enough to seduce the barbarians. His proselytes were many; the men of color of Léogâne and surrounding parishes flocked to the side of this adventurer.[31]

Like Lacroix, Hugo does not give voice to Romaine, thus underscoring violence while muting the human aspirations and spiritual forces behind the Trou Coffy insurgency and by extension the Haitian Revolution itself, world history's only successful national slave rebellion. Romaine never really speaks in the novel but is only spoken of, twice, by Pierrot, an "elderly African leader"[32] of the slave insurrections in the North Province, addressing Biassou and André Rigaud:

> "Biassou, ponder this example! Why all these massacres that oblige the whites to respond with such ferocity? And why resort to trickery for the purpose of whipping our poor comrades into a frenzy when they are already past the boiling point? At Trou Coffy there is a mulatto charlatan by the name of Romaine the Prophetess who goaded a band of

> blacks to the point of fanaticism: he profanes the sacred mass; he persuades his followers that he is in contact with the Virgin Mary, whose supposed oracles he listens to by placing his head in the tabernacle; he incites his comrades to murder and pillage, all in the name of *Maria*!"[33]

After thus mildly plagiarizing Lacroix, Hugo—who clearly had no idea that André Riguad in fact bequeathed the title of commander general to Romaine-la-Prophétesse—next has his narrator "offended and provoked" by "something even more tender than religious devotion in the way Pierrot uttered" Romaine's name.[34] In the following paragraph of the novel, Pierrot suggests that Romaine is an "obi," which was a contemporary term for sorcerer that is one etymological root of the West Indian word "Obeah," and that Romaine is a "trickster."[35] Fear ensued, compelling Pierrot to raise the following question, which reflects Hugo's own racism as much as it does Romaine's silencing: "I am not unaware that you need a common bond when leading an army made up of men from so many regions, but could you not create it through other means than a ferocious fanaticism and ridiculous superstitions? Believe me, Biassou, the whites are less cruel than we are."[36]

Bug Jargal is not the only novel in which Romaine-la-Prophétesse appears, as Cuban author Mayra Montero resuscitates the prophetess as "a bitch" and the "hungry and bloodthirsty" female leader of a "pack of savannah zombies" in her sensationalist thriller *In the Palm of Darkness*.[37] Exoticist, essentialist red flags about this novel are unwittingly raised by three blurbs on its back cover, where Montero is praised for having "used the vivid and ever-volatile palette of Haiti to paint the darkly swirling essences of *the* Caribbean experience, a new world;" for being a "wonderfully accurate . . . portrayal of the smooth and spherical unity of *the* Haitian mind" and of "what *the* Haitian way of being in the world can mean in contact (and contrast) with American styles of thought and action;" a book "in which people plagued by poverty and savage dictatorship love, laugh and survive."[38]

Set in the twentieth century "in the mountains of violence-torn Haiti," the novel is basically about an American scientist named Victor Grigg who is in Haiti on a quest for specimens of an endangered species of frog (if this sounds evocative of Wade Davis' controversial *The Serpent and the Rainbow*, that's because it is).[39] The protagonist is Thierry Adrien, Grigg's Haitian guide and interpreter. Romaine appears in Chapter 6, "The Hunt," where we learn that Thierry's father was, like Grigg, a hunter only not of frogs but, as a courageous member of a noble band called *pwazon rat* (rat poison), of zombies—"savannah zombies," to be precise—a "profession" that required him to be a devotee of the Vodou spirit "Baron La Croix," master of cemeteries.[40] Thierry's father, also named Thierry, meets his match, however, in the reincarnated Romaine-la-Prophétesse:

> My father was killed by an old she-devil named Romaine La Prophetesse, and evil woman in life, you can just imagine what she was like in death. In her day she had been a *mambo*, a priestess, a *madame* with a hard heart. . . .
>
> The day she ambushed my father, Romaine La Prophetesse was travelling with her pack along the trails of Chilotte, a pack of savannah zombies as hungry and bloodthirsty as she was. They caught him far from camp, doing his business in some bushes—that was another of his old habits: My father never let anybody see him shit, he said it was the moment of greatest weakness for a man and he would go away from his people to do it.

Romaine's fictional cowardice in ambushing Thierry *père* in his "moment of greatest weakness" is only surpassed in brutality by the manner in which her ruthless band of bloodthirsty savages finished off the intrepid zombie hunter. Two of the other members of the *pwazon rat* brigade, savannah zombies named Diovine Joseph and (I kid you not) Moses Dumbo discover the ravaged corpse:

> They found it without its skin. Those beasts had flayed him and left him lying in his own shit. Frou Frou washed him anyway, but afterward she complained that her hands had stuck to his raw flesh, that my father's little veins had wrapped around her fingers like worms. A body without skin is disgusting, but even so, Frou Frou dressed him in his shirt.[41]

In her seeming attempt to valorize "the smooth and spherical unity of the Haitian mind," Montero's objectives in *In the Palm of Darkness* are of course quite the opposite of Hugo's racist novel *Bug Jargal*. Although their portraits of Romaine are on the surface very different—Hugo's historical portrait is of Romaine as a fanatical male leader of rebel slaves in 1791 in Saint-Domingue, while Montero's is of a Romaine reincarnated as a female zombie in the hills outside of Bombardopolis (meaning that Romaine's postmortem transmigration took him far to the north from Trou Coffy)—Hugo and Moreno nevertheless both obsess with what they perceive to be Romaine's fanaticism, violence, and charlatanry. Despite his being depicted as a leader in each portrayal, the prophetess speaks in neither account; as in the historical record and in the illustrious annals of Haitian art and letters, Romaine is here largely muted and masked, as are his followers. We are left once again with no glimpse of his appeal, of the powerful dynamics of social healing in African and Creole religious contexts, or of the resounding blow that the prophetess and his thousands of followers dealt to an unspeakably oppressive colonial slaving regime

Conclusion: Peering through the Weeds

On March 5, 2015, Haitian president Michel Martelly and German ambassador to Haiti Klaus Peter Shick were on hand in Léogâne to celebrate the inauguration of La Place de Sainte Rose de Lima, a public park complete with a basketball court, restrooms, leafy promenades, metal benches, a playground, solar-powered lampposts, and an elevated pavilion for musical and theatrical performances. There they addressed a rather unruly crowd that had gathered on the new plaza, some protesting the state's investment in a public square when the city still had no electricity, no hospital, and no courthouse in the lingering, crumbled wake of the tragic 2010 earthquake. Nonetheless, the ribbons were cut, a monument was unveiled, the dignitaries addressed the masses, *et voilà!*: Léogâne had a new park, a symbol of progress to all but the protesters, one of whom was a short, bald, and boisterous man dressed entirely in white, the color in which his head and face were also painted. A living echo of the dead, who in Kongolese cosmology are white, he was front and center that day and separated from the stage by well-armed police officers dressed in military fatigues.

Located directly across the street from the reconstructed church by the same name, Sainte Rose de Lima—the very sanctuary (now reconstructed) in which Romaine-la-Prophétesse was married to Marie Roze in 1785, and where Abbé Ouvière preached on New Year's Day a few years later—the shiny square was hailed as part of a "renaissance" for Haiti, as a phoenix rising out of the rubble of the horrific 2010 earthquake, which had focused its wrath on Léogâne, a city now "reborn out of the ashes." One journalist reported that this was "a brand new public plaza," but that is only partially true.[42] Yes, the park was given a total makeover and a new name, but it had been there for decades in another form, carrying the name La Place Anacaona previously. It had fallen into desuetude long before the earthquake, choked by weeds, covered with debris from floods of years gone by, an impromptu pasture for generations of draught animals and livestock. It was also at times a de facto marketplace for sex workers and fruit vendors alike, a place altogether abandoned by the state,

FIGURE 9.1 The most celebrated of all Native American leaders in Caribbean history, the cacique Anacaona reigned over a large portion of Hispaniola when the Spanish arrived and was a native of the region that would later be ruled by Romaine-la-Prophétesse. *Queen Anacaona, Léogâne.* 1997. Hervé Montreuil. Photograph by Nathan Rey. Courtesy of the author.

a memorial park whose intended significations had long and largely been forgotten by the people.

I had driven or walked by La Place Anacaona hundreds of times when I lived in Haiti in the 1990s without having the slightest clue that Romaine-la-Prophétesse might be memorialized there. But he was. Somewhere beside the goats and beneath the weeds there lay a plaque ensconcing the following heroes of Léogâne: Marie-Claire Heureuse, Catherine Flon, Romaine-la-Prophétesse, Balthazar Inginac, and Carole Demesmin:[43] An empress, a seamstress of the first Haitian flag, an insurrectionary prophetess, a general and statesman, and a celebrated chanteuse and Vodou priestess. And although the plaque is long gone and the park's name has been changed in honor of a Catholic saint, a saint who was one of the first immigrants to ever live in Léogâne, a large statue of the Taino queen Anacaona rises above the plaza, her head covered in feathers, one hand raised to the sky, the other brandishing a scepter, her chest adorned with necklaces. One would not be mistaken to see in her Romaine-la-Prophétesse, even without looking for him.

Conclusion

Kontre zo na gran chemen, sonje vyann te kouvri'l.
—Haitian Proverb[1]

WHEN EXTERMINATING ANGELS were exterminated in the revolutionary Atlantic world, sometimes their heads were cut off and posted on spikes or otherwise exhibited in the public square for all to see. La Place d'Armes, the heart of Saint-Domingue's largest city, Cap-Français, witnessed its fair share of such macabre spectacles during the colony's turbulent history. The most renowned of these was Boukman's, and surely Makandal's head would have been likewise impaled there had the legendary maroon master of poison not escaped execution by morphing into a fly and buzzing off, as legend would have it. Legendary or factual, what almost always goes unmentioned in accounts of Boukman's fate, however, is that shortly after the rebel slave's decapitation Abbé Philémon, curé of the parish of Limbé, was executed by hanging and that "Boukman's head was placed on the galley to parody the intimate liaison that had existed between him and the chief."[2] Also usually passed over in accounts of his fate is that following Boukman's execution another Catholic priest, Abbé Sulpice,[3] the Capuchin pastor of the Le Trou parish and "chaplain of the army of insurgents, celebrated Masses in all of the insurgent parishes that his soul rest in peace."[4]

When fears of slave insurrection, poison, and pillage spiked among the whites and elite free coloreds of the colony, so too did suspicions that the Catholic clergy were in cahoots with the "*scelerats*"—with the "villains." But when celebrating the "[m]any Spartacuses [who] passed through Haiti as exterminating angels, avenging their race for nearly three centuries of persecution," nineteenth-century Haitian historian Thomas Madiou certainly did not have Abbé Sulpice or Abbé Philemon in mind, listing instead the likes of "Pétion, Clervaux, Capoix, Geffrard, Christophe," who "achieved our independence and completed the work that Toussaint Louverture started." Though unwilling to count a white Catholic priest among the "exterminating angels," Madiou interestingly opines that this "warm" African genius of liberating vengeance is what "animated the Augustines, the Cypriens, the Church fathers."

By Madiou's logic, it was thus an African spirit that led to both "the triumph of Christianity" and to the triumph of the Haitian Revolution, "great catastrophes" in which "the core qualities of Africans are manifest."[5] Despite his being a Catholic cleric, Abbé Sulpice, it would seem, is disqualified from such a racialized category of world-transforming genius due entirely to his whiteness. Abbé Ouvière would be too, but what about Romaine-la-Prophétesse? Could he gain entry into this exclusive company in the writing of Haitian history? He was black, after all, and a devout Christian. Not for Madiou, who dismisses Romaine as nothing more than a violent "imposter," guilty of "so many cruelties in Léogâne," of "pillaging, raping, and murdering."[6]

If others who resorted to unspeakable violence to combat oppression were nonetheless still admissible into the pantheon of exterminating angels, why not Romaine-la-Prophétesse? If Christianity was itself inspired by "African genius," furthermore, then wouldn't by extension white Catholic priests like Abbé Sulpice take their place in the hallowed legion of heroes of the Haitian Revolution? Madiou's answer would be no, but the independent Republic of Haiti's first constitution might suggest otherwise. Drafted under the leadership of Jean-Jacques Dessalines, the constitution of 1805 states: "No white person, of whatever nationality, may set foot on this territory in the role of master or proprietor nor in the future acquire any property here," and that all Haitians "will henceforth be known by the generic denomination of blacks." However, "Article 13," as Sybille Fischer points out, "implies that white women, Germans, and Poles can become Haitians by an act of government, which means that they too would count as black."[7]

Madiou restricts the glorious ranks of exterminating angels to those who were black, however, who contributed to the cause of Haitian independence, and who were more "civilized" than Romaine-la-Prophétesse. Yet white people who contributed to the cause could also become black, as ensconced in one of Haiti's first constitutions, hence Abbé Philemon and Abbé Sulpice, technically speaking, could qualify, doubly so Romaine-la-Prophétesse, a free black who in fact wreaked a great deal of havoc against white oppression in Saint-Domingue. What is more important, however, is how the priest and the prophetess understood themselves: *as Catholics and as healers*. Popular Catholicism in the Dominguan religious field had been so Africanized by the late eighteenth century that any affirmation of Romaine's self-identification as Catholic would not imply any refutation of the importance of African religious forms or other cultural manifestations of *"African genius"* in the Trou Coffy insurgency.

It would thus seem that Madiou has inserted an artificial dichotomy into his telling of the history of the Haitian Revolution, one that is not really helpful.

Toward understanding not only the Haitian Revolution but the entire revolutionary Atlantic world, however, certain dichotomies must hold firm, like those between justice and injustice, humanity and inhumanity, peace and violence, order and chaos. This was, after all, an era in which debates over human rights mushroomed into a material realization of Marx's famous assertion that "the point of philosophy is not to interpret the world but to change it."[8] Of course, there were radically divergent interpretations of justice and injustice, of rights and wrongs, then provoking the Atlantic world to indeed become revolutionary and eventually to reshape the entire world. In Saint-Domingue, most planters believed that they had the right to own and to work slaves; free coloreds believed that they had the right to full French citizenship; while many slaves believed that the entire system in which they toiled was profoundly unjust. Much blood was spilled and many heads rolled when those variegated and confrontational interpretations of justice inspired the chaos and violence that often marked the Haitian Revolution, whether the blood pouring from a severed head in La Place d'Armes or on the fence surrounding the insurgent camp at Trou Coffy, or the blood from her own body used as ink on a note written by a mulatta slave to declare: "I leave all justice to God. It belongs only to Him. If justice is slow, it will be exacted more terribly."[9]

The notion that divine justice for Haiti, if left unserved, might intensify over time should haunt us all. Slow to accept the Haitian Revolution as a triumph for human freedom, the world of power has been even slower to admit its complicity in Haiti's suffering.[10] The Christmas 1791 gathering of the priest, the prophetess, and Romaine's officers at Trou Coffy reflects this complicity, just as it reflects the interconnectedness of points, projects, and persons throughout the revolutionary Atlantic world and the centrality of Haiti—and of religion—to the emergence of the hallmarks of modernity, like human rights, the nation state, democracy, sovereignty, capitalism, and freedom.[11] The priest and the prophetess each acted out of concerns with justice and their respective understandings of the will of God, one aiming to "tranquilize" the other, and one aiming to crush the other's very people. Put otherwise, in disparate ways each man sought to heal a sick world. The results were indeed sometimes unspeakably dreadful—and sometimes enthrallingly triumphant.

In the interim, despite the epochal triumph of the Haitian Revolution, on the Atlantic scale, justice was left unserved and remains unserved for Haiti to this day. For the priest and the prophetess were among "those who died for and lived through the Haitian Revolution [who] became part of every society in the Atlantic World," as Laurent Dubois insightfully suggests. "They continue to speak to us, as founders in a long struggle for dignity and freedom that remains incomplete."[12]

Forcefully contributing to this struggle, Romaine-la-Prophétesse and the insurgents who followed him at Trou Coffy certainly caused a good deal of blood to flow, leaving a trail of death and destruction across the Plain of Léogâne and the hills and mountains surrounding Jacmel and Léogâne and in both cities in 1791–1792. Abbé Ouvière tried to bring peace to Léogâne, as someone whom Romaine deeply trusted, clearly to a fault, though later in life, as Doctor Pascalis, he caused blood to flow in quite a different way, administering bloodletting on his yellow fever patients in Philadelphia and New York. Though their respective techniques and results were incomparable, the blood that the priest and the prophetess caused to flow, whether in Léogâne, Jacmel, Philadelphia, or New York, was in every case intended to effect healing, whether the social healing of an ill society or the biophysical healing of a feverish human body. But did their own blood flow in the end? That of the priest? That of the prophetess?

In what was perhaps the most dramatic turn of events in the priest's uncommonly dramatic life, within a period of just two years, Abbé Ouvière managed to twice narrowly escape execution on opposite sides of the Atlantic Ocean. For, as we've seen, collaborations of the kind that he crafted with Romaine-la-Prophétesse resulted in the execution of other Catholic priests in Saint-Domingue in 1791; the next year in France, meanwhile, had he been arrested as a counterrevolutionary priest, he might well have been condemned to death. In the first instance, Ouvière managed to exonerate himself in part by exploiting Romaine's deep religious devotion. In the second, the priest escaped arrest in France by absconding once again to the Caribbean, though he could not—and never would—return to Saint-Domingue. How he endured the next several months of a kind of dual exile in Jamaica is difficult to say; probably the priest relied on the good graces of British authorities and French refugees there from Saint-Domingue. What is as clear as it is remarkable, though, is that the priest twice eluded pending doom and went on to became a prominent physician and scientist in the United States of America, as Doctor Pascalis.

The prophetess was not nearly as fortunate. Betrayed by the priest, abandoned by his followers, and separated from his family, Romaine-la-Prophétesse somehow evaded capture at the hands of the Saint-Léger raid on Trou Coffy in March of 1792, evidently soldiering on in obscurity for a couple more years before perhaps being eliminated by Jean-Jacques Dessalines in 1795.[13] Recalcitrant, religiously creative, black insurgent leaders—and the prophetess certainly fits that bill—were targeted for elimination in the South and West

Provinces that year by the emerging power troika of Toussaint/Christophe/Dessalines. This campaign was carried out by Dessalines, who was tasked by Toussaint with the mission of crushing those elements that he called "obstacles to freedom."[14] Timoléon Brutus views the initiative as being as much an attack on Vodou as on political obstacles, arguing that it was the first Haitian "antisuperstitious campaign," and that Dessalines especially

> had developed repugnance for a superstition that, like a leper, gnawed at the soul of the black across the ages. He deemed as necessary, for his age and in his fashion, a radical curé for this African flaw. . . . Dessalines gave them chase and shot them down, killing a number of them.[15]

Thus Romaine may have been eliminated because of some perceived "African flaw," one that would have lingered through his *créolité*, free status, and reputation as an upstanding coffee planter. That is not certain, nor do we know whether his head might indeed have been cut off. About these things, we can at least speculate with the shards of evidence that do exist. As to whether the prophetess was ever accorded a dignified burial, sadly I doubt it. As to whether one could find his grave, meanwhile, I am convinced that it impossible.

For his part, the priest was buried in New York and probably once had a tombstone bearing his name. Though his was a more dignified passing than that of the prophetess, Ouvière's grave is now, for all intents and purposes, as unmarked as Romaine's, but for quite different reasons. It is very probable that the priest was buried at St. John's Burying Ground, on Varick Street in Manhattan, which is now covered by a softball field, a bocce court, and a water spout. The material remains of the priest and 10,000 other souls lie beneath them, unbeknownst to the softball or bocce players or children frolicking in the fountain. New York's historic Trinity Episcopal Church, which had built St. John's and buried the dead there beginning in the 1830s, when its own cemetery got full, sold the cemetery and its magnificent St. John's Chapel to developers in 1898. The chapel was then demolished, the headstones toppled and discarded, and the cemetery covered with a layer of earth to eventually transform the space into a public park. Today this is James J. Walker Park, affectionately known to New Yorkers as Jimmy Walker Park. For everything else that it is, Jimmy Walker Park is a mass grave with but a single nameless marker for the thousands entombed there.[16] For Félix Pascalis, there is an even sadder irony in that his burial beneath one of the largest cities in the world is precisely the thing that he railed against in one of his most extensive scientific publications, "An Exposition of the danger of Interment in Cities."[17]

FIGURE 10.1 Likely resting place of Félix Pascalis Ouvière (d. 1832). Old St. John's Burying Ground. *Photographic Views of New York City, 1870's–1970's, from the collections of the New York Public Library*. ca.1900. Courtesy of the Milstein Division of United States History, Local History & Genealogy, the New York Public Library, Astor, Lenox and Tilden Foundation.

Despite all the power and influence that Abbé Ouvière and Romaine-la-Prophétesse wielded in this world, thus neither the priest nor the prophetess is commemorated by a marked grave. I have visited both Trou Coffy and Jimmy Walker Park to seek the spirit of each man; the former place a bucolic mountain grove on a tropical island, the latter a noisy urban playground near the mouth of a tunnel, the Holland Tunnel, through which more than 30 million motor vehicles pass each year. They lay dead worlds apart, Abbé Ouvière and Romaine Rivière, neither being commemorated by name in either place, though their lives and deaths powerfully demonstrate just how deeply connected those worlds in reality were and are. Their legacies live on, furthermore. Ouvière's descendants prosper to this day in South Carolina, while it is quite probable that Rivière has living descendants in the Dominican Republic, Haiti, or perhaps somewhere in the Haitian diaspora, like New York or Philadelphia.

What about legacies beyond their DNA? Doctor Pascalis left numerous scientific publications, and while most of them have since been demonstrated to be empirically flawed or superseded by major advances in things like germ science and cellular biology, the man was a pioneering figure in early American medicine and should indeed be celebrated as such. His vision and applied intellect also capture the veritable and venerable spirits of both Enlightenment science and American ingenuity, and at times his efforts were really quite pathbreaking. Whether in being the first naturalist to cultivate silkworm nurseries in the United States, one of the first epidemiologists to actually map disease and think about it on a truly global scale, or the first translator of Benjamin Rush into French, Pascalis forged paths that are today being trudged by scholars and nations seeking to understand and combat things like the Ebola virus and global warming. That is a remarkable legacy indeed.

Equally remarkable is Romaine-la-Prophétesse's legacy as part of Haiti's demonstration of religion's power to combat oppression and to effect social change. The Virgin Mary is at the heart of that legacy, moreover, a pattern in which Marianism has been exploited in Haitian history to extract religious power toward political aims. Within 20 years of the fall of Trou Coffy, for instance, during Haiti's subsequent North-South civil war, Henry Christophe ordered a spy to dress up like the Virgin Mary and climb a tree to announce that his advancing armies were sent by God. Later that century, in 1847, Faustin Soulouque was named emperor of Haiti. Born into slavery in Petit-Goâve in 1782, some of his earliest childhood memories were surely of the Trou Coffy insurgency; so perhaps the emperor had Romaine-la-Prophétesse in mind when two year's into his rule, and following disastrous military campaigns he had launched to conquer the prophetess' native Dominican Republic,

Soulouque sent an artist to clandestinely climb a tree along the Champ de Mars in Port-au-Prince to paint an image of the Virgin Mary—"in such a fashion," scoffed one unconvinced observer, "did heaven bequeath a crown to Soulouque."[18] Thirty-five years later, the Virgin Mary would heal the nation of a deadly small pox epidemic, in 1882, just as she would bring the pope to Haiti in 1983, which helped topple the brutal Duvalier dictatorship in 1986.[19]

Today, as most Haitian Catholics and Vodouists would surely believe, the Virgin Mary is healing their nation anew following the catastrophic earthquake of 2010. The *goudougoudo*, as it is called onomatopoeically in Haitian Creole, toppled not only the Cathedral of Our Lady of the Assumption in Port-au-Prince but also the Church of St. Rose de Lima in Léogâne, the oldest church in Haiti. Abbé Ouvière once preached there, perhaps with Romaine in attendance, while the prophetess himself stood in this sanctuary numerous times as the godfather of newly baptized free colored Dominguan Catholics, and he was married in the sanctuary to Marie Roze Adam, a mulatta slave whose freedom he had purchased and who bore him three children. Masses said at Trou Coffy sometimes used ritual paraphernalia from St. Rose, meanwhile, and it's even possible that the tabernacle and some of the icons in the insurgent camp's chapel derived from the church. In many ways, it was this very church, St. Rose, and the Blessed Virgin Mary that brought the priest and the prophetess together. Following their historic and remarkable Christmas summit of 1791 in Trou Coffy, however, their respective legacies would radically diverge. Though in religion and war, and not in science or medicine, the prophetess was every bit a pathbreaker as the priest. Romaine-la-Prophétesse should thus ever be recognized as occupying a pioneering place in a most impressive heritage of Haitian Marianism and of a universal legacy of religion's capacity to inspire and sustain resistance. Like those of the priest, furthermore, the legacies of the prophetess were amplified and accelerated by the tumults and aspirations of the revolutionary Atlantic world.

Surely with ardency and frequency, the prophetess prayed to the Virgin Mary to understand and achieve her will for a world without slavery; in Saint-Domingue, which he helped transform into Haiti. Presumably, Abbé Ouvière prayed to her there, too, even doing so together with the prophetess and his followers at Trou Coffy on Christmas Eve 1791. Millions of others from throughout Haiti have done so in the ensuing years, beseeching their national patron saint for a wide range of miracles, like deliverance from disease, enslavement, injustice, poverty, dictatorships, and the rubble of earthquakes.[20] The priest and the prophetess prayed to the Virgin for another iteration of these miracles, for social healing, even if each man harbored different visions of justice and of what society should look like. Those prayers, too, would eventually be answered, however incompletely. Thus was Haiti born, a true gift to the world, a cornerstone of human freedom, and an inspiration to all oppressed peoples and those who act in solidarity with them. Catholicism, especially devotion to the Virgin Mary, is very much a part of that inspiration. And if the story of Haiti teaches us anything, it is, in the words of the prophetess' priestly adviser, that "the greater the pain, the greater must be our confidence in the power and energy of life."[21]

Notes

INTRODUCTION

1. "Life is the fruit of chance. And chance is divine." Franketienne, "L'ARBRE MYTHIQUE." *Miraculeuse*, 566. Unless otherwise indicated, all translations in this book are mine.
2. Garran de Coulon, *Rapport sur les troubles de Saint-Domingue, Tome 2*, 494.
3. At this church, Jean-Jacques Dessalines would, with Toussaint Louverture in attendance, be married to Léogâne native and future empress of Haiti Marie-Claire Heureuse Felicité, in October of 1801. Dessalines had the city of Léogâne burned two years later rather than see it conquered anew by the French.
4. Madiou, *Histoire d'Haïti, Tome I*, 15. After this massacre, in which Anacaona was taken prisoner and later hanged, "Ovando . . . in commemoration of his triumph, founded a town near the lake, which he called Santa Maria de la Verdadera Paz (St. Mary of the True Peace)." Irving, *Columbus*, 332.
5. Moreau de Saint-Méry, *Description topographique, Tome Second*, 446.
6. More a village than a city, the town then counted merely 120 residents. Breathett, "The Religious Missions in Colonial French Saint Domingue," 17.
7. Moreau de Saint-Méry, *Description topographique, Tome Second*, 473.
8. Fischer, *Modernity Disavowed*, 2004, 208.
9. De Alcedo, *Diccionario geográfico-histórico de las Indias Occidentales ó América*, 569.
10. James, *The Black Jacobins*, 31. Much of the city was crushed in a 1751 earthquake but rebuilt by 1770, when an even worse earthquake struck and devastated Léogâne anew.
11. Laborie, *The Coffee Planter of Saint-Domingue.*
12. Girod-Chantrans, *Voyage d'un Suisse dans différentes colonies*, 137.
13. Fick, *The Making of Haiti*, 61–63; Farmer, *AIDS and Accusation*, 193–207, 273n5. On the fear that Makandal inspired and its sociopolitical context, also see Pluchon, *Vaudou, sorciers, empoisonneurs*, 165–182.

14. Rey, "Classes of Mary in the Haitian Religious Field."
15. Abeysekara, *Colors of the Robe*, 24.
16. Rey, "The Virgin Mary and Revolution in Saint-Domingue." More recently I published an encyclopedia article on Romaine, "Romaine-la-Prophétesse." In the interim, Robert Taber has analyzed Romaine's economic activity as part of his comparison of Dominguan social life in Saint-Marc and Léogâne, "The Issue of Their Union."
17. Trouillot, *Silencing the Past*, 48.
18. Of course, the Haitian Revolution witnessed blacks taking over the entirety of a former French colony and eventually going on to conquer the whole island of Hispaniola, but I understand "colonial history" in Saint-Domingue/Haiti to have ended with the torching of Cap-Français in June of 1793. On this epochal event, see Popkin, *You Are All Free.*
19. Though I give Romaine precedence in this book by placing his chapter before Ouvière's, for purely poetic reasons I have chosen to entitle the book *The Priest and the Prophetess* rather than *The Prophetess and the Priest.*
20. Blackburn, *The Overthrow of Colonial Slavery*, 58–59.
21. Michel, Bellegarde-Smith, and Racine-Toussaint, "From the Horses' Mouths," 70.
22. In some of my earlier work I uncritically accepted this position and took on face value, and in fact cited approvingly, claims about Vodou's being the key to understanding the outbreak of the Haitian Revolution by scholars like Odette Mennesson-Rigaud, Harold Courlander and Rémy Bastien, and Michel Laguerre. Mennesson-Rigaud, "Le rôle du vaudou dans l'indépendance d'Haïti," 43. Courlander and Bastien, *Religion and Politics in Haiti*, 42. Laguerre, "The Place of Voodoo in the Social Structure of Haiti." I no longer agree with their arguments on this count.
23. For one trenchant critique of such scholarship, see Woodson, "Review of Patrick Bellegarde-Smith's *Haiti: The Breached Citadel*," 156–160. The imbalanced and largely negative portrayal of Catholicism vis-à-vis slavery is by no means unique to the literature on the Haitian Revolution. On this, see Stark, *For the Glory of God.*
24. Fouchard, *Les marrons du syllabaire*, 115.
25. Ibid., 30. For an excellent overview of the question of Vodou's influence on slave insurrection in Saint-Domingue, see Hoffmann, "Le Vodou sous la colonie et pendant les guerres d'indépendance."
26. Without citing a shard of "evidence" himself, for instance, Patrick Bellegarde-Smith asserts that "[t]he evidence surrounding the role of Vodou in the Haitian Revolution and in the history of the nation's early years is incontrovertible." Bellegarde-Smith, "Broken Mirrors," 25.
27. David Geggus opines that although some kind of an uprising did occur, "it does not seem that a place called Bois Caïman has ever existed." Geggus, *Haitian Revolutionary Studies*, 86. In a controversial article, meanwhile,

Léon-François Hoffmann argues that the Bois-Caïman saga is entirely mythic. Hoffmann, "Histoire, mythe et idéologie: la cérémonie du Bois-Caïman," 9–34. Furthermore, much of the scholarly literature confuses the Bwa Kayiman event with another meeting among conspiring slaves that took place slightly earlier on the Lenormand de Mézy Plantation near Morne Rouge. Geggus, *Haitian Revolutionary Studies*, 84–87.

28. Dubois, *Avengers of the New World*, 102.
29. Jacques de Cauna helpfully considers the impact of Freemasonry on Polverel in "Polverel et Sonthonax, deux voies pour l'abolition de l'esclavage." On Toussaint and Freemasonry, see Bell, *Toussaint Louverture*. More generally on Freemasonry in Saint-Domingue, see Buck-Morss, *Hegel, Haiti, and Universal History*. On Jews in Saint-Domingue, see Maurouard, *Les juifs de Saint-Domingue (Haïti)*; and Cahen, "Les juifs dans les colonies françaises au XIIIe siècle"; and Garrigus, "New Christians/'New Whites.'"
30. For example, Maya Deren writes that "all these West Africans had certain basic beliefs in common"; Alfred Métraux underscores that "the annual intake from the African coast consisted mainly of blacks from Dahomey and Nigeria," and thus that "Voodoo … in structure and in spirit has remained essentially Dahomean"; while Karen McCarthy Brown's celebrated 404-page book *Mama Lola* relegates the discussion of Kongo influences on Vodou to one sentence and a single footnote. Deren, *The Divine Horsemen*, 58–59. Métraux, *Voodoo in Haiti*, 26, 29; Brown, *Mama Lola*, 100.
31. Eltis, "Voyages: The Transatlantic Slave Trade Database," http://www.slavevoyages.org; last accessed April 10, 2014. Vodou spirits, or *lwa yo*, generally have various manifestations, which meander along different branches of the pantheon. The main branches, which are called *nanchon* (lit: "nations," sometimes spelled *nasyon*) in Haitian Creole, are *rada*, which derives mostly from West Africa, and *petwo*, which is clearly more of West Central African origins. On this, see Desmangles, *The Faces of the Gods*; and Deren, *The Divine Horsemen*.
32. For explorations of Kongo Catholic influences in Haiti, see Rey "Ancestral and Saintly Root Experiences"; Rey, "A Consideration of Kongolese Catholic Influences on *dominguois*/Haitian Popular Religion"; and Vanhee, "Central African Popular Christianity." For a recent study that challenges affirmative notions of Catholic influences among enslaved Central Africans in Saint-Domingue, see Mobley, "The Kongolese Atlantic."
33. Asad, *Genealogies of Religion*, 29. I must state a sense of wonder, meanwhile, if *any* definition whatsoever *is not* such a product.
34. Tweed, *Crossing and Dwelling*, 54.
35. Abeysekara, *Colors of the Robe*, 24.
36. See, for instance, Bellegarde-Smith, *Haiti: The Breached Citadel*, 21–36. Especially troubling are Bellegarde-Smith's outright denial of a place for Christianity in "Haitian self-identity and cultural heritage" and his insinuation that Christianity

in Haiti is tantamount to "zombification" (21): "If in previous eras one result of converting the people of Haiti to Christianity was to make the people compliant slaves, the objectives of contemporary Western policies and Christian missions might lead the Haitian people to develop a measure of self-hatred and repudiate their indigenous culture and way of life" (33). This was hardly the "result" that Christianity had on the likes of Jean-François, Makaya, Toussaint Louverture, or Romaine-la-Prophétesse; furthermore, the historical evidence clearly indicates that Christianity has always been a central component to Haitians' "indigenous culture and way of life."

37. Lacroix, *Mémoires pour server à l'histoire de la révolution de Saint-Domingue*, 177, 143, italics added.
38. In stating this, I am by no means advancing any apologetic for the slaughter of "innocent victims" in the free colored insurgencies of 1791–1792, even if much of the violence that stormed out of Trou Coffy was in reality beyond Romaine's control, as will be demonstrated in Chapter 6.
39. Sweet, *Domingos Álvares*, 227.
40. Sepinwall, *The Abbé Grégroire*, 6.
41. Furstenberg, *When The United States Spoke French*, 17.
42. Moreau de Saint-Méry, *Description topographique, Tome première.*

CHAPTER 1

1. "Once you are in the slaughterhouse, you have to accept that blood splashes on you."
2. Important exceptions include Fick's *The Making of Haiti*; Garrigus, *Before Haiti*; King, *Blue Coat or Powdered Wig*; Taber, "The Issue of Their Union."
3. Felix Pascalis, "Anecdote historique." New York, 1821. NYAM MS Folio Pascails Ouviere, 1819–1823, 45. Trou Coffy was both a place name and a synecdoche ascribed by contemporary observers to the insurgency that Romaine led as a whole, which was much broader, geographically speaking. Throughout this book, meanwhile, when citing and transcribing archival sources in French in which accents are missing or the spelling is incorrect or archaic, I do not make any alterations to the original texts.
4. It appears that at least one white-owned plantation, that of the DesMarattes family, was willfully offered for use by the Trou Coffy insurgents, as Baudoin DesMarattes was accused by observers as being among their collaborators. Lettre de Lamothe Vedel à l'Assemblée Coloniale, Jacmel, 1 mars 1792. AN DXXV 61 615.
5. Ardouin, *Études sur l'histoire d'Haïti, Tome premier*, 28.
6. Extract of a letter from Les Cayes, 11 February 1792. *Philadelphia Aurora*, March 16, 1792. As cited in Fick, *The Making of Haiti*, 129.
7. Rapport fait a l'assemblee coloniale le 14 fev 1792, signé J. P. M. Bloüet, Curé de Jacmel D.S. AN DXXV 61 615.

8. Position de la province de l'Ouest, 12 mars, 1792. AN DXXV 61 615.
9. One observer estimated that the number of mulatto insurgents camped around the cities of Les Cayes and Grand Goâve to be a total of "four to five thousand." Lettre du M. Calpié, habitant des Orangers, à M. Pinchinat, 3 janvier, 1792. AN DXXV 61 612.
10. Jean-Philippe Garran de Coulon's first mention of the Trou Coffy insurgency opens with a paragraph explaining that the "most violent" of the "furies of the civil war" were to be found "in the eastern part of the [South] province, along the borders of that of the West," suggesting that some white insurgents from the region joined forces with the *gens de couleur* in the sack of Jacmel. The specific individuals he names, however, were not themselves clearly tied to or residents of the South Province, so his meaning here is not entirely clear. Garran de Coulon, *Rapport sur les troubles de Saint-Domingue, Tome 2*, 537–538.
11. As Sidney Mintz puts it, the Revolution's "ideological overtones were not those of Africa against Europe, nor even entirely or consistently of black against white." Mintz, "Introduction," 11.
12. Ibid., 19.
13. Garrigus, *Before Haiti*, 4.
14. Fick, *The Making of Haiti*, 20.
15. "The French Revolution of 1789 offered them [free coloreds] an opportunity to put forward claims for political rights and even to imagine the possibility of displacing whites as the colony's dominant group. In historical perspective, the conflict between whites and the slaves appears as the fundamental issue in the Haitian Revolution, but until June 1793, it was the question of equality for the free people of color that dominated politics in Saint-Domingue and debates about the colony in France." Popkin, *You Are All Free*, 12.
16. Ardouin, *Études sur l'histoire d'Haïti, Tome premier*, 28.
17. Anonymous, *Cahier contenant les plaintes, doléances & réclamations.*
18. Ghachem, *The Old Regime and the Haitian Revolution*, 237–238.
19. Popkin, *You Are All Free*, 36. On Ogé's political machinations and how his background differed from Chavannes's, see Garrigus, "Vincent Ogé Jeune (1757–91)."
20. Raimond and his wife left Saint-Domingue for Paris "In the spring of 1784." Garrigus, "Opportunist or Patriot?," 5.
21. As cited in Popkin, *You Are All Free*, 90. Raimond was walking a political tightrope, and he did so with such great effect that John Garrigus has good reason to state the following: "After Toussaint Louverture, the most important Caribbean-born actor in the Haitian Revolution was Julien Raimond, a free-coloured planter whose proposals for racial reform destabilized the slave regime in Saint-Domingue," Garrigus, "Opportunist or Patriot?" 1.
22. Fick, *The Making of Haiti*, 119.
23. Ibid., 122–123.
24. Ibid., 126.

25. Ardouin, *Études sur l'histoire d'Haïti, Tome premier*, 47–48.
26. Thornton, "'I am the Subject of the King of Congo.'"
27. Popkin, *You Are All Free*, 130.
28. Ibid., 38.
29. Extrait du Registre des declarations de la Municipalité de Jacmel, 1 fevrier 1792. AN DXXV 61 615.
30. L'assemblee provinciale du sud à l'assemblee coloniale. Les Cayes, 5 janvier 1792. AN DXXV 61 612.
31. Exposition qui font MM les commissaires, nommés et envoyés par l'assemblée provinciale du Sud. Les Cayes et Torbeck, 5 fevrier 1791. AN DXXV 61 614.
32. Ibid.
33. "Religious capital" is a term coined by Pierre Bourdieu to designate that form of "symbolic capital" that is operative in the "religious field." Bourdieu, "Genèse et structure du champ religieux." For a full discussion of Bourdieu's theory of religion, see Rey, *Bourdieu on Religion*.
34. "The role of the *commandeur* on the plantations was central, for it was upon him that the rhythm of work in the fields depended and under his direct authority that the vast majority of slaves labored. More often than not, especially toward the end of the colonial period, he was recruited from among the creole slaves and would be a person whose general demeanor projected authority and commanded respect." Fick, *The Making of Haiti*, 30. On *commandeurs* in Saint-Domingue, see also Dubois, *Avengers of the New World*, 36–39.
35. Exposition qui font MM les commissaires, nommés et envoyés par l'assemblée provinciale du Sud. I have found no free colored accounts in the archive of these events that might expose possible exaggerations made by the white authors of the documents cited here.
36. Interrogation du nommé Joseph Blek, St. Louis, 18 fevrier 1792. AN DXXV 61 615. Blek (or Bleck) was of the Bleck family that is discussed briefly by Garrigus in *Before Haiti*, the most notable member being Hyacinthe Bleck, a "free colored saddle maker and entrepreneur" and political agitator for the rights of the *gens de couleur* (233). Meanwhile, ancestry.com names "Joseph Bleck" as Hyacinthe and Guillaume Bleck's brother, indicating that he was a "major de la confederation de l'Ouest," but adding that he died on February 9, 1792, in Les Cayes, more than a week before the interrogation of Joseph Blek. http://www.rootsweb.ancestry.com/~htiwgw/familles/fiches/003827.htm; last accessed December 2, 2103.
37. These slaves *cum* mercenaries were called *Les Suisses* "because, like the Swiss soldiers hired to fight for the royal French army, they were willing to fight for pay." Hundreds of slaves were recruited by free people of color to fight as mercenaries, many of them being in the end abandoned and expelled from the colony. Popkin, *A Concise History of the Haitian Revolution*, 45. On the Swiss, see also Geggus, *Haitian Revolutionary Studies*, 99–118.

38. Ardouin indicates that Narcisse's last name was Rollin and that he was killed during a counterattack on Camp Prou. *Notes sur l'Histoire d'Haïti, Tome premier*, 69.
39. Extrait des minutes de greffe de la commission prevotale de la partie du sud de St Domingue, séante aux Cayes, 20 fevrier 1792. AN DXXV 61 615.
40. Rapport de Bloüet; Lettre de Romaine Rivière la Prophetesse et Elie à Abbé Ouvière, Camp du Trou Coffy, 24 decembre 1791. AN DXXV 110 887.
41. Labat, *Nouveau voyage*, 330–331.
42. H. Leclerq, "Vessels for Holy Oils: Treatment of Vessels Used to Contain Blessed Oils." *The Original Catholic Encyclopedia*. http://oce.catholic.com/index.php?title=Vessels_for_Holy_Oils; last accessed November 30, 2013.
43. Geggus, "Slave Resistance Studies and the Haitian Revolution," 16. It is noteworthy that one of the first plantations to be burned in the North Province during the slave revolt of 1791 was that owned by a Catholic religious order, the Pères de la Charité. Fick, *The Making of Haiti*, 99. The order also ran the hospital in Cap-Français, where one of their slaves, prior to his escape, had been Biassou. Cauna, "Toussaint Louverture," 152. I have found one other act of aggression against a Catholic priest during the period under question, in which a pastor leading a funeral procession was stopped and the burial he had planned was derailed by a group of marauding whites near Saint-Marc, who were alleged to have opened the casket and cannibalized the body. Chanlatte jeune, Viart, Dubourg, and Ouvière, *Suite du mémoire historique des dernières révolutions*, 7.
44. Ardouin, *Études sur l'histoire d'Haïti, Tome premier*, 69n2. Italics in original.
45. L'Assemblee provincial et provisoirement administrative du Sud à l'Assemblee coloniale de la partie française de Saint Domingue. Les Cayes, 11 mars, 1792. AN DXXV 61 615. The Provincial Assembly described Rigaud as "a monster" with a "vicious soul" who is "capable of bringing those around him to the very excess of villainy."
46. La municipalité des Cayes à l'Assemblee colonial, Les Cayes, 19 mars, 1792. AN DXXV 61 615.
47. Fick, *The Making of Haiti*, 156.
48. Rey, "The Virgin Mary and Revolution in Saint-Domingue."
49. For example, one baptismal record from the parish of Léogâne indicates that the godmother was the "wife of Romain Riviere, free black," while a contract for a land transaction into which Romaine entered also identifies him as a free black "of the Spanish nation," while about a half dozen other notarial documents, which were legally binding, concur without exception. Baptême de Pierre Gédeon, mulatre, Léogâne, 10 octobre 1790. ANSOM ECN, SAINT-DOMINGUE- LEOGANE-1790, 24; Vente de Gerault Touneaux mulatre libre à Romain Rivière negre libre, Pardevant des notaires du Roy de Léogâne, Léogâne, 31 octobre 1785. ANSOM DPPC NOT SDOM 1530. I am profoundly grateful to Rob Taber for having shared with me the notarial records pertaining to Romaine's business dealings, as well as his marriage contract, all of which are

treated in much greater detail in Chapter 3. The priest estimated that by 1791 the prophetess was "about forty years old." Pascalis, "Anecdote historique," 45.

50. Lettre de l'Abbé Ouvière aux membres réunis les commissaires de la paroisse et de l'armée combinée de l'Ouest Séante à la Croix de bouquets, Léogâne, 29 decembre 1791. AN DXXV 110 873.
51. Commissaires des Citoyens de Couleur de St. Marc, *Mémoire historique des dernières révolutions*, 102. Saint-Léger, *Compte rendu à l'Assemblée Nationale*, 27. Pascalis, "Anecdote historique," 52.
52. Pascalis, "Anecdote historique," 53.
53. Moreau de Saint-Méry, *Description topographique, Tome second*, 472. Perhaps further confusing matters, there is a village in Fonds d'Oie called Fond Droit.
54. In addition to the names of persons who received sacraments, parish registries generally also include the names of parents, godparents, and witnesses, and often their places of residence are listed as well. Besides the few entries in which Romaine is named as a godfather or witness, there is only one other person said to have resided in Trou Coffy, a 26-year-old free black named Joseph Lacroix, who died in Trou Coffy on May 29, 1791, and was buried in the parish cemetery in Léogâne the next day. Sépulcre de Joseph Lacroix, ANSOM ECN SAINT-DOMINGUE-LEOGANE-1791.
55. Trou Coffy should not be confused with Nan Cofi, a place in the mountains located near Haiti's La Visite National Park.
56. Letter of Father Margat to the General Procurer of the Company of Jesus, July 20, 1743. In Jan, *Collecta, Tome I*, 28–53, 39.
57. Lettre de l'Abbé Ouvière aux membres réunis les commissaires de la paroisse et de l'armée combinée de l'Ouest séante a la Croix de bouquets, Léogâne, 29 decembre 1792. AN DXXV 110 868. A second copy is also found in AN DXXV 110 873. Their texts are identical.
58. Pascalis, "Anecdote historique," 51.
59. "The insurgent leaders Jean-François and Biassou made the importance of African military tactics clear in a letter they wrote late in 1791, in which they asserted that most of their followers were "a multitude of *nègres* from the coast"—that is, from Africa—"most of whom can barely say two words of French but who in their country were accustomed to fighting wars." Dubois, *Avengers of the New World*, 109. See also Thornton, "African Soldiers in the Haitian Revolution."
60. Lettre de l'Abbé Ouvière aux membres réunis les commissaires de la paroisse et de l'armée combinée de l'Ouest séante a la Croix de bouquets.
61. Pascalis, "Anecdote historique," 52.
62. Laborie, *The Coffee Planter of Saint Domingo*, 36.
63. Garrigus, *Before Haiti*, 174.
64. Writing of Romaine's brief appearance in the historical literature, Dubois likewise doesn't question that the prophetess "established himself in an abandoned church." Dubois, *Avengers of the New World*, 106. Dubois seemingly relies on

Fick for this piece of inaccurate information, and Fick (*The Making of Haiti*, 127) draws it from a secondary source, Serge Larose's widely cited article "The Meaning of Africa in Haitian Vodu," 111.

65. Rapport de Bloüet.
66. Pascalis, "Anecdote historique," 50.
67. King, *Blue Coat or Powdered Wig*, 176.
68. See Chapter 2 for further discussion of these and other instances of Romaine's religious participation reflected in the Léogâne parish registries, including full citations.
69. Pascalis, "Anecdote historique," 56.
70. Chanlatte jeune, Viart, Dubourg, and Ouvière, *Mémoire historique des dernières révolutions*, 102–103.
71. Précis des faits qui se sont passés dans la paroisse de Jacmel depuis le commencement de septembre 1791 jusqu'à ce jour—onze mars 1791.
72. Chanlatte jeune, Viart, Dubourg, and Ouvière, *Mémoire historique des dernières révolutions*, 102–103.
73. Précis des fait qui se sont passe dans la paroisse de Jacmel depuis le commencement de septembre 1791 jusqu'au ce jour—onze mars 1791.
74. Courlogne is identified (as "Elie dis Courjelongue") as a free colored in the Léogâne parish records. Baptême de Simon, Léogâne, 15 mai 1790. ANSOM ECN, SAINT-DOMINGUE-LEOGANE, 1790. The name "Jacques Bourssiquot" also appears in these records, likely a relative of Alexandre Boursiquot, and the racial identification is listed as *"mulatre libre."* ANSOM ECN, SAINT-DOMINGUE-LEOGANE, 1791.
75. Lettre de LaMothe Vedel, majeur du district du Cayes Jacmel, à l'Assemblée Coloniale, Jacmel, 1 mars 1792. AN DXXV 61 615.
76. Lettre de Cussan à l'Assemblée Nationale, Jacmel, 15 février, 1792. AN DXXV 61 615.
77. Lettre du S. Deslandes à Delisle de Bressolle, Capitaine Général des Blancs et des Citoyens de Couleur Reunies, n. p., 1 mars 1792. AN DXXV 61 615.
78. Garran de Coulon, *Rapport sur les troubles de Saint-Domingue, Tome 2*, 538.
79. Ibid., 533.
80. As King explains, the title *habitant*, which literally means "resident," was a mark of social privilege in Saint-Domingue, which he translates colloquially as "gentleman farmer" and "planter." *Blue Coat or Powdered Wig*, ix, xviii.
81. Garrigus, *The Making of Haiti*, 229.
82. Rapport de Bloüet.
83. Many people in Haiti today fear the waters off the south coast in and around Jacmel, which has a reputation for strong rip currents and large waves. As an avid surfer who lived in Haiti for six years and often surfed in Jacmel, I can attest to the waves being very powerful there. As for the sharks, sadly sediment from the erosion of Haiti's mountains in recent decades has killed the reefs closest to

shore, meaning that the marine food chain has migrated further out to sea, and so local fisherman assured me that there was no need to fear sharks any longer in the Bay of Jacmel or in Bainet, which is also home to an excellent surf spot.

84. Rapport de Bloüet.
85. Sépulcre de Anguié, Duborg, Dupré, 10 octobre 1791, Bainet. ANSOM ECN SAINT-DOMINGUE-BAYNET-1791, 33.
86. Saint-Léger, *Compte rendu à l'Assemblée Nationale*, 48.
87. Garran de Coulon, *Rapport sur les troubles de Saint-Domingue, Tome 2*, 486–487. The letter cited by Garran in this instance, which I have not seen, is Lettre de Boursiquot et autres hommes de Couleur à Coutarel, commissaire conciliateur de Baynet, 30 decembre 1791.
88. Rapport de Bloüet.
89. Ardouin, *Essais sur l'histoire d' Haïti*, 54. It seems that Vissière had been previously unallied with Trou Coffy, but once Gros Poisson and presumably a multitude of troops from Romaine's redoubt arrived in Camp Pasquet, he had little choice but to acquiesce. Précis des faits qui se sont passés dans la paroisse de Jacmel.
90. Précis des faits qui se sont passés dans la paroisse de Jacmel.
91. Lettre deposée aux archives de l'assemblée provinciale et provisoirement administrative de l'Ouest, Jacmel, 9 janvier 1792. AN DXXV 61 612.
92. Précis des faits qui se sont passés dans la paroisse de Jacmel. Though barely legible, in another document, a letter written by a one Deslandes and ostensibly addressed to "Delisle De Bressolle" and Alexander Boursiquot, opens with the salutation "M. Romaine, mon cher ami, à des amis les citoyens de couleur qui habitant aux environs de son camp" (Mr. Romaine, my dear friend, to the friends the citizens of color who live around his camp). The letter is evidently intended to inform Romaine, Bresolle, and Boursiquot of recent developments around Cap Rouge and to express the opinion that the free colored insurgency in the Jacmel theater would need to hire and arm additional "Swiss," and that some kind of a treaty was being prepared for his consideration. Copie d'une lettre dus S Deslandes a Deslisle de Bressolle, Capitaine Generale des Blancs et des Citoyens des Couleurs reuines, Cap Rouge, 1 mars, 1792. AN DXXV 61 615. Another archival source indicates that the city of Jacmel was "blocked by *gens de couleur* of the area who are frequently reinforced by those from Trou Coffy, Cayes Jacmel, and Baynet," suggesting a fairly large network of insurgencies linked to Romaine and Trou Coffy. Position de la Province de l'Ouest, 12 mars, 1792.
93. Position de la Province de l'Ouest. Members of the DesMarattes family may in fact have offered their plantation to the insurgents and joined their cause, as Garran names "the Desmarrates brothers," along with "Delile—Bressolle" as being among the whites who joined the Trou Coffy insurgency. Garran de Coulon, *Rapport sur les troubles de Saint-Domingue, Tome 2*, 537.

94. Later in the Haitian Revolution, in November of 1799, Camp Pasquet would also serve as the base camp for Toussaint Louverture's siege of Jacmel.
95. Précis des faits qui se sont passés dans la paroisse de Jacmel.
96. La Salle, *Les papiers du général A. N. La Salle*, 45.
97. Précis des faits qui se sont passés dans la paroisse de Jacmel.
98. One secondary source, without attribution, claims that Romaine was in Léogâne during some of the fighting in March of 1792, but I have not been able to find any corroborative evidence for this in the archival material. Cabon, *Histoire d'Haïti*, 89.
99. A *"méssaillé"* (*méssaillée*—fem; *méssailler*—inf.) is someone who is married to a spouse who is deemed to be of a socially inferior class or race. Delisle is identified by this term more than once in the archival sources, though in the roughly 2,000 pages of French archival material that I have studied for this book, the term doesn't appear anywhere else. My sense is that it carried a derogatory connotation in Dominguan society. Lettre de Cussan à l'Assemblée Nationale. Though beyond the scope of the present study, it is noteworthy that Delisle remained a violent menace to the social order in and around Jacmel long after the events discussed here; on this, see La Salle, *Les papiers du général A. N. La Salle*.
100. "The negroes, instead of burying, burn their dead and wounded." "Extract of a letter from Aux-Cayes, dated Feb. 11, 1792." *The Diary or Loudon's Register*, New York, March 19, 1792. Abbé Aubert is discussed in further detail in Chapter 5.
101. Sépulcres, 3 janvier—16 avril, 1792. ANSOM ECN SAINT-DOMINGUE-JACMEL-1792.
102. Précis des faits qui se sont passés dans la paroisse de Jacmel.
103. Déclaration de Luperame [sp?] (Extrait des registres des déclarations de la municipalité de Jacmel), 2 mars, 1792. AN DXXV 61 615. The name of the "black slave" whose testimony is recorded in this document is not entirely legible, but "Luperame" is the closest I can get to deciphering the original handwritten text (from the Latin, this would translate as "Ravaging Wolf"). What is clearer is that Luperame's master was Sieur Savary, who was in attendance when he gave his testimony. On monetary units in Saint-Domingue, see Richard, "A propos de Saint-Domingue"; and Lacombe, "Histoire monétaire de Saint-Domingue et de la République d'Haïti."
104. Lettre de LaMothe Vedel à l'Assemblée Coloniale.
105. Rapport de Bloüet. Sépulcre de Nicolas Caboin, Marigot, 10 mars 1792. ANSOM ECN SAINT-DOMINGUE-JACMEL-1792, 9. Caboin, a plantation manager originally from Bordeaux, was one of several whites killed in a raid on the "fort that the men of color had built in Marigot."

CHAPTER 2

1. Weber, *The Sociology of Religion*, 102.
2. Supplément au détail des faits relatifs aux troubles . . . dans la dépendance de Jacmel depuis onze mars 1792. AN DXXV 62 618. As cited in Fick, *The Making of Haiti*, 307n44.
3. Chanlatte, Viart, Dubourg, and Ouvière. "Suite du mémoire historique," "Suite du mémoire historique (2) des dernières révolutions de l'ouest et du sud de la partie française de Saint-Domingue," 537–540.
4. Earlier drafts of this book contained a discrete section on Marianism at Trou Coffy, but the Virgin Mary is so central to every key aspect of the story of Romaine-la-Prophétesse that I decided to allow her to pervade it rather than setting her apart. A "revitalization movement," as defined by Anthony Wallace in a highly influential and hotly debated article, is "a deliberate, organized, conscious effort by members of a society to construct a more satisfying culture," which is certainly what Romaine's Trou Coffy insurgency was. Wallace, "Revitalization Movements," 265.
5. Vent du Maruice Cavalier et sa femme à Romain Rivière. Pardevant des notaires du Roy à Léogâne, 7 juin 1784. ANSOM DPPC NOT SDOM 1530. I am most grateful to Rob Taber for sharing this and other notarial records in which Romaine is a signer or is otherwise mentioned and for helping me to make sense of them.
6. King. *Blue Coat or Powdered Wig*, 6.
7. Mariage de Romain Riviere et Marie Roze. Léogâne, 23 aout 1785. ANSOM ECN SAINT-DOMINGUE-LEOGANE-1785, 24. Robert Taber raises the possibility that Romaine was actually married more than once and was thus polygamous. Taber, "The Product of their Union," 17.
8. Taber has also uncovered evidence of Romaine's ownership of additional slaves. Taber, "The Mystery of Marie Rose." http://ageofrevolutions.com/2016/01/06/the-mystery-of-marie-rose-family-politics-and-the-origins-of-the-haitian-revolution/; last accessed March 2, 2016.
9. Mariage Romain nègre libre Marie Roze griffe. Léogâne, 22 aout 1784. ANSOM DPPC NOT SDOM 1530. Two entries in the Léogâne parish registry indicate that her name was Marie Roze Adam.
10. Vente de terre de Marie-Jeanne Fougere negresse libre à Romain Riviere negre libre, Pardevant des notaires du Roy de Léogâne, 9 janvier 1787. FR CAOM DPPC NOT SDOM 1532. Vente de terre par Romain Rivière negre libre au Marie-Jeanne Fougere negresse libre, 10 fevrier 1787, Pardevant des notaires du Roy de Léogâne. ANSOM DPPC NOT SDOM 1532. This should not be taken to mean that these transactions involved land near Grande Marre in the Artibonite Valley, but rather more likely land along the Rivière de la Grande Marre, near Cayes Jacmel. The contract of sale also indicates, however, that the Grande Marre in question was located in the "quarters of Citronniers," which

would place it closer to Léogâne than Jacmel. Why Romain would purchase a plantation for 6,600 livres only to sell it back to the person he bought it from one month later for merely 3,600 livres is a mystery that might bespeak a business deal gone horribly wrong. It was a significant loss of income for the prophetess, at any rate.

11. Vente de terre de Gerault Touneaux mulatre libre à Romain Rivière negre libre, Pardevant des notaires du Roy de Léogâne, Léogâne, 31 octobre 1785. ANSOM DPPC NOT SDOM 1530. This information is also stated in both the notarial and parish records of Romaine's marriage to Marie Roze.
12. Pascalis, "Anecdote historique, 48.
13. The Jacmel parish registry contains at least one other case of a Dominican man whose name is Gallicized by the officiating priest at a baptism. On September 15, 1789, Juan Evangelista Gonzalez, a "Spanish mulatto living in Santo Domingo," sponsored a five-week-old freeborn quarteroon named Marie-Marthe Roquet. Though the godfather signed his name in that Hispanic spelling, Father Bloüet recorded it in this entry as "Jean-Evangeliste Gonzales." ANSOM ECN SAINT-DOMINGUE-JACMEL-1789-27.
14. One entry in the Léogâne parish registry indicates Romaine's residence as Citronniers; this, in any event, is very close to Trou Coffy, so it might not mean that he had been actually living anywhere else besides Trou Coffy. Baptême de Anne Augustine, 30 avril 1788. ANSOM ECN SAINT-DOMINGUE-LÉOGÂNE-1788, 13.
15. Furthermore, "To insult the godmother of a black is to cause him the bloodiest harm," and such an insult remains to this day very grave in Haiti. Moreau de Saint-Méry, *Description topographique, Tome Premier*, 55.
16. King, *Blue Coat or Powdered Wig*, 13.
17. Baptême de Jean Baptiste, 12 juin 1789. ANSOM ECN SAINT-DOMINGUE-LEOGANE-1789, 22. Baptême de Marie Elizabeth, 15 août 1788. ANSOM ECN SAINT-DOMINGUE-LEOGANE-1788, 19. Baptême de Jean Joseph, 9 janvier 1787. ANSOM ECN SAINT-DOMINGUE-LEOGANE-1787, 3. Baptême de Anne Augustine, 30 avril 1787. ANSOM ECN SAINT-DOMINGUE-LEOGANE-1787, 13. Baptême de Jean François, 30 avril 1787. ANSOM ECN SAINT-DOMINGUE-LEOGANE-1787, 27. Baptême de Pierre, 12 mai 1786. ANSOM ECN SAINT-DOMINGUE-LEOGANE-1786, 15. Baptême de Jean Joseph, 8 septembre 1786. ANSOM ECN SAINT-DOMINGUE-LEOGANE-1786, 39. Romaine also stood as a witness to a wedding on February 8, 1791. Mariage de Pierre Louis Dimba et Rozette, Leogane, 8 février 1791. ANSOM ECN SAINT-DOMINGUE-LEOGANE-1791, 3–4. Baptême de Pierre Louis, Leogane, 25 juillet 1785. ANSOM ECN SAINT-DOMINGUE-LEOGANE-1785, 21. Baptême de Pierre, Leogane, 21 mai 1785. ANSOM ECN SAINT-DOMINGUE-LEOGANE-1785, 15. Baptême de Pierre Louis, Leogane, 25 juillet 1785. ANSOM ECN SAINT-DOMINGUE-LEOGANE-1785, 21.

18. Baptême de Pierre Louis François, Léogâne, 15 fevrier 1790. ANSOM ECN SAINT-DOMINGUE-LEOGANE-1790, 4. Baptême de Pierre Gédéon, Léogâne, 18 octobre 1790. ANSOM ECN SAINT-DOMINGUE-LEOGANE-1790, 24. Baptême de Marie Elizabeth, 15 août 1788. ANSOM ECN SAINT-DOMINGUE-LEOGANE-1788, 19. Baptême de Jean Joseph, 9 janvier 1787. ANSOM ECN SAINT-DOMINGUE-LEOGANE-1787, 3. It is possible that the first of these was not Romaine's wife, as the godmother is named Marie Rivière and there is no mention of Romaine. In the second, Romaine is indicated to be the godmother's husband.
19. King, *Blue Coat or Powdered Wig*, 9. The Catholic parish records for Jacmel and Léogâne during the period between 1741 and 1791 list hundreds of baptisms, the majority of them for the children of free coloreds and blacks, and without a single exception the godparents are named.
20. Ibid.
21. Baptême de Simon, Léogâne, 24 mai 1790. ANSOM ECN, SAINT-DOMINGUE-LEOGANE-1790, 12. As with many names in the archival sources, Elie's name appears variously, here as "Elie Courjelongue."
22. Lettre d'Elie Courlogne à l'Abbé Ouvière, Trou Coffy, 16 janvier 1792. AN DXXV 110 819. Lettre de l'Abbé Ouvière aux membres réunis les commissaires de la paroisse et de l'armée combinée de l'Ouest séante a la Croix de bouquets, Leogane, 29 decembre 1792. AN DXXV 110 868. As with many names in the archival documents, Soliment's name is spelled variously: "Solimant" by Courlogne and "Soliman" by Ouvière. In my narrative I have chosen to use the spelling "Soliment" because that is how his father-in-law, Romaine, wrote (or had a scribe write) his name. Lettre de Romaine Riviere, la prophetess, commandant general à Monsieur l'Abbé Ouvière, Commissaire Conciliateur à la Croix de Bouquets, Trou Coffy, 26 janvier 1791. AN DXXV 110 887. It is not impossible that Soliment was, or at least was related to, a one Noël Soliman, who is listed as a godfather in the Bainet parish registry in February 1792. Baptême de Rose, 17 février 1792. ANSOM ECN SAINT-DOMINGUE-BAYNET-1792.
23. In the mid-seventeenth century the French Parliament had "raised the age of majority for men (from twenty to thirty) and women (from seventeen to twenty-five)," as Yvonne Fabella explains. However, "Escaping state and parental control of marriage was much easier in Saint-Domingue than in the metropole, in part because of the transient nature of colonial society." Fabella, "Inventing the Creole Citizen," 149–150.
24. Pascalis, "Anecdote historique," 51. Lettre de Romaine Riviere, la prophetess, commandant general a Monsieur l'Abbé Ouvière, 26 janvier 1792. In his 1821 mémoire about Trou Coffy Pascalis mistakenly refers to Soliment as Romaine's "son," whereas earlier correspondence clearly indicates that he was in fact his son-in-law; e.g., Lettre d'Elie Courlogne a l'abbe Ouviere, Trou Coffy, 16 janvier 1792. AN DXXV 110 887.

25. Simpson, *Religious Cults of the Caribbean*, 235.
26. Lettre de l'Abbé Ouvière aux membres réunis les commissaires de la paroisse et de l'armée combinée de l'Ouest séante a la Croix de bouquets.
27. I myself am Hispanic and "look it," and thus I was often called " *panyol*" while living in Haiti in the 1990s, though not as often as simply being called *blan* (lit: white, though a term that is used for foreigners of whatever racial background). Once my Creole became quite fluent, on rare occasions while living in Haiti I was also called an "aysiyen arab" (Arab Haitian), passing for a Haitian of Hadrami or Levantine descent, mistaken for a member of a large and generally economically successful ethnic group in Haiti. When I asked about this on two occasions in the 1990s, I was simply told that people assumed that I couldn't be a *panyol* because my Creole was too good or at least spoken without a Dominican accent.
28. Rapport fait à l'assemblée coloniale le 14 fev 1792, signé J. P. M. Bloüet, Curé de Jacmel D. S. AN DXXV 61 615. "Free people of color and the occasional white malefactor were the only people in Saint-Domingue who rated le nommé or la nommée before their names," while "any white person was Sieur, Dame, or Demoiselle, and the like were reserved for members of the aristocracy." King, *Blue Coat or Powdered Wig*, 163.
29. November 26, 1791, is the last date that Bloüet signed in the Jacmel parish registry. Though Bloüet signed his March 1792 report as "curé of Jacmel," as of November 26 only Father Ferriere was administering sacraments in the parish.
30. Garran de Coulon, *Rapport sur les troubles de Saint-Domingue, Tome 2*, 447–448; Lacroix, *Mémoires pour servir à l'histoire de la révolution de Saint-Domingue*, 142.
31. This is, furthermore, the identifier given for Romaine in Declaration de Marie-Jeanne Harang, 30 mars 1792. AN DXXV 2 14. As cited in Fick, *The Making of Haiti*, 307n41.
32. Précis des faits qui se sont passe dans la paroisse de Jacmel depuis le commencement de septembre 1791 jusqu'au ce jour—onze mars 1791. AN DXXV 61 615.
33. Pascalis, "Anecdote historique," 59.
34. Moreau de Saint-Méry, *Description topographique, Tome Premier*, 94. The quotation marks around "at best" are mine, not Moreau's.
35. Lettre de l'Abbé Ouvière aux membres réunis les commissaires de la paroisse et de l'armée combinée de l'Ouest. Pascalis, "Anecdote historique," 59.
36. Lettre de M. de Villards à l'Abbé Ouvière, 11 janvier 1792. AN DXXV 110 819. There are two letters from Villards to Ouvière that carry this date, one four pages long, the other seven. The cited text is from the longer one. Leslie Desmangles suggests that the transgressive gendered dimension of Romaine's religious leadership reflects a trend in Haitian Vodou in which Ezili, the female divinity of sensuality, resides in the body of a male human being (personal electronic correspondence, November 17, 2013). For an intriguing view of Ezili's gender

transgression in contemporary Haitian Vodou, see the 2002 film *Des hommes et dieux*, by Anne Lescot and Laurence Magloire.

37. Pascalis, "Anecdote historique," 53, 59.
38. Johnson, *The Fear of French Negroes*, 138. On dress among people of color in Saint-Domingue more generally, see also Fouchard, *Les marrons de la liberté*, 62–71; and Moreau de Saint-Méry, *Description topographique, Tome Premier*, 75–77.
39. Desmangles, personal electronic correspondence, November 17, 2013.
40. On Beatriz and the Antonians, see Thornton, *The Kongolese Saint Anthony*; and Fromont, *The Art of Conversion*, 206–212.
41. As James Sweet observes, for instance, "the feminization of these men, as measured by their social and sexual roles as females, rendered them vulnerable to the spirit world." Sweet, "Male Homosexuality and Spiritism in the African Diaspora," 193.
42. See, for instance, Matory, "Is There Gender in Yorùbá Culture?," 544; and Conner, *Queering Creole Spiritual Traditions*, 22.
43. Laguerre, *Voodoo and Politics in Haiti*, 48. Fouchard, *Les marrons du syllabaire*, 115. Rey, "The Virgin Mary and Revolution in Saint-Domingue."
44. Debien, "Le marronnage aux Antilles Françaises au XVIIIe siècle," 6.
45. Moreau de Saint-Méry, *Description topographique, Tome 2*, 497–503.
46. Garran de Coulon, *Rapport sur les troubles de Saint-Domingue, Tome 2*, 537.
47. Précis des fait qui se sont passe dans la paroisse de Jacmel depuis le commencement de septembre 1791 jusqu'au ce jour—onze mars 1791.
48. Moreau de Saint-Méry. *Description topographique, Tome Second*, 500.
49. Ibid., 502.
50. Ibid., 502–503.
51. Matibag, *Haitian-Dominican Counterpoint*, 54.
52. Lettre de Cussan à l'Assemblée Coloniale, Jacmel, 15 février 1792. AN DXXV 61 615.
53. Pascalis, "Anecdote historique," 48.
54. Geggus, "Marronage, voodoo, and the Saint-Domingue Slave Revolt of 1791," 25.
55. Debien, "Le marronnage aux Antilles Françaises au XVIIIe siècle," 17. The term *al mawòn* remains in wide usage in contemporary Haitian Creole to refer to the act of going into hiding to flee political persecution, which roughly one out of every eight Haitian citizens was forced to do at some point during the reign of the murderous junta of Raoul Cédras from 1991–1994. See Rey, "Junta, Rape, and Religion in Haiti, 1993–1994."
56. Debien, "Le marronage aux Antilles Françaises au XVIIIe siècle," 18, 20. Of the 10,863 runaway slave ads listed and transcribed in the remarkable "Marronage in Saint-Domingue" database, 3,490 contain the word "Congo" (several others contain the related words "Angola" or "Angole"), and many of them refer to more than one (and up to eight) Kongolese slaves who had absconded between January 1, 1766, and August 13, 1791. By comparison, 2,602 entries contain the word

"Creole," 690 "Ibo," 393 "Arada," 388 "Mondongue," 120 "Mozambique," and 7 "Nago." Jean-Pierre Le Glaunec and Léon Robichaud, for The French Atlantic History Group, McGill University and Université de Sherbrooke. http://www.marronnage.info/en/index.html; last accessed July 18, 2014.

57. Debien, "Le marronage aux Antilles Françaises au XVIIIe siècle," 1. Leslie Manigat is critical of Debien for his putative tendency "to 'banalize' marronage by denying it any revolutionary content or potential." Manigat, "The Relationship between Marronage and Slave Revolts and Revolution in Saint-Domingue-Haiti," 421–422. Were he able to respond to Manigat's criticism, Debien might suggest that Manigat himself romanticizes marronage by exaggerating its proclivity for fomenting other forms of resistance.
58. It was a time of "frenetic growth" in the region, as John Garrigus explains. "Rising coffee prices up to 1790 attracted many European immigrants, as did the fact that coffee plantations were smaller and less expensive to establish than sugar plantations." Garrigus, *Before Haiti*, 173–174. On coffee planting in Saint-Domingue, see also Trouillot, "Coffee Planters and Coffee Slaves in the Antilles," and Trouillot, "Motion in the System."
59. Max Weber suggests that any examination of religion, past or present, should begin with the question as to what needs people have of it; e.g., "all religions and religious ethics have had to reintroduce cults of saints, heroes or functional gods in order to accommodate themselves to the needs of the masses." Weber, *The Sociology of Religion*, 103.
60. This is not to deny that Romaine's vision, too, was "from the first subject to non-religious, ideological forces of all sorts." Mintz and Trouillot, "The Social History of Haitian Vodou," 138.
61. Pascalis, "Anecdote historique," 48.
62. Rapport de Bloüet. It is worth noting here how faithfully Garran's own Rapport adheres to Bloüet's version of events:

> Léogâne, in this state of abandon, endured all kinds of misfortune that even the most ragged government would want to prevent. Slave uprisings, followed by the same kinds of cruelty that took place in the North, were already taking place in the western part of the South that encloses the city. It was comprised of a substantial gathering in the overlooking mountains. It was led by a Spanish grif, named Romaine Rivière. This man had amassed a great deal of influence by way of fanaticism. It would be very difficult, in spite of all of the accounts that we have of his case, to truly describe the means that this deceiver employed to dupe the blacks into believing in him. It wasn't enough to call himself a prophet; he was a husband and a father; roles that he embraced; and he called himself the godson of the Virgin; and nonetheless he pretended to be a prophetess; he took this as his title; one that was given to him; and the colonial commission is in possession of several letters written in his name that carry the signature Romaine-la-Prophétesse: as if the ending of his name

was enough to redeem such madness. With some hommes de couleur and some Blacks who formed the core of his band, this imposter would repair to a narrow ravine of difficult access called Trou-Coffy. There he had established a kind of sanctuary where he said Mass and pronounced oracles. On the altar was a tabernacle in which he would place his head to consult with supernatural beings. The Virgin Mary responded to him in writing, the answer found in the tabernacle. This absurdity was almost never unaccompanied by cruelty on the path of fanaticism. Romaine commanded murder and pillage in the name of heaven, and his orders were executed blindly because he promised to his disciples certain victory. Garran de Coulon, *Rapport des troubles de Saint-Domingue, Tome 2*, 487–488.

63. On the history of the cult of the Virgin Mary in Haiti, see Rey, *Our Lady of Class Struggle*: and Rey, "The Politics of Patron Sainthood in Haiti."
64. Pascalis, "Anecdote historique," 48, 52–53.
65. Although Catholic doctrines pertaining to the Immaculate Conception and the Assumption of Mary were not formalized until the nineteenth and twentieth centuries, cultic devotion to Mary as immaculate and assumed into heaven date to the Middle Ages and have long been popular in Iberia and France.
66. Rey, *Our Lady of Class Struggle*, 157.
67. Pascalis, "Anecdote historique," 53–54.
68. Lacroix, *Mémoires pour servir à l'histoire de la révolution de Saint-Domingue*, 142; Précis des fait qui se sont passe dans la paroisse de Jacmel depuis le commencement de septembre 1791 jusqu'au ce jour—onze mars 1791. Lettre de M. de Villards à l'Abbé Ouvière, 11 janvier 1792.
69. Madiou. *Histoire d'Haïti, Tome I*, 127. While Madiou was writing some 50 years after Romaine's activities, he nonetheless had access to living witnesses of the Revolution.
70. Trouillot, *Silencing the Past*.
71. Ardouin, *Études sur l'histoire d'Haïti*, 70.
72. James. *The Black Jacobins*, 108. Pluchon, *Vaudou, sorciers, empoisonneurs*, 138. Geggus, "Marronage, Voodoo and the Saint-Domingue Slave Revolt of 1791," 28.
73. Pluchon actually refers to him as an "exalted sorcerer." Pluchon, *Vaudou, sorciers, empoisonneurs*, 138. Geggus, "Marronage, voodoo, and the Saint-Domingue Slave Revolt of 1791," 28. Métraux, *Voodoo in Haiti*, 47.
74. Collection Moreau de Saint-Méry, "Empoisonnements." ANSOM COL F/3/88.
75. Curiosités de St Domingue. n. p., 1788. Collection Moreau de St. Méry, "Minéraux." ANSOM COL F/3/89.
76. Weaver, *Medical Revolutionaries*, 3, 115. James McClellan further explains that the kaperlata healers "arose among and in the service of the free people of color and poor whites. Nothing is known about these 'doctors,' except that they had a name and that official medicine vigorously denounced them." McClellan, *Colonialism and Science*, 136.

77. Durkheim, *The Elementary Forms of Religious Life*, 42. Italics in original. In Central African contexts, poison has also been employed for divinatory purposes. See E. E. Evans-Pritchard's classic *Witchcraft, Oracles and Magic among the Azande*. On poison in Saint-Domingue, see Pluchon, *Vaudou, sorciers, empoisonneurs*, while for a discussion of poison in twentieth-century Haitian religious culture, see Farmer, *AIDS and Accusation*, Chapter 18.
78. Précis des fait qui se sont passe dans la paroisse de Jacmel depuis le commencement de septembre 1791 jusqu'au ce jour—onze mars 1792. Jacmel, 11 mars 1792. AN DXXV 61 615.
79. In Zaire, for instance, from 1986 to 1988 I was a member of a small congregation in the rural northern reaches of the Equator province, among the Ngbaka people, in the village of Bonzale. Once every six months or so, a Belgian priest named Père Gaspard would visit from the nearby Catholic mission of Bobito to say Mass in Bonzale, and while there he would also consecrate a supply of Communion wafers for the catechist to distribute to communicants during the ensuing months. In the Democratic Republic of Congo, meanwhile, in the Roman Catholic Diocese of Boma, where there are nearly 800,000 Catholics, only 305 priests were in service as of 2013, compared with over 2,500 catechists. Conférence Épiscopale Nationale du Congo, Annuaire de l'Église Catholique en DR Congo. Kinshasa: Editions du Secrétariat Générale du CENCO, 2012-13, 49–50. On catechists in the kingdom of Kongo, meanwhile, see Thornton, "The Development of an African Catholic Church."
80. Geggus, "Slave Resistance Studies," 16. For a discussion of one South American religious culture in which shamans are also often sorcerers, see Stirling, "Jivaro Shamanism"; and Brown, "Shamanism and Its Discontents."
81. Eliade, *Shamanism*, 4. It should be noted that Eliade's interpretation, though for more than a generation highly influential, has recently come under attack. See, for instance, Kehoe, *Shamans and Religion*. Meanwhile, Kehoe's efforts to curtail our use of the term shamanism are not entirely convincing. See Marshall, "Review of Alice Beck Kehoe"; and Kendall, "Review of Alice Beck Kehoe."
82. Fick, *The Making of Haiti*, 128.
83. "Theodicy of compensation" is Weber's term for what he sees as a key component of the "religion of non-privileged classes," a category in which Romaine's followers obviously fit. "Resentment is a concomitant of that particular ethic of the disprivileged which, in the sense expanded by Nietzsche and in direct inversion of the ancient belief, teaches that the unequal distribution of mundane goods is caused by the sinfulness and illegality of the privileged, and sooner or later God's wrath will overtake them." Weber, *The Sociology of Religion*, 110.
84. Fick, *The Making of Haiti*, 128. The source cited by Fick here is Supplément au détail des faits relatifs aux troubles . . . dans la dépendance de Jacmel depuis le onze mars 1792. AN DXXV 62, 618.

85. Johnson, *The Fear of French Negroes*, 5.
86. Price-Mars is said by Lorimer Denis and François Duvalier to have expressed this "essential truth" at a meeting of the Société d'histoire et géographie d'Haïti. As cited in Nérestant, *Religion et politique en Haïti*, 28. For his part, Nérestant considers the claim exaggerated, and, though he does not indicate the year of the meeting in question, it was surely between 1923 and 1935, when Price-Mars, one of its founders, was especially active in the Société. In my earlier articles on Romaine, I mistakenly echoed such exaggerations. Rey, "The Virgin Mary and Revolution in Saint-Domingue"; Rey, "Romaine-la-Prophétesse."
87. Larose, "The Meaning of Africa in Haitian Vodu," 111. No archival sources are referenced by Larose.
88. Laguerre, *Voodoo and Politics in Haiti*, 34, 48, 65. Some of these unsubstantiated details are rooted in the work of Milo Rigaud. Specifically, Laguerre cites Rigaud regarding Romaine's supposed talisman, though in Rigaud it is a *coq rangé* (lit: arranged cock; i.e., supernaturally empowered rooster). Rigaud, *La tradition voudou et le voudou haïtien*, 66. Rigaud provides no attribution or evidence for this. Laguerre's earlier source on Romaine is Placide-Justin's 1826 book *Histoire politique et statistique de l'île d'Hayti Saint-Domingue; écrite sur des documents officiels et des notes communiquées par Sir James Barskett*, 200, which only offers one cursory paragraph on the prophetess, also without attribution, which I translate here:

    > Meanwhile, a Spanish mulatto, known by the name Romaine-la-Prophétesse, at the head of a troop of fanaticized blacks and men of color, occupied the area around Léogâne, where, from all over, blacks left their plantations to join them. This new Muhammad, who pretended to have frequent meetings with the Virgin, had amassed enough of a force that the surrounding countryside and the city of Léogâne itself were afraid not to give to his troop everything that was demanded. Rigaud, commander of the men of color of the South, could have mounted some resistance to him, but he fled to the safety of his brothers from Port-au-Prince, where he had established his camp at Bizoton, just outside the walls of that city.

    For more insight into Rigaud's reading of Vodou, see Benoist, "Rencontre avec Milo Rigaud"; and Rey and Richman, "Introduction."
89. It is quite possible that the ribbons, medals, and rosaries were not draped over Romaine's body; instead, they might have been tied to or around him, which would be reflective of a Kongolese religious influence, manifest for instance in the Antonian Movement, that remains central to Haitian Vodou today. See Rey and Richman, "The Somatics of Syncretism."
90. Three white dragoons were killed in the raid, which involved a pursuit of fleeing sectarians toward the Spanish border. Malenfant, *Des colonies et particulièrement de celle de Saint-Domingue*, 217–218. Malenfant observed that most members of the "Vaudou sect" were Aradas, whereas very few Creoles belonged.
91. Ibid.

92. Précis des faits qui se sont passés dans la paroisse de Jacmel depuis le commencement de septembre 1791 jusqu'à ce jour—onze mars 1791.
93. Bonnet. *Souvenirs historiques de Guy-Joseph Bonnet*, 12.
94. Fick, *The Making of Haiti*, 128.
95. Ibid. "A vast assortment of medicinal herbs, empirical therapies, and religious responses to affliction constituted 'slave medicine' in colonial Saint-Domingue," as Paul Brodwin explains. "This was not an indigenous medical system, but rather a reinvented and syncretic one that drew upon African, Amerindian, and European sources." Brodwin, *Medicine and Morality in Haiti*, 40.
96. It should be noted, though, that David Geggus believes that the process may have already been underway "by the 1780s." Geggus, "Saint-Domingue on the Eve of Revolution," 6.
97. Woodson, "Which Beginning Should Be Hindmost?," 47–48.
98. Laguerre, *Voodoo and Politics in Haiti*, 34. In effect, the congregation described by Malenfant at Fonds-Parisien and the one led by Romaine-la-Prophétesse at Trou Coffy were each religious "cells," one of them more African than Catholic and the other more Catholic than African, and it was out of general mergers between such cells that Haitian Vodou would emerge as a religion.
99. Métraux, *Voodoo in Haiti*, 331.
100. Fick, *The Making of Haiti*, 128.
101. Janzen, *Lemba, 1650–1930*, 280. See also Janzen, "Renewal and Reinterpretation in Kongo Religion."
102. Moreau de Saint-Méry, *Description topographique, Tome Premier*, 210–211.
103. Larose, "The Meaning of Africa in Haitian Vodu," 111.
104. Landers, "The Central African Presence in Spanish Maroon Communities," 236. There is a minor spirit, *lwa*, in Haitian Vodou named Limba, whose origins might be in the Lemba cult. Métraux renders the spelling of this divinity as Lemba, but he has nothing else to say about his characteristics, save for the possibility of an iron bar serving as one of his symbols. Métraux, *Voodoo in Haiti*, 166. It is possible that Limba and Lemba are different divinities or that they are two different manifestations of the same *lwa*.
105. Price-Mars, "Lemba-Pétro."
106. Garrigus, *Before Haiti*, 261.
107. Ibid., 202.
108. Thornton, "I Am the Subject of the King of Congo," 189.
109. Wyatt MacGaffey identifies two basic qualities that define prophetism "in popular Kongo consciousness": the prophet's "exercise of healing powers in the public interest. . . . He represents a hierarchical dispensation of healing power mediated through him personally." The ngunza also practices transcendental mediumship with "the invisible world," as Kongo religion assumes "a cosmology describing relationships between the visible and invisible worlds and a limited set of contrasted mediating roles. These assumptions compose the

structure of Kongo religion." MacGaffey, "Cultural Roots of Kongo Prophetism," 179, 192.

110. Lettre de M. de Villards à Ouvière, Léogâne, 13 janvier 1792. AN DXXV 110 819.

111. Desmangles, *The Faces of the Gods*, 143–144. Desmangles further points out that Romaine "parallels the mythological character of Ezili [the leading feminine divinity in Haitian Vodou] as a female character who occupies a male body." Personal electronic correspondence, November 17, 2013. I do not mean here to assert that Ochun, Yemaya, or Oya are important spirits in Haitian Vodou, either today or in the eighteenth century, as they were/are not. Some of Ochun's qualities and those of Yemaya do appear to have been absorbed into Vodou's cult of Ezili, but Oya is, as far as I know, altogether unknown in Haitian religion, whose ruler of all things related to death and dying are the male Gede spirits, especially Bawon Samdi (as well as his manifestations as Bawon Lakwa, Bawon Simitye, and Bawon Kriminel).

112. Writing on his experience as a missionary in the French colony of Martinique, Father Jean-Baptiste DuTerte notes that "a number of (slaves) wear the rosary around their necks." Commenting on difficulties in transmitting the Christian faith to slaves, Liliane Chauleau cites as one impediment the predominance of "the wearing of certain 'ways' (moyens): icons, medals, rosaries, crosses." See Jean-Baptiste DuTerte, *Histoire générale des Antilles*, as cited by Chauleau, "Le baptême á la Martinique au XVIIe siècle," 28.

113. Précis des faits qui se sont passés dans la paroisse de Jacmel et sa dépendance, depuis le commencement septembre 1791 jusqu'à ce jour—onze mars 1792.

114. Lettre de M. Abbé Ouvière aux membres réunis les commissaires de la paroisse et de l'armée combinée de l'Ouest séante à la Croix de bouquets, Léogâne, 29 decembre 1792. AN DXXV 110 868. A second copy of this letter is found in AN DXXV 110 873. It is most likely that Elie Courlogne served as Romaine's scribe, as we know from the Léogâne parish registry that Elie was literate or at least that he could sign his own name, as he did when he became godfather to a mulatto boy named Simon on March 24, 1790. Baptême de Simon, Léogâne, 24 mai 1790. ANSOM ECN, SAINT-DOMINGUE-LÉOGÂNE-1790, 12.

115. Ibid.

116. Dubois, *Avengers of the New World*, 41.

117. Ibid., 107. As Malick Ghachem demonstrates in writing of the Haitian Revolution's outbreak in the North Province, "The royalism for the early slave insurgency was a phenomenon of remarkably diverse origins and manifestations." Ghachem, *The Old Regime*, 274. On royalism in Saint-Domingue, see also Ogle, "The Trans-Atlantic King and Imperial Public Space."

118. Dubois, *Avengers of the New World*, 108.

119. Anonymous, "La Révolution de Saint-Domingue, contenant tout ce qui s'est passé dans la colonie française depuis le commencement de la Révolution jusqu'au départ de l'auteur pour la France, le 8 septembre 1792." As transcribed in Popkin, *Facing Racial Revolution*, 57. Father Cachetan is discussed in much further detail in Chapter 5.
120. Dubois, *Avengers of the New World*, 107.
121. Ibid., 202.
122. Lacroix, *Mémoires pour servir à l'histoire de la révolution de Saint-Domingue*, 253. The passage is also translated and transcribed as "Response of Macaya" in Dubois and Garrigus, *Slave Revolution in the Caribbean*, 128.
123. Thornton, "I Am the Subject of the King of Congo," 189.
124. On religion and royalism in West Africa, see Parrinder, "Divine Kingship in West Africa"; Lloyd, "Sacred Kingship and Government among the Yoruba"; Fagg, *Divine Kingship in Africa*; Wilks, *Forests of Gold*; Pemberton, *Yoruba Sacred Kingship*; Olúpònà, *City of 201 Gods*; and Olúpònà, *Kingship, Rituals and Religion*.
125. Whatever the specific ethnicities of those who followed and surrounded him, Romaine-la-Prophétesse's charisma and healing prowess transformed him into one of a number of inspirational African and Creole religious leaders to emerge in the eighteenth-century Caribbean and lend a hand in the shaping of Afro-Atlantic Christianity. In this sense, the prophetess brings to mind Rebecca Protten, a mixed-race evangelist on the island of St. Thomas: "Chafing cultures gave off the spark of something new," as Jon Sensbach explains in the case of Protten, "melded and fused, picked up new cadences, then spun off into something different again." Sensbach, *Rebecca's Revival*, 5.
126. O'Neil and Rey, "The Saint and Siren."
127. Smith, "Remembering Mary," 525.
128. Fouchard, *Les marrons de la liberté*, 279.
129. Weber, *The Sociology of Religion*, 2, 110.
130. For a transcription of Boukman's alleged sermons, see James, *The Black Jacobins*, 87.
131. Fick, *The Making of Haiti*, 128.
132. I do not mean here to insinuate that Africans alone influenced herbalism or the use of amulets in Saint-Domingue, as there is, of course, a long and prolific history in Europe of such practices, and it is certainly possible that Romaine's creation of amulets reflected European as well as African influences, much like his Catholicism. For insight into relevant European context, see MacLeod and Mees, *Runic Amulets and Magic Objects*; and Müller-Ebeling, Rätsch, and Storl, *Witchcraft Medicine*. For an insightful comparison between African and European forms of sorcery, see Parrinder, *Witchcraft: African and European*.
133. Pascalis, "Anecdote historique," 57.

CHAPTER 3

1. As cited in Stewart, *Stewart's Quotable Africa*, 59.
2. Games, "Atlantic History," 742.
3. Anonymous, "BIOGRAPHY." Middleton, "Felix Pascalis-Ouvière and the Yellow Fever Epidemic of 1797," 497.
4. François Martin, Blancard, Guissard [?], and André Riguad [Sr.], "Attestation." Philadelphia, n.d. NYAM MS 94. Written in 1793 or 1794, this document is in effect a letter of introduction/recommendation that Pascalis secured shortly after his arrival in Philadelphia from several French residents of the city who had known him and/or his family in France. On Jean Joseph Pierre Pascalis, see de Ribbe, *Pascalis*.
5. Anonymous, "PASCALIS OUVIERE (FÉLIX)," 863.
6. "*Extract of a Letter from Dr.* Felix Pascalis, of New York, *to Dr.* Alire R. Delile, *on the subject of the Poisons of the* Upsas Tieute *of Java and other Strychnos.*" In Hosack and Francis, *American Medical and Philosophical Register*, 197–200, 198.
7. Letter of Felix Pascalis to Francisca Pascalis, New York, June 25, 1813. NYAM MS 619—Pascalis Ouviere, Felix.
8. Anonymous, "BIOGRAPHY." Michel Darluc (1717–1783) was a disciple of Swedish naturalist Carl Linnaeus (1707–1778), whose genius Pascalis would later honor in his own storied life by founding and presiding over the New York branch of the Linnaean Society. Darluc is most famous for his work on the natural history of Provence and his three-volume study of the subject, *Histoire naturelle de la Provence, contenant ce qu'il y a de plus remarquable dans les règnes végétal, minéral, animal, et la partie géoponique en trois volumes*. On Darluc, see Collomp, *Un médecin des Lumières*.
9. Shuler, *From the Mayflower to Pole Cat Pond, S. C.*, 53. It is difficult to gauge the credibility of details provided in oral history, such as this document, which was evidently passed down across generations; nevertheless, they are interesting and deserving of the historian's attention.
10. Hitt and Cannon, *Echoes from Pascalina*, 2.
11. "What the French exhibited between 1750 and 1815," writes Roger Williams in a marvelously entitled book, "was an *intensified* passion for the productions of the Vegetable Kingdom, in some individuals reaching mania." Williams, *Botanophilia in Eighteenth Century France*, 1.
12. "BIOGRAPHY: Felix Alexander Ouviere Pascalis."
13. Williams, *Botanophilia in Eighteenth Century France*, 122.
14. Vila, *Enlightenment and Pathology*, 80.
15. "Their personal orientations reveal the polarities of the revolutionary priesthood in 1789: the cranky and secular Sieyès, in fact minimally a priest, trying to bracket religion to bring about a new political era; and the imposing and

pastoral Grégoire trying to reform religion to bring about a new political era as well." Byrnes, *Priests of the French Revolution*, 3.

16. "Officials could not make up their minds whether it was sufficient for Ouvrière [*sic*] to put his name at the end of each copy or if he should add the printer's as well, and whether the granting of a permission to him would offend the Marseille municipality, which might want to exercise some censorship controls of its own." Gough, *The Newspaper Press and the French Revolution*, 33. I have discovered another title from 1789 that is attributed to Abbé Ouvière, one that I have been unable to locate, however: "La Heureuse Journée, ou le triomphe des braves marseillais." Marseille, 1789. The title hardly sounds like it's a royalist tract, to be sure, and it may have been authored by one of Ouvière's critics parading as the priest, using his name as a pseudonym. The source where I found this citation might suggest as much, though its compiler offers no explanation as to why this citation is included in his collection of pseudonyms. Reboul, *Anonymes, pseudonymes et supercheries littéraires de la Provence ancienne et moderne*, 167.
17. Abbé Ouvière, P.S.D.L.S.P., "Les Adieux d'un cosmopolite aux marseillois." n.p., n.d., 1789, 18. Though I have not been able to determine the precise meaning of the abbreviation following his name in this publication, the earliest I have found either by or mentioning Ouvière, Professor Leon-François Hoffmann and Father Ernst Even have suggested to me that the letters might stand for the opening words of a prayer, perhaps in Latin. I am grateful to the Vatican archivists, whose name I do not know, of Father Even's order who alerted us to this possibility. Léon-François Hoffmann and Ernest Even, personal electronic correspondence, November 15, 2009. My thanks to Professor Hoffmann and Father Even for their expert assistance.
18. Scott, "The Urban Bourgeoisie in the French Revolution," 97–98. Scott counts Ouvière as a member of a group of "bold conservatives."
19. Ouvière, "Les Adieux," 2.
20. Felix Pascalis, "Anecdote historique." New York, 1821. NYAM MS Folio Pascails Ouviere, 1819–1823, 49. Martin, Blancard, Guissard, and Riguad, "Attestation."
21. Anonymous, "BIOGRAPHY." The "Archbishop of Belloi" referred to here, evidently mistaking "Belloi" to be a place name in France, was Cardinal Jean-Baptiste de Belloy (1709–1808), Archbishop of Paris, while the surgeon mentioned was most probably Abbé Peyré, with whom Ouvière lived in Port-au-Prince for a period of time, as discussed a bit later in this chapter. A report written by Pinchinat and Beauvais, submitted to the French National Assembly and dated November 29, 1791, indicates that by then Ouvière had been in the colony for "fourteen months." Mavidal et al. (eds.), Assemblée Nationale Législative, *Archives parlementaires de 1787 à 1860*, 318.
22. Pascalis, "Anecdote historique," 50.

23. Shuler, *From the Mayflower to Pole Cat Pond, S. C.*, 53–54. I have found no other mention anywhere of Ouvière's having ever being in Maracaibo, nor that he ever studied at the University of Paris. It is also the case that no one was yet being "beheaded" on the guillotine in France at the time that Ouvière left for Saint-Domingue in 1790.
24. McManners, *Church and Society in Eighteenth Century France*, 647. The practice of tonsure in the Catholic Church ended in 1972, upon Pope Paul VI's signing of the motu proprio *Ministeria quaedam*.
25. Byrnes, *Priests of the French Revolution*, xxiv.
26. McManners, *Church and Society in Eighteenth Century France*, 682n1. The total number of priests in France in 1789 was 60,000; in addition, there were 26,000 monks and 56,000 nuns. Ibid., 473. There may actually have been considerably more, according to a study by Timothy Tackett and Claude Langlois, who estimate that there were a total of over 114,000 French male religious in 1790. Tackett and Langlois, "Ecclesial Structures and Clerical Geography on the Eve of the French Revolution," 357. The total population of France was then roughly 27 million. Andress, *French Society in Revolution*, 19. My thanks to Professor Joseph Burns for bringing the work of Tackett and Langlois to my attention.
27. McManners, *Church and Society in Eighteenth Century France*, 648.
28. Anonymous, "BIOGRAPHY"; Martin, Blancard, Guissard, and Riguad, "Attestation."
29. Byrnes, *Priests of the French Revolution*, xxiv.
30. Anonymous, "BIOGRAPHY." It is unclear how many brothers Ouvière had, but this reference is likely to François Pascalis Ouvière, who wrote to Félix from Nice on August 19, 1792. Lettre de François Pascalis Ouvière à Monsieur l'Abbé Ouvière, Nice, 19 aout 1792. AN DXXV 110 887.
31. Pascalis, "Anecdote historique," 50. Unfortunately, the count's name is illegible in Pascalis' marginal notation of this.
32. Pelissier-Guys and Masson, *Les Bouches-du-Rhône*.
33. McManners, *Church and Society in Eighteenth Century France*, 649. McManners expounds that during "the *ancien régime*, we find clerics who are totally cynical, some scandalous to boot; but there are many more who are paradoxically edifying—unbelievers meticulously fulfilling their duties, dubious characters who change course, routine careerists, believers without enthusiasm who refuse to let the side down, and a multitude of good men and women drawn to the Church for both self-interested reasons and the desire to serve it." Ibid., 2.
34. Ibid., 647.
35. Abbé Ouvière, "Pensionnat colonial établi au Port-au-Prince, par l'Abbé Ouvière, pretre." *Gazette de Saint-Domingue*, 21 janvier 1791.
36. Archival documents suggest that Ouvière said Mass on at least four occasions while in Saint-Domingue: in Croix de Bouquets on December 20, 1791, and one earlier occasion there, at Trou Coffy on Christmas Eve or Christmas Day 1791,

and in Léogâne on New Year's Day 1792. Lettre de Ouvière aux membres réunis les commissaires de la paroisse et de l'armée combinée de l'Ouest séant a la Croix de bouquets, Leogane, 29 decembre 1792, AN DXXV 110 868; Lettre de Baussan à monsieur l'Abbé Ouvière, Leogane, le 2 janvier, 1792, AN DXXV 110 819; Discours prononcé par l'Abbé Ouvière, en présence de l'armée combinée des citoyens de couleur, campée a la Croix des Bouquets, 20 decembre, 1791, AN DXXV 111 881. Abbé Ouvière's sermon at Croix-des-Bouquets suggests that this was not the first Mass that he had celebrated for the Confederate Army. Thirty years later, the former priest would write that he did not say Mass in Trou Coffy, but there is good reason to doubt this claim, as explained in Chapter 6. Pascalis, "Anecdote Historique," 51.

37. Pascalis, "Anecdote Historique," 51.
38. Several letters from his wife to Abbé Ouvière in 1792 are preserved among his papers in the Archives Nationales in Paris, and these are analyzed in Chapter 7.
39. Though extremely rare, married Catholic priests in France at the time were not entirely unheard of, for Byrnes writes of another cleric "who had been married for years: 'I heard the gentle voice of nature. I secretly married a girl of my age, whose virtue and charm have been my greatest happiness for twenty-two years.' Betrayed by a clerical colleague with government connections, he was carried off like a criminal." Byrnes, *Priests of the French Revolution*, 146.
40. Scurr, *Fatal Purity*, 124. By 1793, however, the idea of married priests had gained such wider acceptance that the Legislative Assembly embraced it by putting an end to priestly vows and emptying dozens of monasteries in France of their clerics, many of whom took full advantage of their new liberty and did indeed wed. Some felt pressure to do so by the threat of execution during the Reign of Terror, furthermore, entering marriages "as unconsummated ruses, contracted for self-protection." Sepinwall, *The Abbé Grégoire and the French Revolution*, 146.
41. Shusterman, *The French Revolution*, 206.
42. Ibid., 127.
43. Byrnes, *Priest of the French Revolution*, 258.
44. Lettre de l'Abbé Ouvière à Robespierre, St. Marc, 7 septembre 1790. AN DXXV 111 881.
45. Fouchard, *Les marrons du syllabaire*, 137n202. The letter in question is the only item addressed to or mentioning Robespierre in Ouvière's papers in Paris.
46. Lettre de l'Abbé Ouvière à Robespierre.
47. Sepinwall, *Abbé Grégoire and the French Revolution*, 104.
48. Lacroix, *Mémoires pour servir à l'histoire de la Révolution de Saint-Domingue*, 498.
49. Fouchard, *Les marrons du syllabaire*, 137, n. 202.
50. Laurent Dubois argues that the images were "particularly dangerous" in this regard "since slaves only had to open their eyes ... to understand that people across the Atlantic would support them if they revolted." Dubois, *A Colony of Citizens*, 105.

51. Anonymous, *A Particular Account*, 14.
52. Ibid, 14. The deputies attribute the quoted passage to "*Particulars of the Insurrection in St. Domingo*, printed in the *Jamaica newspapers, but for obvious reasons suppressed in that island.*"
53. In my 1998 article on Romaine-la-Prophétesse, I actually mistook Ouvière for Grégoire. Rey, "The Virgin Mary and Revolution in Saint-Domingue," 350.
54. "Tableau des Membres de la Société des amis des Noirs. Année 1789." In Anonymous, *La Révolution Française et l'Abolition de l'Esclavage*, 1–8.
55. Anonymous, "St. Domingo Disturbance." *Philadelphia General Advertiser*, 321, 3, October 10, 1791, 3. This article is an extract from a letter by Madame de Rouvray to de Lostanges, September 4, 1791, which is reproduced in McIntosh and Wheeler, *Une Correspondance familiale au temps des troubles de Saint-Domingue*, 27. I was unable to review the papers of the Société des Amis des Noirs in Paris and admit that there might be mention of Ouvière therein, though I doubt it.
56. Lacroix. *Mémoires pour server à l'histoire de la révolution de Saint-Domingue*, 142. Less dubiously, Lacroix here also assails Ouvière for his "hatred for the revolution."
57. ANSOM ECN SAINT-DOMINGUE-LEOGANE, 1790, 1791, 1792.
58. ANSOM ECN SAINT-DOMINGUE-PORT-AU-PRINCE, 1790–1792; ANSOM ECN SAINT-DOMINGUE-CROIX-DES-BOUQUETS, 1790–1792.
59. Cabon, *Notes sur l'histoire religieuse d'Haïti*, 46. Cabon also notes that in his research he found no information about any role that Ouvière might have played in the Colonial Assembly or of his "attitude" vis-à-vis the dramatic political events then unfolding in France and in Saint-Domingue. In the interim, I have found much information in this regard, which is detailed in Chapter 7.
60. Ouvière, "Pensionnat colonial établi au Port-au-Prince."
61. Assemblée Nationale Législative. *Archives parlementaires*, 317–318.
62. Ibid.
63. Weaver, *Medical Revolutionaries*, 31. Weaver outlines the status and function of the royal physician, the king's appointee, as follows: "The *médecin du roi* ... verified the degrees of newly arrived doctors, presided at the licensing exams of surgeons, apothecaries, and midwives, assessed pharmacies and the drug supplies of surgeons and apothecaries, and monitored the accounts of their fellow physicians and surgeons."
64. *Observations médicales sur les vertus du quinquina indigène de St-Domingue fait à l'hôpital royal et militaire de Port-au-Prince, par Peyré, médecin du roi, transmises par La Luzerne*. ASRM 191B, dossier 31, Quinquina de Saint-Domingue (1787–1789).
65. McClellan, *Colonialism and Science*, 114.
66. Reçu d'Ouvière la somme de 283 livres pour la vente d'un cheval de Pierre Fronelle, 24 juin 1791, Croix de Bouquets. AN DXXV 110 873. Jean-Philippe Garran de Coulon alludes to a letter from Romaine-la-Prophétesse to Abbé

Ouvière dated November 17, 1791, but I have not found it. Garran de Coulon, *Rapport sur les troubles de Saint-Domingue, Tome 2*, 488.

67. Assemblée Nationale Législative. *Archives Parlementaires*, 317–318. A few pages later, this collection of reports from Saint-Domingue includes one written by Ouvière that is probably the kind of exposé referred to here that had angered some of the political opponents of the mulattoes of Croix-des-Bouquets. Abbé Ouvière, "Suite des événements de la conscription de Port-au-Prince, rédigé par les citoyens de couleurs."
68. Pascalis, "Anecdote Historique," 47.
69. Guerre Civile de la Province de l'Ouest. AN DXXV 110 887. Though unsigned and undated, this document is clearly written in Ouvière's handwriting and appears to be a draft of an edition of the newspaper he was trying to launch. It recounts relevant events of November 22 and 23 and lists the three other members of the council, the "white planters" as Hanus de Jumecourt, D'Aulais [?], and du Chitri. Among other reasons unstated here, the Confederates enlisted the services of these four men because they considered them to be "sincere friends."
70. Lettre de Blanchelande à l'Abbé Ouvière, Cap Français, 28 novembre 1792. AN DXXV 110 819.
71. The formal name of the advisory council was Le conseille de guerre de l'armée des citoyens réuinis de divers paroisses de l'Ouest, campée au bourg de la Croix de Bouquets, extraordinarement assemblée (Council of War of the Army of the Reunited Citizens of Various Parishes of the West, Camped in the City of Croix de Bouquets, Extraordinarily Assembled). Extrait des minutes deposée a la municipalité de port-au-prince, 1 decembre 1791. AN DXXV 61 612.
72. Discours prononcé par l'Abbé Ouvière, en présence de l'armée combinée des citoyens de couleur, campée a la Croix des Bouquets, 20 décembre, 1791. AN DXXV 111 881.
73. Pascalis, "Anecdote Historique," 49.

CHAPTER 4

1. Char, "Transfuges." *Ouevres complètes*, 9.
2. Ghachem, *The Old Regime and the Haitian Revolution*, 246.
3. Fick, *The Making of Haiti*, 86–88.
4. Garrigus, *Before Haiti*, 251. On this subject, see also Fick, *The Making of Haiti*, 137–143.
5. For an excellent discussion of this, see Thornton, "African Soldiers in the Haitian Revolution."
6. Copie de l'interrogation subi par le negre Pierre-Louis, 11 octobre, 1791. AN DXXV 61 610. The interrogation of Pierre-Louis is also included in the French parliamentary records. *Archives Parlementaires, Tome 37*, January 11, 1792, 392. Assemblée Nationale, *Archives Parlementaires de 1787 à 1860*. Paris: Dupont, 1891 (1792), CXLIII, 312–313.

7. For a brief discussion of one particular use of human skulls in Haitian Vodou see McAlister, *Rara!*, 104–106.
8. Other whites were very likely members of the Trou Coffy insurgency from its inception, but I have found no trace of their identities, with the exceptions of Delisle de Bresolle and the DesMarattes brothers.
9. By a little more than a year later, Tavet had become the mayor of Jacmel. See his letter to General La Salle of October 30, 1792. In La Salle, *Papiers du général A.-N. La Salle*, 46–48.
10. Traité de paix entre les citoyens blancs et les citoyens de couleur des quatorze paroisses de la province de l'Ouest, de la partie française de Saint-Domingue, 19 octobre 1791. AN DXXV 111. 881.
11. Throughout the Plain of Léogâne there were already as of 1789 a number of "small groups of insurgents" causing problems for local planters, but there is no evidence that they were at all connected to Trou Coffy. Depréaux, "Le Commandant Baudry des Lozières et la Phalange de Crête Dragons, 1–42, 31. Commander Baudry was wounded by these insurgents. See also Baudry des Lozières, *Second voyage à Louisiane*. On the implications of the Kikongo dictionary that Baudry published while serving in the French military in Saint-Domingue, meanwhile, see Sweet, "New Perspectives on Kongo in Revolutionary Haiti." *The Americas* 74, forthcoming; and Johnson, *The Fear of French Negroes*, 79. I am grateful to Professor Sweet for bringing Baudry to my attention.
12. Fick, *The Making of Haiti*, 127.
13. Garran de Coulon, *Rapport sur les troubles de Saint-Domingue, Tome 2*, 492–493.
14. Lettre de Monsieur Duchemin, officier, à M. Bauchin, Grande Rivière de Léogâne, 19 octobre, 1791. AN DXXV 61 611. Though composed in the first person, this letter also carries the signatures of Messieurs Clery and Malahar.
15. Precis des faits qui se sont passe dans la paroisse de Jacmel depuis le commencement de septembre 1791 jusqu'au ce jour—onze mars 1791. AN DXXV 61 615.
16. Lettre de Labuissonnière, Léogâne, July 16, 1792. In Raimond, *Correspondance de Julien Raimond*, 91–93, 93.
17. Fick, *The Making of Haiti*, 129
18. Garran de Coulon, *Rapport sur les troubles de Saint-Domingue, Tome 2*, 493. Ouvière reported that famine had struck Léogâne in early March of 1792. "Journal de la Guerre Civile à la province de l'Ouest de St. Domingue." AN DXXV 110 887.
19. Lettre de l'Abbé Ouvière aux membres réunis les commissaires de la paroisse et de l'armée combinée de l'Ouest séante a la Croix de bouquets, Léogâne, 29 décembre 1792. AN DXXV 110 868. A second copy of this letter is found in AN DXXV 110 862.
20. Anonymous, "Authentic copy of a letter from a gentleman of character and information in Cape Francois to his correspondent in this city, dated Cape Francois, Dec 28." *National Gazette*, Philadelphia, February 9, 1792. This is the only

intimation of sexual violence in the Trou Coffy insurgency that I have discovered in any primary source.

21. Garran de Coulon, *Rapport sur les troubles de Saint-Domingue, Tome 2*, 492–493. Ouvière's trip to Trou Coffy and the treaty that he brokered with Romaine-la-Prophétesse are discussed in detail in Chapter 6.
22. Delagroix to Saint-Leger [?], Léogâne, February 4, 1792. As cited in Fick, *The Making of Haiti*, 308n52.
23. Garran de Coulon, *Rapport sur les troubles de Saint-Domingue, Tome 2*, 492–493.
24. Lettre du bureau de la police à Monsieur l'Abbé Ouvière, Léogâne, 17 janvier 1792. AN DXXV 110 819.
25. Lettre de Marianne Valde, Léogâne, 2 fevrier 1792. AN DXXV 61 615.
26. Lettre de Villards à Ouvière, Léogâne, 13 janvier 1792. AN DXXV 110 819.
27. Lettre de Villards à Ouvière, Léogâne, 11 janvier, 1792. AN DXXV 110 819. There are actually two letters from Villards to Romaine carrying this date, but I cite them here as one and the same.
28. Lettre de Villards à Ouvière, Léogâne, 13 janvier 1792. AN DXXV 110 819.
29. Garran de Coulon, *Rapport sur les troubles de Saint-Domingue, Tome 2*, 494.
30. Lettre de des Villards à Ouvière, 11 janvier 1792. AN DXXV 110 819.
31. Lettre de Pietemaire [?], Léogâne, 19 janvier 1792.
32. Lettre de des Villards à Ouvière, 11 janvier 1792.
33. Lettre de Villards à Ouvière, Léogâne, 13 janvier 1792. Quite the wordsmith, Villards reveled in his correspondence with Ouvière. In this letter, written in response to a January 9 letter from the priest that is not in the archive, for instance, the enchanted mayor tearfully wrote, "your tender expressions deliciously tickle my own love. . . . The 48 years that weigh upon my head have whitened my hair and deadened my passions, but they have done nothing to dull my sensitivity. To read what a sage writes, the sight of a good man, always deliciously touches my soul." Much later in life, Ouvière would provide one additional bit of information about just who Villards was: *"chev - de St. Louis, Commandant Militaire de la Paroisse."* Felix Pascalis, "Anecdote historique." New York, 1821. NYAM MS Folio Pascalis Ouviere, 1819–1823, 48.
34. Precis des fait qui se sont passe dans la paroisse de Jacmel depuis le commencement de septembre 1791 jusqu'au ce jour—onze mars 1791.
35. Lettre de Baussan à monsieur l'Abbé Ouvière.
36. Lettre d'Elie Courlogne à Ouvière, Trou Coffy, 16 janvier 1792. AN DXXV 110 819.
37. Lettre d'Elie Courlogne à Ouvière, Trou Coffy, 24 janvier 1792. AN DXXV 110 819.
38. Lettre de Elie Courlogne à Ouvière, 16 janvier 1792.
39. Lettre de Romaine Riviere, la prophetess, commandant general à Monsieur l'Abbé Ouvière, Commissaire Conciliateur à la Croix de Bouquets, au Trou Coffy, 26 janvier 1792. AN DXXV 110 887.

40. Interrogation de Joseph Massiat Gibaut Rigaud, n.p., 2 janvier, 1792. AN DXXV 61 614.
41. Lettre de Villards à Ouvière, Léogâne, 28 janvier 1792. AN DXXV 110 819.
42. Lettre de Gauthier à Ouvière, Léogâne, 2 fevrier 1792. AN DXXV 110 819.
43. Interrogation de Gibaut Rigaud; Extrait des pieces deposees aux archives de l'assemblee nationale de la partie francaise de St Domingue. Jacmel le 21 janvier 1792. AN DXXV 61 614.
44. Lettre de Marianne Valde, negresse de Léogâne, 2 février 1792. AN DXXV 61 615.
45. Lettre de D'Audard à Ouvière, Léogâne, 25 janvier 1792. AN DXXV 110 819.
46. Lettre de Pietemaire [?] à l'Abbé Ouvière, Léogâne, 19 janvier 1792. AN DXXV 110 819.
47. Lettre de Villards à l'Abbé Ouvière, Léogâne, 28 janvier 1792. AN DXXV 110 819.
48. "Lettre d'un particulier de Léogâne, du 7 février 1792." In Garran de Coulon, *Rapport sur les troubles de Saint-Domingue, Tome 2*, 492–493.
49. Position de la Province de l'Ouest, 12 mars 1792. AN DXXV 61 615.
50. Letters of Bérouet, June 16, 1792 and July 18, 1792, as transcribed in their entireties in Debien, *Une plantation de Saint-Domingue*, 114–115.

CHAPTER 5

1. In his biography of Toussaint Louverture, Madison Smartt Bell offers that even though it is unclear whether the great revolutionary hero was a slave on any of the Jesuit-owned plantations in Saint-Domingue, "it seems very likely that Toussaint was in a position to imbibe their influence during his youth (he was somewhere between eighteen and twenty-four at the time of their expulsion) and that they had a hand in his education." Bell, *Toussaint Louverture*, 64–65. Charles Frostin even traces a Jesuit influence on the Haitian Constitution of 1801. Frostin, "Méthodologie missionnaire et sentiment religieux en Amérique française," 51. While plausible, because my project does not focus either on Toussaint Louverture or the later stages of the Haitian Revolution and the drafting of Haiti's first constitutions, I am unable to assess the reliability of these suggestions.
2. Letter of Father Margat to the Procurer General of the Company of Jesus, July 20, 1743. In Jan, *Collecta pour l'histoire du diocèse du Cap-Haïtien*, 28–55, 47.
3. Ibid., 50.
4. Once gripped by "a certain incompatibility between the institution of slavery and the Catholic religion or at least as it was taught to slaves by the Jesuits in the eighteenth century," as François Kawas explains, the Jesuit mission became increasingly proactive on behalf of slaves' humanity. Kawas, *Histoire des Jésuites en Haïti*, 13.

5. "Every subordinate group creates . . . a hidden transcript that represents a critique of power spoken behind the back of the dominant." Scott, *Domination and the Arts of Resistance*, xii. Laënnec Hurbon underscores the importance of such Jesuit-sanctioned meetings to the development of revolutionary slave consciousness in Saint-Domingue, meanwhile, and how the church functioned for slaves as a "place of sociality par excellence": "Over and above being a center for the distribution of sacraments or of religious ceremonies, the church was a gathering place, a place for meetings and discussion. . . . During Sunday and feast day sermons, the clergy not only transmitted news of recent arrivals in the colony, but also mediated relations between various social and ethnic groups." Hurbon, *Religions et lien social*, 72.
6. On these admonishments, see also Breathett, "The Religious Missions in Colonial French Saint-Domingue," 116.
7. "Arrêt du Petit-Goave, touchant la Fête de Saint Dominique." Petit-Goave, 5 août 1710. In Moreau de Saint-Méry, *Loix et constitutions des colonies françoises de l'Amérique sous le Vent, Tome 2*, 204–205.
8. "Accords fait entre les Marguilliers du Cap, le Supérieur de la Mission des Jésuites, et le Curé; et Arrêt du Conseil de la même Ville qui les Homologue." Cap Français, 7 janvier/6 février 1719; "Arrêt du Conseil du Cap, contenant modification de celui du 7 janvier précédent de la même Ville qui homologuait le Traité d'entre les Marguilliers et les R.R. P.P." Cap-Français, 3 julliet 1719. In Moreau de Saint-Méry, *Loix et constitutions des colonies françoises de l'Amérique sous le Vent, Tome 2*, 630–632, 632; 649–650, 650.
9. M. Bernard, "Mémoire pour le Conseil de Marine sur Plusieurs Choses qui _______ dans les Isles d'Amérique." Martinique, 25 septembre, 1722. ANSOM COL F3 91.
10. "Mémoire des Préfets Apostoliques et Supérieurs Généreaux des Missionaires Residants aux Iles Françaises." Martinique, 22 septembre, 1722. ANSOM COL F3 91. A similar letter concerning the reduction of the number of feast days written in 1760 in Cayenne provides a comprehensive list of feast days celebrated in that colony on which slaves were free from work. They numbered 30 in all. For some reason, slaves in Cayenne at the time seemingly had, in addition to Sundays, every other Saturday off. All told, this amounted to 108 days a year. Small wonder, then, that slaves generally liked the Church. M. Mailliard, "Lettre aux Ministeres." Cayenne, 26 octobre, 1760. ANSOM COL F3 91. These and related documents are found in the Collection Moreau de Saint-Méry in folders entitled "Fêtes" and "Jésuites."
11. P. Larcher, "Mandement du Préfet Apostolique de la Mission des Jésuites, et Ordonnance du Gouverneur Général pour un retranchement des Fêtes dans le ressort du Conseil du Cap." Cap-Français, 3 julliet 1719. In M. Moreau de Saint-Méry, *Loix et constitutions des colonies françoises de l'Amérique sous le Vent, Tome 3*, 274, 276.

12. "Extrait de la lettre du Ministre aux Administrateurs, sur l'inhumation solennelle d'une Négresse pendue." Cap-Français, 22 octobre 1737. In Moreau de Saint-Méry, *Loix et constitutions des colonies françoises de l'Amérique sous le Vent, Tome 3*, 485.
13. "Arrêt de règlement du Conseil du Cap, sur les abus, en matière de Religion, de la part des Gens de Couleurs." Cap-Français, 18 février 1761. In Moreau de Saint-Méry, *Loix et constitutions des colonies françoises de l'Amérique sous le Vent, Tome 4*, 352–356, 352.
14. Ibid., 355.
15. "Arrêt du Conseil du Cap, qui ordonne que les Jésuites remettront au Greffe de la Cour leurs Constitutions, Statuts, &." Cap-Français, 7 octobre 1762. In Moreau de Saint-Méry, *Loix et constitutions des colonies françoises de l'Amérique sous le Vent, Tome 4*, 505–506.
16. "Arrêt du Conseil Supérieur du Cap-Français Isle de Saint-Domingue qui condamne la Moralité et la Doctrine des Jésuites." In Kawas, *Histoire des Jésuites en Haïti*, 135–150, 135–136, 147. Moreau's *Loix et consitutions* only contains the preamble to this decree, whereas Kawas transcribes it in its entirety.
17. "Arrêt Définitif du Conseil du Cap, qui Prononce l'Extinction des Jésuites, et leur expulsion hors de la Colonie." Cap-Français, 24 novembre 1763. In Moreau de Saint-Méry, *Loix et constitutions des colonies françoises de l'Amérique sous le Vent, Tome 4*, 626–628.
18. Ibid., 628. Bell identifies a one Abbé Leclerc as another Jesuit who remained in the colony after the expulsion, "in quasi hiding," but he provides no source for this claim, while primary source records suggest more persuasively that Leclerc was in fact a Capuchin. Bell, *Toussaint Louverture*, 64; "Demande de poste par le père Leclerc de Saint-Étrain, rappel des services rendus à la mission et de la perte de deux habitations suite une modification de frontière avec la partie espagnol de l'ile (novembre 1776/juin 1777)." ANSOM FR COL F5A 25/4. George Breathett even suggests, without providing evidence, "purportedly some Jesuits who had remained on the island" were present among "a group of enlightened slaves assembled at a pretended voudoun ceremony and planned a general revolt in Haiti" in August of 1791, presumably at Bois Caïman. I think this is unlikely. Breathett, *The Catholic Church in Colonial Haiti (1704–1785)*, 18. Breathett mistakenly notes August 4 as the date of the 1791 ceremony in question, furthermore.
19. On religious and theological interpretations of earthquakes in Haitian history, see Rey, "(Mis)Representations of Religion and Earthquakes in Haiti"; McAlister, "From Slave Revolt to a Blood Pact with Satan"; Richman "Religion at the Epicenter"; Buteau, "Encountering God in Haiti"; and Rey, "Fear and Trembling in Haiti." A meteor shower in Saint-Domingue in 1789, meanwhile, was believed by some to be a curse from on high. One observer of the event, an attorney named Dufouart, scoffed at such belief: "And so it is, ever clinging to their first

impressions, that some men hold to the very end to the absurdities that swaddled their childhood." "Du Port-au-Prince au Rédacteur," Miragoâne, 14 février 1789, *Nouvelles Diverses*, Numéro XX, 7 mars 1789. ANSOM COLONIES F/3/92.

20. The notion of "religious habitus" was developed by Pierre Bourdieu toward understanding the sources and functions of any individual's perception of and disposition toward religion. Bourdieu, *"Genèse et structure du champ religieux."* See also Rey, *Bourdieu on Religion*, 2007.
21. Lettre d M. des Rouaudières à Madame de Marans, au Fond, Isle Saint-Domingue, 20 juin 1770. In Debien, *Lettres des Colons*, 24–26, 25.
22. Janin, *La religion aux colonies françaises*, 130.
23. Ibid.
24. Charles Frostin goes so far as to suggest that, "In the case of Saint-Domingue, the Jesuit experience demands attention in the sense that it prepared from afar and primed in advance the fearsome reckonings of pending Haitian independence." Frostin, "Méthodologie missionnaire et sentiment religieux en Amérique française," 34.
25. The Jesuits returned to Haiti in 1953, only to be expelled anew by François Duvalier in 1964. By 1972, some had returned "in a clandestine manner," and, shortly after the fall of the Duvalier regime, in 1986 the order was permitted to return once again. Kawas, "L'Histoire de la compagnie de Jésus en Haïti." http://www.jesuites.org/Haiti.htm; last accessed May 14, 2010.
26. Levine, "The Future of Liberation Theology in Latin America." http://quod.lib.umich.edu/j/jii/4750978.0002.201?view=text;rgn=main; last accessed March 3, 2016.
27. As Jeremy Popkin observes, in the early stages of the Haitian Revolution "insurgents wanted the help of white priests." Popkin, *Facing Racial Revolution*, 159.
28. Hurbon, "Le clergé catholique et l'insurrection de Saint-Domingue," 32. Italics added. Though it is unclear how he arrives at these numbers, Hurbon specifies that, "no fewer than 16 of the 24 priests in the North had actively or even decisively participated in the insurrection." On this subject, see also Hurbon, "Esclavage et évangélisation"; Adrien, "Notes sur le clergé du nord et la révolte des esclaves en 1791"; and Thibau, *Le temps de Saint-Domingue*.
29. Popkin, *Facing Racial Revolution*, 159.
30. Hurbon, "Le clergé catholique et l'insurrection de Saint-Domingue," 32–34.
31. Landers, *Atlantic Creoles in the Age of Revolutions*, 59.
32. As David Geggus puts it, during all of the death and destruction of the 1791 slave insurrection in the North Province, "priests were always spared and they were sufficiently well treated to have left the reputation, fostered by the planters, who hanged one of them, of being the rebels' active collaborators." Geggus, "Slave Resistance Studies," 16–17. Popkin concurs: "The whites fighting against the uprising were intensely suspicious of these clergymen and sometimes even blamed them for inciting the slaves to rebel." Popkin, *Facing Racial Revolution*, 159.

33. Malouet, *Collections of Memories of the Colonies*, as cited in Parkinson, *"This Gilded African,"* 56.
34. Peabody, "'A Dangerous Zeal,'" 90.
35. I have found no instances in the Dominguan parish registries in which Abbé Aubert signs off as having administered sacraments, though I confess to having not reviewed all the thousands of pages that they comprise, limiting myself to a certain time frame and to certain parishes, like Léogâne, Jacmel, and Cayes-Jacmel. For many parishes, meanwhile, the registries are seemingly lost to history.
36. Thibau, *Le temps de Saint-Domingue*, 319.
37. De Blanchelande, *Supplément au Mémoire de M. de Blanchelande*, 19.
38. Ibid.
39. Anonymous eyewitness account, cited in Thibau, *Le temps de Saint-Domingue*, 311. Thibau combines primary sources in the many lengthy block quotes in his book, evidently weaving in his own imaginative embellishments, leaving it very difficult to track down the original attribution of certain archival texts he analyzes. I have a recollection of seeing this passage in an eighteenth-century French text somewhere, likely the original, though my bibliographic notes fail to indicate exactly where.
40. In Thibau, *Le temps de Saint-Domingue*, 309. Popkin indicates that in some documentation Cachetan's name appears as "Cajétan." Popkin, *Facing Racial Revolution*, 102.
41. Anonymous, "La Révolution de Saint-Domingue, contenant tout ce qui s'est passé dans la colonie française depuis le commencement de la Révolution jusqu'au départ de l'auteur pour la France, le 8 septembre 1792." As transcribed in Popkin, *Facing Racial Revolution*, 49–58, 57.
42. Anonymous, "La Révolution de Saint-Domingue." As cited in Thibau, *Le temps de Saint-Domingue*, 309.
43. Anonymous, "La Révolution de Saint-Domingue," 268–269. As transcribed and translated in Popkin, *Facing Racial Revolution*, 57.
44. Ibid.
45. M. Monchet, "Quelques observations sur l'insurrection des Noir à St. Domingue, sur les causes et les agents secret de cette conspiration." *Service Historique de l'Armée de Terre*, Vincennes. 1 M 589, n. d. I am grateful to Donna Evleth for having found and transcribed this document for me.
46. Delahaye's character receives considerable attention in one of Madison Smart Bell's compelling historical novels of the Haitian Revolution, *Masters of the Crossroads*.
47. Delahaye, *Florindie ou Historie physico-économique des végétaux de la Torride*. Delahaye also provided illustrations for Thierry de Menonville's *Traité de la Culture de Nopal et de l'Éducation de la Cochenille dans les Colonies Françaises de l'Amérique; Précédé d'un Voyage à Guaxaca*. Both of these publications were

financed by Le Cercle des Philosophes, Saint-Domingue's leading scientific institution. On science in Saint-Domingue, see McClellan, *Colonialism and Science.*

48. Darimajou, *La Chasteté Du Clergé Dévoilée,* 63–65.
49. Jan, *Monographie religieuse des Paroisses du Cap-Haïtien,* 210–211.
50. Carteau, *Soirées Bermudiennes,* 82. In addition to Delahaye, Carteau lists several other Catholic priests among the conspirators behind the slave uprising, namely, Abbé Osmond, Abbé Philibert Leblondin, who had both recently "arrived from France for unknown reasons," Abbé Boucher, "curé of Terrier Rouge ... and Sonthonox's right hand man," Father Sulpice, a Capuchin, and "Several curés, under deceptive veneer."
51. Ibid., 235.
52. Benot, "Documents sur l'insurrection des esclaves de Saint-Domingue," para. 2.
53. Bell, *Toussaint Louverture,* 27. Eventually, Jean-François felt that he had no choice but to eliminate Jeannot because of his excessive cruelty, which threatened to disparage the cause for which they were fighting: "his uncontrolled barbarism could seriously jeopardize their imminent negotiations with the white authorities." Fick, *The Making of Haiti,* 113.
54. Gros, *An Historick Recital.* As cited in Popkin, *Facing Racial Revolution,* 135–136. Though the French word "*curé*" should seemingly be translated as "curate," as here, in the Catholic Church it really means "pastor," while "*vicaire*" is likewise not soundly translatable in Catholic contexts as "vicar," but more so as "assistant pastor." I've thus chosen to keep the French originals, even when translating passages into English, throughout this book. My thanks to Professor Joseph Byrnes for pointing out this subtle but important point.
55. Bell, *Toussaint Louverture,* 27.
56. Benot, "The Insurgents of 1791."
57. Interrogation of 1 December 1793 [*sic*], AN DXXV 5. As translated and transcribed in Popkin, *Facing Racial Revolution,* 158–163, 163.
58. Lettre de Biassou à Delahaye, 13 decembre 1792. AN DXXV 12. As transcribed in its entirety by Benot in "The Insurgents of 1791," 20.
59. Interrogation of 1 December 1793 [*sic*], 160.
60. Ibid., 161–162. Popkin suggests that the year of this document is mislabeled and should in fact read 1792. Popkin, *Facing Racial Revolution,* 378n2. Benot notes, meanwhile, that Delahaye was still in Dondon when whites retook the town on January 27, 1793, and that he fled to the Spanish side of the island, only to be arrested later. Benot, "Documents sur l'insurrection des esclaves de Saint-Domingue," 7, http://ahrf.revues.org/2175; last accessed January 10, 2014. There is thus some confusion over certain details surrounding Delahaye's arrest and detainment. At any rate, in the same article, Benot indicates that Abbé Roussel, curé of Grande Anse, was likewise interrogated by Sonthonax and provides the call number for the interrogation as AN DXXV 14.

61. Popkin, *Facing Racial Revolution*, 159.
62. Adolphe Cabon refers to a report that indicates "there were sixteen missionaries lost in the massacres caused by the slave revolts," but he takes this to mean that in addition to the three who were executed by the French and the one who "died of fear," twelve missionaries fled. As such, sixteen were indeed lost, though it is not clear from Cabon whether any of them were killed by rebel slaves. Adolphe Cabon, *Notes sur l'histoire religieuse d'Haïti*, 38. Bell's research, meanwhile, suggests that Delahaye, "Old friend to liberty though he was, [Delahaye] was among the slain." Bell, *Toussaint Louverture*, 237. Pierre Pluchon concurs with Bell, counting Delahaye among the three slain priests, the others being Sulpice and Philippe. Pluchon, *Vaudou, sorciers. empoisonneurs*, 124.
63. Jan, *Monographie religieuse*, 211. Jan attributes the report of blacks killing Delahaye to Cabon; however, Cabon clearly indicates that Delahaye was in fact captured and executed by the French in Cap-Français. Cabon, *Notes sur l'histoire religieuse d'Haïti*, 43. Hurbon follows Cabon in offering that he was drowned, adding that General Rochambeau had ordered the priest's aquatic execution. Hurbon, "Le clergé catholique et l'insurrection," 32. Cabon's texts offer few citations and thus investigating the accuracy of all of his claims is a tall order, if not an impossibility.
64. Cabon, *Notes sur l'histoire religieuse d'Haïti*, 43.
65. Anonymous, *Histoire des désastres de Saint Domingue: tableau de la colonie jusqu'à la révolution de 1789*, 262. This book does not carry the name of any author or date and place of publication, but it is clearly a slightly altered version of Descourlitz, *Histoire des désastres de Saint-Domingue, précédée d'un tableau du régime et des progrès de cette colonie depuis sa fondation jusqu'à l'époque de la Révolution française*. On the authorship of this important book, see Benzaken, "Who Was the Author of *Histoire des désastres de Saint Domingue* in Paris in the Year III?" Benzaken disputes that Descourlitz could have authored the book, suggesting that a one LaPlace, a self-proclaimed "modest coffee planter" in the North Province, wrote it instead.
66. Benot, "Documents sur l'insurrection des esclaves de Saint-Domingue," 7.
67. By 1789, writes Cabon, Catholic priests in Saint-Domingue were "relegated . . . to the ranks of those denied any consideration by colonial prejudice, like petty merchants, property-less whites, *hommes de couleur*; it was expected that they would be judged like these others by a low level police magistrate." Cabon, *Notes sur l'histoire religieuse d'Haïti*, 26. And thus, as Pluchon suspects, this might have been a material reason for some socially and politically marginalized priests like Delahaye "to exploit their relative influence over the slaves. . . . How could one thus not suspect certain colonial priests of having inflamed the fervor of the Blacks?" Pluchon, *Vaudou, sorciers, empoisonneurs*, 124.
68. Copie de la deposition d'Abbé Bienvenu Amonet, n.d., aux archives de l'Assemblée coloniale de la partie française de l'ile de Saint-Domingue. AN DXXV 61 611. Though written in the first person plural tense, Bienvenu is referring to himself alone. Thibau evidently misreads this document to suggest that

Bienvenu asked municipal authorites to go to Dondon. Thibaud, *Le temps de Saint-Domingue*, 318.

69. Copie de la deposition d'Abbé Bienvenu Amonet, n.d., aux archives de l'Assemblée coloniale de la partie française de l'île de Saint-Domingue. These are my summations and not literal translations from Bienvenu's deposition.
70. Gros, *An Historick Recital*, as transcribed in Popkin, *Facing Racial Revolution*, 115–155, 132. The passage is found on page 12 of the French original, Gros, *Précis historique*.
71. Interrogation of 1 December 1793 [*sic*], in Popkin, *Facing Racial Revolution*, 163.
72. Gros, *An Historick Recital*, in Popkin, *Facing Racial Revolution*, 132.
73. Ibid., 139.
74. Ibid., 138.
75. Ibid., 124.
76. La Municipalité de Jacmel à l'Assemblee Coloniale de la partie francaise de St Domingue, Jacmel, 20 janvier 1792. AN DXXV 61 614.
77. Lettre de M. Cussan à l'Assemblée Nationale, Jacmel, 15 février, 1792. AN DXXV 61 615.
78. La Municipalité de Jacmel à l'Assemblee Coloniale de la partie francaise de St Domingue, Jacmel, 20 janvier 1792.
79. Extrait des pièces deposées aux Archives de l'Assemblée Coloniale de la partie Francaise de Saint-Domingue: Extrait du Registre des Déclarations de la Municipalité de Jacmel, Jacmel, 11 fevrier 1792. AN 61 615.
80. Extrait des déclarations fait à la municipalite de Jacmel par Lamy Lartigue, 29 octobre 1792. In La Salle, *Les papiers du général A.N. La Salle*, 50–54, 53–54.
81. Lettre de M. Cussan à l'Assemblée Nationale.
82. Abbé Aubert should not be confused with his contemporary and namesake Abbé Jean-Louis Aubert, the fabulist, dramatist, journalist, and poet who lived from 1731–1814 and, as far as I know, never visited Saint-Domingue. Nor should he be confused with another contemporary Abbé Aubert, curé of Fromentières in France, who was arrested for having refused to sign an oath of allegiance to the Constitution in 1791 and was eventually deported to Cayenne in 1778, a dramatic experience that is recounted in Boitel, *Déportation de M. l'Abbé Aubert*.
83. Acte d'Abjuration de Stephen Charles, Cayes Jacmel, 15 janvier 1786. ANSOM ECN SAINT-DOMINGUE-CAYES-JACMEL, 1786, 2.
84. Mariage de Charles Stephen et Marie Magdalene Lavocat, Cayes Jacmel, 6 février 1786. ANSOM ECN SAINT-DOMINGUE-CAYES-JACMEL, 1786, 2.
85. Lettre de Lamothe Vedel à l'assemblée colonial, Jacmel, 1 mars 1792. AN DXXV 61 615. Vedel had previously collaborated with Blacé as another member of the illegal Saint-Marc assembly, which may have been one of the reasons the major wound up in a Toulouse jail under the weight of a death sentence in 1793. Assemblée générale, *Décret de l'Assemblée générale de la Partie française de Saint-Domingue*. Lamothe-Vedel, *Mémoire pour Lamothe-Vedel*. Paris: Bibliothèque nationale de France, département Philosophie, histoire, sciences de l'homme, 4-LB43-455, 1799–1804.

86. Dubois, *Avengers of the New World*, 86.
87. Lettre de Lamothe Videl à l'assemblée coloniale, Jacmel, 1 mars 1792. AN DXXV 61 615.
88. Ibid.
89. Ibid.
90. King, *Blue Coat or Powdered Wig*, 183. I am grateful to Rob Taber for alerting me to the political significance of these marriages.
91. Correspondence between Luis Penaver y Cardenas and Manuel Gayoso de Lemos, New Orleans, August 9 and 11, 1797. Archives of the Diocese of Louisiana and the Floridas, Roll 6, 6.403—6.410. Notre Dame University, http://archives.nd.edu/mano/17970811.htm; last accessed April 17, 2014.
92. ANSOM ECN SAINT-DOMINGUE-JACMEL-1785-1791.
93. Rapport fait à l'assemblee coloniale le 14 fev 1792, signé J. P. M. Bloüet, Curé de Jacmel D.S. AN DXXV 61 615. When I moved to Haiti shortly after the coup d'état that ousted President Jean-Bertrand Aristide in 1991, I heard very similar arguments among his neo-Duvalierist opponents, incidentally; i.e., that poor Haitians were not able to properly understand democracy because they mistake it for "license," and that therefore the best form of political rule for the country was a strong dictatorship.
94. Ibid.
95. Ibid.
96. Reclamations contre les assertions offensantes de la lettre de M. de St Leger, du 23 fevrier 1792, MM Mirbeck et roume, par les deputes des paroisses de Jacmel, Cayes Jacmel, Leogane, Petit Goave, Grand Goave, la Croix de Bouquet, et St Marc. AN DXXV 61 615. Père Bloüet is one of 14 signers of this rebuttal and is identified as "J. P. M. Bloüet, curé et deputé de Jacmel."
97. De la Bouderie. *Histoire de Bretagne*, 180. This text also suggests that in addition to being a priest, Père Bloüet was a pharmacist, ibid., 119.
98. Inhumation de Lesesteiux, Léogâne, 20 septembre 1790. ANSOM ECN SAINT-DOMINGUE-LEOGANE-1790, 22.
99. Baptême de Marie Elizabeth, Léogâne, 15 août 1788, ANSOM ECN SAINT-DOMINGUE-LEOGANE-1788, 19; Baptême de Jean Baptiste, Léogâne, 12 juin 1789. ANSOM ECN SAINT-DOMINGUE-LEOGANE-1789, 22.
100. Mariage de Romain Riviere et Marie Roze. Léogâne, 23 aout 1785. ANSOM ECN SAINT-DOMINGUE-LEOGANE-1785, 24.
101. Baptême de Pierre Louis François, Léogâne, 15 fevrier 1790. ANSOM ECN SAINT-DOMINGUE-LEOGANE-1790, 7.
102. Baptême de Pierre Louis François, Léogâne, 15 fevrier 1790. ANSOM ECN SAINT-DOMINGUE-LEOGANE-1790, 47.
103. Mariage de Dimba et Rozette, Léogâne, 8 fevrier 1791. ANSOM ECN SAINT-DOMINGUE-LEOGANE-1791, 7. Normally witnesses signed such entries, though Menetrier indicates that Romaine "declared to not know how."
104. Lettre de Romaine Rivière la Prophetesse et Elie à Abbé Ouvière, Camp du Trou Coffy, 24 decembre, 1791. AN DXXV 110 887.

105. Felix Pascalis, "Anecdote Historique." NYAM MS Folio Pascails Ouviere, 1819–1823, 44–61, 50.
106. The first of these masses was on New Year's Day, 1792, to solemnize the treaty signed between Romaine and municipal authorities that placed him in command of the city of Léogâne. Though the sermon was delivered by Abbé Ouvière, Père Menetrier was surely in attendance and perhaps also officiating. Lettre de Baussan à monsieur l'Abbé Ouvière, Léogâne, le 2 janvier, 1792. AN DXXV 110 819. The prophetess demanded that another Mass be said sometime during the second week in January, upon the departure of a ship that he prophesied would bombard Léogâne, though it did not, evidently to thank the Virgin Mary for the city's deliverance from the threat. Lettre de Villards à Ouvière, Leogane, 13 janvier 1792. AN DXXV 110 819.

CHAPTER 6

1. "Beautiful teeth do not bespeak a friend; the teeth are not the heart." Haitian proverb.
2. Fouchard, *Les marrons du syllabaire*, 115. The other historian is Edner Brutus. Brutus, *La Révolution dans Saint Domingue*, 381. Brutus calls Ouvière one of Romaine's "white friends."
3. Rigaud was Pascalis' "relative via marriage by way of my sister's marrying the legitimate son of his father." Felix Pascalis, "Anecdote historique." New York, 1821. NYAM MS Folio Pascails Ouviere, 1819–1823, 49. Commonly, Rigaud's father is said to have been a wealthy French planter by the same name, André Rigaud, but that is clearly contradicted by Pascalis, who indicated that his father was a one "Monsieur Gay." This adds another level of intrigue to the exploration of the question by Michel Doret. Doret, *André Rigaud*, 46–54.
4. François Martin, Blancard, Guissard [?], and André Riguad [Sr.], "Attestation." Philadelphia, n.d. NYAM MS Folio Pascalis Ouviere 94."
5. Lettre de Raimond, mulatre creole d'Aquin et habitant de Jacmel, datée de Paris, rue Meslée, no. 33, le 4 mars 1791. AN DXXV 110 887. Without naming the party in question, in this letter Raimond speaks of having found someone trustworthy of carrying correspondence from France to Saint-Domingue, in response to the mulatto planters' request that he "send someone of confidence; I have found the man, who is going to be so useful to us." Both the timing of the letter and the fact that it was found in the priest's papers would seem to suggest that Ouvière was the man in question. Raimond mentions that his emissary was making a sacrifice in taking on this mission by leaving his wife behind, which might mean that this person couldn't have been a priest, though, as we saw in Chapter 3, Ouvière was married prior to first going to Saint-Domingue. The mention of "children" complicates matters, though, as nowhere else is there any indication that Ouvière had fathered any until his migration to America and second marriage in 1801, and letters to the priest from his first wife in 1792 make no mention of any children.

6. A December 1, 1791, decree by "The War Council of the Army of the Reunited Citizens of Diverse Parishes of the West, camped in the borough of Croix de Bouquets" does not carry Ouvière's signature, hence he must have formally been appointed to this Council shortly thereafter; or perhaps he was simply absent on the day that this decree was signed. Extrait des minutes déposées à la municipalité de Port-au-Prince, 1 decembre 1791. AN DXXV 61 612.
7. Pascalis, "Anecdote historique," 47–48. One wonders if this might have been the first time that the priest had ever heard about the prophetess.
8. Ibid. Ouvière noted that his title for this mission was actually considerably longer: "commissaire conciliateur auprès des citoyens réunis de Leogane, du Trou Cophy, de Jacmel, du Petit Goave et du Grand Goave." Lettre de l'Abbé Ouvière aux membres réunis les commissaires de la paroisse et de l'armée combinée de l'Ouest séante a la Croix de Bouquets, Léogâne, 29 decembre 1791. AN DXXV 110 868. A second copy of this letter is found in AN DXXV 110 873.
9. Pascalis, "Anecdote historique," 49.
10. Ibid.; Lettre de P. Pinchinat à Monsieur l'Abbé Ouvière, Croix de Bouquets, 30 decembre, 1791. AN DXXV 110 887.
11. Pascalis, "Anecdote historique," 49.
12. Discours prononcé par l'Abbé Ouvière, en présence de l'armée combinée des citoyens de couleur, campée a la Croix des Bouquets, 20 decembre, 1791. AN DXXV 111 881. This sermon is detailed in Chapter 3.
13. Pascalis, "Anecdote historique," 49.
14. Ibid.
15. Ibid.
16. Lettre de l'Abbé Ouvière aux membres réunis les commissaires de la paroisse et de l'armée combinée de l'Ouest séante a la Croix de bouquets.
17. Ibid.
18. "Religious capital" is Pierre Bourdieu's term for the power to consecrate that orthodox "religious specialists" uniquely enjoy and employ to market "salvation goods" to the laity and shape and sustain their worldview. Bourdieu, "Genèse et structure du champ religieux." See also Rey, *Bourdieu on Religion*. It should be noted here that the term "religious capital" as used in much American sociology of religion that is influenced by rational choice theory differs considerably from Bourdieu's conceptualization of the term, which is what I mean in employing the term. For one glimpse of the American version, see Stark and Finke, *Acts of Faith*.
19. I am not the first historian to compare Ouvière with Bienvenu, a distinction that belongs to Edner Brutus: "Among his white friends, Romaine counted l'abbé Ouvrière [*sic*], who, at that moment in time, was holed up in Croix-des-Bouquets, among the somewhat liberal colonists of the town, in the midst of the confederated mulattoes and free blacks. The liberal colonists and the affranchis wanted to exploit abbé Ouvrière's [*sic*] relationship with Romaine, and they turned the priest

into a conciliation commissioner charged with the task of capturing for them the terrible gang leader. Upon learning of Saint Léger's arrival, they asked abbé Ouvrière [*sic*] to play the very same role with Romaine that abbé Bienvenu had played with Jean-François and Biassou. An achievement of such stature would have, they believed, favorably impressed the commander and demonstrated to him their control over the slaves." Brutus, *La révolution dans Saint-Domingue*, 381.

20. Lettre de Romaine Rivière et Elie à monsieur l'Abbé Ouvière, Trou Coffy, December 24, 1791. AN DXXV 110 887. The outside of this letter carries the following addendum: "I forgot to tell you that one of our men has been wounded." It is unclear whether Romaine knew that in addition to being a priest Ouvière was also a physician, nor can we know whether Ouvière treated the wounded insurgent in question or any other combatants during his time in Saint-Domingue. In addition to Catholic priests, physicians were also coveted by insurgents. One of them, Dr. Thibal, found himself a prisoner of Jean-François and was asked "not to refuse to aid the sick and the wounded in the nearby camps if they called upon me." Thibal, *Récit historique du citoyen Thibal*, as transcribed in Popkin, *Facing Racial Revolution*, 163–168, 166,
21. Pascalis, "Anecdote historique," 50–51.
22. Lettre de l'abbé Ouvière aux membres réunis les commissaires de la paroisse et de l'armée combinée de l'Ouest séante a la Croix de bouquets.
23. Pascalis, "Anecdote historique," 51. Another account has the party arriving in Trou Coffy "at midnight, to be precise." Commissaires des Citoyens de Couleur de St. Marc, *Mémoire historique*, 104.
24. Lettre de l'abbé Ouvière aux membres réunis les commissaires de la paroisse et de l'armée combinée de l'Ouest séante a la Croix de bouquets. The word that Ouvière uses in the original French, "*soudan*," referred historically to a high-ranking military officer under a caliph. This is one of several instances in which Ouvière employed Islamic metaphors when speaking of the Trou Coffy movement, and as we saw in Chapter 2, the priest was very struck that the prophetess wore a turban and suspected that he was at least minimally influenced by Islam. For instance, Pascails, "Anecdote historique," 59.
25. Lettre de l'Abbé Ouvière aux membres réunis les commissaires de la paroisse et de l'armée combinée de l'Ouest séante a la Croix de bouquets.
26. Pascalis, "Anecdote historique," 52.
27. Ibid. Soliman is referred to as "Soliment" in the 1791–1792 documents but as "Soliman" in Ouvière's 1821 memoir.
28. Ibid., 53.
29. Ibid.
30. "Abandon all hope, ye who enter here." Ibid. Ouvière's citation of Dante's most famous line is somewhat altered, as the original Latin reads "*Lasciate ogni speranza, voi ch'entrate.*" In his typical linguistic and oratory flashiness, Ouvière also added the "Oh" at the beginning of the quote for good measure.

31. Ibid., 53–56. Pages 54–55 in the folio that contains "Anecdote historique" are unrelated documents evidently mistakenly entered, thus the pagination for "Anecdote historique" should actually be 47–53, 56–61.
32. Lettre de l'Abbé Ouvière aux membres réunis les commissaires de la paroisse et de l'armée combinée de l'Ouest séante a la Croix de bouquets.
33. Pascalis, "Anecdote historique," 56–57.
34. Ibid., 58–59.
35. Commissaires des Citoyens, *Mémoire historique*, 104.
36. Lettre de l'Abbé Ouvière aux membres réunis les commissaires de la paroisse et de l'armée combinée de l'Ouest séante a la Croix de bouquets.
37. Pascalis, "Anecdote historique," 59.
38. Ibid. I think he meant "three days earlier," not "four."
39. Pascalis, "Anecdote historique," 59.
40. Ibid. December 31, 1791, was a Saturday. An undated letter from Romaine and Elie Courlogne to Ouvière suggests that the signing was to have occurred the day before but that Romaine requested that it be pushed back a day ("*l'allignet du sejour de vendredi nous est absolument impossible et avons remis a samedi, le 31 du present*"). Lettre de Romaine Riviere et Elie Courlogne à l'Abbé Ouvière, Trou Coffy, n.d. AN DXXV 110 887.
41. Lettre de Baussan à monsieur l'Abbé Ouvière, Léogâne, le 2 janvier, 1792. AN DXXV 110 819.
42. Lettre de Romaine Riviere et Elie Courlogne à l'Abbé Ouvière, Trou Coffy, n.d.
43. Lettre de Boisrond . . . [?] et Depas Medina à Ouvière, Aquin, 3 janvier 1792. AN DXXV 110 819. The first signature on this letter is illegible, though it is followed by the title "President." Medina's name is preceded by what is apparently an abbreviation of his first name, while the title "Secretary" follows his surname.
44. Lettre de Richallet à Ouvière, Fondoi, 1 janvier 1792. DXXV 110 887. "Fondoi" is likely a Gallicized spelling of "Fondwa," which administratively today is a "rural community" in the commune of Léogâne. Trou Coffy is located in this rural community.
45. Lettre de M. de Villards à Ouvière, Léogâne, 6 janvier 1792. AN DXXV 110 819.
46. Lettre de Villards à Ouvière, Léogâne, 11 janvier 1792. AN DXXV 110 819. Lettre de Gauthier à Ouvière, Léogâne, 12 janvier 1792, a dix heures du matin. AN DXXV 110 819.
47. Lettre de Pinchinat à Ouvière, 30 decembre 1792. AN DXXV 110 887.
48. Pascalis, "Anecdote historique," 59.
49. Lettre d'Elie Courlogne à Ouvière, Trou Coffy, 16 janvier 1792. DXXV 110 887.
50. Lettre de Romaine Riviere, la prophetess, commandant general à Monsieur l'Abbé Ouvière, Commissaire Conciliateur à la Croix de Bouquets, au Trou Coffy, 26 janvier 1792. AN DXXV 110 887.
51. Fick, *The Making of Haiti*, 139.
52. Lacroix, *Mémoires pour server à l'histoire de la révolution de Saint-Domingue*, 177.

53. Dalmas, *Histoire de la révolution de Saint-Domingue*, 234.
54. Ouvière, "Journal de la Guerre Civile à la province de l'Ouest de St. Domingue."
55. Bonnet, *Souvenirs historiques de Guy-Joseph Bonnet*, 2. Bonnet was 19-years-old at the time of the fall of Trou Coffy.
56. Ibid., 12. Bonnet would go on to have a distinguished career in the Haitian Revolution and was among the signers, in 1803, of the "Haitian Act of Independence."
57. Saint-Léger, *Compte rendu à l'Assemblée Nationale*, 1. The February 11 decree launched the First Civil Commission and outlined the objectives of its mission in Saint-Domingue.
58. Ibid., 25.
59. Ibid., 26–27.
60. Ibid., 27.
61. Ibid., 27–28.
62. Ibid., 28.
63. Ibid., 29.
64. Bonnet, *Souvenirs historiques de Guy-Joseph Bonnet*, 14.
65. Saint-Léger, *Compte rendu à l'Assemblée Nationale*, 45.
66. Lettre de Saint Léger au Maire de Léogâne, 10 mars 1792. AN DXXV 2 15.
67. Saint-Léger, *Compte rendu à l'Assemblée Nationale*, 45.
68. "Extract of a letter from Port-au-Prince, dated March 14, 1792." *Philadelphia General Advertiser*, 480, April 11, 1792, 2. A longer and redacted version of this letter appeared again in this newspaper on April 25, under the title "Boston April 14: Extract of a letter from Port-au-Prince, to a gentleman of this town, dated March 14, 1792." *Philadelphia General Advertiser*, 491, April 25, 1792, 3.
69. Bonnet, *Souvenirs historiques de Guy-Joseph Bonnet*, 14.
70. Saint-Léger, *Compte rendu à l'Assemblée Nationale*, 46.
71. Ouvière, "Journal de la Guerre Civile à la province de l'Ouest de St. Domingue."
72. Bonnet, *Souvenirs historiques de Guy-Joseph Bonnet*, 14
73. Saint-Léger, *Compte rendu à l'Assemblée Nationale*, 45–46.
74. "Boston April 14: Extract of a letter from Port-au-Prince, to a gentleman of this town, dated March 14, 1792."
75. Ouvière, "Journal de la Guerre Civile à la province de l'Ouest de St. Domingue." It is not clear whether Ouvière was himself an eyewitness to the battle of Léogâne of 1792. I tend to doubt it, however, as he was more likely holed up in Croix-des-Bouquets at the time.
76. "Extract of a letter from Port-au-Prince, dated March 19, 1792."
77. Saint-Léger, *Compte rendu à l'Assemblée Nationale*, 48. The "Boursicot" referred to here was certainly Alexandre Boursiquot, one of the leading figures in the mulatto uprisings around Jacmel and Bainet, whom we met in Chapter 1. That he was arrested at Trou Coffy further illustrates the connections between the two insurgent theaters and the place of primacy that Romaine held in directing the

insurrections in both parishes. A journalistic account has it that when the "rebellion in Léogâne" was "crushed" "[t]wo chiefs have been taken and have suffered," likely referring to Boursiquot and perhaps Elie Courlogne or Gros Poisson. "News from Port-au-Prince." *Columbia Centinel*, March 17, 1792. Garran also identifies Boursiquot as "one of the leaders of Trou-Coffi" and alleges that he was an orchestrator of the Bainet massacre, as discussed in Chapter 1. Garran de Coulon, *Rapport sur les troubles de Saint-Domingue, Tome 2*, 486–487.

78. Ouvière, "Journal de la Guerre Civile à la province de l'Ouest de St. Domingue."
79. Dalmas, *Histoire de la révolution de Saint-Domingue*, 266–267.
80. Saint-Rémy, *Pétion et Haïti*, 61–63.
81. Guthrie, *Nouvelle géographie universelle*, 343.
82. "Lettre au Rédacteur: Extrait d'une lettre de St. Marc, 12 avril 1792," *Mercure de France* 18, May 15, 1792, 69–72, 71. It is quite likely that Ouvière, who was in Saint-Marc at that time, authored this letter, as the reference to Saint-Léger's being saved by an "*homme de couleur* who gave his life to save him, as well as the *Chevalier d'assas à Clostercamp*" appears in his "Journal de la Guerre Civile à la province de l'Ouest de St. Domingue": "*un homme de couleur mouvant comme le chevalier d'assas a sauvé le commissaire.*" This is significant in that it reflects how Ouvière really felt about Romaine and his "infernal doctrine." The "Journal" also reports "Romaine took flight." Despite Trou Coffy's fall, it is possible that Romaine inspired at least one last-ditch, vengeful attack on whites a couple of weeks later. During "the last days of the month of March, 300 armed Blacks descended upon Bois Blanc and attacked the *habitation Foucault*. There they committed incredible cruelties." This plantation was located some 40 miles west of Léogâne, and those who survived the attack managed "to find ships along the coast that brought them to Port-au-Prince." Assemblée Nationale Législative, *Archives Parlementaires*, June 2, 1792, 537. At around this time, Abbé Ouvière resided at the Foucault plantation, thus raising the question as to whether this attack might have been orchestrated by Romaine as an act of revenge against a traitor.
83. Coulon, *Rapport sur les troubles de Saint-Domingue, Tome 2*, 489.
84. Fick, *The Making of Haiti*, 128.
85. The two most influential of all Kongo prophets, Beatriz Kimpa Vita (1684–1706) and Simon Kimbangu (1887–1951), were each capable of vanishing. Beatriz would "visit Heaven frequently. She announced that she would die every Friday and go to heaven, dining with God and 'pleading the cause of the blacks, particularly the restoration of the Kingdom of Kongo' before Him." Thornton, *The Kongolese Saint Anthony*, 166. Meanwhile, "Kimbangu reportedly had many of the powers commonly attributed to prophets in both Kongolese traditional belief systems and biblical prophecy—people believed that he predicted the future, prophesied, healed the sick, could not be harmed by gunfire, and could even disappear when he wanted to." Covington-Ward, "'Your Name Is Written in the

Sky,'" 326. Unlike Beatriz and Kimbangu and other influential prophets in West Central African history, however, both Makaya and Romaine-la-Prophétesse were never imprisoned.

86. Lettre de Carbonnot à Monsieur Abé [*sic*] Ouvière, n.d., n.p., AN DXXV 110 887. Ouvière would later claim that he had already left Saint-Domingue by the time of Saint-Léger's raid on Trou Coffy, but that is simply untrue and underscores the care the priest later took to conceal certain aspects of his past in the colony. Pascalis, "Anecdote historique,"61.
87. Chanlatte, jeune, capitaine générale, Viart, Dubourg. F. Ouvière. P. adjoint à la députation. "Suite du mémoire historique (2) des dernières révolutions de l'ouest et du sud de la partie française de Saint-Domingue."

CHAPTER 7

1. Lettre de P. Pinchinat à Monsieur Abbé Ouvière, Croix de Bouquets, 30 décembre, 1791. AN DXXV 110 887.
2. Viart should not be confused with Villards, the mayor of Léogâne when the Trou Coffy insurgency broke out.
3. Lettre de Pierre Pinchinat à Monsieur Abbé Ouvière, Croix de Bouquets, 26 janvier 1792. AN DXXV 110 887.
4. Lettre de Pierre Pinchinat à Monsieur Abbé Ouvière, Croix de Bouquets, 1 mars 1792. AN DXXV 110 887
5. Mémoire historique des dernières révolutions des Provinces de l'Ouest et du Sud de la partie française de St. Domingue, publié par les commissaires des citoyens de couleurs de St Marc. n. d. AN DXXV 111 872.
6. Lettre de Félix Pascalis Ouvière à Pierre Pinchinat, Kingston, 8 March 1793. NYAM MS 577—Pascalis Ouviere, Felix. Over a quarter century later, Ouvière noted that the deputation had arrived in France "in the middle of the month of May." Felix Pascalis, "Anecdote historique." New York, 1821. NYAM MS Folio Pascails Ouviere, 1819–1823, 61. Unless he was trying to mislead Pinchinat, there is no reason to doubt the more precise indication of 1793.
7. Lettre de Pierre Pinchinat à Julien Raimond, Saint Marc, April 9, 1792. *Correspondance de Julien Raimond*, 65–68.
8. Mémoire historique des dernières révolutions des Provinces de l'Ouest et du Sud de la partie française de St. Domingue, publié par les commissaires des citoyens de couleurs de St Marc. In all likelihood this document is the mémoire attributed also to Pinchinat, which Ouvière had helped write. Also among the papers delivered to the Assemblée was Les membres du conseil d'administration des citoyens de couleur campés à St. Marc aux Messieurs les membres de l'Assemblée Nationale à Paris, St. Marc, 15 décembre 1791. AN DXXV 867.

9. Lettre de LaRoque à M. Ouvière, Marseille, 9 juin 1792. AN DXXV 110 887. This letter alludes to Ouvière's departure for Paris on Friday of the week prior. June 9, 1792, was a Saturday, meaning that Ouvière left Nantes for Paris on June 1.
10. It is, of course, possible that after arriving in France Abbé Ouvière visited his wife, and others, in Marseille prior to travelling to Paris. I doubt this, though, because Madame Ouvière surely would have mentioned such a visit in her initial letter, dated July 4, 1792. Furthermore, the priest had very pressing business to tend to in Paris, business that his wife feared would indeed take precedence over their reunion.
11. Lettre à Monsieur Abbé Ouvière, Député de St. Domingue à Paris, Marseille, 4 juillet 1792. AN DXXV 110 887.
12. Lettre à Monsieur Abbé Ouvière, Député de St. Domingue à Paris, Marseille, 24 juillet 1792. AN DXXV 110 887.
13. Lettre de LaRoque à Ouvière, Marseille, 1 juin, 1792. AN DXXV 110 887. There are two other letters from LaRoque to Ouvière in this same dossier, dated June 12 and 18.
14. Lettre à Monsieur Abbé Ouvière, Député de St. Domingue à Paris, Marseille, 29 juillet 1792. AN DXXV 110 887.
15. Lettre à Abbé Ouvière, Rouen, 7 aout 1792. Unsigned. AN DXXV 110 887.
16. Lacroix, *Mémoires pour server à l'histoire de la révolution de Saint-Domingue*, 142.
17. Lettre à Abbé Ouvière, Rouen, 22 aout 1792. Unsigned. AN DXXV 110 887. This letter carries Ouvière's name on the outer fold, with the instruction that it be relayed to "Algonquin, Creole of the Bourbon Island."
18. Lettre de François Pascalis Ouvière à Monsieur l'Abbé Ouvière, Nice, 19 aout 1792. AN DXXV 110 887. The priest's brother also asked for two additional copies of his controversial newspaper, one for Abbé de Pradine, who had formerly been curé of Port-au-Prince, long before Ouvière had arrived in Saint-Domingue. Demande de recommandation pour l'abbé de Pradine, ancien curé de Port-au-Prince (1786). ANSOM COL F5A 26.
19. Moreover, as John Garrigus demonstrates, growing racial animosity between whites and free coloreds after 1770 led to "increasing use of the term *affranchi* for free people of color. . . . Labelling all free people of color *'affranchis'* was a way of saying that they were all ex-slaves, even those who were born free. For this reason the state required them to produce documents proving their liberty at any time, an idea that had its roots in plantation discipline." Garrigus, *Before Haiti*, 167–168.
20. As cited in ibid., 167.
21. Ibid., 233–234.
22. Raimond, *Correspondance de Julien Raimond*, 65n1.
23. Jean-Philippe Garran de Coulon also refers to Abbé Ouvière's papers as having been seized in Paris. Garran de Coulon, *Rapport sur les troubles de Saint-Domingue, Tome 2*, 490. Garran de Coulon, *Rapport sur les troubles de Saint-Domingue, Tome*

1. It is likely this collection of Ouvière's papers that we find housed today in the Archives Nationales in Paris.

24. The decree is included as part of Raimond's annotation of Pinchinat's letter of April 9, 1792. Raimond, *Correspondance de Julien Raimond*. Emphasis in original.

25. Dated July 19, 1792, the letter of Chanlatte and Viart is included as part of Raimond's annotation of Pinchinat's letter of April 9, 1792. Ibid.

26. Lettre de Chanlatte et Viart aux Messieurs Dubourg et Ouvière, La Rochelle, 26 juin 1792. AN DXXV 110 887.

27. The last preserved letter I have found that is addressed to Ouvière while he was in Paris that year is dated August 26, 1792. Lettre de Caraïbe à Algonquin, Rouen, 26 août 1792. AN DXXV 110 887. It is of course possible that the priest had already fled France by then. In a 1793 letter written from Kingston to Pinchinat, Ouvière indicates that he was in London as of October 1792. Lettre de Félix Pascalis Ouvière à Pierre Pinchinat, Kingston, 8 mars 1793.

28. Unfortunately, I have found no extant copy of this report, which would be a great historical interest.

29. Lettre de Félix Pascalis Ouvière à Pierre Pinchinat, Kingston, 8 mars 1793.

30. Popkin, *You Are All Free*, ix.

31. Anonymous, "BIOGRAPHY."

32. Anonymous, "PERSONS LEAVING THE ISLAND." *Royal Gazette*, Kingston, Jamaica, May 18, 1793.

33. Williams, *The French Assault on American Shipping*, 92

34. Anonymous, "BIOGRAPHY."

35. Williams, *The French Assault on American Shipping*, 92.

36. Ibid. The official US government record of this incident has the date as June 11, 1793, and informs that *L'Embuscade* captured a second vessel in the attack, the *Morning Star*. US House of Representatives, *Congressional Series of United States Public Documents, Volume 1521*, 231.

37. Anonymous, "BIOGRAPHY."

38. US House of Representatives, *Congressional Series of United States Public Documents, Volume 1521*, 321.

39. Ibid. The mouth of the Delaware Bay is 87 miles from Philadelphia, so any point in the Atlantic off the Jersey Shore would have been farther than that. Blank, Lubchenco, and Kennedy, *Distances Between United States Ports*, 9, 11.

40. "Letter from Madame de Mauduit to George Washington, 8 May 1793," FONA http://founders.archives.gov/documents/Washington/05-12-02-0440. In Patrick and Pinheiro (eds.), *The Papers of George Washington*, 558–559. Coincidentally, a French soldier who had been arrested for his involvement in the killing of Colonel Mauduit was languishing "in a horrible dungeon" in Léogâne at the very time when the priest was visiting Trou Coffy, in late December 1791. Pascalis, "Anecdote historique," 60.

41. Furstenberg, *When the United States Spoke French*, 145.

42. Larousse, *Grand dictionnaire universel du XIXe siècle*, 1356.
43. James, *The Black Jacobins*, 83.
44. Ibid.
45. Zizek, "'*Plum de fer*,'" 619.
46. Prudhomme, *Histoire générale*, 416–417.
47. Garran de Coulon, *Rapport sur les troubles de Saint-Domingue, Tome 2*, 491.
48. Ibid., 490.
49. Fournier and Bégim, "*Marais*," 561.
50. Provoked by Fournier and Begim to set the record straight, in 1821 Pascalis would write his "Anecdote historique," which is one of the most valuable eyewitness accounts of the 1791 free colored insurrection in Saint-Domingue yet to be uncovered. Pascalis, "Anecdote historique." It is cited extensively elsewhere in this book, especially in the preceding chapter.

CHAPTER 8

1. "To try to understand a life as a unique and self-sufficient series of events with no links other than the association with a subject whose constancy is no doubt merely that of a proper name, is nearly as absurd as trying make sense of a route in the metro without taking into account the structure of the subway, that is, the matrix of objective relations between the different train stations." Bourdieu, "L'Illusion biographique," 71.
2. While at the peak of his powers, Pascalis was an internationally renowned physician and scientist. "In 1820 he received a diploma from the Société Royale de Médecine de Marseille, and in 1821 from the Société Linnéenne de Paris. In this country he was similarly recognized by the South Carolina Medical Society in 1806 and the New Orleans Medical Society in 1818." Annan, "The Academy of Medicine of New York," 119. For a glimpse of Pascalis' influence on public health policy, see Arner, "Making Global Commerce into International Health Diplomacy."
3. Bolton, "Early American Chemical Societies," 719.
4. Branson and Patrick, "Étrangers dans un Pays Étrange," 194.
5. Letter of Felix Pascalis, MD, to Mons. Petit de Villers, New York, November 8, 1827. HSP, Letters of Dr. Felix Pascalis. Petit de Villers had served alongside Pascalis as a member of the free colored Confederacy's advisory council in Croix de Bouquets in 1791–1792. Arrêté du conseile de guerre de l'armée des citoyens réunis de divers paroisses de l'Ouest, campée au bourg de la Croix de Bouquets, extraordinairement assemblée, Croix de Bouquets, 1 decembre 1791. AN DXXV 61 612.
6. "To George Washington from Madame de Mauduit, 8 May 1793," FONA, http://founders.archives.gov/documents/Washington/05-12-02-0440; last accessed May 24, 2014. This letter is transcribed entirely and more fully discussed in Chapter 7.

7. François Martin, Blancard, Guissard [sp?], and André Riguad [Sr.]. "Attestation," Philadelphia, n.d., NYAM MS 94.
8. Letter of Recommendation for Dr. Felix Pascalis from Governor Thomas McKean, Philadelphia, 27 April 1800. NYAM, SAFE.
9. Anonymous, "Information for Aiken Museum: Felix Pascalis Ouviere, MD, 1762-1833—age 71." n.d., n.p. ACPL.
10. Letters of Felix Pascalis to Francisca Pascalis, New York, May 18, 19, 20, 1813. NYAM. MS 619—Pascalis Ouviere, Felix.
11. Letter from John J. Audubon to Felix Pascalis, New York, 13 May 1829. NYAM MS 95—Audubon.
12. Branson and Patrick, "Étrangers dans un Pays Étrange," 205n1. Duff Cooper informs us of "a small French colony" in late eighteenth-century Philadelphia, "the center of which was a book shop kept by Moreau de Saint-Méry at number 84 First Street. Here about nightly took place animated reunions of French refugees, who discussed over their host's Madeira the present and the future of their country." Moreau had arrived in 1790 from France after evading arrest in his native Martinique, and he resided in Philadelphia until 1799. It was there that he published his widely cited *Description topographique et politique de la partie espagnole et de la partie française de l'ile de Saint-Domingue*, which contains the earliest historical reference to African religious practices referred to by the name "*vaudou*." Another prominent resident of the city was the priest-*cum*-diplomat and legendary womanizer Charles Maurice Talleyrand-Périgord. Duff Cooper, *Talleyrand*. New York: Grove, 74. On the French presence in late eighteenth- and early nineteenth-century Philadelphia particularly and the United States in general, see Furstenberg, *When the United States Spoke French*. For additional context, see White, *Encountering Revolution*.
13. Pascalis renounced his French citizenship and was sworn in as a naturalized US citizen on April 28, 1807. Naturalization Document, Felix Pascalis Ouviere, City of New York, April 28, 1807. NYAM Box 15, Folder 31.
14. Hebert, "The Pennsylvania French in the 1790s," 73.
15. Ibid., 74.
16. Felix Pascalis to James Rush, New York, July 5, 1819. HSP Rush 25 MS 14-18. On Moreau in Philadelphia, see Furstenberg, *When the United States Spoke French*.
17. Stafford, *The Philadelphia Directory for 1801*, 108. Pascalis had prior lived at 47 North Fourth Street, in 1797. By 1802, the *Philadelphia Directory* has him listed as residing at 78 Cedar Street (Cedar Street and South Street are the same), in 1802 and 1803, and at 281 South Front in 1804. Robinson, *The Philadelphia Directory, City and County Register for 1802*, 188; *The Philadelphia Directory, City and County Register for 1803*, 193; *The Philadelphia Directory, City and County Register* (1804), 178.
18. Hebert. "The Pennsylvania French in the 1790s," 99.

19. On religion and politics in early America, see Lambert, *The Founding Fathers and the Place of Religion in America.*
20. As Hebert explains, "Of the four settled at Asylum, none had asked permission from Bishop Carroll to assume their priestly role," instead pursuing farming and other business enterprises. "One Abbé Colin may have officiated for a while, for he ordered altar stones and a missal, and had set aside a lot for a chapel," but by 1805 a visiting priest named Father Dithert "noted that the remaining settlers had done without the support of religion for very long. Thus, if the residing priests had given unofficial services, their efforts were short lived." Hebert, "The Pennsylvania French in the 1790s," 65.
21. Felix Pascalis, "Anecdote Historique," New York, 1821. NYAM MS Folio Pascails Ouviere, 1819–1823, 47–61, 51.
22. For insight into the Catholic practice of Dominguan blacks in Philadelphia, see Davies, "Class, Culture, and Color"; and Davies, "Vodou in the Early Republic," http://usreligion.blogspot.com/2013/11/vodou-in-early-republic-more-questions.html; last accessed July 3, 2014.
23. "Archdiocese of Philadelphia," *New Advent: The Catholic Encyclopedia.* http://www.newadvent.org/cathen/11793b.htm. Last accessed 7 October, 2009.
24. Hebert, "The Pennsylvania French in the 1790s," 7. In effect, the war "increased such feelings, Catholic France being viewed as evil personified, and Catholic Frenchmen as the agents of the devil." Ibid., 5.
25. Ibid., 11.
26. Anonymous, "Information for Aiken Museum." It is likely that his first wife, the unnamed woman whom we met in Chapter 7, was dead by the time Pascalis reached Philadelphia in 1793, as in one of her letters to him in the summer of 1792 she discusses her failing health and her sense that she would soon die. Lettre à Monsieur Abbé Ouvière, Deputé de St. Domingue à Paris, Marseille, 29 juillet 1792. AN DXXV 110 887. Cyril Shuler suggests that McKlintock was a native Philadelphian but doubts a rumor that Aaron Burr had once been her fiancé. Shuler, *From the Mayflower to Pole Cat Pond, S. C.*, 52.
27. Hitt and Cannon, *Echoes from Pascalina*, 32. It was common for French immigrants in early republican America to marry local women, which "helped them learn the English language, provided them with the support of a family, and contributed to their adjustment and attachment to the new environment." Hebert, "The Pennsylvania French in the 1790s," 26. It should be noted that Pascalis was likely already quite conversant in English prior to his arrival in the United States, as his first publication includes passages that he himself translated from English. Ouvière, P.S.D.L.S.P., "Les Adieux d'un cosmopolite aux marseillois," 11–14. Judging from the satirical caricature in Image 8.1, meanwhile, it would seem that he spoke the language with a heavy French accent during the entire part of his life in America.

28. Philadelphia Genealogical Society of Pennsylvania, *Records of Christ Church in Philadelphia*, 178. Shuler mistakenly indicates that Bishop William White, then senior pastor at Christ Church, married the couple, but this was indeed also mistakenly reported in a wedding announcement that appeared in the *New York Weekly Museum* on March 21, 1801. Shuler, *From the Mayflower to Pole Cat Pond, S. C.*, 52. Hitt and Cannon, *Echoes from Pascalina*, 32. The three other signers of the Declaration of Independence entered at Christ Church Burial Ground are Joseph Hewes, Francis Hopkinson, and George Ross.
29. Hitt and Cannon, *Echoes from Pascalina*, 50. Shuler, *From the Mayflower to Pole Cat Pond, S.C.*, 52. In his 1827 letter to Petit de Villers, Pascalis notes that his "only son" was then 17-years-old. Felix was a sickly child who seemingly died before reaching adulthood. Letter of Felix Pascalis, MD, to Mons. Petit de Villers, New York, November 8, 1827. HSP, Letters of Dr. Felix Pascalis.
30. Marquis Who's Who on the Web. "Felix Pascalis," http://search.marquiswhoswho.com.libproxy.temple.edu/executable/SearchResults.aspx?db=H,W; last accessed September 28, 2009. William Middleton suggests, quite plausibly, that Pascalis moved to New York to collaborate with Dr. Samuel Latham Mitchill, another pioneering figure in early American medicine. Middleton, "Felix Pascalis-Ouvière and the Yellow Fever Epidemic of 1797," 514. Pascalis lived in at least five different locations in New York: Courtland Street, 47 Nassau Street, Chatham Street, Upper Reed Street, and Pearl Street. Anonymous, "Removal," *New York Gazette*, 1 May 1807; Anonymous, "Removal," *The Columbian*, 4 May 1810.
31. Anonymous, "BIOGRAPHY," 123.
32. On the fateful voyage of *The Hankey*, see Smith, *Ship of Death*.
33. Powell, *Bring Out Your Dead*, 159. Devèze himself had twice contracted yellow fever while in Saint-Domingue, where he frequently treated the disease. He fled Saint-Domingue in July of 1793 and arrived in Philadelphia on August 7, 1793, just as the epidemic was about to engulf the city. Like Pascalis, Devèze published his observations on the yellow fever epidemic: *An Enquiry into, and Observations Upon the Causes and Effects of the the Epidemic Disease Which raged in Philadelphia from the month of August till towards the middle of December 1793*.
34. Built around 1740, Bush Hill Mansion had previously served as the residence for Vice President John Adams, from 1790 to 1792.
35. Letter of Felix Pascalis to Jean Devèze, New York, 20 July 1820. NYAM MS Folio Pascalis Ouviere, 1819–1823. The following claim is thus dubious: "The [Bush Hill] hospital was put under his [Devèze's] care and Dr. Pascalis was made an associate, for he was deeply read in the history and nature of the disease, as it had appeared in different ages and countries." Anonymous, "BIOGRAPHY," 123. It should be noted that Devèze did occasionally bleed his patients, though nowhere as aggressively as Rush or Pascalis. For his part, while he endorsed and

practiced bloodletting, Pascalis did think that at times Rush pushed the method too far. Pascalis-Ouvière, *An Account of the Yellow Fever Epidemic*, 50–51.

36. Powell, *Bring Out Your Dead*, 117.
37. Pascalis, "Account of an Abscess of the Liver," 158.
38. Kelly, "Félix A. Pascalis-Ouvrière [*sic*]," 894.
39. Koehler, "Heavy Metal Medicine," 61–65. http://pubs.acs.org/subscribe/journals/tcaw/10/i01/html/01chemch.html; last accessed, January 30, 2014. Pascalis also underwent massive bloodletting after a fall from a horse that left him unconscious in 1813. Letter of Felix Pascalis to Francisca Pascalis, New York, September 1813 [day unclear]. NYAM MS 619—Pascalis Ouviere, Felix. The following year, he also proposed bloodletting for his young son Felix, who was then suffering from some kind of renal ailment. Letter of Felix Pascalis to Elizabeth Pascalis, 22 January 1814. NYAM MS 141/142/143—Pascalis Ouviere, Felix.
40. College of Physicians of Philadelphia, *Transactions*, cxvii.
41. By contrast, in 1800 Philadelphia counted 135 potters, 169 soap boilers, and 196 weavers. Anonymous, *The New Trade Directory for Philadelphia Anno 1900*, 31.
42. Rush cites Pascalis' treatment of yellow fever patients in his treatise on the senses. Carlson, Wollock, and Noel, *Benjamin Rush's Lectures on the Mind*, 282. Pascalis' publications also circulated in Europe, as evinced by his French critics and by Adolph Callisen's list of 19 titles by Pascalis in his 1833 German bibliography. Callisen, *Medicinisches Schriftsteller-Lexicon der jetzt lebenden Aerzte, Wundärzte, Geburtshelfer, Apotheker und Naturforscher aller gebildeten Völker*, 331–333.
43. Drawing upon his experience of the disease in Saint-Domingue, Pascalis published an earlier essay on yellow fever in the United States that won an award from the Medical Society of Connecticut. The award-winning essay, presented in 1795, was entitled "What are the chymichal properties of the effluvia of contagion of the epidemic of New York, in the year 1795; and does said epidemic differ from the usual fevers of this country except in degree?" William Middleton explains that Pascalis included data for this study "from his observations of yellow fever patients at Bush Hill, the country house of the Tory William Hamilton near Philadelphia that had been commandeered as a hospital for the isolation and care of victims of the epidemic in 1793." Middleton, "Felix Pascalis-Ouvière and the Yellow Fever Epidemic of 1797," 498.
44. Pascalis-Ouvière, *An Account of the Yellow Fever Epidemic*, 2. Pascalis identifies himself on the inner title page of this study as "Corresponding Member of the Medical Society of Connecticut, and Resident Member of the Philadelphia Academy of Medicine."
45. Shannon, "Disease Mapping and Early Theories of Yellow Fever," 221. Miller and Pencak provide different figures for the epidemic in Philadelphia, stating that in 1798 "only 20 percent of the city's nearly 60,000 inhabitants remained in town, and of these 4,500 died." Miller and Pencak, *Pennsylvania*, 144.

46. Pascalis-Ouviere, *An Account of the Yellow Fever Epidemic*, 17. Rush held similar miasmic ideas, only he placed the blame for the epidemic on a pile of rotting coffee that had been abandoned on the Arch Street wharf. Powell, *Bring Out Your Dead*, 12.
47. Pascalis-Ouviere, *An Account of the Yellow Fever Epidemic*, 107. Pascalis makes the same recommendation for stone wharves in his later study of yellow fever in New York. Pascalis-Ouvière, *A Statement of the Occurrence during the Malignant Yellow Fever*, 49. See also Kopperman, "'Venerate the Lancet.'"
48. Felix Pascalis, "Remarks on a Spanish Pamphlet," 5.
49. Miller and Pencak, *Pennsylvania*, 144. President John Adams and his cabinet also abandoned Philadelphia during the 1797 outbreak of yellow fever.
50. Anonymous, "BIOGRAPHY," 123. I have found no other evidence to corroborate these recollections that Jefferson financed Pascalis' trip to Spain, but I also have no reason to doubt that this may have been the case.
51. *Biographie universelle et portative des contemporains*, 863. Though Pascalis never published *Pyrroloimoglia*, he did publish a short article on his observations of the disease in Cadiz and Gibraltar. Pascalis, "Observations on the Non-Importation of the Yellow Fever into Spain." The passport that Pascalis carried on his 1805 trip to Spain is housed in the New York Academy of Medicine. NYAM MS 144—Passport. It was valid for five months.
52. "Pascalis was, moreover, given to proposing schemes that he never carried out. Witness the grandiose 'Universal College of Medicine,' with its 'Great Dean' who was to hold a chair in London, its twelve 'Consistories' scattered over the face of the globe whose functions were to regulate medical instruction that would be uniform throughout the civilized world, the surplus from whose fees was to be sufficient for pensions and relief for superannuated physicians. This gigantic scheme seems to have died in October 1823, with Pascalis' hope that he would soon publish the list of persons to form consistories in Europe and America." Olmsted, "A Letter from Felix Pascalis of New York to François Magendie in 1826," 374.
53. Letter of Felix Pascalis Ouvière to Thomas Jefferson, New York, July 31, 1806. TCJP.
54. Letter, 1806 August 16, of Thomas Jefferson, to Dr. Felix Pascalis, TCJP. Pascalis, "Proposals for Publishing by Subscription." Evidently Pascalis sought to raise funds for this ambitious project, soliciting pre-orders in the amount of "Five dollars the set, or handsomely bound and lettered at Six dollars."
55. Pascalis-Ouvière, *A Statement of the Occurrence during the Malignant Yellow Fever*.
56. Ibid., 20.
57. Tom Koch provides a detailed discussion of the significance of a map that Pascalis created for his 1819 New York study of yellow fever. Koch, *Disease Maps*, 87–91. See also Koch, *Cartographies of Disease*; Jarcho, "Yellow Fever, Cholera, and the Beginnings of Medical Cartography"; and Shannon, "Disease Mapping

and Early Theories of Yellow Fever." I'm grateful to Professor Sergio Rey, my brother, for his expert insight into the history of medical cartography.

58. Pascalis, "What are the chymical processes of the effluvia of contagion of the epidemic of New York, in the year 1795; and does said epidemic differ from the Usual Fevers of this Country except in degree?" Cited in Middleton, "Félix Pascalis-Ouvière and the Yellow Fever Epidemic of 1797," 498; Pascalis, *An Account of the Contagious Epidemic Yellow Fever.*
59. Apel, "Feverish Bodies, Enlightened Minds," 106–107.
60. In this capacity he issued citations, for instance, one dated July 13, 1803, and addressed to "Mr. Jonathan Meredith [will] take notice that unless the nuisance existing on your premises in Front Street, Below Lombard, which is a privy in the cellar, (~~unusual~~) very offensive an injurious to the tenants . . . [you] will incur the penalty of law." HSP Gratz AL 1800-24.
61. The College of Physicians and Surgeons merged with Columbia University on April 1, 1811. Though a member of the College, "Pascalis' name does not appear on the faculty list" of Columbia University." Middleton, "Felix Pascalis-Ouvière and the Yellow Fever Epidemic of 1797," 514.
62. Pascalis, "Eulogy on the Life and Character of the Honorable Samuel Latham Mitchill," 15 October 1831.
63. Middleton, "Felix Pascalis-Ouvière and the Yellow Fever Epidemic of 1797," 515. For a brief discussion of the influence and context of Pascalis' study on burials, see Hoglund, "Hidden Agendas."
64. Felix Pascalis, "An Exposition of the danger of Interment in Cities,"118–123.
65. Manly, Pascalis, and Steel, "A System of Medical Ethics."
66. "The sacred duty or privilege of a catholic priest is not compellable to disclose the secrets of auricular confession was maintained by a decision of the court of sessions of New-York, 14th of June, 1813. In the case of the Rev. Mr. K. refusing his testimony on a matter of felony. (Vid, cathol. Quest. Report. By wm. Sampson, Esq.)."
67. Veatch, *Disputed Dialogues,* 109.
68. In some circles, Pascalis is celebrated as the first person to cultivate silk worms in America, and he promoted the practice in a short book entitled *Practical Instructions and Directions for Silkworm Nurseries, and for the Culture of the Mulberry Tree.* Never one to lack confidence, so enthused was he about the future of this industry in America that he launched a quarterly journal dedicated to the science underlying it, *The Silk Culturist.* He also held the position of "Chairman of the Silk Committee of the American Institute" and conducted experiments with electricity in efforts "to promote the growth of silk worms." H. Meigs and James Talimadge, "Electricity Applied to Vegetation." *New York Daily Tribune,* April 30, 1845. In an 1829 letter, Pascalis speaks of his "experiments on electricity: . . . I have on my desk some superb specimens of silk from my worms electrified to different degrees." Felix Pascalis letter to Peter S. Du Ponceau, New York, July 29, 1829. HSP Gratz ALS 1824–29.

69. Fournier and Bégim,"*Marais*," 561.
70. Letter of Felix Pascalis to Jean Devèze, New York, 8 November 1819. NYAM Folio Pascalis Ouviere, 1819–1923. Interestingly, the priest blamed Moreau for having been in part responsible for "this foul calumny," that is, of Fournier and Begim's attempt to slander him.
71. Letter of Felix Pascalis to Jean Devèze, 12 July 1820, NYAM Folio Pascalis Ouviere, 1819–1823.
72. Pascalis, "Anecdote historique."
73. Affidavit of Jean Devèze, Paris, 20 February 1820. NYAM MS 17—Deveze.
74. Pascalis to James Rush, July 5, 1819.
75. Zundel, *History of Old Zion Lutheran Evangelical Church*, 45–46.
76. *The Gazette of the United States*, XVIII, 2511, October 14, 1800, 4. $100 would today be worth $1,886.74. davemanuel.com/inflation-calculator.php; last accessed February 25, 2015.
77. Miller and Pencak, *Pennsylvania*, 140.
78. "Dr. Felix Pascalis" became a member on January 2, 1800. Pennsylvania Society for Promoting the Abolition of Slavery, *Centennial Anniversary of the Pennsylvania Society*, 60. His election certificate is signed by James Pemberton. ACHM Pascalis Binder, Old Hill Box 1. The world's first abolitionist organization, the Society was founded in 1775, and later lauded by Richard Allen as "the friend of those who hath no helper." Among its notable members were Benjamin Franklin, who became the Society's president in 1787, Benjamin Rush, Robert Morris, and John Greenleaf Whittier. Inspired by earlier Quaker abolitionist efforts, the Society played an important role in the realization of the Pennsylvania Gradual Abolition Act of 1780, "the first abolition society anywhere in the western world." Newman, "The Pennsylvania Abolitionist Society," 7.
79. The US Census indicates that there was one free colored female living with Pascalis' white family of four in 1820 and two free colored males living with his white family of three in 1830, suggesting that Pascalis had hired live-in servants for his household there rather than contracting other indentured servants, and perhaps reflecting his upward social mobility. 1820 US Census: New York Ward 6, New York, New York, Page: 484; NARA Roll: M33-77; Image 252; 1830 US Census: New York Ward 2, New York, New York, Page: 60; NARA Roll: M19-96; Family History Film: 0017156. A letter from an acquaintance who had lodged at Pascalis' house on Pearl Street in New York, at a time when Pascalis was unexpectedly out of town, suggests that one of the servants' names was Rosa, and also indicates that the home had a garden and caged birds. Letter of Edward W. Wells to Felix Pascalis, New York, 23 September 1823. NYAM MS 176/177—Wells E. W. Wells was in town to take his medical examination and stayed at the house for a week.
80. It should be added, however, that by 1800 "all but 55 of Philadelphia's 6,500 blacks were free." Randall M. Miller and William Pencak, *Pennsylvania: A History of the Commonwealth*. University Park, PA: Penn State University Press, 2002, 139-140.

81. Aptheker, "The Quakers and Negro Slavery," 356. For further insight into Quaker negotiation of slavery during the period in question, see Soderlund, *Quakers and Slavery*; Carey and Plank, *Quakers and Abolition*; and Carey, *From Peace to Freedom*.
82. Certificate of the election of Felix Pascalis to the Pennsylvania Society for Promoting the Abolition of Slavery, the Relief of Free Negroes Unlawfully Held in Bondage, and for Improving the Condition of the Negro Race. Philadelphia, February 2, 1800. ACHM Pascalis Binder, Ola Hitt Box 1 [photocopy].
83. On Rush's abolitionism, see Kloos, *A Sense of Deity*; and Newman, *Freedom's Prophet*.
84. "A Letter from the Famous Dr. Pascalis, to the Author," in Hawkins, *A History of a Voyage to the Coast of Africa*, iii–iv. The letter was republished in *The Columbian Phoenix and Boston Review*, May 1, 1800. Hailing from Charleston, South Carolina, Hawkins was a young captain of a slave ship who describes in his book in some detail the "grief" and hardship of the slaves that he purchased and brought to the Americas, though he fell far short of the abolitionist conclusion that Pascalis drew from his observations. Though having "rebuked" himself for "having embarked in the African trade," Hawkins instead concluded he was "fully convinced the removal of these poor wretches, even to the slavery of the West Indies, would be an act of humanity, rather than one exposed to censure." Hawkins, *A History of a Voyage to the Coast of Africa*, 93–94. It would be his only venture in the trade, as the captain contracted some ophthalmological ailment that afflicted many of the slaves on his ship, and he went blind at age 23.
85. As David Geggus explains, "The Haitian Revolution occurred at a time when the antislavery movement, liberation ideology, and humanitarianism were gaining ground but when scientific enquiry was undermining concepts of the oneness of mankind, so preparing the way for the 'scientific racism' of the nineteenth century." Geggus, "Preface," xv.
86. In another pseudo-scientific essay, "The Albiness," Pascalis opined that albinism is caused by "nothing more than a defect or imperfection in system of circulation, which deprives the ratina of the *pigmentium nigrim* and the hair of its coloring matter. Pascalis, "The Albiness," *The National Register* 5, 23, June 6, 1818, 357.
87. Pascalis, "Desultory Remarks," 366.
88. City of New-York, *The Commissioners of the Almshouse v. Alexander Whistelo*, 2.
89. Ibid., 6.
90. Ibid., 3.
91. Ibid., 4.
92. In Latin, *rete mucosum* literally translates as "mucus net," though more conventionally referred to in dermatology as the Malpighian layer. Late eighteenth-/early nineteenth-century scientists like Pascalis and Benjamin Rush considered this to be "the fictional skin layer," as put by Harriett Washington. Washington, *Medical Apartheid*, 80. See also Curran, *The Anatomy of Blackness*.

93. City of New-York, *The Commissioners of the Almshouse v. Alexander Whistelo*, 22–23.
94. Ibid., 41. James Jay was the brother of John Jay, the first chief justice of the United States.
95. Ibid. The Latin passage in the mayor's verdict translates as "Let no God intervene unless a knot come worthy of such a deliverer."
96. Pascalis, "Memorial on the Upward Forces of Fluids," 116. Many of these views that Pascalis had concerning religion are also reflected in his "An Adress [*sic*] to the Benevolent Society delivered on the 4th of March—1803." NYAM MS 226/ MS 557—Pascalis Ouviere, Felix. He adds in this address, "The precepts of that Religion are to heal the wounds and alleviate the suffering of the unfortunate."
97. Pascalis-Ouvière, *Annual Oration*, 6.
98. Ibid., 10. Further evincing Pascalis' evolutionist view of religious history, in 1823 he wrote: "Among ancient nations, however, little advance beyond the infancy of civilization, or among barbarous tribes, or destruction of the remains of the dead were shockingly cruel, absurd or contradictory; and well calculated to illustrate the superstitions of the times." Pascalis, "An Exposition of the Danger of Interment in Cities." The secularization thesis has been one of the dominant issues in the sociology of religion since the 1960s and has its roots in Max Weber's argument that advances in science lead inevitably to the "disenchantment of the world." Weber, "Science as Vocation," 155–156. Weber first published this essay in the German original in 1922.
99. Ibid., 48.
100. Pascal, "Linnaean Society of Paris," 383.
101. Several letters from Felix Pascalis to his wife are preserved in the archives of the New York Academy of Medicine, and they reflect financial hardship. For instance, on October 11, 1813, he responded to his wife's complaints about the autumn chill by assuring her that he was arranging to have a shawl made for her, while at the same time sending some stockings for her to mend. Letter of Felix Pascalis to Elizabeth Pascalis, New York, 11 October 1813. NYAM MS 141/142/143—Pascalis Ouviere, Felix. In an undated letter that seems to have been sent a few months later, he wrote to his daughter the following: "children who do not belong to rich parents must be contented with what is decent and comfortable." Letter of Felix Pascalis to Francisca Pascalis, New York, n.d. NYAM MS 141/142/143—Pascalis Ouviere, Felix.
102. Letter of Felix Pascalis to Francisca Pascalis, 13 December 1813. NYAM MS 141/142/143—Pascalis Ouviere, Felix. It is not clear if and/or why people in Virginia might have then been eating more pork than were their compatriots elsewhere in America.
103. Letter of Felix Pascalis to Francisca Pascalis, 31 December 1813. NYAM MS 141/142/143—Pascalis Ouviere, Felix.

104. Letter of Felix Pascalis to Francisca Pascalis, 26 January 1814. NYAM MS 141/142/143—Pascalis Ouviere, Felix.
105. Francesca Canfield died on May 23, 1833, though Griswold mistakenly posts the date of her demise 10 years earlier, going on to explain that her father outlived his daughter by "ten disconsolate years." Griswold, *The Female Poets of America*, 135. In fact, Canfield died just a couple of months before her father, "cut off by a lingering disease," as her obituary reads, "in the course of which, she manifested many traits of character which peculiarly recommended her to the sympathies and affectionate recollection of her friends, although not of a nature to be enumerated in a public journal." *The New-York Mirror, Vol. X.* New York, June 8, 1833, 391. Her given name was in fact Francisca. Letter of Felix Pascalis to Francisca Pascalis, New York, 16 December 1813. NYAM MS 141/142/143—Pascalis Ouviere, Felix.
106. Griswold, *The Female Poets of America*, 135.
107. Felix Pascalis to Archibold McIntyre, New York, February 1, 1824. HSP Gratz ALS 1824–29.
108. Anonymous, "Birthday of Linnaeus," *The Minerva; or, Literary, Entertaining and Scientific Journal*, May 31, 1832, 60.
109. Ibid., 60. Pascalis was a founder of the New York Linnaeus Society. Jefferson had previously, in 1822, been made an honorary member of the Linnaean Society of Paris. Aymonin, "Thomas Jefferson et les naturalistes français," 304. Pascalis had also been in touch with Jefferson in 1819/1820, in an attempt to have Jefferson acquire for the University of Virginia "a large Collection of natural curiosities .... Shells, Crustacea, fishes, Minerals, Birds; some living animals, etc." for a bargain price of "less than 2000 doll." Jefferson responded to Pascalis two weeks later, expressing his regret that the "institution is not yet in a sufficient state of forwardness to avail ourselves of the advantage, our buildings are not yet half finished: and, until they are compleated, our whole funds must be applied to that object." "To Thomas Jefferson from Felix Pascalis Ouviere, 15 December 1819," FONA, http://founders.archives.gov/documents/Jefferson/98-01-02-0963, ver. 2014-05-09); last accessed July 3, 2014. "From Thomas Jefferson to Felix Pascalis Ouviere, 2 January 1820," FONA, http://founders.archives.gov/documents/Jefferson/98-01-02-1001; last accessed May 9, 2014.
110. Griswold, *The Female Poets of America*, 136.
111. Anonymous, "Birthday of Linnaeus." Italics added.
112. Anonymous, "Doctor Pascalis; Federal; Philosopher; Jefferson." *Philadelphia Gazette*, 10 February 1801.
113. Pascalis, "Observations and Practical Remarks," 3. It is not unworth speculating that Pascalis had expressed similar ideas in his anticelibacy writings that may have resulted in his excommunication from the Catholic Church over 40 years earlier, as discussed in Chapter 3. The implications of Pascalis' views on venereal disease, meanwhile, are contextualized by William Benemann,

who observes how Pascalis understood that "a woman's vagina emits an invisible vapor which can transmit venereal disease if a man even comes near her." Benemann, *Male-Male Intimacy in Early America*, 142.

114. Pascalis, "Remarks on a Spanish Pamphlet."
115. Pascalis-Ouvière, *A Statement of the Occurrence during the Malignant Yellow Fever*, 21.
116. Ibid., 26.
117. Episcopal Church, Diocese of New York, *Journals*, 317.
118. At least part of Pascalis' library has been preserved and is on display at the Aiken County Historical Museum in South Carolina, in the Pascalis Room. The collections of sermons are by Joseph Stevens Buckminster (1784–1812), a Unitarian minister from Boston who once occupied the Chair of Scripture at Harvard, and John Newton (1725–1807), an English Anglican priest and prominent abolitionist who is also quite famous for having written one of the most beloved of all Christian hymns, "Amazing Grace." Joseph S. Buckminster, *Sermons by the Late Joseph S. Buckminster with a Memoir on his Life and Character* (Boston: Wells and Lilly, 1821). John Newton, *Posthumous Works of the Late Rev. John Newton* (Philadelphia: Woodward, 1809). An inventory of the books from the Pascalis library in Aiken is found in the ACHM Pascalis Binder, Ola Hitt Box 1. The collection includes 11 volumes of the *Medical Repository*. The oldest item is Benito Geronymo Feyjoo y Montenegro, *Cartas, Eruditas, y Curiosas*... (Madrid: Marin, 1774).
119. Pascalis, "An Exposition of the danger of Interment in Cities," 3.
120. Pascalis' descendants in South Carolina were once in possession of an original portrait painting of the man whose "picture frame had a pocket in the back in which his Masonic apron and his Masonic gloves were kept." Shuler, *From the Mayflower to Pole Cat Pond, S.C.*, 38. With that said, Pascalis is not listed in the membership records of the Grand Masonic Lodges of New Jersey, New York, or Pennsylvania, though this does not mean he never participated at any or all of these lodges as an active Freemason. Immigrant Freemasons in early republican American frequently retained their homeland lodge membership while participating in lodges in cities like Philadelphia and New York. For their expert insight into these matters and for having checked through their respective archives for Pascalis, I am most grateful to Glennys A. Waldman, chief librarian and the Masonic Temple Grand Lodge in Philadelphia (personal electronic communication, January 14, 2010); Thomas Savini, director of the Chancellor Robert R. Livingston Library of Grand Lodge in New York (personal electronic communication, June 30, 2014; July 2, 2014); and Brian Johnson, Grand Lodge administrator in Trenton (personal electronic communication, July 2, 2014).
121. Felix Pascalis, "History of Two Remarkable Cases of Mania," 365.
122. "Although a follower of Benjamin Rush, Pascalis' interests were limited more narrowly to medical questions, such as Rush's theory of the origin of disease. . . .

Whatever contacts he had with Rush (who was four years his senior), they did not influence him in the direction of Rush's interest in the philosopher/theologians of the Scottish Enlightenment." Veatch, *Disrupted Dialogue*, 109.

123. "From the Diary of Rev. J. T. Cornish, St. Thaddeus Episcopal Church, 1846–1870." ACPL—Pascalis Family Folder.
124. Felix Pascalis to Benjamin Rush, New York, April 24, 1805. HSP 13 Rush MS 14-18.
125. Felix Pascalis to Benjamin Rush, New York, March 8, 1812. HSP 13 Rush MS 20-23. This letter also notes that Pascalis was having some of Rush's work translated into French. Pascalis also makes mention of a brother in Italy, "the principal Officer depouté [*sic*] of the army in that new section of the French empire." Pascalis sailed to Europe that year "in the Fregate John Adams," a US naval ship that would see action in the Barbary Wars, the War of 1812, the Mexican-American War, and the US Civil War, not to be confused with the second USS *John Adams*, a naval submarine.
126. Pascalis-Ouvière, *Medico-chymical dissertations on the causes of the epidemic called yellow fever*, 3.
127. Pascalis, "Remarks on the Theory of Pain," 79. Cabanis was a professor of medicine at the University of Paris, and his remarks on pain, quoted here by Pascalis, were published just two years before Pascalis published his own theory of pain. Cabanis, *Rapport du physique de et du moral de l'homme*.
128. Middleton, "Felix Pascalis-Ouvière and the Yellow Fever Epidemic of 1797," 514.
129. Pascalis, "Eulogy on the Life and Character of the Hon. Samuel Latham Mitchill, M.D." October 15, 1831. The Latin quote is from Horace and translates as "I have raised a monument more permanent than bronze."
130. Felix Pascalis letter to Doctor (John) Ferguson. September 7, 1832. UPRB, PU-SP Ms Coll 75, E. F. Smith Collection, 540.4. This letter, which is an expression of condolences on the passing of Ferguson's father and of regret for being unable to attend his funeral, is the last document written by Pascalis that I have found, with the exception of his last will and testament.
131. Last Will and Testament of Felix Pascalis. New York, 31 May 1833. ACPL Pascalis Family Folder.
132. *New York Evening Post*, July 22, 1833. *Who's Who in American History* indicates the 29th as his date of death, http://search.marquiswhoswho.com.libproxy.temple.edu/executable/SearchResults.aspx?db=H,W; last accessed September 28, 2009. Kelly indicates the date as the 27th. Kelly, "Félix A. Pascalis-Ouvrière [*sic*]."
133. The plantation was located in Montmorenci, Aiken County, South Carolina. The master's house is an official historical landmark in the State of South Carolina. See the Historical Marker Database, http://www.hmdb.org/marker.asp?marker=9797; last accessed April 28, 2010. It is of course possible that McKlintock possessed some wealth independently and might have combined it with whatever that Dr. Pascalis may have left her. The decision to move to

South Carolina was one that likely involved their son's prior experience there as an engineer. Shuler indicates that Cyril, along with a business partner, purchased the plantation in 1832 and sold it to his mother in 1835. Shuler, *From the Mayflower to Pole Cat Pond, S.C.*, 57. Shuler's text also contains a copy of a bill of sale for a slave girl that Eliza Pascalis, the priest's wife, purchased in 1843. Ibid., 61. Eliza adopted the four orphaned children of Francisca Canfield and raised them in South Carolina. See also Hitt and Cannon, *Echoes from Pascalina*.

134. Geggus, "Slave Resistance Studies and the Saint-Domingue Revolt," 1.
135. New York Historical Society, "Slavery and the Making of New York." http://www.slaveryinnewyork.org/about_exhibit.htm; last accessed July 2, 2010. More than 40 percent of New York's households at the time owned at least one slave, contrasted with a figure of "just" 2 percent in Philadelphia.

CHAPTER 9

1. "A wayward child still grows up before Bawon." Bawon is the chief Vodou spirit of the cemetery.
2. Price-Mars, *Ainsi parla l'oncle*, 20.
3. Romaine is mistaken to have been a woman in a number of texts, both scholarly and fictional. See, for an example of the former, Matthews, "Female Maroons of the West Indies," http://www.caribbean-atlas.com/en/themes/waves-of-colonization-and-control-in-the-caribbean/resistance-to-imperialism-and-emancipation/female-maroons-of-the-west-indies.html; last accessed February 6, 2016. For an example of the latter, see Deive, *Viento negro, Bosque del Caimán*, 68. On Deive's novel, see Fumagalli, "Servants Turned Masters."
4. Péan, "Haïti: Le père Dessalines et les sans repères," http://www.alterpresse.org/spip.php?article17215#nb2; last accessed, February 7, 2016.
5. Auguste, "Les Congos dans la Révolution Haïtienne, " 35.
6. Thus, certainly, we should not confuse Romain with Romaine-la-Prophétesse. Because he was evidently executed in Saint-Domingue in 1802, furthermore, nor should we confuse the Romain discussed by Auguste with a slave from Saint-Domingue named Romain, who committed suicide by slitting his throat in Trenton, New Jersey, in 1802. On the latter and the significance of his life and death in the revolutionary Atlantic world, see Johnson, *The Fear of French Negroes*, xv–xxii.
7. Strauss. *The Christ of Faith and the Jesus of History*. Strauss is more famous for his masterpiece *The Life of Jesus, Critically Examined*.
8. Trouillot, *Silencing the Past*, 175–176n65.
9. Anacaona is honored in additionally myriad ways, such as by the Léogâne-based women's soccer club Anacaona FC, the Anacaona Boutique Hotel in Anguilla, the Daughters of Anacaona Writing Project in New York City, and an award-winning novel by Edwidge Danticat, *Anacaona*, as well as in folk music, sculpture, and children's books, place names, etc. Danticat, *Anacaona, Golden Flower*.

10. Richman, "Innocent Imitations?," 222.
11. This is a comment that Breton left in the guest book at the Haitian Center of Art in Port-au-Prince in 1945. As cited in Geis, "Myth, History, and Repetition." For further insight into Breton's reading of Vodou, especially spirit possession, see Benedicty, *Spirit Possession in French, Haitian, and Vodou Thought*, 117–126.
12. Trouillot, *Silencing the Past*, 67.
13. Ibid., 67.
14. Péan, "Les élections du 25 octobre et le changement en Haïti," http://www.alterpresse.org/spip.php?article19232#.VqloLPkrKUk; last accessed February 1, 2016.
15. Jean Métellus, "Pour Mumia Abu-Jamal," *L'Humanité dimanche*, January 9–15, 2014, 90.
16. Daréus, "Haïti/Guerre de l'Indépendance: Bois-Caïman, On s'en souvient," http://radiotelevision2000.com/home/?p=20003; last accessed February 2, 2016.
17. Thoreau, *The Journal of Henry David Thoreau, 1837–1861*, 65.
18. Brown, *Mama Lola*, 229.
19. "Visual piety" is David Morgan's term for "the constructive operation of seeing that looks for, makes room for, the transcendent in daily life." Morgan, *The Sacred Gaze*, 6. On visual piety in Haitian Miami, see Rey and Stepick, "Visual Culture and Visual Piety."
20. Farmer, *AIDS and Accusation*, 101.
21. Campbell, *The Hero's Journey*. 58.
22. I thank Sam Strong for having raised this interesting question.
23. On homophobia in Haiti, see Hoffmann, *Haïti: Couleurs, croyances, créole*; and, for something more recent, see Gaestel, "Haiti's Fight for Gay Rights." http://projects.aljazeera.com/2014/haiti-lgbt/; last accessed February 14, 2016; and Rey, "Fear and Trembling in Haiti." For further insight into the struggle for gay rights in Haiti, see http://www.kouraj.org/; last accessed February 14, 2016.
24. Tinsley, "Ezili Danto: A Lesbian History of Haiti?" http://smallaxe.net/sxvisualities/cqv/provocations/tinsley-ezili-danto; last accessed February 11, 2016.
25. Fournier and Bégim. "*Marais*," 561. François Fournier de Pescay (1771–1833) is celebrated as one of the first persons "of color" to have ever practiced medicine in France and all of Europe. J. A. Rogers, *World's Great Men of Color, Volume II* (New York: Touchstone, 1947), 553.
26. Hoffmann, "Representations of the Haitian Revolution in French Literature," 342. Toumson, *Bug Jargal*. As cited in de Cauna, "Les sources historiques de Bug Jargal," http://www.msha.fr/celfa/article/DeCauna01.pdf; last accessed October 16, 2009. For his part, de Cauna disagrees with Toumson's reading.
27. Fumagalli, *On the Edge*, 64.
28. Hoffmann, "Representations of the Haitian Revolution in French Literature." 343.
29. Ibid., 344.
30. Chris Bongie, in Hugo, *Bug-Jargal*, 210n95.

31. Lacroix, *Mémoires pour server à l'histoire de la révolution de Saint-Domingue*, 142.
32. Geggus, *Haitian Revolutionary Studies*, 126.
33. Hugo, *Bug Jargal*, 162.
34. Ibid., 163.
35. "Obi" was a term used in Saint-Domingue for sorcery, to judge from the term's entry in the brief glossary with which Lacroix's *Mémoires* opens: "Obi, synonym of sorcery, and sometimes of hex." Lacroix, *Mémoires pour servir à l'histoire de la révolution de Saint-Domingue*, vii. For an excellent collection of essays on the subject of Obeah in the Caribbean, see Paton and Forde, *Obeah and Other Powers*; and Handler and Bilby, *Enacting Power*. The term "ndoki" was also used in the colony to connote banditry, sorcery, and slavery itself, as James Sweet indicates. Sweet, "New Perspectives on Kongo in Revolutionary Haiti."
36. Hugo, *Bug Jargal*, 163.
37. Montero, *In the Palm of Darkness*, 55. For a brief but insightful scholarly commentaries on Montero's treatment of Romaine, see Braham, "The Monstrous Caribbean," 46, and Braham, *From Amazons to Zombies*, 160–161. Another novel in which Romaine has a cameo as a "great priestess," like Anacaona, who was capable of assembling an army of zombies toward mounting resistance to white, and to male, domination, is Stéphane Prandini's *La main du diable*, 92–93.
38. The blurbs are by Bob Shacochis, Madison Smartt Bell, and Rosario Ferré, respectively. Italics added.
39. Davis, *The Serpent and the Rainbow*. Romaine actually also makes a brief, sensational appearance in Davis' deeply problematic book as an insurgent leader who "marched to the music of drums and conque shells behind an entourage of houngan [*sic*] chanting that the weapons of the whites, their cannon and muskets were bamboo, their gunpowder but dust; his personal guard carried only long cowtails blessed by the spirits and thus capable of deflecting the bullets of the whites" (202). For a compelling analysis of Davis' research on Haiti and its implications, see Ingliss, "Putting the Undead to Work."
40. Montero, *In the Palm of Darkness*, 11.
41. Ibid., 55.
42. Claude Bernard Sérant, "La Place Anacaona de Léogâne: Où sont passées les neiges d'antant?" *Le Nouvelliste*, January 23, 2006.
43. Ibid.

CONCLUSION

1. "When encountering a bone in the big road, remember that flesh once covered it." I thank Drexel Woodson for bringing this proverb to my attention many years ago at a place in Haiti called PIRÈD. It also appears in Woodson, "Which Beginning Should Be Hindmost."

2. Thibau, *Le temps de Saint-Domingue*, 319. See also Hurbon, "Le clergé catholique et l'insurrection," 34. The display of severed heads was not uncommon in Saint-Domingue: "there has been a mortal hatred between the whites and the mulattoes; but the former seem to be most exasperated and implacable, having frequently cut off the heads of the others and carried them about on bayonets and poles." Anonymous, "News from Port-au-Prince," *Columbia Centinel*, March 17, 1792.
3. Alexis, *Black Liberator*, 48.
4. Madiou, *Histoire d'Haïti, Tome I*, 97.
5. Ibid., x.
6. Ibid., 128. Though it is plausible that Romaine's followers may have committed acts of sexual violence, there is no clear reference to rape in any of the primary source literature about the Trou Coffy insurgency. On rape in Haitian history more generally, see Rey, "Junta, Rape, and Religion in Haiti."
7. Fisher, *Modernity Disavowed*, 232. The passages from the first Haitian constitution cited here are also found on this page in *Modernity Disavowed*. Jane Gordon insightfully points out that the 1805 constitution, in effect, contributed to a "creolization of Enlightenment" ideas in which "'Black' therefore became, as it would in the Black Consciousness movement in South Africa in the mid-1960s, a political rather than a racial identity." Gordon, *Creolizing Political Theory*, 213.
8. Marx, "Theses on Feuerbach," 15.
9. As cited in Girod-Chantrans, *Voyage d'un Suisse dans différentes colonies d'Amérique*, 170.
10. In 1825, France demanded a sum of 150 million francs in reparations for French property lost or destroyed during the Haitian Revolution, which in today's fiscal measures would be worth more than 12 billion US dollars! France held recognition of Haiti's independence hostage, delivering their ransom demand on a fleet of heavily armed warships. In 2003, Haitian president Jean-Bertrand Aristide petitioned that his nation be reimbursed for the roughly 90 million francs that Haiti did in fact pay. On this lurid saga, see Ives, "Haiti: Independence Debt, Reparations for Slavery and Colonialism, and International Aid," http://www.globalresearch.ca/haiti-independence-debt-reparations-for-slavery-and-colonialism-and-international-aid/5334619; last accessed March 7, 2014.
11. On this point, I am in agreement with David Scott's argument that "the narrative of revolution is inseparable from the larger narrative of modernity and ... categories such as 'nation,' 'sovereignty,' 'progress,' 'reason,' and so on." Scott, *Conscripts of Modernity*, 89.
12. Dubois, *Avengers of the New World*, 306.
13. "Haiti—Historique: 1492–1992." http://www.nilstremmel.com/haiti/; last accessed October 16, 2006. Also, http://demokrasikreyol.blogspot.com/2008_07_01_archive.html; last accessed July 12, 2009. The Louverture Project, a

Wikipedia-related website on the Haitian Revolution also indicates 1795 as the year of Romaine's death, but this is not indicated in either of the sources that its scant page on Romaine cites. http://thelouvertureproject.org/index.php?title=Romaine-la-Proph%C3%A9tesse; last accessed April 8, 2010.

14. As Carolyn Fick explains, "[b]ecause Dessalines embraced political independence, because he became the military leader of independence, and because independence was indeed achieved under his military leadership, it is generally assumed, after the facts, that the violent elimination of these independent maroon and voodoo leaders was therefore a justifiable, if unfortunate, necessity in the name of national unity." Fick, *The Making of Haiti*, 233. See also Dayan, *Haiti, History, and the Gods*, 23–24.
15. Brutus, *L'Homme d'Airain*, 132–133. Neither Brutus nor Fick names Romaine among the victims: "Almost all of their leaders, like Sylla, Sans-Souci, Petit-Noël Prieur, and Macaya in the North, or Lamour Dérance in the West, were African and refused to be commanded by the creole generals." Fick, *The Making of Haiti*, 231. On antisuperstitious campaigns in Haitian history, see Ramsey, *The Spirits and the Law*.
16. Trinity does have record of Pascalis' burial. Register of Burials in the Parish of Trinity Church, New York, "Felix A. B. Pascalis," Age 72, 22 July 1833. As photocopied in Hitt and Cannon, *Echoes from Pascalina*, 164. The exact site of the priest's grave is lost to history, however, as 120 of the 10,000 bodies at St. John's were exhumed and buried at a large cemetery uptown. There is no indication that Pascalis was one of them. Gwynned Canan (personal electronic correspondence, May 14, 2010, May 18, 2010). On the sad demise of St. John's Chapel and Burying Ground, see Christopher Gray, "A Chapel the City Fought to Save," *New York Times*, April 27, 2008.
17. Pascalis, "An Exposition of the danger of Interment in Cities."
18. Rey, "The Politics of Patron Sainthood in Haiti," 527–529.
19. Ibid. See also Rey, *Our Lady of Class Struggle*.
20. Rey, *Our Lady of Class Struggle*. Rey and Stepick, *Crossing the Water and Keeping the Faith*.
21. Pascalis, "Remarks on the Theory of Pain."

Bibliography

ARCHIVES CONSULTED

Aiken County Historical Museum (ACHM); Aiken, SC
Aiken County Public Library (ACPL); Aiken, SC
American Philosophical Society (APS); Philadelphia, PA
Archives de la Société Royale de la Médecine (ASRM); Paris, France
Archives Nationales de France (AN); Paris, France
Archives Nationales de France—Section Outre-Mer (ANSOM); Aix-en-Provence, France
Archives of the Diocese of Louisiana and the Floridas (ADLF); Notre Dame, IN
Founders Online, National Archives (FONA); Washington, DC
Historical Society of Pennsylvania (HSP); Philadelphia, PA
New York Academy of Medicine (NYAM); New York, NY
Papers of Thomas Jefferson (POTJ); Princeton, NJ
Service Historique de la Défense (SHD); Paris, France
Trinity Episcopal Church, Burial Records (TEC); New York, NY
Tucker-Coleman Collection, Jefferson Papers (TCJP); Williamsburg, VA
University of Pennsylvania Rare Books and Manuscripts Collection (UPRB); Philadelphia, PA

NEWSPAPERS

Affiches Américaines
American Argus
American Masonick Record and Albany Saturday Magazine
Columbia Centinel
Gazette de Saint-Domingue
Journal de Saint-Domingue

Mercure de France
National Gazette
New York Daily Tribune
New York Evening Post
New York Gazette
New York Weekly Museum
Nouvelles Diverses
Philadelphia Aurora
Philadelphia General Advertiser
The Columbian Phoenix and Boston Review
The Diary or Loudon's Register
The Gazette of the United States
The National Register
The Minerva
The New-York Mirror
The Royal Gazette
True American and Commercial Advertiser

PUBLISHED PRIMARY SOURCES

Anonymous. n.d. *Histoire des désastres de Saint Domingue: Tableau de la colonie jusqu'à la révolution de 1789*. n.p.

———. 1968. "Tableau des Membres de la Société des amis des Noirs. Année 1789." In Anonymous, *La Révolution Française et l'Abolition de l'Esclavage: Textes et Documents, Tome VI*. Paris: Éditions d'Histoire Sociales, 1–8.

———. 1789. *Cahier, contenant les plaintes, doléances & réclamations des citoyens libres & propriétaires de couleur, des Îles & Colonies françaises*. Paris: n.p.

———. 1789. *Heureuse (l') journée, ou le triomphe des braves marseillais*. Marseille: n.p.

———. 1791–1792. *A Particular Account of the Insurrection of the Negroes of St. Domingo begun in August 1791* [microform]: translated from the French: speech made to the National Assembly the third of November, 1791, by the deputies from the General Assembly of the French part of St. Domingo. London: n.p.

———. 1792. "La Révolution de Saint-Domingue, contenant tout ce qui s'est passé dans la colonie française depuis le commencement de la Révolution jusqu'au départ de l'auteur pour la France." n.p.

———. 1799. *The New Trade Directory for Philadelphia Anno 1800*. Philadelphia: Way & Groff.

———. 1822. "For the Minerva CAMDEN. Case of Aneurism of the Left Areola." *The Minerva*, 86.

———. 1826. "PASCALIS OUVIERE (FÉLIX)." *Biographie universelle et portative des contemporains, ou Dictionnaire historique des hommes célèbres de toutes les nations, morts ou vivants*, 2, 2. Paris: Bureau de la Biographie.

———. 1833–1834. "BIOGRAPHY: Felix Alexander Ouviere Pascalis." In Samuel Hazard (ed.), *Hazard's Registry of Pennsylvania, Volume 12*. Philadelphia: WM. F. Geddes, 123–124.

Assemblée générale de la Partie française de Saint-Domingue. 1799–1804 (1790). *Décret de l'Assemblée générale de la Partie française de Saint-Domingue, rendu à l'unanimité, en sa séance du 28 mai 1790*. Saint-Marc: Imprimerie de l'Assemblée Générale.

Assemblée Nationale Législative. 1891–1894. *Archives Parlementaires de 1787 à 1860*. Paris: Dupont.

Baudry des Lozières, Louis-Narcisse. 1803. *Second voyage à Louisiane: Faisant suite au premier de l'auteur de 1794 à 1798*. Vol. 2. Paris: Charles.

Bonnet, Edmond. 1864. *Souvenirs historiques de Guy-Joseph Bonnet, Premier partie*. Paris: Durand.

Breathett, George (ed.). 1983. *The Catholic Church in Colonial Haiti (1704–1785): Selected Letters, Memoirs, and Documents*. Salisbury: Documentary Publications.

Cabanis, P. J. G. 1824. *Rapport du physique et du moral de l'homme*. Paris: J. B. Baillière.

Carlson, Eric T., Jeffrey L. Wollock, and Patricia S. Noel (eds.). 1981. *Benjamin Rush's Lectures on the Mind*. Philadelphia: American Philosophical Society.

Carteau, Félix. 1802. *Soirées Bermudiennes*. Bordeaux: Pellier-Lawalle.

Chanlatte jeune, Viart, Dubourg, and F. Ouvière. 1792. *Mémoire historique des dernières révolutions des provinces de l'ouest et du sud de la partie française de Saint-Domingue*. Archives Parlementaires, 1787–1860, Assemblée Nationale Législative. Paris, Dupont, 1890–1897, 518–537.

———. 1792. *Suite du mémoire historique des dernières révolutions des provinces de l'ouest et du sud de la partie française de Saint-Domingue. Suite*. Paris: Imprimerie du Patriote Français.

———. 1894. "Suite du mémoire historique (2) des dernières révolutions de l'ouest et du sud de la partie française de Saint-Domingue." In M. J. Mavidal and M. E. Laurent, *Archives parlementaires, de 1768 à 1860. Tome XLIV*. Paris: Dupont, 537–540.

City of New-York. 1879 (1808). *The Commissioners of the Almshouse v. Alexander Whistelo, (a black man); Being a Remarkable Case of Bastardy*. General sessions, New York, 1808. Burlington: Burlington Book Co.

College of Physicians of Philadelphia. 1887. *Transactions of the College of Physicians of Philadelphia, Third Series, Volume the Ninth*. Philadelphia: Blakiston.

Commissaires des Citoyens de Couleur de St. Marc. 1792. *Mémoire historique des dernières révolutions des provinces de l'ouest et du sud de la partie française de Saint-Domingue*. Paris: Imprimerie du Patriote Français.

Darimajou, Dominique. 1790. *La chasteté du clergé dévoilée: ou Procès-verbaux des séances du clergé chez les filles de Paris, trouvés à la Bastille, Première partie*. Rome: Imprimerie de la Propagande.

Darluc, Michel. 1782–1786. *Histoire naturelle de la Provence, contenant ce qu'il y a de plus remarquable dans les règnes végétal, minéral, animal, et la partie géoponique en trois volumes.* Avignon: J. J. Niel.

De Alcedo, Don Antonio. 1787. *Diccionario geográfico-histórico de las Indias Occidentales ó América: es á saber: de los reynos del Perú, Nueva España, Tierra Firme, Chile, y Nuevo reyno de Granada.* Tomo dos. Madrid: Manuel Gonzalez.

———. 1812. *The Geographic and Historical Dictionary of America and the Americas and the West Indies. Vol. II.* Trans. G. A. Thompson. New York: Burt Franklin.

De Blanchelande, Philibert-François Rouxel. 1791. *Supplément au Mémoire de M. de Blanchelande.* n.p.

De Menonville, Thierry. 1787. *Traité de la Culture de Nopal et de l'Éducation de la Cochenille dans les Colonies Françaises de l'Amérique; Précédé d'un Voyage à Guaxaca.* Cap François: Chez la veuve Herbault.

Debien, Gabriel (ed.). 1965. *Lettres des Colons.* Laval: Madiot/Université de Dakar, Faculté de Lettres et Sciences Humaines.

Delahaye, Abbé. 1788. *Florindie ou Historie physico-économique des végétaux de la Torride.* Cap François: Imprimerie Royal.

Descourlitz, Michel-Étienne. 1795. *Histoire des désastres de Saint-Domingue, précédée d'un tableau du régime et des progrès de cette colonie depuis sa fondation jusqu'à l'époque de la Révolution française.* Paris: Garnery.

Devèze, Jean. 1794. *An Enquiry into, and Observations Upon the Causes and Effects of the Epidemic Disease Which raged in Philadelphia from the month of August till towards the middle of December 1793.* Philadelphia: Parent.

Episcopal Church, Diocese of New York. 1844. *Journals on the Convention of the Protestant Episcopal Diocese of New York.* New York: H. M. Onderdonk.

Fournier and Bégim. 1818. "Marais." In Adleon et al. (eds.), *Dictionnaire des sciences médicales, Tome trentième.* Paris: C. L. F. Panckoucke, Mai-Mar, 516–580.

Garran de Coulon, Jean-Philippe. 1797a. *Rapport sur les troubles de Saint-Domingue, fait au nom de la Commission des Colonies, des Comités du Salut Public, de Législation et de Marine, réunis. Tome 1,* Paris: Imprimerie Nationale.

———. 1797b. *Rapport sur les troubles de Saint-Domingue, Tome 2.* Paris: Imprimerie Nationale.

———. 1798. *Rapport sur les troubles de Saint-Domingue, Tome 4.* Paris: Imprimerie Nationale.

Girod-Chantrans, Justin. 1785. *Voyage d'un Suisse dans différentes colonies.* Neufchatel: Imprimerie de la Société Typographique.

Gros, M. 1792. *An Historick Recital, of the Different Occurrences in the Camps of Grande Reviere [sic], Dondon, Sainte-Suzanne, and others, from the 26th of October, 1791, to the 4th of December of the Same Year.* Baltimore: Samuel & John Adams.

———. 1793. *Précis historique, qui expose dans le plus grand jour les manœuvres contre-révolutionnaires employées contre St. Domingue; qui désigne & faire connoître les principaux agents de tous les massacres, incendies, vols, & dévastations qui s'y sont commis;*

le but qu'ils se proposoient en autorisant & faisant exécuter un tissu d'horreurs, dont la seule description fait frémir la nature: faits qui sont à la connaissance de la colonie entière; qui ont acquis toute l'authenticité possible, par la déposition publique du citoyen Gros, procureur-syndic de Valière, prisonnier des brigands, & confirmée sur les lieux par celle de plusieurs autres témoins, juridiquement faite. Paris: Imprimerie de L. Potier de Lille.

Guthrie, William. 1802. *Nouvelle géographie universelle, tome VI, partie II.* Trans. Fr. Noel. Paris: Langlois.

Hawkins, Joseph. 1797. *A History of a Voyage to the Coast of Africa, and Travels into the Interior of that Country; Containing Particular Descriptions of the Climate and Inhabitants, and Interesting Particulars Concerning the Slave Trade.* Troy: Pratt.

Hosack, David and John W. Francis (eds.) 1814. *American Medical and Philosophical Register, or Annals of Medicine, Natural History, Agriculture and the Arts, First Volume.* New York: C. S. Van Winkle.

Jan, Jean-Marie (ed.). 1955. *Collecta pour l'histoire du diocèse du Cap-Haïtien, Tome I.* Port-au-Prince: Deschamps.

Labat, Jean-Baptiste. 1722. *Nouveau voyage aux îles de l'Amérique. Tome VI.* Paris: Cavelier.

Laborie, P. J. 1798. *The Coffee Planter of Saint Domingo with an appendix, containing a view of the constitution, government, laws, and state of that Colony, previous to the year 1789. To which are added, some hints on the present state of the Island, under the British Government.* London: T. Cadell and W. Davies.

Lacroix, Baron Pamphile. 1819. *Mémoires pour server à l'histoire de la révolution de Saint-Domingue, Tome premier.* Paris: Pillet Ainé.

Lamothe-Vedel. n.d. *Mémoire pour Lamothe-Vedel.* Toulouse: n.p.

Larousse, Pierre. 1866–1877. *Grand dictionnaire universel du XIXe siècle: Français, historique, géographique, mythologique, bibliographique.... Tome X.* Paris: Administration du grand Dictionnaire historique.

La Salle (marquis de), Adrien Nicolas Piedefer. 1897 (1792–1793). *Les papiers du général A. N. La Salle, Saint-Domingue, 1792–1793.* Ed. Armand Corre. Quimper: Imprimerie C. Cotonnec, 1897.

Linn, John B. and William H. Egle (eds.). 1896. *Pennsylvania Archives, Second Series, Vol. 8.* Harrisburg: State Printer of Pennsylvania.

Malenfant, Colonel. 1814. *Des colonies et particulièrement de celle de Saint-Domingue.* Paris: Audibert.

Manly, James R., Felix Pascalis, and John H. Steel. 1823. "A System of Medical Ethics." Albany: Medical Society of the State of New York.

Mavidal, M. J. et al. (eds.). 1891. Assemblée Nationale Législative, *Archives parlementaires de 1787 à 1860: Recueil complet des débats législatifs et politiques des chambres françaises, Tome XXXVII.* Paris: Société d'Imprimerie et Librairie Administrative.

McIntosh, M. E. and B. C. Wheeler (eds.). 1959. *Une Correspondance Familiale au temps des troubles de Saint-Domingue.* Paris: Société d'Histoire des Colonies Françaises.

Mitchill, Samuel. 1803. "Medical and Philosophical News." *The Medical Repository* 6, 6, 449–450.

Mitchill, Samuel L., Felix Pascalis, and Samuel Akerly. 1813. "A Critical Analysis of Recent Publications on these Departments of Knowledge, and their Auxiliary Branches." *The Medical Repository* 1, 1.

Moreau de Saint-Méry, Méderic Louis Elie. 1784–1790. *Loix et constitutions des colonies françoises de l'Amérique sous le Vent.* 6 vols. Paris: Quillau, Méquignon Jeune.

———. 1797. *Description topographique, physique, civile, politique et historique de la partie française de l'isle Saint-Domingue, Tome Second.* Philadelphia Chez l'Auteur.

———. 1958 (1797–1798). *Description topographique, physique, civile, politique, et historique de la partie française de l'isle Saint-Domingue, Tome Premier.* Paris: Société de l'Histoire des Colonies Françaises.

Ouvière P.S.D.L.S.P., Abbé. 1789. "Les Adieux d'un cosmopolite aux marseillois." n.p.

Pascalis, Félix. 1805. "Account of an Abscess of the Liver, terminating favourably by Evacuation through the Lungs." In John Redman Coxe (ed.). *The Philadelphia Medical Museum* 1, 2. Philadelphia: Bartram, 158–162.

———. 1806a. "Proposals for Publishing by Subscription, By I. Riley & Co. No I, City-Hotel, New-York, Pyrroloimoglia, or; Inquiries into the Pestilence Called Yellow Fever." New York: I. Riley.

———. 1806b. "Observations on the Non-Importation of the Yellow Fever into Spain." *The Medical Repository* 3, 2, August–October, 376–380.

———. 1823. "An Exposition of the dangers of Interment in Cities; illustrated by an account of the Funeral Rites and Customs of the Hebrews, Greeks, Romans, and primitive Christians; by ancient and modern ecclesiastical canons, civil statutes and municipal regulations; and by chemical and physical principles. Chiefly from the works of Vicq D'Azyr, of France, and Prof. Scipione Piattoli, of Modena; with additions." *The Philadelphia Journal of the Medical and Physical Sciences,* 7, 14, 1820–1827.

———. 1826a. "Remarks on the Theory of Pain." *The North American Medical and Surgical Journal* 1, 1, 79–89.

———. 1826b. "Linnaean Society of Paris." *American Journal of Science and Arts, Volume 11.* New Haven: Maltby, 380–384.

———. 1826c. "Memorial on the Upward Forces of Fluids, and their Applicability to Several Arts and Sciences." *American Journal of Sciences and Arts* 1, 1, 110–116.

———. 1829. *Practical Instructions and Directions for Silkworm Nurseries, and for the Culture of the Mulberry Tree.* New York: J. Seymour.

———. 1831. "Eulogy on the Life and Character of the Honorable Samuel Latham Mitchill." New York: *American Argus.*

Pascalis-Ouvière, Félix. 1796. *Medico-chymical dissertations on the causes of the epidemic called yellow fever; and on the best antimonial preparations for the use in medicine.* Philadelphia: Snowden and McCorkle.

———. 1798. *An Account of the Yellow Fever Epidemic, Which Prevailed in Philadelphia in the Summer and Autumn of 1797; Comprising The Questions of its Causes and Domestic Origin, Characters, Medical Treatments, and Prevention.* Philadelphia: Snowden and McCorkle.

———. 1812. "Observations and Practical Remarks on the Nature, Progress and Operation of the Venereal Disease." *The Medical Repository*, November 1811–January 1812, 3298–3335.

———. 1819. *A Statement of the Occurrence during the Malignant Yellow Fever, in the city of New-York, in the Summer and Autumnal Months of 1819; and of the Check given to its Progress, by the Measures Adopted by the Board of Health.* New York: W. A. Mercein.

———. 1822. *Annual Oration Delivered Before the Chemical Society of Philadelphia, January 31st 1801.* Philadelphia: John Bioren.

———. 1823. "History of Two Remarkable Cases of Mania," (From the Memoirs of the Royal Academy of Marseille)." In Anonymous, *The Medical Repository of Original Articles and Intelligence, Relative to Physic, Surgery, Chemistry, and Natural History* 7, 3.

Patrick, Christine Sternberg and John C. Pinheiro (eds.). 2005. *The Papers of George Washington, Presidential Series, vol. 12, 16 January 1793–31 May 1793.* Charlottesville: University of Virginia Press.

Pennsylvania Society for Promoting the Abolition of Slavery. 1875. *Centennial Anniversary of the Pennsylvania Society, for Promoting the Abolition of Slavery, the Relief of Free Negroes Unlawfully Held in Bondage, and for Improving the Condition of the African Race.* Philadelphia: Grant, Faires, and Rodgers.

Peyré, Abbé. 1787–1789. *Observations médicales sur les vertus du quinquina indigène de St-Domingue fait à l'hôpital royal et militaire de Port-au-Prince, par Peyré, médecin du roi, transmises par La Luzerne.* Paris: Société Royale de la Médecine.

Philadelphia Genealogical Society of Pennsylvania. 1907. *Records of Christ Church in Philadelphia: Marriages, Confirmations and Communicants, Vol. 180.* Philadelphia: Genealogical Society of Pennsylvania.

Prudhomme, Louis-Marie. 1797. *Histoire générale et impartial des erreurs des fautes et des crimes commis pendant la Révolution Française, Tome II.* Paris: Convention Nationale.

Raimond, Julien. 1793. *Correspondance de Julien Raimond avec ses frères de Saint-Domingue, et les pièces qui ont été adressées par eux.* Paris: Imprimerie du Cercle Sociale.

Robinson, James. 1802. *The Philadelphia Directory, City and County Register.* Philadelphia: Oswald.

———. 1803. *The Philadelphia Directory, City and County Register for 1803.* Philadelphia: Woodward.

———. 1804. *The Philadelphia Directory, City and County Register for 1802*. Philadelphia: Woodward.

Saint-Léger, M. [Edmond de]. 1792. *Compte rendu à l'Assemblée Nationale*. Paris: Imprimerie Nationale.

Société des Amis des Noirs and Jean-Antoine-Nicolas de Caritat de Condorcet. 1968 (1789). *Règlement de la Société des Amis des Noirs, Suivi d'un "Tableau des Membres de la Société des amis des Noirs. Année 1789." La Révolution Française et l'Abolition de l'Esclavage: Textes et Documents, Tome VI*. Paris: Éditions d'Histoire Sociale.

Stafford, C. W. 1801. *The Philadelphia Directory for 1801, Containing the Names, Occupations, and Places of Abode of the Citizens*. Philadelphia: Woodward.

Thibal. 1797. *Récit historique du citoyen Thibal, médecin et habitant de la paroisse Sainte-Suzanne, détenu prisonnier, par les brigands, depuis 16 mois*. In *Récit historique sur les événements qui se sont succédés dans les camps de Grande Rivière, du Dondon, de Ste.-Suzanne et autres, depuis le 26 Octobre 1791 jusqu'au 27 Décembre de la même année*. Cap Français: Parent.

United States Census. 1820. New York Ward 6, New York, New York. Page 484; NARA Roll: M33-77; Image 252.

———. 1830. New York Ward 2, New York, New York. Page 60; NARA Roll: M19-96; Family History Film: 0017156.

United States House of Representatives. 1871–1872. *Congressional Series of United States Public Documents, Volume 1521*. Washington, DC: GPO.

SECONDARY SOURCES

Abeysekara, Ananda. 2002. *Colors of the Robe: Religion, Identity, and Difference*. Columbia: University of South Carolina Press.

Adrien, Antoine. 1992. "Notes sur le clergé du nord et la révolte des esclaves en 1791." In Conférence Haïtienne des Religieux (eds.), *Évangélisation d'Haïti: 1492–1992, Tome 2, La révolution de 1791: Libération hier et aujourd'hui*. Port-au-Prince: Le Natal, 47–56.

Aldridge, Susan. n.d. "John and Ben Williams family-White Pond, SC and Capt. W.W. Williams of Barnwell and Aiken." http://genealogytrails.com/scar/aiken/johnben_williams_family.htm; last accessed May 1, 2011.

Alexis, Stephen. 1949. *Black Liberator: The Life of Toussaint Louverture*. Trans. William Sterling. New York: MacMillan.

Andress, David. 1999. *French Society in Revolution*. Manchester: Manchester University Press.

Annan, Gertrude L. 1948. "The Academy of Medicine of New York, 1825–1830, and Its Contemporary, The New York Medical Academy." *Bulletin of the Medical Library Association* 36, 2, 117–123.

Ardouin, Beaubrun. 1958 (1853). *Études sur l'histoire d'Haïti, Tome Premier*. Port-au-Prince: Dalencourt.

Ardouin, C. N. 1865. *Essais sur l'histoire d'Haïti*. Port-au-Prince: Bouchereau.

Apel, Thomas. 2012. "Feverish Bodies, Enlightened Minds: Yellow Fever and Common Sense Natural Philosophy in the Early Republic, 1793–1805." Ph.D. diss., Georgetown University.

Aptheker, Herbert. 1940. "The Quakers and Negro Slavery." *Journal of Negro History* 25, 3, 331–362.

Arner, Katherine. 2013. "Making Global Commerce into International Health Diplomacy: Consuls and Disease Control in the Age of Revolutions." *Journal of World History* 24, 4, 771–796.

Asad, Talal. 1993. *Genealogies of Religion: Discipline and Reasons of Power in Christianity and Islam*. Baltimore and London: Johns Hopkins University Press.

Auguste, Claude B. 1990. "Les Congos dans la Révolution Haïtienne." *Revue de la Société Haïtienne d'Histoire et de Géographie* 168, 11–42.

Aymonin, Gérard. 1977. "Thomas Jefferson et les naturalistes français: un épisode des relations scientifiques franco-américaines." *Annales de Bretagne* 84, 3, 303–306.

Bell, Madison Smartt. 2004. *Masters of the Crossroads*. New York: Vintage.

———. 2007. *Toussaint Louverture: A Biography*. New York: Pantheon.

Bellegarde-Smith, Patrick. 1990. *Haiti: The Breached Citadel*. Boulder: Westview.

———. 2006. "Broken Mirrors: Mythos, Memories, and National History." In Patrick Bellegarde-Smith and Claudine Michel (eds.), *Haitian Vodou: Spirit, Myth, and Reality*. Bloomington and Indianapolis: Indiana University Press, 19–31.

Benedicty, Alessandra. 2015. *Spirit Possession in French, Haitian, and Vodou Thought*. Lanham and London: Lexington Books.

Benemann, William E. 2014. *Male-Male Intimacy in Early America: Beyond Romantic Friendships*. London: Routledge.

Benoist, Jean. 2010. "Rencontre avec Milo Rigaud." *Études créoles*, Octobre, 1–19.

Benot, Yves. 2005. "Documents sur l'insurrection des esclaves de Saint-Domingue: lettres de Biassou, Fayette ... ". *Annales historiques de la révolution française* 339, 137–150.

———. 2009. "The Insurgents of 1791, Their Leaders, and the Concept of Independence." In David Patrick Geggus and Norman Fiering (eds.), *The World of the Haitian Revolution*. Bloomington and Indianapolis: Indiana University Press, 99–110.

Benzaken, Jean-Charles. 2009. "Who Was the Author of *Histoire des désastres de Saint Domingue* in Paris in the Year III?" *French History* 23, 2, 261–267.

Blackburn, Robin. 1988. *The Overthrow of Colonial Slavery, 1776–1848*. London and New York: Verso.

Blank, Rebecca M., Jane Lubchenco, and David M. Kennedy. 2012. *Distances Between United States Ports*, 12th ed. Washington, DC: National Oceanic and Atmospheric Administration.

Boitel, Abbé (ed.). 1868. *Déportation de M. l'Abbé Aubert, curé de Fromentières, à Cayenne*. Châlons-sur-Marne: Le Roy.

Bolton, H. Carrington. 1897. "Early American Chemical Societies." *Journal of the American Chemical Society* 19, 9, 717–732.

Bourdieu, Pierre. 1971a. "Genèse et structure du champ religieux." *Revue française de sociologie* 12, 2, 295–334.

———. 1971b. "Une interprétation de la théorie de la religion selon Max Weber." *Archives européennes de sociologie* 12, 1, 3–21.

———. 1986. "L'Illusion biographique." *Actes de la Recherche en Sciences Sociales* 62/63, 69–72.

Braham, Persephone. 2013. "The Monstrous Caribbean." In Asa Simon Mittman and Peter J. Dendle (eds.), *The Ashgate Research Companion to Monsters and the Monstrous*. Farnham and Burlington: Ashgate, 17–48.

———. 2015. *From Amazons to Zombies: Monsters in Latin America*. Lewisburg: Bucknell University Press.

Branson, Susan and Leslie Patrick. 2001. "Étrangers dans un Pays Étrange: Saint-Domingan Refugees of Color in Philadelphia." In David P. Geggus (ed.), *The Impact of the Haitian Revolution in the Atlantic World*. Columbia: University of South Carolina Press, 193–208.

Breathett, George. 1954. "The Religious Missions in Colonial French Saint Domingue." Ph.D. diss., Iowa State University.

Brodwin, Paul. 1996. *Medicine and Morality in Haiti: The Contest for Healing Power*. Cambridge and New York: Cambridge University Press.

Brown, Karen McCarthy. 1991. *Mama Lola: A Vodou Priestess in Brooklyn*. Los Angeles and Berkeley: University of California Press.

Brown, Michael Forbes. 1988. "Shamanism and Its Discontents." *Medical Anthropology Quarterly* 2, 2, 102–120.

Brutus, Edner. 1969. *Révolution dans Saint-Domingue*. Paris: Éditions du Panthéon.

Brutus, Timoléon. 1946. *L'Homme d'Airain: Étude monographique sur Jean-Jacques Dessalines, fondateur de la nation haïtienne. Histoire de la vie d'un esclave devenu empereur jusqu'à sa mort, le 17 octobre 1806, Deuxième volume*. Port-au-Prince: N. A. Théodore.

Buck-Morss, Susan. 2009. *Hegel, Haiti, and Universal History*. Pittsburgh: University of Pittsburgh Press.

Buteau, Emmanuel. 2015. "Encountering God in Haiti: A Postcolonial Practical Theology." Ph.D. diss., St. Thomas University.

Byrnes, Joseph F. 2014. *Priests of the French Revolution: Saints and Renegades in a New Political Era*. University Park: Pennsylvania State University Press.

Cabon, Adolphe. 1920–1927. *Histoire d'Haïti: cours professé au Petit Séminaire-Collège Saint-Martial, Tome 3*. Port-au-Prince: La Petite Revue.

———. 1933. *Notes sur l'histoire religieuse d'Haïti: De la révolution au concordat (1789–1860)*. Port-au-Prince, Petit Séminaire Collège Saint-Martial.

Cahen, Abraham. 1882. "Les juifs dans les colonies françaises au XIIIe siècle." *Revue des études juives* 4, 127–145, 236–248; 5, 68–92, 258–272.

Callisen, Adolph Carl Peter. 1833. *Medicinisches Schriftsteller-Lexicon der jetzt lebenden Aerzte, Wundärzte, Geburtshelfer, Apotheker und Naturforscher aller gebildeten Völker. Vierzehnter Band. Nie-Pfen*. Copenhagen: Harald Fisher.

Campbell, Joseph. 1990. *The Hero's Journey*. Novato: New Life Library.

Carey, Brycchan. 2012. *From Peace to Freedom: Quaker Rhetoric and the Birth of American Antislavery, 1657–1761*. New Haven: Yale University Press.

Carey, Brycchan and Geoffrey Plank (eds.). 1988. *Quakers and Abolition*. Champaign: University of Illinois Press.

Char, René. 1983. *Ouvres complètes*. Paris: Gaillamard.

Chauleau, Liliane. 1989. "Le baptême á la Martinique au XVIIe siècle." In Laënnec Hurbon (ed.), *Le phénomène religieux dans la Caraïbe: Guadeloupe, Guyane, Haïti, Martinique*. Montréal: CIDIHCA, 23–56.

Collomp, Alain. 2011. *Un médecin des Lumières. Michel Darluc, naturaliste provençal*. Rennes: Presses Universitaires de Rennes.

Conférence Épiscopale Nationale du Congo. 2012–2013 *Annuaire de l'Église Catholique en DR Congo*. Kinshasa: Editions du Secrétariat Générale du CENCO.

Conner, Randy P., with David Hatfield Sparks. 2004. *Queering Creole Spiritual Traditions: Lesbian, Gay, Bisexual, and Transgender Participation in African Derived Traditions in the Americas*. Binghamton: Harrington Park Press.

Cooper, Duff. 1932. *Talleyrand*. New York: Grove Press.

Covington-Ward, Yolanda. 2014. "'Your Name Is Written in the Sky': Unearthing the Story of Kongo Female Prophets in the Colonial Belgian Congo." *Journal of Africana Religions* 2, 3, 317–346.

Courlander, Harold and Rémy Bastien. 1966. *Religion and Politics in Haiti*. Washington, DC: Institute for Cross Cultural Research.

Curran, Andrew S. 2011. *The Anatomy of Blackness: Science and Slavery in an Age of Enlightenment*. Baltimore: Johns Hopkins University Press.

Dalmas, Antoine. 1814. *Histoire de la révolution de Saint-Domingue*. Paris: Mame Frères.

Danticat, Edwidge. 2005. *Anacaona, Golden Flower*. New York: Scholastic Press.

Daréus, Daniel. 2012. "Haïti/Guerre de l'Indépendance: Bois-Caïman, On s'en souvient." *Radio Vision 2000*, August 20. http://radiotelevision2000.com/home/?p=20003; last accessed February 2, 2016.

Davies, John. 2008. "Class, Culture, and Color: Black Saint-Dominguan Refugees and African-American Communities in the Early Republic." Ph.D. diss., University of Delaware.

———. 2013. "Vodou in the Early Republic: More Questions than Answers." *Religion in American History*. http://usreligion.blogspot.com/2013/11/vodou-in-early-republic-more-questions.html; last accessed December 23, 2014.

Davis, Wade. 1985. *The Serpent and the Rainbow: A Harvard Scientist's Astonishing Journey into the Secret Societies of Haitian Voodoo, Zombies, and Magic*. New York: Simon and Schuster.

Dayan, Joan. 1995. *Haiti, History, and the Gods*. Berkeley and Los Angeles: University of California Press.

De Balzac, Honoré. 1830. *La Comédie humaine*. Paris: Mame Delaunay.

De Cauna, Jacques. 1985. "Les sources historiques de Bug Jargal: Hugo et la révolution haïtienne." *Conjonction* 166, 21–66.

———. 1997. "Polverel et Sonthonax, deux voies pour l'abolition de l'esclavage." In Marcel Dorigny (ed.), *Léger-Félicité Sonthonax: La première abolition de l'esclavage, La Révolution française et la Révolution de Saint-Domingue*. Saint-Denis and Paris: Société française d'histoire d'outre-mer and Association pour l'étude de la colonisation européenne, 47–53.

———. 2007. "Toussaint Louverture et le déclenchement de l'insurrection des esclaves du Nord en 1791: Un retour aux sources." In Alain Yacou (ed.), *Saint-Domingue espagnol et la révolution nègre d'Haïti*. Paris: Karthala, 135–155.

De la Bouderie. M. 1803. *Histoire de Bretagne*. Paris et Nantes: Société des Bibliophiles Bretons.

De Ribbe, Charles. 1854. *Pacalis: Étude sur la fin de la Constitution Provençale, 1787–1790*. Paris: Dentu.

Debien, Gabriel. 1941. *Une plantation de Saint-Domingue: La sucrerie Galbaud du Fort (1690–1801)*. Cairo: Institut Français d'Archéologie Orientale.

———. 1966. "Le marronnage aux Antilles Françaises au XVIIIe siècle." *Caribbean Studies* 6, 3, 3–43.

Deive, Carlos Esteban. 2000. *Viento negro, Bosque del Caimán*, Santo Domingo: Editoria Centenario.

Deren, Maya. 1953. *The Divine Horsemen: The Living Gods of Haiti*. New York: Vanguard Press.

Depréaux, Albert. 1924. "Le Commandant Baudry des Lozières et la Phalange de Crête Dragons (Saint-Domingue, 1789–1792)." *Revue de l'histoire de colonies françaises* 17, 1–42.

Desmangles, Leslie G. 1992. *The Faces of the Gods: Vodou and Roman Catholicism in Haiti*. Chapel Hill: University of North Carolina Press.

Dubois, Laurent. 2004. *Avengers of the New World: The Story of the Haitian Revolution*. Cambridge, MA and London: Harvard University Press.

———. 2006. *A Colony of Citizens: Revolution and Slave Emancipation in the French Caribbean*. Chapel Hill: University of North Carolina Press.

Dubois, Laurent and John D. Garrigus. 2006. *Slave Revolution in the Caribbean, 1789–1804: A Brief History with Documents*. Boston and New York: Bedford/St. Martin's.

Durkheim, Émile. 1995 (1912). *The Elementary Forms of Religious Life*. Trans. Karen E. Fields. New York: Free Press.

Eliade, Mircea. 1964. *Shamanism: Archaic Techniques of Ecstasy*. Princeton: Princeton University Press.

Eltis, David. 2008–2009. *Voyages: The Transatlantic Slave Trade Database*. http://www.slavevoyages.org/; last accessed January 12, 2013.

Evans-Pritchard, E. E. 1976. *Witchcraft, Oracles and Magic among the Azande*. New York: Oxford University Press.

Fabella, Yvonne Eileen. 2008. "Inventing the Creole Citizen: Race, Sexuality, and the Colonial Order in Pre-Revolutionary Saint-Domingue." Ph.D. diss., Stony Brook University.

Fagg, William Buller. 1978 (1970). *Divine Kingship in Africa*. London: British Museum Press.

Farmer, Paul. 1992. *AIDS and Accusation: Haiti and the Geography of Blame*. Berkeley and Los Angeles: University of California Press.

Fick, Carolyn E. 1991. *The Making of Haiti: The Saint-Domingue Revolution from Below*. Knoxville: University of Tennessee Press.

Fischer, Sybille. 2004. *Modernity Disavowed: Haiti and the Cultures of Slavery in the Age of Revolution*. Durham: Duke University Press.

Forsyth, David P. 1964. *The Business Press in America, 1750–1865*. Philadelphia and New York: Chilton.

Fouchard, Jean. 1984. *Les marrons du syllabaire: Quelques aspects du problème de l'instruction et de l'éducation des esclaves et affranchis de Saint-Domingue*. Port-au-Prince: Deschamps.

———. 1988. *Les marrons de la liberté*. Port-au-Prince: Deschamps.

Franketienne. 2003. *Miraculeuse: Spirale 2003, Fragmentaires I*. Port-au-Prince: Éditions des Antilles.

Fromont, Cécile. 2014. *The Art of Conversion: Christian Visual Culture in the Kingdom of the Kongo*. Chapel Hill: University of North Carolina Press.

Frostin, Charles. 1979. "Méthodologie missionnaire et sentiment religieux en Amérique française aux 17e et 18e siècles: Le cas de Saint-Domingue." *Cahiers d'histoire* 24, 1, 19–43.

Fumagalli, Maria Cristiana. 2012. "Servants Turned Masters: Carlos Esteban Deive's *Viento negro, Bosque del Caimán* and the Future of Hispaniola." *Journal of Haitian Studies* 18, 2, 100–118.

———. 2015. *On the Edge: Writing the Border Between Haiti and the Dominican Republic*. Liverpool: Liverpool University Press.

Furstenberg, François. 2014. *When the United States Spoke French: Five Refugees Who Shaped a Nation*. Baltimore: Johns Hopkins University Press.

Gaestel, Allyn. 2014. "Haiti's Fight for Gay Rights." *Al Jazeera*, November 8. http://projects.aljazeera.com/2014/haiti-lgbt/; last accessed February 14, 2016.

Games, Alison. 2006. "Atlantic History: Definitions, Challenges, and Opportunities." *American Historical Review* 3, 3, 741–757.

Garrigus, John D. 2001. "New Christians /'New Whites': Sephardic Jews, Free People of Color, and Citizenship in French Saint-Domingue, 1760–1789." In Paolo

Bernadini and Norman Fiering (eds.), *The Jews and the Expansion of Europe to the West: 1450 to 1800*. New York: Berghahn Books, 314–332.

———. 2007. "Opportunist or Patriot? Julien Raimond (1744–1801) and the Haitian Revolution." *Slavery and Abolition* 28, 1, 1–21.

———. 2010. *Before Haiti: Race and Citizenship in French Saint-Domingue*. New York: Palgrave MacMillan.

———. 2011. "Vincent Ogé Jeune (1757–91): Social Class and Free Colored Mobilization on the Eve of the Haitian Revolution." *The Americas* 68, 1, 33–62.

Geggus, David (Patrick). 1983. "Slave Resistance Studies and the Haitian Revolution: Some Preliminary Considerations." Latin American and Caribbean Center Occasional Paper Series. Miami: Florida International University.

———. 1992. "Marronage, voodoo, and the Saint-Domingue Slave Revolt of 1791." In Patricia Galloway and Philippe Boucher (eds.), *Proceedings of the Fifteenth Meeting of the French Historical Society, Martinique and Guadalupe, 1989*. Lanham: University Press of America, 22–35.

———. 2001. "Preface." In David P. Geggus (ed.), *The Impact of the Haitian Revolution in the Atlantic World*. Columbia: University of South Carolina Press, ix–xviii.

———. 2002. *Haitian Revolutionary Studies*. Bloomington and Indianapolis: Indiana University Press.

———. 2009. "Saint-Domingue on the Eve of the Haitian Revolution." In David Patrick Geggus and Norman Fiering (eds.), *The World of the Haitian Revolution*. Bloomington and Indianapolis: Indiana University Press, 3–20.

Geis, Terri. 2015. "Myth, History, and Repetition: André Breton and Vodou in Haiti." *South Central Review* 32, 1, 56–75.

Ghachem, Malick W. 2012. *The Old Regime and the Haitian Revolution*. New York: Cambridge University Press.

Gough, Hugh. 1988. *The Newspaper Press and the French Revolution*. London: Routledge.

Griswold, Rufus Wilmot. 1849. *The Female Poets of America*. Philadelphia: Carey and Hart.

Handler, Jerome S. and Kenneth S. Bilby. 2012. *Enacting Power: The Criminalization of Obeah in the Anglophone Caribbean, 1760–2011*. Kingston: University of the West Indies Press.

Hebert, Anne Catherine Bieri. 1981. "The Pennsylvania French in the 1790s." Ph.D. diss., University of Texas at Austin.

Hitt, Wayne Wade and Doris Rollins Cannon. 1997. *Echoes from Pascalina*. Charlotte: Jostens Graphics.

Hoffmann, Léon-François. 1987. "Le Vodou sous la colonie et pendant les Guerres d'Indépendance." *Conjonction: Revue franco-haïtienne*, 173, 109–135.

———. 1989. *Haïti: Couleurs, croyances, créole*. Montréal: CIDHICA.

———. 1990. "Histoire, mythe et idéologie: la cérémonie du Bois-Caïman." *Études créoles* 13, 9–34.

———. 2009. "Representations of the Haitian Revolution in French Literature." In David Patrick Geggus and Norman Fiering (eds.), *The World of the Haitian Revolution*. Bloomington and Indianapolis: Indiana University Press, 339–351.

Hoglund, Sarah. 2013. "Hidden Agendas: The Secret to Early Nineteenth-Century British Burial Reform." In Albert D. Pionke and Denise Tischler Millstein (eds.), *Victorian Secrecy: Economies of Knowledge and Concealment*. Surrey and Burlington: Ashgate, 15–28.

Hugo, Victor. 2004 (1826). *Bug Jargal*. Trans. Chris Bongie. Peterborough: Broadview.

Hurbon, Laënnec. 1989. "Présentation: Le continent 'Religion' dans les Îles de la Caraïbe." In Laënnec Hurbon (ed.), *Le phénomène religieux dans la caraïbe: Guadeloupe, Guyane, Haïti, Martinique*. Montréal: CIDHICA, 11–18.

———. 1991. "Esclavage et évangélisation: point de départ pour une méthodologie de l'histoire de l'église d'Haïti." In Conférence Haïtienne des Religieux (eds.), *Évangélisation d'Haïti, Tome 1: Esclavage et évangélisation*. Port-au-Prince: Le Natal, 43–71.

———. 2000. "Le clergé catholique et l'insurrection de Saint-Domingue." In Laënnec Hurbon (ed.), *L'Insurrection des esclaves de Saint-Domingue*. Paris: Karthala, 29–39.

———. 2004. *Religions et lien social: L'Église et l'état moderne en Haïti*. Paris: Éditions du Cerf.

Ingliss, David. 2011. "Putting the Undead to Work: Wade Davis, Haitian Vodou, and the Social Uses of the Zombie." In Cristopher M. Moreman and Cory James Rushton (eds.), *Race, Oppression and the Zombie: Essays on the Cross-Cultural Appropriations of the Caribbean Tradition*. Jefferson: McFarland, 42–59.

Irving, Washington. 1828. *A History of the Life and Voyages of Christopher Columbus*. London: John Murray.

Ives, Kim. 2013. "Haiti: Independence Debt, Reparations for Slavery and Colonialism, and International Aid." *Global Research*. Centre for Research on Globalization. http://www.globalresearch.ca/haiti-independence-debt-reparations-for-slavery-and-colonialism-and-international-aid/5334619; last accessed March 7, 2014.

James, C. L. R. 1963. *The Black Jacobins: Toussaint L'Ouverture and the San Domingo Revolution*. New York, Vintage.

Jan, Jean-Marie. 1950. *Monographie religieuse des paroisses du Cap-Haïtien*. Port-au-Prince: Deschamps.

Janin, Joseph. 1942. *La religion aux colonies françaises sous l'Ancien Régime: de 1629 à la Révolution*. Paris: D'Auteuil.

Janzen, John. 1982. *Lemba, 1650–1930: A Drum of Affliction in Africa and the New World*. New York: Garland.

———. 2013. "Renewal and Reinterpretation in Kongo Religion." In Susan Cooksey, Robin Poynor, and Hein Vanhee (eds.), *Kongo Across the Water*. Gainesville: University Press of Florida, 132–142.

Jarcho, Saul. 1970. "Yellow Fever, Cholera, and the Beginnings of Medical Cartography." *Journal of the History of Medicine and Allied Sciences* 25, 2, 131–142.

Johnson, Sara E. 2012. *The Fear of French Negroes: Transcolonial Collaboration in the Revolutionary Americas.* Berkeley, Los Angeles, and London: University of California Press.

Kawas, François. n.d. "L'Histoire de la compagnie de Jésus en Haïti: Une histoire brève mais mouvementée." http://www.jesuites.org/Haiti.htm; last accessed May 14, 2010.

———. 2006. *Histoire des Jésuites en Haïti aux XVIIIe et XXe siècles.* Paris: L'Harmattan.

Kehoe, Alice Beck. 2000. *Shamans and Religion: An Anthropological Exercise in Critical Thinking.* Prospect Heights: Waveland Press, 2000.

Kelly, Howard A. 1912. "Félix A. Pascalis-Ouvrière." In Howard A. Kelly (ed.), *A Cyclopedia of American Medical Biography: Comprising the Lives of Eminent Deceased Physicians and Surgeons, from 1610 to 1910, Volume II.* Philadelphia and London: W. B. Saunders, 894.

Kendall, Laura. 2002. "Review of Alice Beck Kehoe, *Shamans and Religion: An Anthropological Exercise in Critical Thinking.*" *American Anthropologist* 104, 1, 359–360.

King, Stewart R. 2001. *Blue Coat or Powdered Wig: Free People of Color in Pre-Revolutionary Saint Domingue.* Athens and London: University of Georgia Press.

Kloos, Jr., John M. 1991. *A Sense of Deity: The Republican Spirituality of Dr. Benjamin Rush.* New York: Carlson.

Koch, Tom. 2005. *Cartographies of Disease: Maps, Mapping, and Medicine.* New York and Redlands: ESRI.

———. 2011. *Disease Maps: Epidemics on the Ground.* Chicago: University of Chicago Press.

Koehler, Christopher S. W. 2001. "Heavy Metal Medicine." *Today's Chemist* 10, 1, 61–65.

Kopperman, Paul E. 2004. "'Venerate the Lancet': Benjamin Rush's Yellow Fever Therapy in Context." *Bulletin of the History of Medicine* 78, 3, 539–574.

Knapp, Samuel L. 1834. *Female Biography; Containing Notices of Distinguished Women, in Different Nations and Ages.* New York: Carpenter.

Lacombe, Robert. 1956. "Histoire monétaire de Saint-Domingue et de la République d'Haïti, de ses origines à 1874." *Revue d'histoire des colonies* 42, 152–153, 273–337.

Laguerre, Michel S. 1973. "The Place of Voodoo in the Social Structure of Haiti." *Caribbean Quarterly* 19, 3, 36–50.

———. 1989. *Voodoo and Politics in Haiti.* New York: St. Martin's Press.

Lambert, Frank. 2006. *The Founding Fathers and the Place of Religion in America.* Princeton: Princeton University Press.

Landers, Jane G. 2002. "The Central African Presence in Spanish Maroon Communities." In Linda M. Heywood (ed.), *Central Africans and Cultural*

Transformations in the American Diaspora. New York and Cambridge, UK: Cambridge University Press, 227–242.

———. 2010. *Atlantic Creoles in the Age of Revolutions*. Cambridge, MA and London: Harvard University Press.

Larose, Serge. 1977. "The Meaning of Africa in Haitian Vodu." In Iaon M. Lewis (ed.), *Symbols and Sentiments: Cross Cultural Studies in Symbolism*. London: Academic Press, 85–116.

Le Glaunec, Jean-Pierre and Léon Robichaud. n.d. "Marronage in Saint-Domingue" (database). The French Atlantic History Group, McGill University and Université de Sherbrooke. http://www.marronnage.info/en/index.html; last accessed February 12, 2015.

Leclerq, H. 1913. "Vessels for Holy Oils: Treatment of Vessels Used to Contain Blessed Oils." *The Original Catholic Encyclopedia*. http://oce.catholic.com/index.php?title=Vessels_for_Holy_Oils; last accessed November 30, 2013.

Lescot, Anne and Laurence Magloire. 2002. *Des hommes et dieux* (film). DigitAL AM.

Lloyd, C. 1960. "Sacred Kingship and Government among the Yoruba." *Africa: Journal of the International African Institute* 30, 3, 221–237.

Loughlin, James. 1911. "Archdiocese of Philadelphia." *The Catholic Encyclopedia*. *Vol 11*. New York: Robert Appleton. http://www.newadvent.org/cathen/11793b.htm; last accessed December 20, 2014.

MacGaffey, Wyatt. 1977. "Cultural Roots of Kongo Prophetism." *History of Religions* 17, 2, 177–193.

MacLeod, Mindy and Bernard Mees. 2006. *Runic Amulets and Magic Objects*. Woodbridge: Boydell Press.

Madiou, Thomas. 1989 (1847). *Histoire d'Haïti, Tome I, 1492–1799*. Port-au-Prince: Deschamps.

Manigat, Leslie F. 1977. "The Relationship between Marronage and Slave Revolts and Revolution in Saint-Domingue-Haiti." *Annals of the New York Academy of Sciences* 292, 420–438.

Marquis Who's Who on the Web. n.d. "Felix Pascalis." https://cgi.marquiswhoswho.com/OnDemand/Default.aspx?last_name=Pascalis&first_name=Felix; last accessed September 28, 2009.

Marshall, Jon. 2003. "Review of Alice Beck Kehoe, *Shamans and Religion: An Anthropological Exercise in Critical Thinking*." *Australian Journal of Anthropology* 14, 3, 425–426.

Marx, Karl. 1969 (1845). "Theses on Feuerbach." In Karl Marx and Friedrich Engels, *Marx/Engels: Selected Works, Volume I*. Moscow: Progress, 13–15.

Matibag, Eugenio. 2003. *Haitian-Dominican Counterpoint: Nation, Race, and State on Hispaniola*. New York: Palgrave Macmillan.

Matthews, Gelien. 2013. "Female Maroons of the West Indies." In Romain Cruse and Kevon Rhiney (eds.), *Caribbean Atlas*. http://www.caribbean-atlas.com/en/themes/waves-of-colonization-and-control-in-the-caribbean/

resistance-to-imperialism-and-emancipation/female-maroons-of-the-west-indies.html; last accessed February 6, 2016.

Matory, J. Lorand. 2008. "Is There Gender in Yorùbá Culture?" In Jacob K. Olupona and Terry Rey (eds.), *Òrìsà Devotion as World Religion: The Globalization of Yorùbá Religious Culture*. Madison: University of Wisconsin Press, 513–558.

Maurouard, Elvire. 2008. *Les juifs de Saint-Domingue (Haïti)*. Paris: Éditions du Cygne.

McAlister, Elizabeth. 2002. *Rara! Vodou, Power, and Performance in Haiti and Its Diaspora*. Berkeley and Los Angeles: University of California Press.

———. 2012. "From Slave Revolt to a Blood Pact with Satan: The Evangelical Rewriting of Haitian History." *Studies in Religion/Sciences Religieuses* 41, 2, 187–215.

McClellan III, James E. 1992. *Colonialism and Science: Saint Domingue in the Old Regime*. Baltimore and London: Johns Hopkins University Press.

McManners, John. 1999. *Church and Society in Eighteenth Century France, Volume I: The Clerical Establishment and Its Social Ramifications*. New York: Oxford University Press.

Mennesson-Rigaud, Odette. 1958. "Le rôle du vaudou dans l'indépendance d'Haïti." *Présence africaine* 17–18, 43–67.

Métellus, Jean. "Pour Mumia Abu-Jamal." 2014. *L'Humanité dimanche*, January 9–15, 90.

Métraux, Alfred. 1972 (1959). *Voodoo in Haiti*. Trans. Hugo Charteris. New York: Schocken.

Michel, Claudine, Patrick Bellegarde-Smith, and Marlène Racine-Toussaint. 2006. "From the Horses' Mouths: Women's Words/Women's Worlds." In Patrick Bellegarde-Smith and Claudine Michel (eds.), *Haitian Vodou: Spirit, Myth, and Reality*. Bloomington and Indianapolis: Indiana University Press, 70–83.

Middleton, William S. 1964. "Felix Pascalis-Ouvière and the Yellow Fever Epidemic of 1797." *Bulletin of the History of Medicine* 38, 497–515.

Miller, Randall M. and William Pencak. 2002. *Pennsylvania: A History of the Commonwealth*. University Park: Penn State University Press

Mintz, Sidney and Michel-Rolph Trouillot. 1972. "Introduction." In Alfred Métraux (ed.), *Voodoo in Haiti*. New York: Schocken, 1–15.

———. 2005. "The Social History of Haitian Vodou." In Donald J. Cosentino (ed.), *Sacred Arts of Haitian Vodou*. Los Angeles: UCLA Fowler Museum of Cultural History, 122–147.

Mobley, Christina Frances. 2015. "The Kongolese Atlantic: Central African Slavery and Culture from Mayombe to Haiti." Ph.D. diss., Duke University.

Montero, Mayra. 1997 (1995). *In the Palm of Darkness*. Trans. Edith Grossman. New York: Harper Collins.

Morgan, David. 2005. *The Sacred Gaze: Religious Visual Culture in Theory and Practice*. Berkeley and Los Angeles: University of California Press.

Müller-Ebeling, Claudia, Christian Rätsch, and Wolf-Dieter Storl. 2003 (1996). *Witchcraft Medicine: Healing Arts, Shamanic Medicine, and Forbidden Plants.* Trans. Annabel Lee. Rochester: Inner Traditions.

Nérestant, Micial M. 1997. *Religion et politique en Haïti.* Paris: Karthala.

New York Historical Society. n.d. "Slavery and the Making of New York." http://www.slaveryinnewyork.org/about_exhibit.htm; last accessed July 2, 2010.

Newman, Richard S. 2005. "The Pennsylvania Abolitionist Society: Restoring a Group to Glory." *Pennsylvania Legacies* 6, 2, 6–10.

———. 2008. *Freedom's Prophet: Bishop Richard Allen, the AME Church, and the Black Founding Fathers.* New York: New York University Press.

Ogle, Gene E. 2009. "The Trans-Atlantic King and Imperial Public Space." In David Patrick Geggus and Norman Fiering (eds.), *The World of the Haitian Revolution.* Bloomington: Indiana University Press, 79–96.

Olmsted, J. M. D. 1940. "A Letter from Felix Pascalis of New York to François Magendie in 1826." *Annals of Medical History* 2, 371–374.

Olúpònà, Jacob K. 1991. *Kingship, Rituals and Religion in a Nigerian Community: A Phenomenological Study of Ondo Yoruba Festivals.* Stockholm: Almqvist & Wiksell International, 1991.

———. 2012. *City of 201 Gods: Ilé-Ifẹ̀ in Space, Time, and the Imagination.* Berkeley, Los Angeles, and London: University of California Press.

O'Neil, Deborah and Terry Rey. 2012. "The Saint and Siren: Liberation Hagiography in a Haitian Village." *Studies in Religion/Sciences Religieuses* 41, 2, 166–186.

Packard, Francis R. 1954. "Felix Pascalis-Ouvrière." In Dumas Malone (ed.), *Dictionary of American Biography* 14. New York: Charles Scribner's Sons, 286–287.

Parkinson, Wenda. 1970. *"This Gilded African": Toussaint Louverture.* New York: Quartet.

Parrinder, Geoffrey. 1956. "Divine Kingship in West Africa." *Numen: International Review for the History of Religion* 3, 2, 111–121.

———. 1963. *Witchcraft: African and European.* New York: Barnes and Noble, 1963.

Paton, Diana and Maarit Forde (eds.). 2012. *Obeah and Other Powers: The Politics of Caribbean Religion and Healing.* Durham: Duke University Press.

Peabody, Sue. 2002. "'A Dangerous Zeal': Catholic Missions to Slaves in the French Antilles, 1635–1899." *French Historical Studies* 25, 1, 53–90.

Péan, Leslie. 2014. "Haïti: Le père Dessalines et les sans repères." *Alterpresse*, October 25. http://www.alterpresse.org/spip.php?article17215#nb2; last accessed, February 7, 2016.

———. 2015. "Les élections du 25 octobre et le changement en Haïti." *Alterpresse*, November 18. http://www.alterpresse.org/spip.php?article19232#.VqloLPkrKUk; last accessed 1 February 2016.

Pelissier-Guys, Henri and Paul Masson. 1925. *Les Bouches-du-Rhône: 10: Encyclopédie départementale: Le Mouvement sociale.* Aix-en-Provence: Bibliothèque Méjanes.

Pemberton III, John. 1996. *Yoruba Sacred Kingship.* Washington, DC: Smithsonian.

Placide-Justin. M. 1826. *Histoire politique et statistique de l'île d'Hayti Saint-Domingue; écrite sur des documents officiels et des notes communiquées par Sir James Barskett.* Paris: Brières.

Pluchon, Pierre. 1987. *Vaudou, sorciers, empoisonneurs: de Saint-Domingue à Haïti.* Paris, Karthala.

Popkin, Jeremy D. 2007. *Facing Racial Revolution: Eyewitness Accounts of the Haitian Insurrection.* Chicago: University of Chicago Press.

———. 2010. *You Are All Free: The Haitian Revolution and the Abolition of Slavery.* New York: Cambridge University Press.

———. 2012. *A Concise History of the Haitian Revolution.* Chichester: Wiley-Blackwell.

Powell, J. M. 1949. *Bring Out Your Dead: The Great Plague of Yellow Fever in Philadelphia in 1793.* Philadelphia: University of Pennsylvania Press.

Prandini, Stéphane. 2010. *La main du diable.* Paris: Éditions Le Manuscrit, 2010.

Price-Mars, Jean. 1928. *Ainsi parla l'oncle: Essais d'ethnologie.* New York: Parapsychology Foundation.

———. 1938. "Lemba-Pétro: Un culte secret, son histoire, sa localisation géographique, son symbolisme." *Revue de la Société d'histoire et de géographie d'Haïti* 9, 28, 12–31.

Ramsey, Kate. 2011. *The Spirits and the Law: Vodou and Power in Haiti.* Chicago and London: University of Chicago Press.

Reboul, Robert. 1973 (1878). *Anonymes, pseudonymes et supercheries littéraires de la Provence ancienne et moderne.* Geneva: Slatkine.

Rey, Terry. 1996. "Classes of Mary in the Haitian Religious Field: A Theoretical Analysis of the Effects of Socio-Economic Class on the Perception and Uses of a Religious Symbol." Ph.D. diss., Temple University.

———. 1998. "The Virgin Mary and Revolution in Saint-Domingue: The Charisma of Romaine-la-Prophétesse." *Journal of Historical Sociology* 11, 3, 341–369.

———. 1999a. *Our Lady of Class Struggle: The Cult of the Virgin Mary in Haiti.* Trenton and Asmara: Africa World Press.

———. 1999b. "Junta, Rape, and Religion in Haiti, 1993–1994." *Journal of Feminist Studies in Religion,* 15, 2, 73–100.

———. 2001. "A Consideration of Kongolese Catholic Influences on *dominguois/* Haitian Popular Religion." In Linda M. Heywood (ed.), *Central Africans and Cultural Transformations in the Atlantic Diaspora.* New York: Cambridge University Press, 265–285.

———. 2002. "The Politics of Patron Sainthood in Haiti: 500 Years of Iconic Struggle." *The Catholic Historical Review* 81, 4, 519–545.

———. 2005a. "Romaine-la-Prophétesse." In Colin Palmer (ed.), *Encyclopedia of African-American Culture and History.* New York: MacMillan Reference USA, 1972–1973.

———. 2005b. "Ancestral and Saintly Root Experiences in Afro-Atlantic Christianity: From Kongo to Saint-Domingue." In José Curto and Renée

Soulodre-La France (eds.), *Africa and the Americas: Interconnections During the Slave Era*. Trenton and Asmara: Africa World Press, 215–230.

———. 2005c. "Habitus et Hybridité: Une interprétation du syncrétisme dans la religion afro-catholique d'après Bourdieu." *Social Compass: International Review of Sociology of Religion* 52, 4, 453–462.

———. 2007. *Bourdieu on Religion: Imposing Faith and Legitimacy*. London: Routledge.

———. 2011. "(Mis)Representations of Religion and Earthquakes in Haiti." *Revue de la Société haïtienne d'histoire, de géographie et de géologie*, nos. 241–244, 178–192.

———. Forthcoming. "Fear and Trembling in Haiti: A Charismatic Catholic Prophecy of the 2010 Earthquake." In Stan Chu Ilo (ed.), *Fire From Heaven: Pentecostalism, Catholicism, and the Spirit in the World*. Eugene: Cascade Press.

Rey, Terry and Karen Richman. 2010. "The Somatics of Syncretism: Tying Body and Soul in Haitian Religion." *Studies in Religion/Sciences Religieuses* 39, 3, 379–403.

———. 2012. "Introduction." *Studies in Religion/Sciences Religieuses* 41, 2, 145–147.

Rey, Terry and Alex Stepick. 2010. "Visual Culture and Visual Piety in Little Haiti: The Sea, the Tree, and the Refugee." In Paul DiMaggio and Patricia Fernández-Kelly (eds.), *Art in the Lives of Immigrant Communities in the United States*. New Brunswick: Rutgers University Press, 229–248.

———. 2013. *Crossing the Water and Keeping the Faith: Haitian Religion in Miami*. New York: New York University Press.

Richard, Robert. 1954. "À propos de Saint-Domingue: la monnaie dans l'économie coloniale (1674–1803)." *Revue d'histoire des colonies* 41, 142, 22–46.

Richman, Karen. 2008. "Innocent Imitations? Authenticity and Mimesis in Haitian Vodou Art, Tourism, and Anthropology." *Ethnohistory* 55, 2, 203–227.

———. 2012. "Religion at the Epicenter: Agency and Affiliation in Léogâne after the Earthquake." *Studies in Religion/Sciences Religieuses* 41, 2, 148–165.

Rigaud, Milo. 1953. *La tradition voudou et le voudou haïtien: Son temple, ses mystères, sa magie*. Paris: Niclaus.

Saint-Rémy, Joseph. 1965. *Pétion et Haïti: Étude monographique et historique*. Paris: Berger-Levrault.

Scott, David. 2004. *Conscripts of Modernity: The Tragedy of Colonial Enlightenment*. Durham, NC and London, UK: Duke University Press.

Scott, James C. 1990. *Domination and the Arts of Resistance: Hidden Transcripts*. New Haven: Yale University Press.

Scott, William. 1991. "The Urban Bourgeoisie in the French Revolution: Marseille, 1789–1792." In Allen Forest and Peter Jones (eds.), *Reshaping France: Town, Country, and Region in the Revolution*. New York: Manchester University Press, 86–104.

Scurr, Ruth. 2007. *Fatal Purity: Robespierre and the French Revolution*. New York: MacMillan.

Sensbach, Jon. F. 2005. *Rebecca's Revival: Creating Black Christianity in the Atlantic World*. Cambridge, MA and London, UK: Harvard University Press.

Sepinwall, Alyssa Goldstein. 2005. *The Abbé Grégroire and the French Revolution: The Making of Modern Universalism*. Berkeley and Los Angeles: University of California Press.

Sérant, Claude Bernard. 2006. "La place Anacaona de Léogâne: Où sont passées les neiges d'autant?" *Le Nouvelliste*, January 23.

Shannon, Gary W. 1981. "Disease Mapping and Early Theories of Yellow Fever." *Professional Geographer* 33, 3, 221–227.

Shuler, Cyril O. 1997. *From the Mayflower to Pole Cat Pond, S. C.: A Family History Which Includes the Cushman, Lemar, Martin, Pascalis, Shuler, Wade and Woodward Families*. Clemson: C. O. Shuler.

Shusterman, Noah. 2014. *The French Revolution: Faith, Desire, and Politics*. Oxon and New York: Routledge.

Simpson, George Eaton. 1965. *Religious Cults of the Caribbean: Trinidad, Jamaica, and Haiti*. Caribbean Monograph Series, 15. San Juan: University of Puerto Rico.

Smith, Billy G. 2013. *Ship of Death: A Voyage That Changed the Atlantic World*. New Haven and London: Yale University Press.

Smith, Mark M. (ed.). 2001. "Remembering Mary: Reconsidering the Stono Rebellion." *Journal of Southern History* 67, 3, 513–534.

———. 2005. *Stono: Documenting and Interpreting a Southern Slave Revolt*. Columbus: University of South Carolina Press.

Soderlund, Jean R. 1988. *Quakers and Slavery: A Divided Spirit*. Princeton: Princeton University Press.

Somerset Publishing. 1999. "PASCALIS-OUVRIERE, FELIX (1750–1833)." *Pennsylvania Biographical Dictionary*. 3rd ed., Vol. 1. St. Claire Shores: Somerset, 281–282.

Stark, Rodney. 2006. *For the Glory of God: How Monotheism Led to Reformations, Science, Witch-Hunts, and the End of Slavery*. Princeton: Princeton University Press.

Stark, Rodney and Roger Finke. 2000. *Acts of Faith: Explaining the Human Side of Religion*. Berkeley and Los Angeles: University of California Press.

Stewart, Julia. 2004. *Stewart's Quotable Africa*. London: Penguin, 2004.

Stirling, Matthew W. 1933. "Jivaro Shamanism." *Proceedings of the American Philosophical Society* 72, 3, 137–145.

Stoddard, T. Lothrop. 1979 (1914). *The French Revolution in San Domingo*. Westport: Negro Universities Press.

Strauss, David Friedrich. 1902 (1848). *The Life of Jesus, Critically Examined*. Trans. George Eliot. London: Swan Sonnenschein.

———. 1977 (1865). *The Christ of Faith and the Jesus of History: A Critique of Schleiermacher's* The Life of Jesus. Trans. Leander E. Keck. Philadelphia: Fortress Press.

Sweet, James H. 1996. "Male Homosexuality and Spiritism in the African Diaspora." *Journal of the History of Sexuality* 7, 2, 184–202.

———. 2011. *Domingos Álvares, African Healing, and the Intellectual History of the Atlantic World*. Chapel Hill: University of North Carolina Press.

———. 2017. "New Perspectives on Kongo in Revolutionary Haiti." *The Americas* 74, forthcoming.

Taber, Robert D. 2015. 'The Issue of Their Union: Family, Law, and Politics in Western Saint-Domingue, 1777–1789." Ph.D. diss., University of Florida.

———. 2016. "The Mystery of Marie Rose: Family, Politics, and the Origins of the Haitian Revolution." *Age of Revolution*, January 16. http://ageofrevolutions.com/2016/01/06/the-mystery-of-marie-rose-family-politics-and-the-origins-of-the-haitian-revolution/; last accessed March 2, 2016.

Tackett, Timothy and Claude Langlois. 1980. "Ecclesiastical Structures and Clerical Geography on the Eve of the French Revolution." *French Historical Studies* 11, 3, 352–370.

Thibaud, Jacques. 1989. *Le temps de Saint-Domingue: L'esclavage et la révolution française*. Paris: Lattes.

The Louverture Project. 2008. "Haiti—Historique: 1492–1992." http://www.nilstremmel.com/haiti/; last accessed July 12, 2009.

Thoreau, Henry David. 2009. *The Journal of Henry David Thoreau, 1837–1861*. Ed. Damion Searls. New York: New York Review of Books.

Thornton, John K. 1984. "The Development of an African Catholic Church in the Kingdom of Kongo, 1491–1750." *Journal of African History* 25, 2, 147–167.

———. 1991a. "African Soldiers in the Haitian Revolution." *Journal of Caribbean History* 25, 1–2, 58–80.

———. 1991b. "African Dimensions of the Stono Rebellion." *American Historical Review* 96, 4, 1991, 1101–1113.

———. 1993. "'I Am the Subject of the King of Congo': African Political Ideology and the Haitian Revolution." *Journal of World History* 4, 2, 181–214.

———. 1998. *The Kongolese Saint Anthony: Dona Beatriz Kimpa Vita and the Antonian Movement, 1684–1706*. New York: Cambridge University Press.

Thornton, John K. and Linda M. Heywood. 2007. *Central Africans, Atlantic Creoles, and the Foundation of the Americas*. New York: Cambridge University Press.

Tinsley, Omise'eke Natasha. n.d. "Ezili Danto: A Lesbian History of Haiti?" *Small Ax Visualities*. http://smallaxe.net/sxvisualities/cqv/provocations/tinsley-ezili-danto; last accessed February 11, 2016.

Toumson, Roger. 1979. *Bug Jargal: Ou, la révolution haïtienne vue par Victor Hugo*. Fort-de-France: Desormeaux.

Trouillot, Michel-Rolph. 1982. "Motion in the System: Coffee, Color, and Slavery in Eighteenth Century Saint-Domingue." *Review* 3, 331–388.

———. 1993. "Coffee Planters and Coffee Slaves in the Antilles: The Impact of a Secondary Crop." In Ira Berlin and Philip Morgan (eds.), *Cultivation and Culture: Labor and the Shaping of Slave Life in the Americas*. Charlottesville: University Press of Virginia, 124–137.

———. 1995. *Silencing the Past: Power and the Production of History*. Boston: Beacon.

Tweed, Thomas A. 2006. *Crossing and Dwelling: A Theory of Religion*. Cambridge, MA and London: Harvard University Press.

Vanhee, Hein. 2002. "Central African Popular Christianity and the Making of Haitian Vodou Religion." In Linda M. Heywood (ed.), *Central Africans and Cultural Transformations in the American Diaspora*. New York: Cambridge University Press, 243–264.

Veatch, Robert M. 2004. *Disputed Dialogues: Medical Ethics and the Collapse of the Physician-Humanist Connection (1770–1989)*. New York: Oxford University Press.

Vila, Anne C. 1998. *Enlightenment and Pathology: Sensibility in the Literature and Medicine of Eighteenth Century France*. Baltimore and London: Johns Hopkins University Press.

Wallace, Anthony F. C. 1956. "Revitalization Movements." *American Anthropologist* 58, 2, 264–281.

Washington, Harriet A. 2008. *Medical Apartheid: The Dark History of Medical Experiments on African Americans from Colonial Times to the Present*. New York: Knopf.

Weaver, Karol K. 2006. *Medical Revolutionaries: The Enslaved Healers of Eighteenth-Century Saint Domingue*. Urbana and Chicago: University of Illinois Press.

Weber, Max. 1946 (1922). "Science as Vocation." In Hans H. Gerth and C. Wright Mills (eds. and trans.), *From Max Weber: Essays in Sociology*. New York: Oxford University Press, 129–156.

———. 1963 (1922). *The Sociology of Religion*. Trans. Ephraim Fischoff. Boston: Beacon.

White, Ashli. 2012. *Encountering Revolution: Haiti and the Making of the Early Republic*. Baltimore: Johns Hopkins University Press.

Wilks, Ivor. 1995. *Forests of Gold: Essays on the Akan and the Kingdom of the Asante*. Athens: Ohio University Press.

Williams, Greg H. 2009. *The French Assault on American Shipping, 1793–1813: A History and Comprehensive Record of Merchant Marine Losses*. Jefferson: McFarland.

Williams, Robert L. 2001. *Botanophilia in Eighteenth Century France*. Dordrecht: Kluwer.

Woodson, Drexel G. 1992. "Which Beginning Should Be Hindmost? Surrealism in Appropriations of Facts about Haitian Contact Culture." Paper delivered to the American Anthropological Association, San Francisco, December 2.

———. 1993. "Review of Patrick Bellegarde-Smith's *Haiti: The Breached Citadel*." *New West Indian Guide/Nieuw Westindische Gids* 67, 1, 156–160.

Zizek, Joseph. 2003. "'*Plum de fer*': Louis-Marie Prudhomme Writes of the French Revolution." *French Historical Studies* 26, 4, 619–660.

Zundel, William Artel. 1922. *History of Old Zion Lutheran Evangelical Church, in Hempfield Township, Westmoreland County, Pennsylvania, Near Harrold's*. The Church Council, n.p.

Index

Printed in the USA
CPSIA information can be obtained
at www.ICGtesting.com
CBHW031352060724
11234CB00011B/122/J